FUTURE
MEDIA

Future Media
© 2011 by Rick Wilber

Cover design by Josh Beatman
Interior design by Elizabeth Story

Tachyon Publications
1459 18th Street #139
San Francisco, CA 94107
(415) 285-5615
www.tachyonpublications.com
tachyon@tachyonpublications.com

Series Editor: Jacob Weisman
Project Editor: Jill Roberts

ISBN 10: 1-61696-020-5
ISBN 13: 978-1-61696-020-9

Printed in the United States of America by Worzalla
First Edition: 2011
0 9 8 7 6 5 4 3 2 1

FUTURE MEDIA

tachyon publications / san francisco

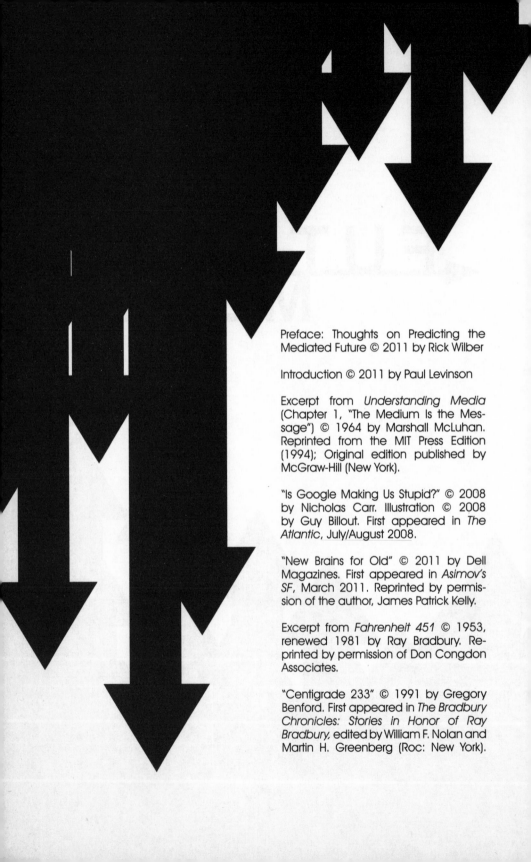

CONTENTS

About the Editor

Rick Wilber is a long-time college journalism professor and the author of several college textbooks, including *Magazine Feature Writing* (St. Martin's Press), *The Writer's Handbook for Editing and Revision* (McGraw Hill), and *Modern Media Writing* (Cengage). He is at work on an innovative introductory media text in an e-book format, *Media Matters*, for Allyn & Bacon/Pearson Publishing. He is a journalism professor at the University of South Florida, where he heads the magazine major.

Wilber has also been writing science fiction short stories for various magazines and anthologies since the early 1980s. Some fifty of his short stories have appeared in *Analog*, *Asimov's SF*, *Fantasy & Science Fiction*, and many other magazines in the science fiction field, as well as a variety of literary magazines like *Cencrastus* (Scotland), *Gulf Stream*, and others where he has also published several dozen poems.

His thriller novel *Rum Point* came out to good reviews in 2010 (McFarland), his thriller *The Cold Road* (Forge, 2003) was also well-reviewed in 2003, and his short story collection, *To Leuchars* (Wildside, 2000) was called a "minor classic" by SF Site.

Thoughts on Predicting the Mediated Future
Rick Wilber

The origins of this collection lie in conversations I had beginning in 2009 with Tachyon publisher Jacob Weisman and his colleague Bernie Goodman, and it was Bernie who took the lead in urging me to think about a book that played to my deep and abiding interest in two seemingly different fields: the mass media, where I have enjoyed a long career as a professor and as a textbook author; and in science fiction, where I've also been fortunate enough to enjoy a long career as a writer and have happily spent a lifetime as a devoted reader. I have been teaching mass-media courses at various universities since the mid-1970s, and while I make no claim to real scholarship in the field, I enjoy teaching what I've learned from those scholars who have made major contributions to our understanding of the often worrisome power of the media. Similarly, in the science fiction genre I've enjoyed a mildly successful career as a writer and editor since my first published short story in 1980, and I happily admit to being a great admirer of the field's many excellent writers and their work.

It was Bernie who pointed out an obvious connection between science fiction writers and mass-media scholarship. In both cases there has long been an interest in where the media are going in the future, and what the social implications of that mediated future will be. Science fiction writers tend to follow one troubled individual into that mediated future while mass-media scholars tend to take a broader, wider point of view; but both are certainly interested in the mass media of the future and its impact on us all.

And so this anthology attempts to take a glimpse at both the forest and the trees of the future of the media, offering various kinds of material from scholars, science fiction authors, popular essayists, media theorists and inventors, performance artists, and others. Their material ranges from memoranda and addresses to Congress, to performance pieces that are meant to be staged, to short stories, to novel excerpts, to blogs, and more.

On the fiction side there are excerpts from classic novels that feature the mass media, including Norman Spinrad's famous *Bug Jack Barron*, Aldous Huxley's dystopian *Brave New World*, Ray Bradbury's classic *Fahrenheit 451*, and the very recent *Makers*, by award-winning blogger, novelist, and futurist Cory Doctorow. There are also a number of entertaining, and often fretful, short stories by some of the most famous names in science fiction, as well as a pair of important, and very edgy, performance pieces, one by Guillermo Gomez-Pena and the other a play by Joe Haldeman, one of the most honored writers in science fiction, who pays his respects to Huxley in his "feelie script."

On the nonfiction side there are journal articles, a blog entry, several important magazine articles, a few chapters excerpted from important books focused on media criticism, and even some testimony given before the U.S. House of Representatives.

There is, in these various offerings, a wide diversity of opinion about the promise or peril of the mass media. For instance, while Gregory Benford, James Patrick Kelly, and Nicholas Carr take a worrisomely dark view of what's happening to us as we read less and surf the Web more, Cory Doctorow and Timothy Berners-Lee find the emergence of easy access to information and global interconnectedness to be profoundly positive in many respects, so much so that these benefits do much, for them, to outweigh the cultural losses. And while Kit Reed and Norman Spinrad predict a dark side of television entertainment that seems to have come true in many ways, Henry Jenkins finds much to admire in an environment that blends movies and television into the digital online future that offers access to inventive storytellers who work outside the old mediated systems to find ample audience.

In terms of structure, the book opens and closes with material from Marshall McLuhan. The opening essay is the very famous chapter "The Medium Is the Message," from his seminal book *Understanding Media*, and it is in this chapter that he coins the phrase "the medium is the message" and explains it, setting the parameters very nicely for what is to come in the book you hold in your hand. Later, at the back of the book, another famous McLuhan essay (and the concluding chapter from that same book) closes this collection with McLuhan's thoughts on what was, for him in the mid-1960s, the "new electric age," which offers total interdependence even as it promotes the pursuit of independent thought and independent work. With McLuhan firmly wrapping the contents, the book then generally alternates fiction and nonfiction, paying attention to how the two forms interact thematically. For instance, Ray Bradbury's *Fahrenheit 451* and Gregory Benford's homage to Bradbury, "Centigrade 233," pose questions about the decline of reading and its implications that are then discussed in James Patrick Kelly's "New Brains for Old" and "Nicholas Carr's "Is Google Making Us Stupid?" Similar ties to immersive and interactive media where the audience has a direct connection to—and sometimes a hand in directly modifying—the content are found in stories or essays by Pat Cadigan, Kate Wilhelm, James Patrick Kelly, Judy Wacjman, Allucquére Rosanne Stone, and others.

The inclusion of significant material from decades in the past does, I hope, lend an interesting viewpoint to the future that these gifted writers saw up ahead somewhere. Has television become the artificial reality that Kit Reed predicted in the 1960s, where it's possible to order in everything you need to live your life? Do we have television hosts who shout at and denigrate their guests, as Jack Barron does in the excerpt from Norman Spinrad's famous novel? Are there television game shows that follow men and women in peril as they struggle to stay alive, as in Robert Sheckley's famous short story? Was Vannevar Bush right in what he saw in 1945 as the future of computing and its impact on society? Did McLuhan and Neil Postman (as his son, Andrew, notes wryly), predict with disturbing precision some of the issues that confront us today, and will confront us in the future, when it comes to media use? The answer seems self-evident.

Ultimately, it's my hope that this collection serves two important functions. One is to celebrate the inventive social commentary of some of science fiction's best writers and to compare their work to the deep conjecture of scholars and writers of various kinds who have given thought to the future of the mass media and raised perceptive questions about the societal implications of mass media not only today but into the future. The other is to present readers, especially undergraduate readers taking courses in media studies, with a mix of entertaining, if often quite profound, science fiction stories centered around the mass media, and add in a similar mix of significant nonfiction articles about the mass media written by important scholars and other thoughtful critics of the field. Several of the articles reprinted here have formed the basic root structure of mass-media studies, and it is interesting to see how accurate McLuhan and others were in their seminal work. Other, more recent, pieces offer predictions of where the media might be in the future and what the implications may be for society should those predictions come true. Will the media in the future live up to the promise that Doctorow, Jenkins, Berners-Lee, and others see? It's going to be fun to see—or more likely, to immerse ourselves in—isn't it?

Rick Wilber

February 2011

Acknowledgements

A book of this nature, one that collects and reprints material from living authors and scholars as well as classic material from decades ago is something of a team effort. I am indebted to a number of people who offered advice, encouragement, and suggestions. John Kessel was especially helpful in offering suggestions about several important science fiction stories that are included. My colleagues in the School of Mass Communications at the University of South Florida, especially Ken Killebrew, were equally helpful in offering suggestions about significant mass-media theorists and their work that might be included. Bernie Goodman and Tachyon Publisher Jacob Weisman were extremely helpful in working out the mix of fiction and nonfiction, and Tachyon's Managing Editor Jill Roberts somehow managed to be both patient and persistent in moving the project forward. The entire Tachyon staff, in fact, was outstanding in all regards.

All of the writers and theorists I communicated with personally were, without exception, supportive and helpful as I sought permission for their work, and the permissions departments at a number of book publishers and journal publishers were responsive and communicative as I sought to find ways to stay within a reasonable budget and still acquire important work.

Paul Levinson, novelist, science fiction writer, media scholar, professor and administrator, musician, essayist, blogger, and more, was kind enough to contribute the introduction to this book, and I am most appreciative of his remarks.

As always, I owe a special thanks to my wife, Dr. Robin Wilber of St. Petersburg College, and my college daughter Samantha, and my special son, Richard, Jr., all of whom were understanding and supportive of the demands on a writer and editor who needs to meet his deadlines.

And, finally, I am always in the process of acquiring a new appreciation for the mass media by seeing them anew each semester through the eyes of several hundred undergraduates in the introductory course I have been teaching by one course name or another for more than thirty years. Incredibly, I have, I'm guessing, taught somewhere in excess of eight thousand students about the future of the mass media. This book is, in good part, a reflection of that long history of teaching, and I owe a great debt to the many students who have sat patiently through my lectures.

Any errors of fact in the introductory material are, of course, my own.

This book is dedicated to the several professors who had a great impact on me as an undergraduate and then graduate student: William G. Ward, Dickie Spurgeon, Roberta Bosse, Hans Juergensen, and Donald Baden.

Rick Wilber
February 2011

Introduction
Paul Levinson

Media scholar and science fiction author Paul Levinson is the Professor of Communication and Media Studies at Fordham University. His nonfiction books include *The Soft Edge* (Routledge, 1998), *Digital McLuhan* (Routledge, 1999), and *New New Media* (Allyn & Bacon, 2009). His science fiction novels include *The Silk Code* (Tor, 1999), which won the Locus Award for best first novel; *The Pixel Eye* (Tor, 2003); and *The Plot to Save Socrates* (Tor, 2006), and his short stories have been nominated for Nebula, Hugo, Edgar, and Sturgeon awards. He appears regularly on several national and international TV and radio programs, hosts three popular podcasts, and was listed in *The Chronicle of Higher Education* as one of Twitter's Top 10 High Flyers in 2009.

Predictions of the future—ranging from scholarly to science fiction—have been hazardous, to say the least. The British Admiralty did its utmost in the early nineteenth century to stave off the deployment of steam power in naval warfare. Marshal Foch in France less than a century later was sure that air flight would have no major military application at all. Science fiction has thus far missed the boat completely in its projections of time travel and teleportation in future societies and, with the exception of Murray Leinster's "A Logic Named Joe" in the 1940s, pretty much missed the personal computer revolution, too.

So why bother with predicting the future? Well, sometimes the predictions have been spot on. Vannevar Bush's article in 1945 about the "memex" foresaw the Internet, and Arthur C. Clarke's article in the same year proposed the use of satellites for world-wide telecommunication. In science fiction, Jules Verne got the submarine, H. G. Wells saw what genetic engineering could in effect do (in *The Island of Dr. Moreau*), and a myriad of writers predicted voyages to the moon and beyond.

In addition to those satisfactions, predicting the future is fun. And, probably of most importance, fathoming the future inevitably provides a great snapshot of the state of society at the time the predictions are made.

Future Media fires on all these cylinders. The anthology offers predictions from throughout the twentieth century to the present, from nonfiction as well as science fiction, about our modes of communication or media—the ways in which we prepare and package our information and messages for transmission to another place or preservation into the future.

In the nonfiction theater, Vannevar Bush's 1945 "As We May Think" from *The Atlantic Monthly* is, in fact, included here in its entirety, along with a sampling of work from some of the most creative and perceptive thinkers of the past sixty years. They range from Marshall McLuhan, who deservedly has not one but two entries, to Andrew Postman about his father Neil's work (Neil Postman was my doctoral dissertation mentor at New York University in the late 1970s). Tim Berners-Lee, who unlike other claimants actually did invent a significant part of the Internet, has an entry here, as do Cory Doctorow and James Patrick Kelly, who are also represented as science fiction writers. Judy Wacjman presents a balanced analysis of what our new media revolution should mean for women in particular.

Note that you don't have to agree with these predictions and analyses to find them of keen value. For example, I often jest-in-truth that Neil Postman, the best teacher I ever had, was also my greatest failure in my exuberant attempt to get him to think more optimistically (and, I would say, correctly) about the future of media. But Neil Postman's writing from more than two decades ago, and Andrew's introduction to it from 2006, are no less worthy of consideration and enjoyable to read. I did not share McLuhan's pessimism, either, but his two contributions to *Future Media* are, like all of his writing, just chock-full of exploding insights in every line and made me glad once again that I wrote a whole book, *Digital McLuhan* (1999), about this master's work. If the classes I teach at Fordham University are an indication, McLuhan's work is as relevant today in understanding media as it was more than four decades ago.

Speaking of enjoyment, the science fiction reproduced in this volume provides an even higher octane mix of pleasure and contemplation of serious issues regarding the future of communication because, well, fiction is by and large intrinsically more fun to read. Aldous Huxley's *Brave New World* is as relevant today as when it was first published in 1932—in fact, more so, given our advances in genetic engineering. And the communicative possibilities of "soma" are as appealing as ever and even more pertinent to our current world than the 1930s, as Joe Haldeman's "Fantasy for Six Electrodes and One Adrenaline Drip" (written in 1972 but not published until the twenty-first century) makes clear. Gregory Benford's "Centigrade 233" from 1991 is more literally predictive of our array of media today and where they may be going and wraps up all of that in a nod to Ray Bradbury's *Fahrenheit 451* (1953), which is excerpted here and is probably the most media-savvy science fiction novel ever written. "Tech-Illa Sunrise," by Rafael Lozano-Hemmer and Guillermo Gómez-Peña, provides a trenchant, fictional McLuhan-esque analysis in the tradition of John Brunner's *Stand on Zanzibar* (1969) and John Varley's "Press Enter" (1985), except from south of the border, replete with a memorable reference to Arturo Rosenbleuth's "gringo colleague Norbert Weiner." Robert Sheckley's "The Prize of Peril" gives us his patented take—piercing and droll—on the future of television, which is all but already here, as does Kit Reed's "At Central" from 1967.

The effective partnership of nonfiction and science fiction in *Future Media*—the ease with which musings about the future and fictional relationships in the future cohabit and work together in this volume—brings home a point I often make when someone asks me how it is that I write nonfiction about the media *and* science fiction about the media and lots of other things. My answer is that the two are not all that different—at least, not to me. For nonfiction to read well, to captivate its audience enough to receive its messages, the nonfiction should be presented in a commanding narrative. Similarly, there is no reason that science fiction has to be about bug-eyed monsters from deep in the Earth or way beyond Earth in outer space. From its very beginnings with Mary Shelley through Verne, Wells, and the present, science fiction has been and continues to be about more, indeed about our human capacity to not only receive but to change the universe, which I take to be the signature characteristic of our species.

I often joke that my critics say that my nonfiction reads like science fiction, because it takes such flights of fancy, and my science fiction reads like nonfiction, because my fiction is so weighted with heavy ideas, but the truth is no one (that I know of) has ever said this, and if someone did, I would take it as a real compliment. But given the élan of the writings in *Future Media* and the deft way they mix profundity into the spinning worlds described, I have no doubt that critics, students, professors, and anyone up for a good, provocative read about communications and the future will be in for a treat with this anthology. And—peering a bit or farther into the future—I expect that readers will be perusing and learning from this anthology, and using it in their classrooms, in formats and on devices you are currently holding, on media described and foreseen in this volume, and via modes of communication that possibly no one has as yet even envisioned.

Excerpt from *Understanding Media*
The Medium is the Message
Marshall McLuhan

Marshall McLuhan (1911–1980) was the first media scholar to achieve mainstream recognition for his work. His *Understanding Media: The Extensions of Man* (McGraw-Hill, 1964) was a global bestseller and introduced the idea that "the medium is the message" to millions. It is in this opening chapter of *Understanding Media* that McLuhan used this often quoted—and often misunderstood—concept. McLuhan had one thing in mind and the world, all too often, seemed to have another when it came to understanding that the medium is, indeed, the message.

In a culture like ours, long accustomed to splitting and dividing all things as a means of control, it is sometimes a bit of a shock to be reminded that, in operational and practical fact, the medium is the message. This is merely to say that the personal and social consequences of any medium—that is, of any extension of ourselves—result from the new scale that is introduced into our affairs by each extension of ourselves, or by any new technology. Thus, with automation, for example, the new patterns of human association tend to eliminate jobs, it is true. That is the negative result. Positively, automation creates roles for people, which is to say depth of involvement in their work and human association that our preceding mechanical technology had destroyed. Many people would be disposed to say that it was not the machine, but what one did with the machine, that was its meaning or message. In terms of the ways in which the machine altered our relations to one another and to ourselves, it mattered not in the least whether it turned out cornflakes or Cadillacs. The restructuring of human work and association was shaped by the technique of fragmentation that is the essence of machine technology. The essence of automation technology is the opposite. It is integral and decentralist in depth, just as the machine was fragmentary, centralist, and superficial in its patterning of human relationships.

The instance of the electric light may prove illuminating in this connection. The electric light is pure information. It is a medium without a message, as it were, unless it is used to spell out some verbal ad or name. This fact, characteristic of all media, means that the "content" of any medium is always another medium. The content of writing is speech, just as the written word is the content of print, and print is the content of the telegraph. If it is asked, "What is the content of speech?," it is necessary to say, "It is an actual process of thought, which is in itself nonverbal." An abstract painting represents direct manifestation of creative thought processes as they might appear in computer designs. What we are considering here, however, are the psychic and social consequences of the designs or patterns as they amplify or accelerate existing processes. For the "message" of any medium or technology is the change of scale or pace or pattern that it introduces into human affairs. The railway did not introduce movement or transportation or wheel or road into human society, but it accelerated and enlarged the scale of previous human functions, creating totally new kinds of cities and new kinds of work and leisure. This happened whether the railway functioned in a tropical or a northern environment, and is quite independent of the freight or content of the railway medium. The airplane, on the other hand, by accelerating the rate of transportation, tends to dissolve the railway form of city, politics, and association, quite independently of what the airplane is used for.

Let us return to the electric light. Whether the light is being used for brain surgery or night baseball is a matter of indifference. It could be argued that these activities are in some way the "content" of the electric light, since they could not exist without the electric light. This fact merely underlines the point that "the medium is the message" because it is the medium that shapes and controls the scale and form of human association and action. The content or uses of such media are as diverse as they are ineffectual in shaping the form of human association. Indeed, it is only too typical that the "content" of any medium blinds us to the character of the medium. It is only today that industries have become aware of the various kinds of business in which they are engaged. When IBM discovered that it was not in the business of making office equipment or business machines, but that it was in the business of processing information, then it began to navigate with clear vision. The General Electric Company makes a considerable portion of its profits from electric light bulbs and lighting systems. It has not yet discovered that, quite as much as AT&T, it is in the business of moving information.

The electric light escapes attention as a communication medium just because it has no "content." And this makes it an invaluable instance of how people fail to study media at all. For it is not till the electric light is used to spell out some brand name that it is noticed as a medium. Then it is not the light but the "content" (or what is really another medium) that is noticed. The message of the electric light is like the message of electric power in industry, totally radical, pervasive, and decentralized. For electric light and power are separate from their uses, yet they eliminate time and space factors in human association exactly as do radio, telegraph, telephone, and TV, creating involvement in depth.

A fairly complete handbook for studying the extensions of man could be made up from selections from Shakespeare. Some might quibble about whether or not he was referring to TV in these familiar lines from *Romeo and Juliet*:

> But soft! what light through yonder window breaks?
> It speaks, and yet says nothing.

In *Othello*, which, as much as *King Lear*, is concerned with the torment of people transformed by illusions, there are these lines that bespeak Shakespeare's intuition of the transforming powers of new media:

> Is there not charms
> By which the property of youth and maidhood
> May be abus'd? Have you not read, Roderigo,
> Of some such thing?

In Shakespeare's *Troilus and Cressida*, which is almost completely devoted to both a psychic and social study of communication, Shakespeare states his awareness that true social and political navigation depend upon anticipating the consequences of innovation:

> The providence that's in a watchful state
> Knows almost every grain of Plutus' gold,
> Finds bottom in the uncomprehensive deeps,

> Keeps place with thought, and almost like the gods
> Does thoughts unveil in their dumb cradles.

The increasing awareness of the action of media, quite independently of their "content" or programming, was indicated in the annoyed and anonymous stanza:

> In modern thought, (if not in fact)
> Nothing is that doesn't act,
> So that is reckoned wisdom which
> Describes the scratch but not the itch.

The same kind of total, configurational awareness that reveals why the medium is socially the message has occurred in the most recent and radical medium theories. In his *The Stress of Life*, Hans Selye tells of the dismay of a research colleague on hearing of Selye's theory:

> When he saw me thus launched on yet another enraptured description of what I had observed in animals treated with this or that impure, toxic material, he looked at me with desperately sad eyes and said in obvious despair: "But Selye, try to realize what you are doing before it is too late! You have now decided to spend your entire life studying the pharmacology of dirt!"

As Selye deals with the total environmental situation in his "stress" theory of disease, so the latest approach to media study considers not only the "content" but the medium and the cultural matrix within which the particular medium operates. The older unawareness of the psychic and social effects of media can be illustrated from almost any of the conventional pronouncements.

In accepting an honorary degree from the University of Notre Dame a few years ago, General David Sarnoff made this statement: "We are too prone to make technological instruments the scapegoats for the sins of those who wield them. The products of modern science are not in themselves good or bad; it is the way they are used that determines their value." That is the voice of the current somnambulism. Suppose we were to say, "Apple pie is in itself neither good nor bad; it is the way it is used that determines its value." Or,

"The smallpox virus is in itself neither good nor bad; it is the way it is used that determines its value." Again, "Firearms are in themselves neither good nor bad; it is the way they are used that determines their value." That is, if the slugs reach the right people firearms are good. If the TV tube fires the right ammunition at the right people it is good. I am not being perverse. There is simply nothing in the Sarnoff statement that will bear scrutiny, for it ignores the nature of the medium, of any and all media, in the true Narcissus style of one hypnotized by the amputation and extension of his own being in a new technical form. General Sarnoff went on to explain his attitude to the technology of print, saying that it was true that print caused much trash to circulate, but it had also disseminated the Bible and the thoughts of seers and philosophers. It has never occurred to General Sarnoff that any technology could do anything but *add* itself on to what we already are.

Such economists as Robert Theobald, W. W. Rostow, and John Kenneth Galbraith have been explaining for years how it is that "classical economics" cannot explain change or growth. And the paradox of mechanization is that although it is itself the cause of maximal growth and change, the principle of mechanization excludes the very possibility of growth or the understanding of change. For mechanization is achieved by fragmentation of any process and by putting the fragmented parts in a series. Yet, as David Hume showed in the eighteenth century, there is no principle of causality in a mere sequence. That one thing follows another accounts for nothing. Nothing follows from following, except change. So the greatest of all reversals occurred with electricity, that ended sequence by making things instant. With instant speed the causes of things began to emerge to awareness again, as they had not done with things in sequence and in concatenation accordingly. Instead of asking which came first, the chicken or the egg, it suddenly seemed that a chicken was an egg's idea for getting more eggs.

Just before an airplane breaks the sound barrier, sound waves become visible on the wings of the plane. The sudden visibility of sound just as sound ends is an apt instance of that great pattern of being that reveals new and opposite forms just as the earlier forms reach their peak performance. Mechanization was never so vividly fragmented or sequential as in the birth of the movies, the moment that translated us beyond mechanism into the world of growth and organic interrelation. The movie, by sheer speeding up the mechanical, carried us from the world of sequence and connections into the world of creative configuration and structure. The message of the movie medium is that of transition from lineal connections to configurations. It is the transition that produced the now quite correct observation: "If it works, it's obsolete." When electric speed further takes over from mechanical movie sequences, then the lines of force in structures and in media become loud and clear. We return to the inclusive form of the icon.

To a highly literate and mechanized culture the movie appeared as a world of triumphant illusions and dreams that money could buy. It was at this moment of the movie that cubism occurred, and it has been described by E. H. Gombrich (*Art and Illusion*) as "the most radical attempt to stamp out ambiguity and to enforce one reading of the picture—that of a man-made construction, a colored canvas." For cubism substitutes all facets of an object simultaneously for the "point of view" or facet of perspective illusion. Instead of the specialized illusion of the third dimension on canvas cubism sets up an interplay of planes and contradiction or dramatic conflict of patterns, lights, textures that "drives home the message" by involvement. This is held by many to be an exercise in painting, not in illusion.

In other words, cubism, by giving the inside and outside, the top, bottom, back, and front and the rest, in two dimensions, drops the illusion of perspective in favor of instant sensory awareness of the whole. Cubism, by seizing on instant total awareness, suddenly announced that *the medium is the message.* Is it not evident that the moment that sequence yields to the simultaneous, one is in the world of the structure and of configuration? Is that not what has happened in physics as in painting, poetry, and in communication? Specialized segments of attention have shifted to total field, and we can now say, "The medium is the message" quite naturally. Before the electric speed and total field, it was not obvious that the medium is the message. The message, it seemed, was the "content," as people used to ask what a painting was *about.* Yet they never thought to ask what a melody was about, nor what a house or a dress was about. In such matters, people retained some sense of the whole pattern, of form and function as a unity. But in the electric age this integral idea of structure and configuration has become so prevalent that educational theory has taken up the matter. Instead of working with specialized "problems" in arithmetic, the structural approach now follows the linca of force in the field of number and has small children meditating about number theory and "sets."

Cardinal Newman said of Napoleon, "He understood the grammar of gunpowder." Napoleon had paid some attention to other media as well, especially the semaphore telegraph that gave him a great advantage over his enemies. He is on record for saying that "Three hostile newspapers are more to be feared than a thousand bayonets."

Alexis de Tocqueville was the first to master the grammar of print and typography. He was thus able to read off the message of coming change in France and America as if he were reading aloud from a text that had been handed to him. In fact, the nineteenth century in France and in America was just such an open book to de Tocqueville because he had learned the grammar of print. So he, also, knew when that grammar did not apply. He was asked why he did not write a book on England, since he knew and admired England. He replied:

> One would have to have an unusual degree of philosophical folly to believe oneself able to judge England in six months. A year always seemed to me too short a time in which to appreciate the United States properly, and it is much easier to acquire clear and precise notions about the American Union than about Great Britain. In America all laws derive in a sense from the same line of thought. The whole of society, so to speak, is founded upon a single fact; everything springs from a simple principle. One could compare America to a forest pierced by a multitude of straight roads all converging on the same point. One has only to find the center and everything is revealed at a glance. But in England the paths run criss-cross, and it is only by travelling down each one of them that one can build up a picture of the whole.

De Tocqueville, in earlier work on the French Revolution, had explained how it was the printed word that, achieving cultural saturation in the eighteenth century, had homogenized the French nation. Frenchmen were the same kind of people from north to south. The typographic principles of uniformity, continuity, and lineality had overlaid the complexities of ancient feudal and oral society. The Revolution was carried out by the new literati and lawyers.

In England, however, such was the power of the ancient oral traditions of common law, backed by the medieval institution of Parliament, that no uniformity or continuity of the new visual print culture could take complete hold. The result was that the most important event in English history has never taken place; namely, the English Revolution on the lines of the French Revolution. The American Revolution had no medieval legal institutions to discard or to root out, apart from monarchy. And many have held that the American Presidency has become very much more personal and monarchical than any European monarch ever could be.

De Tocqueville's contrast between England and America is clearly based on the fact of typography and of print culture creating uniformity and continuity. England, he says, has rejected this principle and clung to the dynamic or oral commonlaw tradition. Hence the discontinuity and unpredictable quality of English culture. The grammar of print cannot help to construe the message of oral and nonwritten culture and institutions. The English aristocracy was properly classified as barbarian by Matthew Arnold because its power and status had nothing to do with literacy or with the cultural forms of typography. Said the Duke of Gloucester to Edward Gibbon upon the publication of his *Decline and Fall*: "Another damned fat book, eh, Mr. Gibbon? Scribble, scribble, scribble, eh, Mr. Gibbon?" De Tocqueville was a highly literate aristocrat who was quite able to be detached from the values and assumptions of typography. That is why he alone understood the grammar of typography. And it is only on those terms, standing aside from any structure or medium, that its principles and lines of force can be discerned. For any medium has the power of imposing its own assumption on the unwary. Prediction and control consist in avoiding this subliminal state of Narcissus trance. But the greatest aid to this end is simply in knowing that the spell can occur immediately upon contact, as in the first bars of a melody.

A Passage to India by E. M. Forster is a dramatic study of the inability of oral and intuitive oriental culture to meet with the rational, visual European patterns of experience. "Rational," of course, has for the West long meant "uniform and continuous and sequential." In other words, we have confused reason with literacy, and rationalism with a single technology. Thus in the electric age man seems to the conventional West to become irrational. In Forster's novel the moment of truth and dislocation from the typographic trance of the West comes in the Marabar Caves. Adela Quested's reasoning powers cannot cope with the total inclusive field of resonance that is India. After the Caves: "Life went on as usual, but had no consequences, that is to say, sounds did not echo nor thought develop. Everything seemed cut off at its root and therefore infected with illusion."

A Passage to India (the phrase is from Whitman, who saw America headed Eastward) is a parable of Western man in the electric age, and is only incidentally related to Europe or the Orient. The ultimate conflict between sight and sound, between written and oral kinds of perception and organization of existence is upon us. Since understanding stops action, as Nietzsche observed, we can moderate the fierceness of this conflict by understanding the media that extend us and raise these wars within and without us.

Detribalization by literacy and its traumatic effects on tribal man is the theme of a book by the psychiatrist J. C. Carothers, *The African Mind in Health and Disease* (World Health Organization, Geneva, 1953). Much of his material appeared in an article in *Psychiatry* magazine, November, 1959: "The Culture, Psychiatry, and the Written Word." Again, it is electric speed that has revealed the lines of force operating from Western technology in the remotest areas of bush, savannah, and desert. One example is the Bedouin with his battery radio on board the camel. Submerging natives with floods of concepts for which nothing has prepared them is the normal action of all of our technology. But with electric media Western man himself experiences exactly the same inundation as the remote native. We are no more prepared to encounter radio and TV in our literate milieu than the native of Ghana is able to cope with the literacy that takes him out of his collective tribal world and beaches him in individual isolation. We are as numb in our new electric world as the native involved in our literate and mechanical culture.

Electric speed mingles the cultures of prehistory with the dregs of industrial marketeers, the nonliterate with semiliterate and the postliterate. Mental breakdown of varying degrees is the very common result of uprooting and inundation with new information and endless new patterns of information. Wyndham Lewis made this a theme of his group of novels called *The Human Age.* The first of these, *The Childermass*, is concerned precisely with accelerated media change as a kind of massacre of the innocents. In our own world as we become more aware of the effects of technology on psychic formation and manifestation, we are losing all confidence in our right to assign guilt. Ancient prehistoric societies regard violent crime as pathetic. The killer is regarded as we do a cancer victim. "How terrible it must be to feel like that," they say. J. M. Synge took up this idea very effectively in his *Playboy of the Western World.*

If the criminal appears as a nonconformist who is unable to meet the demand of technology that we behave in uniform and continuous patterns, literate man is quite inclined to see others who cannot conform as somewhat pathetic. Especially the child, the cripple, the woman, and the colored person appear in a world of visual and typographic technology as victims of injustice. On the other hand, in a culture that assigns roles instead of jobs to people—the dwarf, the skew, the child create their own spaces. They are not expected to fit into some uniform and repeatable niche that is not their size anyway. Consider the phrase "It's a man's world." As a quantitative observation endlessly repeated from within a homogenized culture, this phrase refers to the men in such a culture who have to be homogenized Dagwoods in order to belong at all. It is in our I.Q. testing that we have produced the greatest flood of misbegotten standards. Unaware of our typographic cultural bias, our testers assume that uniform and continuous habits are a sign of intelligence, thus eliminating the ear man and the tactile man.

C. P. Snow, reviewing a book of A. L. Rowse (*The New York Times Book Review*, December 24, 1961) on *Appeasement* and the road to Munich, describes the top level of British brains and experience in the 1930s. "Their I.Q.'s were much higher than usual among political bosses. Why were they such a disaster?" The view of Rowse, Snow approves: "They would not listen to warnings because they did not wish to hear." Being anti-Red made it impossible for them to read the message of Hitler. But their failure was as nothing compared to our present one. The American stake in literacy as a technology or uniformity applied to every level of education, government, industry, and social life is totally threatened by the electric technology. The threat of Stalin or Hitler was external. The electric technology is within the gates, and we are numb, deaf, blind, and mute about its encounter with the Gutenberg technology, on and through which the American way of life was formed. It is, however, no time to suggest strategies when the threat has not even been acknowledged to exist. I am in the position of Louis Pasteur telling doctors that their greatest enemy was quite invisible, and quite unrecognized by them. Our conventional response to all media, namely that it is how they are used that counts, is the numb stance of the technological idiot. For the "content" of a medium is like the juicy piece of meat carried by the burglar to distract the watchdog of the mind. The effect of the medium is made strong and intense just because it is given another medium as "content." The content of a movie is a novel or a play or an opera. The effect of the movie form is not related to its program content. The "content" of writing or print is speech, but the reader is almost entirely unaware either of print or of speech.

Arnold Toynbee is innocent of any understanding of media as they have shaped history, but he is full of examples that the student of media can use. At one moment he can seriously suggest that adult education, such as the Workers' Educational Association in Britain, is a useful counterforce to the popular press. Toynbee considers that although all of the oriental societies have in our time accepted the industrial technology and its political consequences: "On the cultural plane, however, there is no uniform corresponding tendency." (Somervell, 1. 267) This is like the voice of the literate man, floundering in a milieu of ads, who boasts, "Personally, I pay no attention to ads." The spiritual and cultural reservations that the oriental peoples may have toward our technology will avail them not at all. The effects of technology do not occur at the level of opinions or concepts, but alter sense ratios or patterns of perception steadily and without any resistance. The serious artist is the only person able to encounter technology with impunity, just because he is an expert aware of the changes in sense perception.

The operation of the money medium in seventeenth-century Japan had effects not unlike the operation of typography in the West. The penetration of the money economy, wrote G. B. Sansom (in *Japan*, Cresset Press, London, 1931) "caused a slow but irresistible revolution, culminating in the breakdown of feudal government and the resumption of intercourse with foreign countries after more than two hundred years of seclusion." Money has reorganized the sense life of peoples just because it is an extension of our sense lives. This change does not depend upon approval or disapproval of those living in the society.

Arnold Toynbee made one approach to the transforming power of media in his concept of "etherialization," which he holds to be the principle of progressive simplification and efficiency in any organization or technology. Typically, he is ignoring the *effect* of the challenge of these forms upon the response of our senses. He imagines that it is the response of our opinions that is relevant to the effect of media and technology in society, a "point of view" that is plainly the result of the typographic spell. For the man in a literate and homogenized society ceases to be sensitive to the diverse and discontinuous life of forms. He acquires the illusion of the third dimension and the "private point of view" as part of his Narcissus fixation, and is quite shut off from Blake's awareness or that of the Psalmist, that we become what we behold.

Today when we want to get our bearings in our own culture, and have need to stand aside from the bias and pressure exerted by any technical form of human expression, we have only to visit a society where that particular form has not been felt, or a historical period in which it was unknown. Professor Wilbur Schramm made such a tactical move in studying *Television in the Lives of Our Children*. He found areas where TV had not penetrated at all and ran some tests. Since he had made no study of the peculiar nature of the TV image, his tests were of "content" preferences, viewing time, and vocabulary counts. In a word, his approach to the problem was a literary one, albeit unconsciously so. Consequently, he had nothing to report. Had his methods been employed in 1500 A.D. to discover the effects of the printed book in the lives of children or adults, he could have found out nothing of the changes in human and social psychology resulting from typography. Print created individualism and nationalism in the sixteenth century. Program and "content" analysis offer no clues to the magic of these media or to their subliminal charge.

Leonard Doob, in his report *Communication in Africa*, tells of one African who took great pains to listen each evening to the BBC, news, even though he could understand nothing of it. Just to be in the presence of those sounds at 7 p.m. each day was important for him. His attitude to speech was like ours to melody—the resonant intonation was meaning enough. In the seventeenth century our ancestors still shared this native's attitude to the forms of media, as is plain in the following sentiment of the Frenchman Bernard Lam expressed in *The Art of Speaking* (London, 1696):

> 'Tis an effect of the Wisdom of God, who created Man to be happy, that whatever is useful to his conversation (way of life) is agreeable to him...because all victual that conduces to nourishment is relishable, whereas other things that cannot be assimilated and be turned into our substance are insipid. A Discourse cannot be pleasant to the Hearer that is not Basic to the Speaker; nor can it be easily pronounced unless it be heard with delight.

Here is an equilibrium theory of human diet and expression such as even now we are only striving to work out again for media after centuries of fragmentation and specialism.

Pope Pius XII was deeply concerned that there be serious study of the media today. On February 17, 1950, he said:

> It is not an exaggeration to say that the future of modern society and the stability of its inner life depend in large part on the maintenance of an equilibrium between the strength of the techniques of communication and the capacity of the individual's own reaction.

Failure in this respect has for centuries been typical and total for mankind. Subliminal and docile acceptance of media impact has made them prisons without walls for their human users. As A. J. Liebling remarked in his book *The Press*, a man is not free if he cannot see where he is going, even if he has a gun to help him get there. For each of the media is also a powerful weapon with which to clobber other media and other groups. The result is that the present age has been one of multiple civil wars that are not limited to the world of art and entertainment. In *War and Human Progress*, Professor J. U. Nef declared: "The total wars of our time have been the result of a series of intellectual mistakes...."

If the formative power in the media are the media themselves, that raises a host of large matters that can only be mentioned here, although they deserve volumes. Namely, that technological media are staples or natural resources, exactly as are coal and cotton and oil. Anybody will concede that society whose economy is dependent upon one or two major staples like cotton, or grain, or lumber, or fish, or cattle is going to have some obvious social patterns of organization as a result. Stress on a few major staples creates extreme instability in the economy but great endurance in the population. The pathos and humor of the American South are embedded in such an economy of limited staples. For a society configured by reliance on a few commodities accepts them as a social bond quite as much as the metropolis does the press. Cotton and oil, like radio and TV, become "fixed charges" on the entire psychic life of the community. And this pervasive fact creates the unique cultural flavor of any society. It pays through the nose and all its other senses for each staple that shapes its life.

That our human senses, of which all media are extensions, are also fixed charges on our personal energies, and that they also configure the awareness and experience of each one of us, may be perceived in another connection mentioned by the psychologist C. G. Jung:

> Every Roman was surrounded by slaves. The slave and his psychology flooded ancient Italy, and every Roman became inwardly, and of course unwittingly, a slave. Because living constantly in the atmosphere of slaves, he became infected through the unconscious with their psychology. No one can shield himself from such an influence.
>
> (*Contributions to Analytical Psychology*, London, 1928)

Is Google Making Us Stupid?

What the Internet is doing to our brains

Nicholas Carr

Nicholas Carr writes about technology and culture. He is the author of *The Big Switch: Rewiring the World from Edison to Google* (W.W. Norton & Co., 2008) and *Does IT Matter? Information Technology and the Corrosion of Competitive Advantage* (Harvard Business School Publishing Co., 2004). His most recent book, *The Shallows: What the Internet Is Doing to Our Brains* (W.W. Norton & Co., 2010), is a *New York Times* bestseller. Carr has been a columnist for the *Guardian* and has written for *The Atlantic*, the *New York Times*, the *Wall Street Journal*, *Wired*, the *London Times*, the *New Republic*, the *Financial Times*, *Die Zeit*, and other periodicals. In this essay, Carr worries about changes in the way we read and think. Are our brains literally changing? Are we losing our ability to concentrate and to contemplate? Is Google making us stupid? This essay ran in the July/August 2008 issue of *The Atlantic*.

Illustration by Guy Billout

"Dave, stop. Stop, will you? Stop, Dave. Will you stop, Dave?" So the super-computer HAL pleads with the implacable astronaut Dave Bowman in a famous and weirdly poignant scene toward the end of *Stanley Kubrick's 2001: A Space Odyssey*. Bowman, having nearly been sent to a deep-space death by the malfunctioning machine, is calmly, coldly disconnecting the memory circuits that control its artificial "brain. "Dave, my mind is going," HAL says, forlornly. "I can feel it. I can feel it."

I can feel it, too. Over the past few years I've had an uncomfortable sense that someone, or something, has been tinkering with my brain, remapping the neural circuitry, reprogramming the memory. My mind isn't going—so far as I can tell—but it's changing. I'm not thinking the way I used to think. I can feel it most strongly when I'm reading. Immersing myself in a book or a lengthy article used to be easy. My mind would get caught up in the narrative or the turns of the argument, and I'd spend hours strolling through long stretches of prose. That's rarely the case anymore. Now my concentration often starts to drift after two or three pages. I get fidgety, lose the thread, begin looking for something else to do. I feel as if I'm always dragging my wayward brain back to the text. The deep reading that used to come naturally has become a struggle.

I think I know what's going on. For more than a decade now, I've been spending a lot of time online, searching and surfing and sometimes adding to the great databases of the Internet. The Web has been a godsend to me as a writer. Research that once required days in the stacks or periodical rooms of libraries can now be done in minutes. A few Google searches, some quick clicks on hyperlinks, and I've got the telltale fact or pithy quote I was after. Even when I'm not working, I'm as likely as not to be foraging in the Web's info-thickets, reading and writing e-mails, scanning headlines and blog posts, watching videos and listening to podcasts, or just tripping from link to link to link. (Unlike footnotes, to which they're sometimes likened, hyperlinks don't merely point to related works; they propel you toward them.)

For me, as for others, the Net is becoming a universal medium, the conduit for most of the information that flows through my eyes and ears and into my mind. The advantages of having immediate access to such an incredibly rich store of information are many, and they've been widely described and duly applauded. "The perfect recall of silicon memory," *Wired*'s Clive Thompson has written, "can be an enormous boon to thinking." But that boon comes at a price. As the media theorist Marshall McLuhan pointed out in the 1960s, media are not just passive channels of information. They supply the stuff of thought, but they also shape the process of thought. And what the Net seems to be doing is chipping away my capacity for concentration and contemplation. My mind now expects to take in information the way the Net distributes it: in a swiftly moving stream of particles. Once I was a scuba diver in the sea of words. Now I zip along the surface like a guy on a Jet Ski.

I'm not the only one. When I mention my troubles with reading to friends and acquaintances—literary types, most of them—many say they're having similar experiences. The more they use the Web, the more they have to fight to stay focused on long pieces of writing. Some of the bloggers I follow have also begun mentioning the phenomenon. Scott Karp, who writes a blog about online media, recently confessed that he has stopped reading books altogether. "I was a lit major in college, and used to be [a] voracious book reader," he wrote. "What happened?" He speculates on the answer: "What if I do all my reading on the web not so much because the way I read has changed, i.e. I'm just seeking convenience, but because the way I THINK has changed?"

Bruce Friedman, who blogs regularly about the use of computers in medicine, also has described how the Internet has altered his mental habits. "I now have almost totally lost the ability to read and absorb a longish article on the web or in print," he wrote earlier this year. A pathologist who has long been on the faculty of the University of Michigan Medical School, Friedman elaborated on his comment in a telephone conversation with me. His thinking, he said, has taken on a "staccato" quality, reflecting the way he quickly scans short passages of text from many sources online. "I can't read *War and Peace* anymore," he admitted. "I've lost the ability to do that. Even a blog post of more than three or four paragraphs is too much to absorb. I skim it."

Anecdotes alone don't prove much. And we still await the long-term neurological and psychological experiments that will provide a definitive picture of how Internet use affects cognition. But a recently published study of online research habits, conducted by scholars from University College London, suggests that we may well be in the midst of a sea change in the way we read and think. As part of the five-year research program, the scholars examined computer logs documenting the behavior of visitors to two popular research sites, one operated by the British Library and one by a U.K. educational consortium, that provide access to journal articles, e-books, and other sources of written information. They found that people using the sites exhibited "a form of skimming activity," hopping from one source to another and rarely returning to any source they'd already visited. They typically read no more than one or two pages of an article or book before they would "bounce" out to another site. Sometimes they'd save a long article, but there's no evidence that they ever went back and actually read it. The authors of the study report:

> It is clear that users are not reading online in the traditional sense; indeed there are signs that new forms of "reading" are emerging as users "power browse" horizontally through titles, contents pages and abstracts going for quick wins. It almost seems that they go online to avoid reading in the traditional sense.

Thanks to the ubiquity of text on the Internet, not to mention the popularity of text-messaging on cell phones, we may well be reading more today than we did in the 1970s or 1980s, when television was our medium of choice. But it's a different kind of reading, and behind it lies a different kind of thinking—perhaps even a new sense of the self. "We are not only *what* we read," says Maryanne Wolf, a developmental psychologist at Tufts University and the author of *Proust and the Squid: The Story and Science of the Reading Brain*. "We are *how* we read." Wolf worries that the style of reading promoted by the Net, a style that puts "efficiency" and "immediacy" above all else, may be weakening our capacity for the kind of deep reading that emerged when an earlier technology, the printing press, made long and complex works of prose commonplace. When we read online, she says, we tend to become "mere decoders of information." Our ability to interpret text, to make the rich mental connections that form when we read deeply and without distraction, remains largely disengaged.

Reading, explains Wolf, is not an instinctive skill for human beings. It's not etched into our genes the way speech is. We have to teach our minds how to translate the symbolic characters we see into the language we understand. And the media or other technologies we use in learning and practicing the craft of reading play an important part in shaping the neural circuits inside our brains. Experiments demonstrate that readers of ideograms, such as the Chinese, develop a mental circuitry for reading that is very different from the circuitry found in those of us whose written language employs an alphabet. The variations extend across many regions of the brain, including those that govern such essential cognitive functions as memory and the interpretation of visual and auditory stimuli. We can expect as well that the circuits woven by our use of the Net will be different from those woven by our reading of books and other printed works.

Sometime in 1882, Friedrich Nietzsche bought a typewriter—a Malling-Hansen Writing Ball, to be precise. His vision was failing, and keeping his eyes focused on a page had become exhausting and painful, often bringing on crushing headaches. He had been forced to curtail his writing, and he feared that he would soon have to give it up. The typewriter rescued him, at least for a time. Once he had mastered touch-typing, he was able to write with his eyes closed, using only the tips of his fingers. Words could once again flow from his mind to the page.

But the machine had a subtler effect on his work. One of Nietzsche's friends, a composer, noticed a change in the style of his writing. His already terse prose had become even tighter, more telegraphic. "Perhaps you will through this instrument even take to a new idiom," the friend wrote in a letter, noting that, in his own work, his "'thoughts' in music and language often depend on the quality of pen and paper."

"You are right," Nietzsche replied, "our writing equipment takes part in the forming of our thoughts." Under the sway of the machine, writes the German media scholar Friedrich A. Kittler, Nietzsche's prose "changed from arguments to aphorisms, from thoughts to puns, from rhetoric to telegram style."

The human brain is almost infinitely malleable. People used to think that our mental meshwork, the dense connections formed among the 100 billion or so neurons inside our skulls, was largely fixed by the time we reached adulthood. But brain researchers have discovered that that's not the case. James Olds, a professor of neuroscience who directs the Krasnow Institute for Advanced Study at George Mason University, says that even the adult mind "is very plastic." Nerve cells routinely break old connections and form new ones. "The brain," according to Olds, "has the ability to reprogram itself on the fly, altering the way it functions."

As we use what the sociologist Daniel Bell has called our "intellectual technologies"—the tools that extend our mental rather than our physical capacities—we inevitably begin to take on the qualities of those technologies. The mechanical clock, which came into common use in the 14th century, provides a compelling example. In *Technics and Civilization*, the historian and cultural critic Lewis Mumford described how the clock "disassociated time from human events and helped create the belief in an independent world of mathematically measurable sequences." The "abstract framework of divided time" became "the point of reference for both action and thought."

The clock's methodical ticking helped bring into being the scientific mind and the scientific man. But it also took something away. As the late MIT computer scientist Joseph Weizenbaum observed in his 1976 book, *Computer Power and Human Reason: From Judgment to Calculation*, the conception of the world that emerged from the widespread use of timekeeping instruments "remains an impoverished version of the older one, for it rests on a rejection of those direct experiences that formed the basis for, and indeed constituted, the old reality." In deciding when to eat, to work, to sleep, to rise, we stopped listening to our senses and started obeying the clock.

The process of adapting to new intellectual technologies is reflected in the changing metaphors we use to explain ourselves to ourselves. When the mechanical clock arrived, people began thinking of their brains as operating "like clockwork." Today, in the age of software, we have come to think of them as operating "like computers." But the changes, neuroscience tells us, go much deeper than metaphor. Thanks to our brain's plasticity, the adaptation occurs also at a biological level.

The Internet promises to have particularly far-reaching effects on cognition. In a paper published in 1936, the British mathematician Alan Turing proved that a digital computer, which at the time existed only as a theoretical machine, could be programmed to perform the function of any other information-processing device. And that's what we're seeing today. The Internet, an immeasurably powerful computing system, is subsuming most of our other intellectual technologies. It's becoming our map and our clock, our printing press and our typewriter, our calculator and our telephone, and our radio and TV.

When the Net absorbs a medium, that medium is re-created in the Net's image. It injects the medium's content with hyperlinks, blinking ads, and other digital gewgaws, and it surrounds the content with the content of all the other media it has absorbed. A new e-mail message, for instance, may announce its arrival as we're glancing over the latest headlines at a newspaper's site. The result is to scatter our attention and diffuse our concentration.

The Net's influence doesn't end at the edges of a computer screen, either. As people's minds become attuned to the crazy quilt of Internet media, traditional media have to adapt to the audience's new expectations. Television programs add text crawls and pop-up ads, and magazines and newspapers shorten their articles, introduce capsule summaries, and crowd their pages with easy-to-browse info-snippets. When, in March of this year, the *New York Times* decided to devote the second and third pages of every edition to article abstracts, its design director, Tom Bodkin, explained that the "shortcuts" would give harried readers a quick "taste" of the day's news, sparing them the "less efficient" method of actually turning the pages and reading the articles. Old media have little choice but to play by the new-media rules.

Never has a communications system played so many roles in our lives—or exerted such broad influence over our thoughts—as the Internet does today. Yet, for all that's been written about the Net, there's been little consideration of how, exactly, it's reprogramming us. The Net's intellectual ethic remains obscure.

About the same time that Nietzsche started using his typewriter, an earnest young man named Frederick Winslow Taylor carried a stopwatch into the Midvale Steel plant in Philadelphia and began a historic series of experiments aimed at improving the efficiency of the plant's machinists. With the approval of Midvale's owners, he recruited a group of factory hands, set them to work on various metalworking machines, and recorded and timed their every movement as well as the operations of the machines. By breaking down every job into a sequence of small, discrete steps and then testing different ways of performing each one, Taylor created a set of precise instructions—an "algorithm," we might say today—for how each worker should work. Midvale's employees grumbled about the strict new regime, claiming that it turned them into little more than automatons, but the factory's productivity soared.

More than a hundred years after the invention of the steam engine, the Industrial Revolution had at last found its philosophy and its philosopher. Taylor's tight industrial choreography—his "system," as he liked to call it—was embraced by manufacturers throughout the country and, in time, around the world. Seeking maximum speed, maximum efficiency, and maximum output, factory owners used time-and-motion studies to organize their work and configure the jobs of their workers. The goal, as Taylor defined it in his celebrated 1911 treatise, *The Principles of Scientific Management*, was to identify and adopt, for every job, the "one best method" of work and thereby to effect "the gradual substitution of science for rule of thumb throughout the mechanic arts." Once his system was applied to all acts of manual labor, Taylor assured his followers, it would bring about a restructuring not only of industry but of society, creating a utopia of perfect efficiency. "In the past the man has been first," he declared; "in the future the system must be first."

Taylor's system is still very much with us; it remains the ethic of industrial manufacturing. And now, thanks to the growing power that computer engineers and software coders wield over our intellectual lives, Taylor's ethic is beginning to govern the realm of the mind as well. The Internet is a machine designed for the efficient and automated collection, transmission, and manipulation of information, and its legions of programmers are intent on finding the "one best method"—the perfect algorithm—to carry out every mental movement of what we've come to describe as "knowledge work."

Google's headquarters, in Mountain View, California—the Googleplex— is the Internet's high church, and the religion practiced inside its walls is Taylorism. Google, says its chief executive, Eric Schmidt, is "a company that's founded around the science of measurement," and it is striving to "systematize everything" it does. Drawing on the terabytes of behavioral data it collects through its search engine and other sites, it carries out thousands of experiments a day, according to the *Harvard Business Review*, and it uses the results to refine the algorithms that increasingly control how people find information and extract meaning from it. What Taylor did for the work of the hand, Google is doing for the work of the mind.

The company has declared that its mission is "to organize the world's information and make it universally accessible and useful." It seeks to develop "the perfect search engine," which it defines as something that "understands exactly what you mean and gives you back exactly what you want." In Google's view, information is a kind of commodity, a utilitarian resource that can be mined and processed with industrial efficiency. The more pieces of information we can "access" and the faster we can extract their gist, the more productive we become as thinkers.

Where does it end? Sergey Brin and Larry Page, the gifted young men who founded Google while pursuing doctoral degrees in computer science at Stanford, speak frequently of their desire to turn their search engine into an artificial intelligence, a HAL-like machine that might be connected directly to our brains. "The ultimate search engine is something as smart as people—or smarter," Page said in a speech a few years back. "For us, working on search is a way to work on artificial intelligence." In a 2004 interview with *Newsweek*, Brin said, "Certainly if you had all the world's information directly attached to your brain, or an artificial brain that was smarter than your brain, you'd be better off." Last year, Page told a convention of scientists that Google is "really trying to build artificial intelligence and to do it on a large scale."

Such an ambition is a natural one, even an admirable one, for a pair of math whizzes with vast quantities of cash at their disposal and a small army of computer scientists in their employ. A fundamentally scientific enterprise, Google is motivated by a desire to use technology, in Eric Schmidt's words, "to solve problems that have never been solved before," and artificial intelligence is the hardest problem out there. Why wouldn't Brin and Page want to be the ones to crack it?

Still, their easy assumption that we'd all "be better off" if our brains were supplemented, or even replaced, by an artificial intelligence is unsettling. It suggests a belief that intelligence is the output of a mechanical process, a series of discrete steps that can be isolated, measured, and optimized. In Google's world, the world we enter when we go online, there's little place for the fuzziness of contemplation. Ambiguity is not an opening for insight but a bug to be fixed. The human brain is just an outdated computer that needs a faster processor and a bigger hard drive.

The idea that our minds should operate as high-speed data-processing machines is not only built into the workings of the Internet, it is the network's reigning business model as well. The faster we surf across the Web—the more links we click and pages we view—the more opportunities Google and other companies gain to collect information about us and to feed us advertisements. Most of the proprietors of the commercial Internet have a financial stake in collecting the crumbs of data we leave behind as we flit from link to link—the more crumbs, the better. The last thing these companies want is to encourage leisurely reading or slow, concentrated thought. It's in their economic interest to drive us to distraction.

Maybe I'm just a worrywart. Just as there's a tendency to glorify technological progress, there's a countertendency to expect the worst of every new tool or machine. In Plato's *Phaedrus*, Socrates bemoaned the development of writing. He feared that, as people came to rely on the written word as a substitute for the knowledge they used to carry inside their heads, they would, in the words of one of the dialogue's characters, "cease to exercise their memory and become forgetful." And because they would be able to "receive a quantity of information without proper instruction," they would "be thought very knowledgeable when they are for the most part quite ignorant." They would be "filled with the conceit of wisdom instead of real wisdom." Socrates wasn't wrong—the new technology did often have the effects he feared—but he was shortsighted. He couldn't foresee the many ways that writing and reading would serve to spread information, spur fresh ideas, and expand human knowledge (if not wisdom).

The arrival of Gutenberg's printing press, in the 15th century, set off another round of teeth gnashing. The Italian humanist Hieronimo Squarciafico worried that the easy availability of books would lead to intellectual laziness, making men "less studious" and weakening their minds. Others argued that cheaply printed books and broadsheets would undermine religious authority, demean the work of scholars and scribes, and spread sedition and debauchery. As New York University professor Clay Shirky notes, "Most of the arguments made against the printing press were correct, even prescient." But, again, the doomsayers were unable to imagine the myriad blessings that the printed word would deliver.

So, yes, you should be skeptical of my skepticism. Perhaps those who dismiss critics of the Internet as Luddites or nostalgists will be proved correct, and from our hyperactive, data-stoked minds will spring a golden age of intellectual discovery and universal wisdom. Then again, the Net isn't the alphabet, and although it may replace the printing press, it produces something altogether different. The kind of deep reading that a sequence of printed pages promotes is valuable not just for the knowledge we acquire from the author's words but for the intellectual vibrations those words set off within our own minds. In the quiet spaces opened up by the sustained, undistracted reading of a book, or by any other act of contemplation, for that matter, we make our own associations, draw our own inferences and analogies, foster our own ideas. Deep reading, as Maryanne Wolf argues, is indistinguishable from deep thinking.

If we lose those quiet spaces, or fill them up with "content," we will sacrifice something important not only in our selves but in our culture. In a recent essay, the playwright Richard Foreman eloquently described what's at stake:

> I come from a tradition of Western culture, in which the ideal
> (my ideal) was the complex, dense and "cathedral-like" structure
> of the highly educated and articulate personality—a man or
> woman who carried inside themselves a personally constructed

and unique version of the entire heritage of the West. [But now] I see within us all (myself included) the replacement of complex inner density with a new kind of self—evolving under the pressure of information overload and the technology of the "instantly available."

As we are drained of our "inner repertory of dense cultural inheritance," Foreman concluded, we risk turning into "'pancake people'—spread wide and thin as we connect with that vast network of information accessed by the mere touch of a button."

I'm haunted by that scene in *2001*. What makes it so poignant, and so weird, is the computer's emotional response to the disassembly of its mind: its despair as one circuit after another goes dark, its childlike pleading with the astronaut—"I can feel it. I can feel it. I'm afraid"—and its final reversion to what can only be called a state of innocence. HAL's outpouring of feeling contrasts with the emotionlessness that characterizes the human figures in the film, who go about their business with an almost robotic efficiency. Their thoughts and actions feel scripted, as if they're following the steps of an algorithm. In the world of *2001*, people have become so machinelike that the most human character turns out to be a machine. That's the essence of Kubrick's dark prophecy: as we come to rely on computers to mediate our understanding of the world, it is our own intelligence that flattens into artificial intelligence.

New Brains For Old
James Patrick Kelly

James Patrick Kelly is a prolific and award-winning novelist, short story writer, essayist, reviewer, poet, and playwright. In 2007, he won the Nebula Award for his novella, *Burn*. In 1996, he won the Hugo Award for his famous novelette "Think Like a Dinosaur," and then the Hugo again in 2000 for his novelette "Ten to the Sixteenth to One." He writes a regular column about the Internet and the digital future for *Asimov's Science Fiction* magazine, and this essay is from that magazine's March 2011 issue. Kelly, citing Nicholas Carr and others, worries about our brains and our ability to concentrate at length. He wonders if long books are passé. No more *War and Peace*, no more *Dune*?

remembering

When I began writing this column back in the last century (yikes!), what I *thought* I was about was finding websites that readers of *Asimov's* might like to check out. I've lost track of how many URLs I have commended to your attention—probably close to a thousand. But as time passed it became clear that the net was not only a vast digital library, but also a toolset for remaking culture. E-books and webzines and podcasts and blogs and Facebook and Creative Commons and free content have changed the way you and I relate to one another, to this magazine, to science fiction, and, yes, to society in general. So while the emphasis has remained on poking around cyberspace, from time to time we have stepped back to look at trends and technologies that affect everybody, no matter whether your favorite author is Isaac Asimov (asimovonline.com/asimov_home_page.html), John Updike (achievement. org/autodoc/page/upd0bio-1) or Dr. Seuss (seussville.com). Well, here we go again.

In the last installment, you may recall, we considered the proposition that the Net is not only changing what we do, but is changing who we are. Nicolas Carr, in a book called *The Shallows: What the Internet Is Doing to Our Brains* (theshallowsbook.com) and a website called Rough Type (roughtype. com) asserts that, largely unbeknownst to us, the Internet is reprogramming our brains and thus privileging certain cognitive abilities over others. While some of his claims are more persuasive than others, his central thesis makes sense not only of social trends but also of some interesting scientific research. If nothing else, Carr's arguments will tickle your science fiction sensibilities. For over a century now, we SF writers have been thinking hard about what a Posthuman (io9.com/5530409/the-essential-posthuman-science-fiction-reading-list) might look like.

Perhaps all we need do is peer deep into our flatscreens.

brainy

In order to understand the implications of what Carr is saying, let's divide his argument into three parts and consider each separately. First: is the net really reprogramming our brains? Second: if so then what exactly is changing? Third: are these changes good or bad?

It may come as a surprise to some readers that our brains can be reprogrammed at all. Until the 1970s, orthodox neuroscience held that the structure of the adult brain was fixed and the only change possible was degenerative. As we aged we would lose mental capacity; the best we could hope for would be to slow the inevitable erosion. This view has been largely discredited. We now know that the brain remains plastic; it can be profoundly remade throughout life. And according to the theory of neuroplasticity, what we experience can change the very structure and functioning of our brain. Connections within our brains are continually being pruned and created. Links can come and go in as little as a week. You will remember during the early days of the World Wide Web that those annoying Under Construction Icons (textfiles.com/underconstruction) were everywhere? So it is with your cerebral cortex, which is similarly in a state of perpetual overhaul.

A key insight of neuroplasticity theory is that our brains are structured and restructured by our experiences. "It's what you pay attention to. It's what's rewarding to you," according to Michael Merzenich (en.wikipedia.org/wiki/Michael_Merzenich), one of the leading researchers in brain plasticity. In a 2004 TED talk (ted.com/talks/lang/eng/michael_merzenich_on_the_elastic_brain.html) he goes on to say, "It's all about cortical processing and forebrain specialization. And that underlies your specialization. That is why you, in your many skills and abilities, are a unique specialist. A specialist who is vastly different in your physical brain, in detail, from the brain of an individual a hundred years ago, enormously different in the details from the brain of an average individual a thousand years ago."

We interrupt this column for a brief rant. Why doesn't everyone know about the non-profit TED (ted.com), the best source of science popularization anywhere? Americans have a huge stake in knowing how the world works and yet our understanding of basic science is abysmal. In a 2009 California Academy of Sciences poll (calacademy.org/newsroom/releases/2009/scientific_literacy.php) only 53% of adults knew how long it takes for the Earth to revolve around the Sun, only 59% knew that the earliest humans and dinosaurs did not live at the same time and only 47% could roughly approximate the percent of the Earth's surface that is covered with water. Help! Do the world a favor and turn someone on to TED today.

We now return to your regularly scheduled column.

In 2008 neuroscientist Gary Small (drgarysmall.com) released the findings of a study (newsroom.ucla.edu/portal/ucla/ucla-study-finds-that-searching-64348.aspx) he had conducted at UCLA. His team worked with seniors ranging from fifty-five and seventy-six, half of whom were seasoned net users and half of whom had no net experience. He found that the experienced netizens "registered a twofold increase in brain activation when compared with those with little Internet experience. The tiniest measurable unit of brain activity registered by the fMRI is called a voxel. Scientists discovered that during Internet searching, those with prior experience sparked 21,782 voxels, compared with only 8,646 voxels for those with less experience." Six days later, Small brought both groups back to repeat the experiment. In the interim he'd had the net novices practice Googling around the net for an hour a day. The results? The newbies' brains now showed increased activity in the same neural circuits as the netizens'. They had effectively rewired their brains.

In five days. Clicking around the net for just one hour a day.

Going back to a point he made in his TED talk, Michael Merzenich posted the following to his blog *On The Brain* (merzenich.positscience.com/?p=177),

"When culture drives changes in the ways that we engage our brains, it creates DIFFERENT brains." Speaking of Google and the net, he goes on to write, "THEIR HEAVY USE HAS NEUROLOGICAL CONSEQUENCES. No one yet knows exactly what those consequences are."

Note: Dr. Merzenich isn't usually quite so heavy handed with the CAPS LOCK key.

who reads Tolstoy?

So what exactly is the net doing to your brain? The prefrontal regions of increased activity in the Small experiment are centers of problem-solving and decision-making. A 2009 New Zealand study (unitec.ac.nz/?1A61532B-FED5-4C57-85C3-60163A08462F) reported that people playing the first-person shooter computer game Counter Strike (store.steampowered.com/app/10/) for eight hours a week increased their ability to multitask up to two and a half times. Patricia Greenwell, a developmental psychologist at UCLA, cites the New Zealand study in her review of the literature published in *Science* (tvturnoff. org/images/fbfiles/images/greenfield%20science%202009.pdf). Researchers have indeed discovered a "new profile of cognitive skills"—including increases in non-verbal IQ and facility at multitasking—among heavy users of "the informal learning environments of television, video games, and the Internet." But she points to other studies which document the tradeoffs of the ongoing reorganization of our brains. "Although the visual capabilities of television, video games, and the Internet may develop impressive visual intelligence, the cost seems to be deep processing: mindful knowledge acquisition, inductive analysis, critical thinking, imagination, and reflection."

Which is apparently what sent Nicolas Carr to his keyboard to write *The Shallows*. Understand that Carr is no Luddite; he concedes the many wonderful uses of the net. He is himself a blogger and a social networker and logs many hours in front of a screen. When he first began to notice that it was difficult to pay attention for more than a few minutes, he wrote it off to "middle-age mind rot." But now he attributes the greater part of his lack of concentration, his tendency to skip and skim and most important, his struggle to read and comprehend entire *books,* to what the internet is doing to his brain. The internet is transforming us into multitaskers and "heavy media multitaskers performed worse on a test of task-switching ability, likely due to reduced ability to filter out interference from the irrelevant task set," according to a 2009

Stanford University Study (pnas.org/content/early/2009/08/21/0903620106. full.pdf). Clifford Nass (stanford.edu/~nass/), lead researcher on the study, put it in layman's terms in an NPR interview (npr.org/templates/story/story. php?storyId=112334449&ft=1&f=5): "It's very frightening to us, and I think the reason it's so frightening is we actually didn't study people while they were multitasking. We studied people who were chronic multitaskers, and even when we did not ask them to do anything close to the level of multitasking they were doing, their cognitive processes were impaired. So basically, they are worse at most of the kinds of thinking not only required for multitasking but what we generally think of as involving deep thought."

So what? says Clay Shirky. You may recall Shirky from the previous installment; he wrote the book *Cognitive Surplus*, which makes the case that the change that the net is effecting throughout society is mostly benign—and besides, it's inevitable. Too bad if deep reading has become a lost skill. Get used to the idea that the age of the book is passing. "No one reads *War and Peace*," he writes in an *Encyclopedia Britannica* blog post (britannica.com/blogs/2008/07/why-abundance-is-good-a-reply-to-nick-carr): "It's too long, and not so interesting." Yes, he's being polemical, but the science suggests that he is half right. It doesn't matter whether Tolstoy's books are interesting or not; their real problem is that they are *long* and that they are *books*.

If books that are "too long" are passé, then we must consign some of our cherished classics to the dustbin of history. The one volume *Lord of the Rings* runs 1216 pages. The Fortieth Anniversary edition of *Dune* is 544 pages. And then there are the works of some of my most talented contemporaries—I'm looking at you, George R. R. Martin (georgerrmartin.com) and Connie Willis (sftv.org/cw) and Kim Stanley Robinson (sfsite.com/lists/ksr.htm) and Susanna Clarke (jonathanstrange.com/).

exit

Excuse me, I got distracted thinking about *Jonathan Strange and Mr. Norrell*. I remember feeling a sense of loss as I read the last page, mourning that my long and lovely encounter with English magic was over. Great book. And so very interesting!

So, what the hell were we talking about...? Was it brains? Something that was supposed to be either good or bad, right? I don't know why I find it so hard to concentrate these days.

The fact is, we don't know whether our new brains will be better than the old ones. What we do know is that they are constantly adapting to the cognitive environment we live in. Maybe it's time to take charge of that environment? Otherwise it's definitely going to mess with our heads.

Excerpt From *Fahrenheit 451*

Ray Bradbury

Ray Bradbury has been awarded the World Fantasy Award for Lifetime Achievement, the Grand Master Award from the Science Fiction Writers of America, the O. Henry Memorial Award, the Benjamin Franklin Award, and the PEN Center USA West Lifetime Achievement Award, among others. In 2000, the National Book Foundation Medal for Distinguished Contribution to American Letters was conferred upon Mr. Bradbury at the National Book Awards Ceremony in New York City. *Fahrenheit 451*, published in 1953, is considered by many critics and readers to be his masterpiece. This excerpt is from Part One: The Hearth and the Salamander, where the novel's protagonist, Montag, is in a conversation with his boss, Captain Beatty, in which Montag finds out the truth about books, and burning, and firemen.

From Part One: *The Hearth and the Salamander*

Montag fell back in bed. He reached under his pillow. The hidden book was still there.

"Mildred, how would it be if, well, maybe, I quit my job awhile?"

"You want to give up everything? After all these years of working, because, one night, some woman and her books—"

"You should have seen her, Millie!"

"She's nothing to me; she shouldn't have had books. It was her responsibility, she should have thought of that. I hate her. She's got you going and next thing you know we'll be out, no house, no job, nothing."

"You weren't there, you didn't see," he said. "There must be something in books, things we can't imagine, to make a woman stay in a burning house; there must be something there. You don't stay for nothing."

"She was simple-minded."

"She was as rational as you and I, more so perhaps, and we burned her."

"That's water under the bridge."

"No, not water; fire. You ever seen a burnt house? It smolders for days. Well, this fire'll last me the rest of my life. God! I've been trying to put it out, in my mind, all night. I'm crazy with trying."

"You should have thought of that before becoming a fireman."

"Thought!" he said. "Was I given a choice? My grandfather and father were firemen. In my sleep, I ran after them."

The parlor was playing a dance tune.

"This is the day you go on the early shift," said Mildred. "You should have gone two hours ago. I just noticed."

"It's not just the woman that died," said Montag. "Last night I thought about all the kerosene I've used in the past ten years. And I thought about books. And for the first time I realized that a man was behind each one of the books. A man had to think them up. A man had to take a long time to put them down on paper. And I'd never even thought that thought before." He got out of bed.

"It took some man a lifetime maybe to put some of his thoughts down, looking around at the world and life, and then I came along in two minutes and boom! it's all over."

"Let me alone," said Mildred. "I didn't do anything."

"Let you alone! That's all very well, but how can I leave myself alone? We need not to be let alone. We need to be really bothered once in a while. How long is it since you were *really* bothered? About something important, about something real?"

And then he shut up, for he remembered last week and the two white stones staring up at the ceiling and the pump-snake with the probing eye and the two soap-faced men with the cigarettes moving in their mouths when they talked. But that was another Mildred, that was a Mildred so deep inside this one, and so bothered, really bothered, that the two women had never met. He turned away.

Mildred said, "Well, now you've done it. Out front of the house. Look who's here."

"I don't care."

"There's a phoenix car just driven up and a man in a black shirt with an orange snake stitched on his arm coming up the front walk."

"Captain Beatty?" he said.

"Captain Beatty."

Montag did not move, but stood looking into the cold whiteness of the wall immediately before him.

"Go let him in, will you? Tell him I'm sick."

"Tell him yourself!" She ran a few steps this way, a few steps that, and stopped, eyes wide, when the front door speaker called her name, softly, softly, Mrs. Montag, Mrs. Montag, someone here, someone here, Mrs. Montag, Mrs. Montag, someone's here. Fading.

Montag made sure the book was well hidden behind the pillow, climbed slowly back into bed, arranged the covers over his knees and across his chest, half-sitting, and after a while Mildred moved and went out of the room and Captain Beatty strolled in, his hands in his pockets.

"Shut the 'relatives' up," said Beatty, looking around at everything except Montag and his wife.

This time, Mildred ran. The yammering voices stopped yelling in the parlor.

Captain Beatty sat down in the most comfortable chair with a peaceful look on his ruddy face. He took time to prepare and light his brass pipe and puff out a great smoke cloud. "Just thought I'd come by and see how the sick man is."

"How'd you guess?"

Beatty smiled his smile which showed the candy pinkness of his gums and the tiny candy whiteness of his teeth. "I've seen it all. You were going to call for a night off."

Montag sat in bed.

"Well," said Beatty, "*take* the night off!" He examined his eternal matchbox, the lid of which said GUARANTEED: ONE MILLION LIGHTS IN THIS IGNITER, and began to strike the chemical match abstractedly, blow out, strike, blow out, strike, speak a few words, blow out. He looked at the flame. He blew, he looked at the smoke. "When will you be well?"

"Tomorrow. The next day maybe. First of the week."

Beatty puffed his pipe. "Every fireman, sooner or later, hits this. They only need understanding, to know how the wheels run. Need to know the history of our profession. They don't feed it to rookies like they used to. Damn shame." Puff. "Only fire chiefs remember it now." Puff. "I'll let you in on it."

Mildred fidgeted.

Beatty took a full minute to settle himself in and think back for what he wanted to say.

"When did it all start, you ask, this job of ours, how did it come about, where, when? Well, I'd say it really got started around about a thing called the Civil War. Even though our rule-book claims it was founded earlier. The fact is we didn't get along well until photography came into its own. Then—motion pictures in the early twentieth century. Radio. Television. Things began to have *mass*."

Montag sat in bed, not moving.

"And because they had mass, they became simpler," said Beatty. "Once, books appealed to a few people, here, there, everywhere. They could afford to be different. The world was roomy. But then the world got full of eyes and elbows and mouths. Double, triple, quadruple population. Films and radios, magazines, books leveled down to a sort of pastepudding norm, do you follow me?"

"I think so."

Beatty peered at the smoke pattern he had put out on the air. "Picture it. Nineteenth-century man with his horses, dogs, carts, slow motion. Then, in the twentieth century, speed up your camera. Books cut shorter. Condensations. Digests. Tabloids. Everything boils down to the gag, the snap ending."

"Snap ending." Mildred nodded.

"Classics cut to fit fifteen-minute radio shows, then cut again to fill a two-minute book column, winding up at last as a ten- or twelve-line dictionary resume. I exaggerate, of course. The dictionaries were for reference. But many were those whose sole knowledge of *Hamlet* (you know the title certainly, Montag; it is probably only a faint rumor of a title to you, Mrs. Montag) whose sole knowledge, as I say, of *Hamlet* was a one-page digest in a book that claimed: 'Now at last you can read all the classics; keep up with your neighbors.' Do you see? Out of the nursery into the college and back to the nursery; there's your intellectual pattern for the past five centuries or more."

Mildred arose and began to move around the room, picking things up and putting them down. Beatty ignored her and continued.

"Speed up the film, Montag, quick. *Click? Pic? Look, Eye, Now, Flick, Here, There, Swift, Pace, Up, Down, In, Out, Why, How, Who, What, Where, Eh? Uh! Bang! Smack! Wallop, Bing, Bong, Boom!* Digest-digests, digest-digest-digests. Politics? One column, two sentences, a headline! Then, in mid-air, all vanishes! Whirl man's mind around about so fast under the pumping hands of publishers, exploiters, broadcasters, that the centrifuge flings off all unnecessary, time-wasting thought!"

Mildred smoothed the bedclothes. Montag felt his heart jump and jump again as she patted his pillow. Right now she was pulling at his shoulder to try to get him to move so she could take the pillow out and fix it nicely and put it back. And perhaps cry out and stare or simply reach down her hand and say, "What's this?" and hold up the hidden book with touching innocence.

"School is shortened, discipline relaxed, philosophies, histories, languages dropped, English and spelling gradually neglected, finally almost completely ignored. Life is immediate, the job counts, pleasure lies all about after work. Why learn anything save pressing buttons, pulling switches, fitting nuts and bolts?"

"Let me fix your pillow," said Mildred.

"No!" whispered Montag.

"The zipper displaces the button and a man lacks just that much time to think while dressing at dawn, a philosophical hour, and thus a melancholy hour."

Mildred said, "Here."

"Get away," said Montag.

"Life becomes one big pratfall, Montag; everything bang; boff, and wow!"

"Wow," said Mildred, yanking at the pillow.

"For God's sake, let me be!" cried Montag passionately.

Beatty opened his eyes wide.

Mildred's hand had frozen behind the pillow. Her fingers were tracing the book's outline and as the shape became familiar her face looked surprised and then stunned. Her mouth opened to ask a question...

"Empty the theatres save for clowns and furnish the rooms with glass walls and pretty colors running up and down the walls like confetti or blood or sherry or sauterne. You like baseball, don't you, Montag?"

"Baseball's a fine game."

Now Beatty was almost invisible, a voice somewhere behind a screen of smoke.

"What's this?" asked Mildred, almost with delight. Montag heaved back against her arms. "What's this here?"

"Sit down!" Montag shouted. She jumped away, her hands empty. "We're talking!"

Beatty went on as if nothing had happened. "You like bowling, don't you, Montag?"

"Bowling, yes."

"And golf?"

"Golf is a fine game."

"Basketball?"

"A fine game."

"Billiards, pool? Football?"

"Fine games, all of them."

"More sports for everyone, group spirit, fun, and you don't have to think, eh? Organize and organize and superorganize super-super sports. More cartoons in books. More pictures. The mind drinks less and less. Impatience. Highways full of crowds going somewhere, somewhere, somewhere, nowhere. The gasoline refugee. Towns turn into motels, people in nomadic surges from place to place, following the moon tides, living tonight in the room where you slept this noon and I the night before."

Mildred went out of the room and slammed the door. The parlor "aunts" began to laugh at the parlor "uncles."

"Now let's take up the minorities in our civilization, shall we? Bigger the population, the more minorities. Don't step on the toes of the dog-lovers, the cat-lovers, doctors, lawyers, merchants, chiefs, Mormons, Baptists, Unitarians, second-generation Chinese, Swedes, Italians, Germans, Texans, Brooklynites, Irishmen, people from Oregon or Mexico. The people in this book, this play, this TV serial are not meant to represent any actual painters, cartographers, mechanics anywhere. The bigger your market, Montag, the less you handle controversy, remember that! All the minor minor minorities with their navels to be kept clean. Authors, full of evil thoughts, lock up your typewriters. They *did*. Magazines became a nice blend of vanilla tapioca. Books, so the damned snobbish critics said, were dishwater. No *wonder* books stopped selling, the critics said. But the public, knowing what it wanted, spinning happily, let the comic books survive. And the three-dimensional sex magazines, of course. There you have it, Montag. It didn't come from the Government down. There was no dictum, no declaration, no censorship, to start with, no! Technology, mass exploitation, and minority pressure carried the trick, thank God. Today, thanks to them, you can stay happy all the time, you are allowed to read comics, the good old confessions, or trade journals."

"Yes, but what about the firemen, then?" asked Montag.

"Ah." Beatty leaned forward in the faint mist of smoke from his pipe. "What more easily explained and natural? With school turning out more runners, jumpers, racers, tinkerers, grabbers, snatchers, fliers, and swimmers instead of examiners, critics, knowers, and imaginative creators, the word 'intellectual,' of course, became the swear word it deserved to be. You always dread the unfamiliar. Surely you remember the boy in your own school class who was exceptionally 'bright,' did most of the reciting and answering while the others sat like so many leaden idols, hating him. And wasn't it this bright boy you selected for beatings and tortures after hours? Of course it was. We must all be alike. Not everyone born free and equal, as the Constitution says, but everyone *made* equal. Each man the image of every other; then all are happy, for there are no mountains to make them cower, to judge themselves against. So! A book is a loaded gun in the house next door. Burn it. Take the shot from the weapon. Breach man's mind. Who knows who might be the target of the well-read man? Me? I won't stomach them for a minute. And so when houses were finally fireproofed completely, all over the world (you were correct in your assumption the other night) there was no longer need of firemen for the old purposes. They were given the new job, as custodians of our peace of mind, the focus of our understandable and rightful dread of being inferior; official censors, judges, and executors. That's you, Montag, and that's me."

Centigrade 233

Gregory Benford

Gregory Benford is an award-winning science fiction author and a professor of physics at the University of California–Irvine, where his research is focused on plasma turbulence theory and astrophysics. He has twice won the Nebula Award from the Science Fiction Writers of America and has also won the Lord Foundation Award for achievement in the science. He is the author of nearly two dozen novels, four short story collections, a number of books on popular science, and dozens of short stories. "Centigrade 233" was first published in an anthology honoring Bradbury's *Fahrenheit 451*.

It was raining, of course. Incessantly, gray and gentle, smoothing the rectangular certainties of the city into moist matters of opinion. It seemed to Alex that every time he had to leave his snug midtown apartment, the heavens sent down their cold, emulsifying caresses.

He hurried across the broad avenue, though there was scant traffic to intersect his trajectory. Cars were as rare as credible governments these days, for similar reasons. Oil wells were sucking bone dry, and the industrial conglomerates were sucking up to the latest technofix. That was as much as Alex knew of matters worldly and scientific.

He took the weather as a personal affront, especially when abetted by the 3D 'casters who said things like, "As we all know, in the Greater Metropolitan Area latitudinal overpressures have precipitated (ha ha) a cyclonic bunching of moist offshore cumulus—" and on and on into the byzantine reaches of garish, graphically assisted meteorology. Weather porn.

What they meant, Alex told himself as cold drops trickled under his collar, was the usual damp-sock dismality: weather permanently out of whack, thanks to emissions from the fabled taxis that were never there when you needed them. Imagine what these streets were like only thirty years ago! Less than that! Imagine these wide avenues inundated to the point of gridlock, that lovely antique word. Cars parked along every curb, right out in the open, without guards to prevent joyriding.

"Brella?" a beggar mumbled, menacing Alex with a small black club.

"Get away!" Alex overreacted, patting the nonexistent shoulder holster beneath his trenchcoat. The beggar shrugged and limped away.

Small triumph, but Alex felt a surge of pride. Onward!

He found the decaying stucco apartment building on a back street, cowering beside a blocky factory. The mail slot to 2F was stuffed with junk mail. Alex went up creaky stairs, his nose wrinkling at the damp reek of old rugs and incontinent pets. He looked automatically for signs that the plywood frame door to 2F had been jimmied. The grain was as clear as the skin of a virgin spinster.

Well, maybe his luck was improving. He fished the bulky key from his pocket. The lock stuck, rasped, and then turned with a reluctant thump; no electro-security here. He held his breath as the door swung open. Did he see looming forms in the musky murk beyond?

This was the last and oldest of Uncle Herb's apartments. Their addresses were all noted in that precise, narrow handwriting of the estate's list of assets. The list had not mentioned that Uncle Herb had not visited his precious vaults for some years. The others had all been stripped, plundered, wasted, old beer cans and debris attesting to a history of casual abuse by neighborhood gangs.

At the Montague Street apartment, Alex had lingered too long mourning the lost trove described in the list. Three slit-eyed Hispanics had kicked in the door as he was inspecting the few battered boxes remaining of his uncle's bequest. They had treated him as an invader, cuffed him about and extorted "rent," maintaining with evil grins that they were the rightful owners and had been storing the boxes for a fee.

"The People owns this 'parmen' so you pays the People," the shortest of the three had said.

At last they went away, chuckling evilly. There had been scanty wealth in any of the three apartments, and now, one last hope opened to the click of a worn key.

The door creaked. His fingers fumbled and found the wall switch. Vague forms leaped into solid, unending ranks—books! Great gray steel shelves crammed the room, anchored at floor and ceiling against the Earth's shrugs. He wondered how the sagging frame of this apartment building could support such woody weight. A miracle.

Alex squeezed between the rows and discovered wanly lit rooms beyond, jammed alike. A four-bedroom apartment stripped of furniture, blinds drawn, the kitchen recognizable only by the stumps of disconnected gas fittings. But no, no—in the back room cowered a stuffed chair and storklike reading lamp. Here was Uncle Herb's sanctuary, where his will said he had "idled away many a pleasant afternoon in the company of eras lost." Uncle Herb had always tarted up his writing with antique archness, like the frilly ivory-white shade on the stork lamp.

Alex sniffed. Dust lingered everywhere. The books were squeezed on their shelves so tightly that pulling one forth made Alex's forearm muscles ache. He opened the seal of the fogged polymer jacket and nitrogen hissed out.

Preserved! A signed and dated *Martian Chronicles*!

Alex fondled the yellowed pages carefully. The odor of aging pulp, so poignant and indefinable, filled him. A first edition. Probably worth a good deal. He slipped the book back into its case, already regretting his indulgence at setting it free of its inert gas protection.

He hummed to himself as he inched down the rows of shelves, titles flowing past his eyes at a range of inches. *The Forever War* with its crisp colors. A meter-long stretch of E. E. "Doc" Smith novels, all very fine in jackets. *Last and First Men* in the 1930 first edition.

Alex had heard it described as the first ontological epic prose poem, the phrase sticking in his mind. He had not read it, of course. And the pulps! Ranks of them, gaudy spines shouting at customers now gone to dust. Alex sighed.

Everything in the twencen had apparently been astounding, thrilling, startling, astonishing, even spicy. Heroines in distress, their skirts invariably hiked up high enough to reveal a fetching black garter belt and the rich expanse of sheer hose. Aliens of grotesque malignancy. Gleaming silver rockets, their prows no less pointed than their metaphor.

The pulps took the largest bedroom. In the hallway began the slicks. Alex could not resist cracking open a *Collier's* with Bonestell full-colors depicting (the text told him breathlessly) Wernher von Braun's visionary space program. Glossy pages grinned at their first reader in a century. To the moon!

Well, Alex had been there, and it wasn't worth the steep prices. He had sprained an arm tumbling into a wall while swooping around in the big wind caverns. The light gravity had been great, the perfect answer for one afflicted with a perpetual diet, but upon return to Earth he had felt like a bowling ball for a month.

Books scraped him fore and aft as he slid along the rows. His accountant's grasp of numbers told him there were tens of thousands here, the biggest residue of Uncle Herb's collection.

"Lord knows what was in the other apartments," he muttered as he extracted himself from the looming aisles. The will had been right about this apartment—it was all science fiction. Not a scrap of fantasy or horror polluted the collection. Uncle Herb had been a bug about distinctions that to Alex made no difference at all. No novels combining rockets and sword-wielding barbarians. No voluptuous vampires at all, to judge from the covers.

Alex paused at the doorway and looked back, sighing. Bright remnants of a lost past.

He recalled what awe that Brit archeologist had reported feeling, upon cracking into Tut's tomb. Only this time the explorer owned the contents.

He made his way into the chilly drizzle, clucking contentedly to himself. He shared with Uncle Herb the defective gene of bibliophilia, but a less rampant case. He loved the crisp feel of books, the supple shine of aged leather, the *snick snick snick* of flipped pages. But to read? No one did that anymore.

And surely the value of a collectable did not depend on its mere use, not in this Tits 'n Glitz age.

In less than an hour, Alex reclined on a glossy Korean lounger, safely home, speaking to Louise Keppler on his wall screen. Her face showed signs of a refurb job still smoothing out, but Alex did not allow even a raised eyebrow to acknowledge the fact; one never knew how people took such things. Louise was a crafty, careful dealer, but in his experience such people had hidden irrationalities, best avoided.

"You got the index?" she wanted to know.

He wanted to close this deal quickly. Debts awaited, compounding, and Uncle Herb had been a long time dying.

Alex nodded eagerly. "Sure. I ran it through my assessing program just now."

She was swift, eyes darting over the inventory he had e-sent. He shivered and wished he had paid his heating bill this month. His digital thermometer read Centigrade 08. A glance at the window showed the corners filmed by ice. "I hope we can agree on a fair market price," he said, hoping the timbre didn't seem too hopeful.

Louise smiled, eyes at last pinning him with their assessing blue. He thumbed a close-up and found that they were true color, without even a film to conceal bloodshot veins, the sullen residue of the City's delights.

"Alex, we've dealt before. You know me for no fool."

He blinked. "What's wrong?"

"Books, Alex? Early videos, yes. First generation CDs, sure—nobody realized they had only a seven-year lifetime, unless preserved. Those are rare." Her mouth twisted wryly. "But books? These are even earlier, much—"

"Sure, but who cares?" He had to break in.

"Linear reading, Alex?" Sardonic now.

"You should try it," he said swiftly.

"Have you?" she asked with an arched eyebrow. He wondered if she had closeupped him, seen his own red eyes.

"Well, sure...a little..."

"Kids still do, certainly," she said. "But not long enough to get attached to the classic twencen physical form."

"But this was, well, the literature of the future."

"Their future, our past—what of it?" Her high cheekbones lent her lofty authority. She tugged her furs about her. "That's not *our* future."

His knowledge of science fiction came mostly from the myriad movids available. Now that the genre was dead, there was interest in resurrecting the early, naive, strangely grand works—but only in palatable form, of course—to repay the expense of translation into movids.

"They do have a primitive charm," he said uncertainly. "I find them—"

"So torpid! So unaware of what can be done with dramatic line." She shook her head.

Alex said testily, "Look, I didn't call for an exchange of critical views."

She made a show of a yawn. "Quite so. I believe you wanted a bid."

"Yes, but immediately payable. There are, ah, estate expenses."

"I can go as high as twelve hundred euros."

He blinked. "Twelve—" For the first time in his life Alex did not have to act out dismay at an opening price. He choked, sputtered, gasped.

Louise added, "*If* you provide hauling out of that neighborhood and to a designated warehouse."

"Haul—" He coughed to clear his head. Twelve hundred was only two months' rent, or three months of heating oil, with the new tax.

"My offer is good for one day."

"Louise! You're being ridiculous."

She shook her head.

"You haven't been keeping up. Items like this, they were big maybe a decade back. No more. Nostalgia market."

"My uncle spent a fortune on those magazines alone! A complete set of *Amazing Stories*. I can remember when he got the last of it, the rare slab-sheeted numbers."

She smiled with something resembling fondness. "Oh yes, a passing technical fancy, weren't they?"

He stared at her. There were now linear reader portables that expanded right in your hand. A text popped out into a thin sheet, clear and self-lit. Great engineering.

She didn't notice his silence. "But boring, I'm told. Even those worn out magazines were well past the great age of linear writing."

"That doesn't matter," Alex said, recovering slowly and trying to find a wedge to undermine her composure. He drew his coverlet tight, sitting amid the revelry and swank. Entertainment was essential these forlorn days, when all who could have already fled to warmer climes.

Even they had met with rising ocean levels, giving the staybehinds delicious, sardonic amusement. Alex tired of the main plot thread, a sordid romance. He was distracted by his troubles. He opened the book-like reader and began scanning the moving pictures inside. The reader had only one page. The cylinder in its spine projected a 3D animated drama, detailing background and substories of some of the main movid's characters. He popped up sidebar text on several historical details, reading for long moments while the action froze on the walls. When he turned the book's single sheet, it automatically cycled to the next page.

Alex had been following the intricately braided story-streams of Mohicans for months now. Immersion in a time and place blended the fascinations of fiction, spectacle, history, and philosophy. Facets of the tangled tale could be called up in many forms, whole subplots altered at will. Alex seldom intruded on the action, disliking the intensely interactive features. He preferred the supple flows of time, the feeling of inexorable convergence of events. The real world demanded more interaction than he liked; he certainly did not seek it in his recreation.

The old-fashioned segments were only a few paragraphs of linear text, nothing to saturate the eye. He even read a few, interested at one point in the menu which an Indian was sharing with a shapely white woman. Corn mush, singularly unappealing. The woman smacked her lips with relish, though, as she slipped her bodice down before the brave's widening eyes. Alex watched the cooking fire play across her ample breasts, pertly perched like rich yellow-white pears in the flickering, smoky glow, and so the idea came to him.

"Alex," the Contessa said, "they're *marvelous.*"

"Absolute rarities," he said, already catching on that the way to handle these people was to act humble and mysterious. "Hard to believe, isn't it?"

The Contessa gave her blond tresses a saucy little flip. "That people were that way?"

Alex had no idea what way she meant, but he answered, "Oh, yes, nothing exceeds like excess," with what he hoped was light wit. Too often his humor seemed even to himself to become, once spoken, a kind of pig irony—but the Contessa missed even this much, turning away to greet more guests.

He regarded them with that mixture of awe and contempt which those who feel their lights are permanently obscured under bushels know only too well. For here, resplendent, came the mayor and his latest rub, a saffron-skinned woman of teenage smoothness and eyes eons old. They gyred into the ample uptown apartment as if following an unheard gavotte, pirouetting between tight knots of gushing supplicants. The mayor, a moneyed rogue, was a constant worldwide talk show maven. His grinning image played upon the artificial cloud formations that loomed over his city at sunset, accompanied by the usual soft drink advertisements. Impossibly, this glossy couple spun into Alex's orbit.

"Oh, we've heard!" the mayor's rub squeezed out with breathless ardor. "You are so inventive!"

The mayor murmured something which instantly eluded Alex, who was still entranced by the airy, buoyant woman. Alex coughed, blinked, and said, "It's nothing, really."

"I can hardly wait," the perfectly sculpted woman said with utterly believable enthusiasm. Alex opened his mouth to reply, ransacking his mind for some witticism—and then she was gone, whisked away on the mayor's arm as if she had been an illusion conjured up by a street magician. Alex sighed, watching the nape of her swanlike neck disappear into the next knot of admiring drones.

"Well, nice of them to talk to you longer than that," Louise said at his elbow. She was radiant. Her burnt-rust hair softly flexed, caressing her shoulders, cooing and whispering as the luxuriant strands slid and seethed, the newest in biotech cosmetics.

Alex hid his surprise. "It was much longer than I expected," he said cautiously.

"Oh no, you've become the rage." She tossed her radiant hair. "When I accepted the invitation to, well, come and do my little thing, I never expected to see such, such—"

"Such self-luminous beings?" Alex helped her along with the latest term for celebrities.

Louise smiled demurely in sympathy. "I knew—that's why I strong-armed the Contessa for an invitation."

"Ah," Alex said reservedly. He was struggling to retain the sense that his head had not in fact left his body and gone whirling about the room, aloft on the sheer gauzy power of this place.

Through the nearest transparent wall he saw brutal cliffs of glass, perspectives dwindling down into the gray wintry streets of reality.

Hail drummed at him only a foot away. *Skyscraper*, he thought, was the ugliest word in the language. Yet part of a city's charm was its jagged contrasts: the homeless coughing blood outside restaurant windows where account executives licked their dessert spoons, hot chestnut vendors serving laughing couples in tuxes and gowns, winos slouched beside smoked-glass limos.

Even in this clogged, seemingly intimate party there were contrasts, though filmed by politeness. In a corner stood a woman who, by hipshot stance and slinky dress, told everyone that she was struggling to make it socially on the Upper West Side while living on the Lower East. Didn't she know that dressing skimpily to show that you were oblivious to the chilly rooms was last year's showy gesture? Even Alex knew that.

Alex snuggled into his thick tweed jacket, rented for the occasion. "—and I never would have thought of actually just making the obvious show of it you did," Louise concluded a sentence that had nearly whizzed by him. He blinked.

Incredibly, Louise gazed at him with admiration. Until this instant he had been ice-skating over the moments, Alex realized. Now her pursed-mouth respect struck him solidly, with heady effect, and he knew that her lofty professionalism was not all he had longed for. Around him buzzed the endless churn of people whose bread and butter were their cleverness, their nerves, their ineffable sense of fleeting style. He cared nothing for them. Louise—her satiny movements, her acerbic good sense—*that*, he wanted. And not least, her compact, silky curves, so deftly implying voluptuous secrets.

The Contessa materialized like one of the new fog-entertainments, her whispery voice in his ear. "Don't you think it's...time?"

Alex had been lost in lust. "Oh. Oh, yes."

She led. The crowd flowed, parting for them like the Red Sea. The Contessa made the usual announcements, set rules for the silent auction, then gave a florid introduction. Sweating slightly despite the room's fashionable level of chill, Alex opened his briefcase and brought out the first.

"I give you *Thrilling Wonder Stories*, June 1940, featuring 'The Voyage to Nowhere.' Well, I suppose by now we've arrived." Their laughter was edgy with anticipation. Their pencils scribbled on auction cards. "Next, *Startling Stories*, with its promise, 'A Novel of the Future Complete in This Issue.' And if you weren't startled, come back next issue."

That got another stylish laugh from them. As more lurid titles piled up, he warmed to his topic. "And now, novels. *Odd John*, about a super-genius, showing that even in those days it was odd to be intelligent. Both British and American first editions here, all quite authentic."

He could tell he had them. Louise watched him approvingly. He ran through his little jokes about the next dozen novels. Utopian schemes, techno-dreams.

Butlers circulated, collecting bids on the demure pastel cards. The Contessa gave him a pleased smile, making an O with her thumb and forefinger to signal success. Good. The trick lay in extracting bids without slowing the entertainment. He kept up his line of patter.

"I'm so happy to see such grand generosity," Alex said, moving smoothly on. "Remember, your contributions will establish the first fully paperless library for the regrettable poor. And now—"

Dramatic pause. They rustled with anticipation. A touch more of tantalizing to sharpen matters, Alex judged: more gaudy magazines. A fine copy of *Air Wonder Stories*, April 1930, showing a flying saucer like a buzz saw cutting through an airplane. Finally, an *Amazing Stories* depicting New York's massive skyline toppling beneath an onslaught of glaciers. Laughter.

"We won't have that, will we?" Alex asked.

"Nooooo!" the crowd answered, grinning.

"Then let the past protect us!" he cried, and with a pocket lighter bent down to the stack he had made in the apartment's fireplace. The magazines went off first—whoosh!—erupting into billowing orange-yellow flame.

Burning firewood had of course been outlawed a decade ago. Even disposing of old furniture was a crime. They'd tax the carbon dioxide you exhaled if they could.

But no one had thought of this naughtiness. The crisp old pulps, century-dried, kindled the thick novels. Their hardcover dust wrappers blackened and then the boards crackled. Volumes popped open as the glue in their spines ignited. Lines of type stood starkly on the open pages as the fierce radiance illuminated them, engulfed them, banished them forever from a future they had not foretold. The chilly room rustled as rosy heat struck the crowd's intent faces. Alex stepped away from the growing pyre. This moment always came. He had been doing this little stunt only a few weeks, but already its odd power had hummed up and down the taut stretched cables of the city's social stresses. What first began as a minor amusement had quickened into fevered fashion. Instant fame, all doors opening to him—all for the price of a pile of worthless paper.

Their narrowed faces met the dancing flames with rapt eyes, gazes turned curiously inward. He had seen this transformation at dozens of parties, yet only now began to get a glimmer of what it meant to them. The immediate warmth quickened in them a sense of forbidden indulgence, a reminder of lush eras known to their forefathers. Yet it also banished that time, rejecting its easy optimism and unconscious swank. Yes, there it emerged—the cold-eyed gaze that came over them, just after the first rush of blazing heat. The *Amazing Stories* caught and burst open with sharp snaps and pops. On its lurid cover New York's glaciers curled down onto Manhattan's towers—and then into black smoke.

Revenge. That was what they felt. Revenge on an era that had unthinkingly betrayed them. Retribution upon a time that these same people unconsciously sought to emulate, yet could not, and so despised. The Age of Indulgence Past.

"Let's slip away," Louise whispered. Alex saw that the mayor and his newest rub were entranced. None of these people needed him any longer. His treason was consummated, Uncle Herb betrayed yet again.

They edged aside, the fire's gathering roar covering their exit. Louise snuggled against him, a promise of rewards to come. Her frosty professionalism had melted as the room warmed, the radiance somehow acting even on her, a collector.

As Alex crossed the thick carpet toward the door, he saw that this was no mere freakish party trick. The crowd basked in the glow, their shoulders squaring, postures straightening. He had given these people permission to cast off the past's dead hand. The sin of adding carbon dioxide to the burdened air only provided the spice of excitement.

Unwittingly, Alex had given them release. Perhaps even hope. With Louise he hurried into the cold, strangely welcoming night.

Excerpt from *Brave New World*
Aldous Huxley

Aldous Huxley (1894–1963) came to prominence with 1921's *Crome Yellow* and followed that with a series of similar social satires playing on the pretensions of the upper classes in England. In 1932, he published his most famous novel, *Brave New World*, which exposed a future culture dependent on medical breeding expertise and constant psychological conditioning to produce a society with an imperturbable caste system and an economy utterly dependent on consumerism. In this excerpt from chapter eleven of *Brave New World*, John, the Savage, from an untouched reservation comes to London and encounters Huxley's vision of the mass media entertainment of the future, the "feelie."

Chapter Eleven

After the scene in the Fertilizing Room, all upper-caste London was wild to see this delicious creature who had fallen on his knees before the Director of Hatcheries and Conditioning—or rather the ex-Director, for the poor man had resigned immediately afterwards and never set foot inside the Centre again—had flopped down and called him (the joke was almost too good to be true!) "my father." Linda, on the contrary, cut no ice; nobody had the smallest desire to see Linda. To say one was a mother—that was past a joke: it was an obscenity. Moreover, she wasn't a real savage, had been hatched out of a bottle and conditioned like any one else: so couldn't have really quaint ideas. Finally—and this was by far the strongest reason for people's not wanting to see poor Linda—there was her appearance. Fat; having lost her youth; with bad teeth, and a blotched complexion, and that figure (Ford!)—you simply couldn't look at her without feeling sick, yes, positively sick. So the best people were quite determined *not* to see Linda. And Linda, for her part, had no desire to see them. The return to civilization was for her the return to *soma*, was the possibility of lying in bed and taking holiday after holiday, without ever having to come back to a headache or a fit of vomiting, without ever being made to feel as you always felt after *peyotl*, as though you'd done something so shamefully anti-social that you could never hold up your head again. *Soma* played none of these unpleasant tricks. The holiday it gave was perfect and, if the morning after was disagreeable, it was so, not intrinsically, but only by comparison with the joys of the holiday. The remedy was to make the holiday continuous. Greedily she clamoured for ever larger, ever more frequent doses. Dr. Shaw at first demurred; then let her have what she wanted. She took as much as twenty grammes a day.

"Which will finish her off in a month or two," the doctor confided to Bernard. "One day the respiratory centre will be paralyzed. No more breathing. Finished. And a good thing too. If we could rejuvenate, of course it would be different. But we can't."

Surprisingly, as every one thought (for on *soma*-holiday Linda was most conveniently out of the way), John raised objections.

"But aren't you shortening her life by giving her so much?"

"In one sense, yes," Dr. Shaw admitted. "But in another we're actually lengthening it." The young man stared, uncomprehending. "*Soma* may make you lose a few years in time," the doctor went on. "But think of the enormous, immeasurable durations it can give you out of time. Every *soma*-holiday is a bit of what our ancestors used to call eternity."

John began to understand. "Eternity was in our lips and eyes," he murmured.

"Eh?"

"Nothing."

"Of course," Dr. Shaw went on, "you can't allow people to go popping off into eternity if they've got any serious work to do. But as she hasn't got any serious work..."

"All the same," John persisted, "I don't believe it's right."

The doctor shrugged his shoulders. "Well, of course, if you prefer to have her screaming mad all the time..."

In the end John was forced to give in. Linda got her *soma*. Thenceforward she remained in her little room on the thirty-seventh floor of Bernard's apartment house, in bed, with the radio and television always on, and the patchouli tap just dripping, and the *soma* tablets within reach of her hand—there she remained; and yet wasn't there at all, was all the time away, infinitely far away, on holiday; on holiday in some other world, where the music of the radio was a labyrinth of sonorous colours, a sliding, palpitating labyrinth, that led (by what beautifully inevitable windings) to a bright centre of absolute conviction;

where the dancing images of the television box were the performers in some indescribably delicious all-singing feely; where the dripping patchouli was more than scent—was the sun, was a million saxophones, was Popé making love, only much more so, incomparably more, and without end.

"No, we can't rejuvenate. But I'm very glad," Dr. Shaw had concluded, "to have had this opportunity to see an example of senility in a human being. Thank you so much for calling me in." He shook Bernard warmly by the hand.

It was John, then, they were all after. And as it was only through Bernard, his accredited guardian, that John could be seen, Bernard now found himself, for the first time in his life, treated not merely normally, but as a person of outstanding importance. There was no more talk of the alcohol in his blood-surrogate, no gibes at his personal appearance. Henry Foster went out of his way to be friendly; Benito Hoover made him a present of six packets of sex-hormone chewing-gum; the Assistant Predestinator came out and cadged almost abjectly for an invitation to one of Bernard's evening parties. As for the women, Bernard had only to hint at the possibility of an invitation, and he could have whichever of them he liked.

"Bernard's asked me to meet the Savage next Wednesday," Fanny announced triumphantly.

"I'm so glad," said Lenina. "And now you must admit that you were wrong about Bernard. Don't you think he's really rather sweet?"

Fanny nodded. "And I must say," she said, "I was quite agreeably surprised."

The Chief Bottler, the Director of Predestination, three Deputy Assistant Fertilizer-Generals, the Professor of Feelies in the College of Emotional Engineering, the Dean of the Westminster Community Singery, the Supervisor of Bokanovskification—the list of Bernard's notabilities was interminable.

"And I had six girls last week," he confided to Helmholtz Watson. "One on Monday, two on Tuesday, two more on Friday, and one on Saturday. And if I'd had the time or the inclination, there were at least a dozen more who were only too anxious..."

Helmholtz listened to his boastings in a silence so gloomily disapproving that Bernard was offended.

"You're envious," he said.

Helmholtz shook his head. "I'm rather sad, that's all," he answered.

Bernard went off in a huff. Never, he told himself, never would he speak to Helmholtz again.

The days passed. Success went fizzily to Bernard's head, and in the process completely reconciled him (as any good intoxicant should do) to a world which, up till then, he had found very unsatisfactory. In so far as it recognized him as important, the order of things was good. But, reconciled by his success, he yet refused to forego the privilege of criticizing this order. For the act of criticizing heightened his sense of importance, made him feel larger. Moreover, he did genuinely believe that there were things to criticize. (At the same time, he genuinely liked being a success and having all the girls he wanted.) Before those who now, for the sake of the Savage, paid their court to him, Bernard would parade a carping unorthodoxy. He was politely listened to. But behind his back people shook their heads. "That young man will come to a bad end," they said, prophesying the more confidently in that they themselves would in due course personally see to it that the end was bad. "He won't find another Savage to help him out a second time," they said. Meanwhile, however, there was the first Savage; they were polite. And because they were polite, Bernard felt positively gigantic—gigantic and at the same time light with elation, lighter than air.

"Lighter than air," said Bernard, pointing upwards.

Like a pearl in the sky, high, high above them, the Weather Department's captive balloon shone rosily in the sunshine.

"...the said Savage," so ran Bernard's instructions, "to be shown civilized life in all its aspects..."

He was being shown a bird's-eye view of it at present, a bird's-eye view from the platform of the Charing-T Tower. The Station Master and the Resident Meteorologist were acting as guides. But it was Bernard who did most of the talking. Intoxicated, he was behaving as though, at the very least, he were a visiting World Controller. Lighter than air.

The Bombay Green Rocket dropped out of the sky. The passengers alighted. Eight identical Dravidian twins in khaki looked out of the eight portholes of the cabin—the stewards.

"Twelve hundred and fifty kilometres an hour," said the Station Master impressively. "What do you think of that, Mr. Savage?"

John thought it very nice. "Still," he said, "Ariel could put a girdle round the earth in forty minutes."

"The Savage," wrote Bernard in his report to Mustapha Mond, "shows surprisingly little astonishment at, or awe of, civilized inventions. This is partly due, no doubt, to the fact that he has heard them talked about by the woman Linda, his m——."

(Mustapha Mond frowned. "Does the fool think I'm too squeamish to see the word written out at full length?")

"Partly on his interest being focussed on what he calls 'the soul,' which he persists in regarding as an entity independent of the physical environment, whereas, as I tried to point out to him..."

The Controller skipped the next sentences and was just about to turn the page in search of something more interestingly concrete, when his eye was caught by a series of quite extraordinary phrases. "...though I must admit," he read, "that I agree with the Savage in finding civilized infantility too easy or, as he puts it, not expensive enough; and I would like to take this opportunity of drawing your fordship's attention to..."

Mustapha Mond's anger gave place almost at once to mirth. The idea of this creature solemnly lecturing him—*him*—about the social order was really too grotesque. The man must have gone mad. "I ought to give him a lesson," he said to himself; then threw back his head and laughed aloud. For the moment, at any rate, the lesson would not be given.

It was a small factory of lighting-sets for helicopters, a branch of the Electrical Equipment Corporation. They were met on the roof itself (for that circular letter of recommendation from the Controller was magical in its effects) by the Chief Technician and the Human Element Manager. They walked downstairs into the factory.

"Each process," explained the Human Element Manager, "is carried out, so far as possible, by a single Bokanovsky Group."

And, in effect, eighty-three almost noseless black brachycephalic Deltas were cold-pressing. The fifty-six four-spindle chucking and turning machines were being manipulated by fifty-six aquiline and ginger Gammas. One hundred and seven heat-conditioned Epsilon Senegalese were working in the foundry. Thirty-three Delta females, long-headed, sandy, with narrow pelvises, and all within 20 millimetres of 1 metre 69 centimetres tall, were cutting screws. In the assembling room, the dynamos were being put together by two sets of

Gamma-Plus dwarfs. The two low work-tables faced one another; between them crawled the conveyor with its load of separate parts; forty-seven blonde heads were confronted by forty-seven brown ones. Forty-seven snubs by forty-seven hooks; forty-seven receding by forty-seven prognathous chins. The completed mechanisms were inspected by eighteen identical curly auburn girls in Gamma green, packed in crates by thirty-four short-legged, left-handed male Delta-Minuses, and loaded into the waiting trucks and lorries by sixty-three blue-eyed, flaxen and freckled Epsilon Semi-Morons.

"O brave new world..." By some malice of his memory the Savage found himself repeating Miranda's words. "O brave new world that has such people in it."

"And I assure you," the Human Element Manager concluded, as they left the factory, "we hardly ever have any trouble with our workers. We always find..."

But the Savage had suddenly broken away from his companions and was violently retching, behind a clump of laurels, as though the solid earth had been a helicopter in an air pocket.

"The Savage," wrote Bernard, "refuses to take *soma*, and seems much distressed because of the woman Linda, his m————, remains permanently on holiday. It is worthy of note that, in spite of his m————'s senility and the extreme repulsiveness of her appearance, the Savage frequently goes to see her and appears to be much attached to her—an interesting example of the way in which early conditioning can be made to modify and even run counter to natural impulses (in this case, the impulse to recoil from an unpleasant object)."

At Eton they alighted on the roof of Upper School. On the opposite side of School Yard, the fifty-two stories of Lupton's Tower gleamed white in the sunshine. College on their left and, on their right, the School Community Singery reared their venerable piles of ferro-concrete and vita-glass. In the centre of the quadrangle stood the quaint old chrome-steel statue of Our Ford.

Dr. Gaffney, the Provost, and Miss Keate, the Head Mistress, received them as they stepped out of the plane.

"Do you have many twins here?" the Savage asked rather apprehensively, as they set out on their tour of inspection.

"Oh, no," the Provost answered. "Eton is reserved exclusively for upper-caste boys and girls. One egg, one adult. It makes education more difficult of course. But as they'll be called upon to take responsibilities and deal with unexpected emergencies, it can't be helped." He sighed.

Bernard, meanwhile, had taken a strong fancy to Miss Keate. "If you're free any Monday, Wednesday, or Friday evening," he was saying. Jerking his thumb towards the Savage, "He's curious, you know," Bernard added. "Quaint."

Miss Keate smiled (and her smile was really charming, he thought); said Thank you; would be delighted to come to one of his parties. The Provost opened a door.

Five minutes in that Alpha Double Plus classroom left John a trifle bewildered.

"What *is* elementary relativity?" he whispered to Bernard. Bernard tried to explain, then thought better of it and suggested that they should go to some other classroom.

From behind a door in the corridor leading to the Beta-Minus geography room, a ringing soprano voice called, "One, two, three, four," and then, with a weary impatience, "As you were."

"Malthusian Drill," explained the Head Mistress. "Most of our girls are freemartins, of course. I'm a freemartin myself." She smiled at Bernard. "But we have about eight hundred unsterilized ones who need constant drilling."

In the Beta-Minus geography room John learnt that "a savage reservation is a place which, owing to unfavourable climatic or geological conditions, or poverty of natural resources, has not been worth the expense of civilizing." A click; the room was darkened; and suddenly, on the screen above the Master's head, there were the *Penitentes* of Acoma prostrating themselves before Our Lady, and wailing as John had heard them wail, confessing their sins before Jesus on the Cross, before the eagle image of Pookong. The young Etonians fairly shouted with laughter. Still wailing, the *Penitentes* rose to their feet, stripped off their upper garments and, with knotted whips, began to beat themselves, blow after blow. Redoubled, the laughter drowned even the amplified record of their groans.

"But why do they laugh?" asked the Savage in a pained bewilderment.

"Why?" The Provost turned towards him a still broadly grinning face. "*Why?* But because it's so extraordinarily funny."

In the cinematographic twilight, Bernard risked a gesture which, in the past, even total darkness would hardly have emboldened him to make. Strong in his new importance, he put his arm around the Head Mistress's waist. It yielded, willowily. He was just about to snatch a kiss or two and perhaps a gentle pinch, when the shutters clicked open again.

"Perhaps we had better go on," said Miss Keate, and moved towards the door.

"And this," said the Provost a moment later, "is Hypnopædic Control Room."

Hundreds of synthetic music boxes, one for each dormitory, stood ranged in shelves round three sides of the room; pigeon-holed on the fourth were the paper sound-track rolls on which the various hypnopædic lessons were printed.

"You slip the roll in here," explained Bernard, interrupting Dr. Gaffney, "press down this switch..."

"No, that one," corrected the Provost, annoyed.

"That one, then. The roll unwinds. The selenium cells transform the light impulses into sound waves, and..."

"And there you are," Dr. Gaffney concluded.

"Do they read Shakespeare?" asked the Savage as they walked, on their way to the Bio-chemical Laboratories, past the School Library.

"Certainly not," said the Head Mistress, blushing.

"Our library," said Dr. Gaffney, "contains only books of reference. If our young people need distraction, they can get it at the feelies. We don't encourage them to indulge in any solitary amusements."

Five bus-loads of boys and girls, singing or in a silent embracement, rolled past them over the vitrified highway.

"Just returned," explained Dr. Gaffney, while Bernard, whispering, made an appointment with the Head Mistress for that very evening, "from the Slough Crematorium. Death conditioning begins at eighteen months. Every tot spends two mornings a week in a Hospital for the Dying. All the best toys are kept there, and they get chocolate cream on death days. They learn to take dying as a matter of course."

"Like any other physiological process," put in the Head Mistress professionally.

Eight o'clock at the Savoy. It was all arranged.

On their way back to London they stopped at the Television Corporation's factory at Brentford.

"Do you mind waiting here a moment while I go and telephone?" asked Bernard.

The Savage waited and watched. The Main Day-Shift was just going off duty. Crowds of lower-caste workers were queued up in front of the monorail station—seven or eight hundred Gamma, Delta and Epsilon men and women, with not more than a dozen faces and statures between them. To each of them, with his or her ticket, the booking clerk pushed over a little cardboard pillbox. The long caterpillar of men and women moved slowly forward.

"What's in those" (remembering *The Merchant of Venice*) "those caskets?" the Savage enquired when Bernard had rejoined him.

"The day's *soma* ration," Bernard answered rather indistinctly; for he was masticating a piece of Benito Hoover's chewing-gum. "They get it after their work's over. Four half-gramme tablets. Six on Saturdays."

He took John's arm affectionately and they walked back towards the helicopter.

Lenina came singing into the Changing Room.

"You seem very pleased with yourself," said Fanny.

"I *am* pleased," she answered. Zip! "Bernard rang up half an hour ago." Zip, zip! She stepped out of her shorts. "He has an unexpected engagement." Zip! "Asked me if I'd take the Savage to the feelies this evening. I must fly." She hurried away towards the bathroom.

"She's a lucky girl," Fanny said to herself as she watched Lenina go.

There was no envy in the comment; good-natured Fanny was merely stating a fact. Lenina *was* lucky; lucky in having shared with Bernard a generous portion of the Savage's immense celebrity, lucky in reflecting from her insignificant person the moment's supremely fashionable glory. Had not the Secretary of the Young Women's Fordian Association asked her to give a lecture about her experiences? Had she not been invited to the Annual Dinner of the Aphroditeum Club? Had she not already appeared in the Feelytone News—visibly, audibly and tactually appeared to countless millions all over the planet?

Hardly less flattering had been the attentions paid her by conspicuous individuals. The Resident World Controller's Second Secretary had asked her to dinner and breakfast. She had spent one week-end with the Ford Chief-Justice, and another with the Arch-Community-Songster of Canterbury. The President of the Internal and External Secretions Corporation was perpetually on the phone, and she had been to Deauville with the Deputy-Governor of the Bank of Europe.

"It's wonderful, of course. And yet in a way," she had confessed to Fanny, "I feel as though I were getting something on false pretences. Because, of course, the first thing they all want to know is what it's like to make love to a Savage. And I have to say I don't know." She shook her head. "Most of the men don't believe me, of course. But it's true. I wish it weren't," she added sadly and sighed. "He's terribly good-looking; don't you think so?"

"But doesn't he like you?" asked Fanny.

"Sometimes I think he does and sometimes I think he doesn't. He always does his best to avoid me; goes out of the room when I come in; won't touch me; won't even look at me. But sometimes if I turn round suddenly, I catch him staring; and then—well, you know how men look when they like you."

Yes, Fanny knew.

"I can't make it out," said Lenina.

She couldn't make it out; and not only was bewildered; was also rather upset.

"Because, you see, Fanny, *I* like him."

Liked him more and more. Well, now there'd be a real chance, she thought, as she scented herself after her bath. Dab, dab, dab—a real chance. Her high spirits overflowed in a song.

> *"Hug me till you drug me, honey;*
> *Kiss me till I'm in a coma:*
> *Hug me, honey, snuggly bunny;*
> *Love's as good as* soma."

The scent organ was playing a delightfully refreshing Herbal Capriccio—rippling arpeggios of thyme and lavender, of rosemary, basil, myrtle, tarragon; a series of daring modulations through the spice keys into ambergris; and a slow return through sandalwood, camphor, cedar and newmown hay (with occasional subtle touches of discord—a whiff of kidney pudding, the faintest suspicion of pig's dung) back to the simple aromatics with which the piece began. The final blast of thyme died away; there was a round of applause; the lights went up. In the synthetic music machine the sound-track roll began to unwind. It was a trio for hyper-violin, super-cello and oboe-surrogate that now filled the air with its agreeable languor. Thirty or forty bars—and then, against this instrumental background, a much more than human voice began to warble; now throaty, now from the head, now hollow as a flute, now charged with yearning harmonics, it effortlessly passed from Gaspard's Forster's low record on the very frontiers of musical tone to a trilled bat-note high above the highest C to which (in 1770, at the Ducal opera of Parma, and to the astonishment of Mozart) Lucrezia Ajugari, alone of all the singers in history, once piercingly gave utterance.

Sunk in their pneumatic stalls, Lenina and the Savage sniffed and listened. It was now the turn also for eyes and skin.

The house lights went down; fiery letters stood out solid and as though self-supported in the darkness. THREE WEEKS IN A HELICOPTER. AN ALL-SUPER-SINGING, SYNTHETIC-TALKING, COLOURED, STEREOSCOPIC FEELY. WITH SYNCHRONIZED SCENT-ORGAN ACCOMPANIMENT.

"Take hold of those metal knobs on the arms of your chair," whispered Lenina. "Otherwise you won't get any of the feely effects."

The Savage did as he was told.

Those fiery letters, meanwhile, had disappeared; there were ten seconds of complete darkness; then suddenly, dazzling and incomparably more solid-looking than they would have seemed in actual flesh and blood, far more real than reality, there stood the stereoscopic images, locked in one another's arms, of a gigantic negro and a golden-haired young brachycephalic Beta-Plus female.

The Savage started. That sensation on his lips! He lifted a hand to his mouth; the titillation ceased; let his hand fall back on the metal knob; it began again. The scent organ, meanwhile, breathed pure musk. Expiringly, a sound-track super-dove cooed "Oo-ooh"; and vibrating only thirty-two times a second, a deeper than African bass made answer: "Aa-aah." "Ooh-ah! Ooh-ah!" the stereoscopic lips came together again, and once more the facial erogenous zones of the six thousand spectators in the Alhambra tingled with almost intolerable galvanic pleasure. "Ooh..."

The plot of the film was extremely simple. A few minutes after the first Oohs and Aahs (a duet having been sung and a little love made on that famous bearskin, every hair of which—the Assistant Predestinator was perfectly right—could be separately and distinctly felt), the negro had a helicopter accident, fell on his head. Thump! what a twinge through the forehead! A chorus of *ow*'s and *aie*'s went up from the audience.

The concussion knocked all the negro's conditioning into a cocked hat. He developed for the Beta blonde an exclusive and maniacal passion. She protested. He persisted. There were struggles, pursuits, an assault on a rival, finally a sensational kidnapping. The Beta blonde was ravished away into the sky and kept there, hovering, for three weeks in a wildly anti-social *tête-à-tête* with the black madman. Finally, after a whole series of adventures and much aerial acrobacy three handsome young Alphas succeeded in rescuing her. The negro was packed off to an Adult Re-conditioning Centre and the film ended happily and decorously, with the Beta blonde becoming the mistress of all her three rescuers. They interrupted themselves for a moment to sing a synthetic quartet, with full super-orchestral accompaniment and gardenias on the scent organ. Then the bearskin made a final appearance and, amid a blare of saxophones, the last stereoscopic kiss faded into darkness, the last electric titillation died on the lips like a dying moth that quivers, quivers, ever more feebly, ever more faintly, and at last is quiet, quite still.

But for Lenina the moth did not completely die. Even after the lights had gone up, while they were shuffling slowly along with the crowd towards the lifts, its ghost still fluttered against her lips, still traced fine shuddering roads of anxiety and pleasure across her skin. Her cheeks were flushed. She caught hold of the Savage's arm and pressed it, limp, against her side. He looked down at her for a moment, pale, pained, desiring, and ashamed of his desire. He was not worthy, not... Their eyes for a moment met. What treasures hers promised! A queen's ransom of temperament. Hastily he looked away, disengaged his imprisoned arm. He was obscurely terrified lest she should cease to be something he could feel himself unworthy of.

"I don't think you ought to see things like that," he said, making haste to transfer from Lenina herself to the surrounding circumstances the blame for any past or possible future lapse from perfection.

"Things like what, John?"

"Like this horrible film."

"Horrible?" Lenina was genuinely astonished. "But I thought it was lovely."

"It was base," he said indignantly, "it was ignoble."

She shook her head. "I don't know what you mean." Why was he so queer? Why did he go out of his way to spoil things?

In the taxicopter he hardly even looked at her. Bound by strong vows that had never been pronounced, obedient to laws that had long since ceased to run, he sat averted and in silence. Sometimes, as though a finger had plucked at some taut, almost breaking string, his whole body would shake with a sudden nervous start.

The taxicopter landed on the roof of Lenina's apartment house. "At last," she thought exultantly as she stepped out of the cab. At last—even though he *had* been so queer just now. Standing under a lamp, she peered into her hand mirror. At last. Yes, her nose *was* a bit shiny. She shook the loose powder from her puff. While he was paying off the taxi—there would just be time. She rubbed at the shininess, thinking: "He's terribly good-looking. No need for him to be shy like Bernard. And yet... Any other man would have done it long ago. Well, now at last." That fragment of a face in the little round mirror suddenly smiled at her.

"Good-night," said a strangled voice behind her. Lenina wheeled round. He was standing in the doorway of the cab, his eyes fixed, staring; had evidently been staring all this time while she was powdering her nose, waiting—but what for? or hesitating, trying to make up his mind, and all the time thinking, thinking—she could not imagine what extraordinary thoughts. "Good-night, Lenina," he repeated, and made a strange grimacing attempt to smile.

"But, John... I thought you were... I mean, aren't you?..."

He shut the door and bent forward to say something to the driver. The cab shot up into the air.

Looking down through the window in the floor, the Savage could see Lenina's upturned face, pale in the bluish light of the lamps. The mouth was open, she was calling. Her foreshortened figure rushed away from him; the diminishing square of the roof seemed to be falling through the darkness.

Five minutes later he was back in his room. From its hiding-place he took out his mouse-nibbled volume, turned with religious care its stained and crumbled pages, and began to read *Othello*. Othello, he remembered, was like the hero of *Three Weeks in a Helicopter*—a black man.

Drying her eyes, Lenina walked across the roof to the lift. On her way down to the twenty-seventh floor she pulled out her *soma* bottle. One gramme, she decided, would not be enough; hers had been more than a one-gramme affliction. But if she took two grammes, she ran the risk of not waking up in time to-morrow morning. She compromised and, into her cupped left palm, shook out three half-gramme tablets.

Fantasy for Six Electrodes and One Adrenaline Drip

(A Play in the Form of a Feelie Script)

Joe Haldeman

What would the script look like for something like the kind of "feelie" that the Savage viewed in the excerpt from *Brave New World*? Joe Haldeman, one of the most honored writers in science fiction, has given us that script. Haldeman, a Grand Master in science fiction and a multiple Hugo and Nebula Award winner, has given us a murder mystery, full of sex and violence and soma, wrapped inside a "feelie" script. To be sure, Haldeman's story is an artistic improvement over the "feelie" that the Savage experienced in Huxley's book, and one does have to wonder whether *Brave New World* might have taken on a whole different tone had the "feelie" been as much fun to experience as Haldeman's script promises to be.

ESTABLISHING SHOT I: Slow DOLLY down buffet table loaded with rare and expensive foods. Linger on certain items: purple Denebian caviar in crushed ice with pattern of thin lemon circles; a whole grouper jellied in crystal aspic; pepper-roasted bison haunch, partially sliced, pink and steaming; platoons of wine bottles ranked at end of table, some on ice (use stock SMELL for simulated items, linen tablecloth FEEL down to wine bottles; switch to cool smooth moist glass FEEL at end).

NARRATOR

SEXY CULTURED VOICE

There are almost ten million people on Earth with personal worth over ten million credits. Nine million, nine hundred and ninety-nine thousand of them are just too poor to be invited to this party.

PAUSE AT BISON HAUNCH

Of the remaining thousand, say, roughly half are too new to the game of super-rich to be considered.

SUBLIMINALS: Feel and smell of money.

Half of the eligible five hundred either have unfortunate politics or are simply disliked by the host.

SOUND under NARRATOR: polite early cocktail party chatter.

The rest were all invited. Many were off-planet, some did not care for the host, some had pressing business elsewhere. Eighty-three of them have never appeared in public, and this party seemed too public.

Ninety-four came, some with wives or husbands or concubines or friends; a total of one hundred and fifty-one fortunate people. We are interested in only a few of them.

CUT from wine bottles to HAZLIK. HOLD glass FEEL in right hand. SOUND UP. FEEL expensive clothing on SOMATIC: healthy though no longer young male body. TASTE of fine wine and SMELL of good dope. ADD SOMATIC: dope 0.20.

TIGHT on HAZLIK who is talking animatedly, but his voice is lost in SOUND.

                              NARRATOR

You have never heard of Theophilus Hazlik. His anonymity costs him over ten million credits per year. He owns an interstellar shipping agency, seven industrial combines and two countries on two planets. One of them is on Earth.

He is the host.

CUT TO: MEDIUM TWO SHOT of HAZLIK and CELIA OBRAVILLA. FEEL dopestick in CELIA's left hand, HOLD glass FEEL in right. FEEL cool airco breeze on exposed breasts, silk cape over shoulders, silk trousers and no underclothing. Mix TASTE good dope and wine. SOMATIC: dope 0.30, female sexual tension 0.10. (CELIA is about forty but looks half that. See if Special Effects can get across a somatic subliminal of cosmetic surgery; face and body.)

NARRATOR

Celia Obravilla. Born into big money, married bigger. Husband died and she invested wisely. She would be the most sought-after woman at the party...except there were certain questions about her husband's death...of course, it would be gauche to suggest...and dangerous...

SOUND UNDER and TIGHT on CELIA

CELIA

GESTURING with DOPESTICK

...tiresome, tiresome. I told him, Professor, if *I* can't buy it, nobody can; and if it can't be bought, I don't want it.

SOUND UP and CUT to SAUL MORENO. He is a small dark man, sitting alone in a corner. FEEL tight formal clothes that don't quite fit, heat from coffee mug in right hand. TASTE aftertaste of bitter coffee. SOMATIC NULL.

TIGHT on MORENO

NARRATOR

You might have heard of this man, if your profession involves prostitution or wholesale distribution of smuggled interstellar goods. He is Saul Moreno...

MORENO sips coffee. TASTE real coffee flavored with honey and cardamom.

NARRATOR

...and he is not the only criminal here. For instance—

CUT to FREDRIKA OBLIMOV, talking seriously to someone off-camera. She is very old, but beautiful in a cool elegant way. SOMATIC: generalized aches and twinges of old age. Strong TASTE of gin, though she isn't holding a glass. SUBLIMINALS: feel of spiderwebs and smell of mildew.

NARRATOR

This is Fredrika Oblimov, who is the oldest person at the party and probably the most dangerous. She owns an army, but it is not a conventional one. She has made a moderately large fortune by arranging to have very important people murdered. These by verbal contracts, paid in advance, books juggled in advance to hide her fee, hypnotic wipe of memory of agreement. No money-back guarantee, but she claims never to have failed. She has a contract on one of the people at this party.

Watch now: she is telling a joke.

SOUND OUT and explosive laughter. CAMERA CUTS from person to person, six people standing around FREDRIKA, all laughing desperately. FEEL, SMELL, TASTE, SOMATIC: NULL. HOLD SUBLIMINALS and ADD ADRENALINE: 0.10.

CAMERA HOLDS on seventh man, who is not laughing, but has a small innocent smile.

NARRATOR

Do you see this man?

HOLD NULL and SUBLIMINAL DISSOLVE TO SUBLIMINAL: Feel of cold marble and ADD ADRENALINE: 0.12. DOLLY to BIG CLOSE-UP on face: no movement whatsoever except eyes, slowly scanning from left to right.

NARRATOR

He works for Fredrika. Or, if you prefer, he is her husband.
This week.

CAMERA PANS down arm to left hand. BIG CLOSE-UP on hand, thumb rubbing across fingertips.

NARRATOR

This is not a hand. It's a prosthetic device: the fingernails are harder than steel and keener than razors. Underneath the fingernails, a fast-acting nerve poison.

ADD ADRENALINE: 0.15 and ADD SOMATIC SUBLIMINAL: nausea. SOUND UP as laughing dies.

NARRATOR

He is careful whom he touches.

CUT TO: MEDIUM SHOT OF FREDRIKA and the people surrounding her.

FREDRIKA

You are all so kind.

CUT TO: MEDIUM SHOT of HAZLIK. FEEL, TASTE as before, ADRENALINE and SUBLIMINALS OUT.

HAZLIK

LOUDLY, WELL OVER SOUND

All right, everybody. Let the feast begin!

FADE TO COMMERCIAL

COMMERCIAL (One minute Stiffener © spot)

FADE IN ESTABLISHING SHOT II: Same scene as first establishing shot, but buffet table is now a confusion of empty serving dishes, picked bones, empty bottles, etc. SMELL and TASTE: Good food and drink, tang of dope and tobacco smoke. SOMATIC: Pleasantly full, satisfied feeling. SOUND of slightly more animated conversation over subdued clatter of dishes as servants clean off table.

CUT TO: MEDIUM SHOT of HAZLIK standing, talking to an attractive woman seated on a cushion. FREDRIKA and her companion approach.

FREDRIKA

Pardon me, Theo...

CUT TO: MEDIUM CLOSE-UP of HAZLIK as he turns, carefully does not react, smiles warmly. SOMATIC: Small shiver and ADRENALINE: 0.05.

HAZLIK

Ah, Fredrika.

CUT TO: MEDIUM GROUP SHOT of HAZLIK, FREDRIKA and COMPANION.

FREDRIKA

Theo, I don't think you've met my husband, George.

HAZLIK knows exactly what GEORGE is. As they shake hands: ADRENALINE: 0.10, SUBLIMINAL: Feel and smell of clotted blood. FEEL of rough skin against rough skin.

HAZLIK

URBANE: HONEST OPEN SMILE, CRINKLED EYES.

My pleasure.

GEORGE

COLD SMILE

Yes.

MEDIUM TWO SHOT from George's point of view: HAZLIK and FREDRIKA silently regard each other just a moment longer than politeness would allow. ADRENALINE, SUBLIMINAL OUT. SOMATIC: Nerve in neck begins throbbing.

HAZLIK

QUESTIONING

Business has been good.

FREDRIKA

No worse than usual.

PAUSE AND IRONIC SMILE

Men still pay for my services. Fatal attraction.

HAZLIK does not smile. ADRENALINE: 0.12, SOMATIC: Nausea of fear.

HAZLIK drinks large gulp, TASTE and SMELL of warm brandy going down. NAUSEA UP and ADD SOMATIC: gagging reflex.

                              HAZLIK

COUGHS

    Pardon me. (COUGHS AGAIN) Have to cut down on my dope.

                              FREDRIKA

    I can recommend a good hypnotist.

                              HAZLIK

CATCHING REFERENCE TO F'S BUSINESS METHODS

    I've tried that. Several times, I think.

                              FREDRIKA

MERRILY, GLIDING AWAY

    You're right, you're right.

SUBLIMINAL: Feel of cobwebs and sound of batwings.

HAZLIK turns back to young lady. ADRENALINE HOLD and SUBLIMINAL OUT. SOMATIC: Male sexual tension 0.10. INTERCUT CLOSE-UPS, HAZLIK and GIRL.

                              HAZLIK

    You were saying?

Girl is wearing gossamer chemise. FEEL of silk against nipples and thighs. SOMATIC: Female sexual tension 0.20. SMELL of vaginal musk and perfume. GIRL runs tongue between lips rapidly. TASTE and FEEL of warm flesh.

GIRL

Not what I was saying. What I was thinking...

HAZLIK

BACK IN CONTROL

Do you think often?

GIRL

IGNORES JIBE

I was wondering what it would be like to make love to a billionaire.

HAZLIK

SOMATIC: Male sexual tension 0.30.

Seven times over.

GIRL

CONFUSED

Seven *times?*

HAZLIK

CHUCKLES. SOMATIC: Male sexual tension 0.40.

No, no—seven billion.

GIRL

GIGGLES

I thought...

HAZLIK

SOMATIC: Male sexual tension 0.50, SMELL: Male musk, FEEL: erection fighting clothes.

LAUGHS

Anything's possible.

LAP DISSOLVE to HAZLIK and girl making love on lawn.

(Avoid stock intercourse stimulus/response package. The important thing to get across is the idea that Hazlik is sexually potent yet emotionally empty.)

(Consider the following sequence merely as a guide to the director. Much, of course, depends on the individual actors' feelings for one another—Stiffener © or no!)

STROBE ALTERNATION

GIRL: FEEL: soles of feet, buttocks, shoulder blades, back of head all on grass— going back and forth a couple of centimeters with each thrust; HAZLIK's chest hair rubbing against breasts, hairy legs gently abrading inside thighs; slightly painful bumping contact between pubic bones, faces not in contact, his hands pressed against small of back. SMELL: Male musk under dope and wine. SOMATIC: Penis rigid inside vagina, active but controlled, very long thrusts alternating with short quick ones; her sexual response during minute of ALTERNATION before orgasm equals $0.50 + .006667t(\sin\{t/7.78\}$), t in seconds. Then four orgasms, decreasing in intensity as they increase in painfulness, separated by 8, 6, and 4 seconds...then SMELL: Female musk UP and add perspiration. FEEL: Pain from pubic bone contact UP on last two orgasms. SUBLIMINAL: Taste of blood. HAZILIK: FEEL: Elbows to forearms on grass, sharing weight with knees. Fingertips move from buttock cleavage to lumbar dimples. Vagina is almost excessively moist; penis slipping forward and back with almost no resistance. Breasts moving regularly, deforming under his chest. Toenails digging into dirt. SMELL: Vaginal musk and perspiration, grass. TASTE: Aftertaste of good dope and brandy. SOMATIC: Constant male sexual tension 0.75 throughout pre-orgasm minute (distracted, enjoying stiffness of penis more than he is the loving). Slightly painful rhythmic contact between testicles and GIRL's buttocks. Simultaneously with GIRL's last orgasm, HAZLIK ejaculates without joy. SUBLIMINAL: Carrying heavy weight. *BOTH*: Stock SOUND of intercourse.

HAZLIK and GIRL remain joined for about thirty seconds, panting wordlessly after last orgasm. FADE OUT HAZLIK: FEEL, SMELL, SOMATIC. GIRL: FEEL: HAZLIK slipping out of her, she clasps legs over his body.

                    GIRL

    You were very good.

                    HAZLIK

PATS SHOULDER AWKWARDLY AND SLIPS OUT OF HER

    So were you, child.

                    GIRL

LITTLE VOICE

    Don't you want to talk? Sit here a minute and... maybe...

                    HAZLIK
DRESSING, CHUCKLES

Not right now, no...I'm host of this thing, remember? Have
to get back and mix.

GIRL stretches out on her side, watching HAZLIK dress. FEEL: Grass prickling
arm, head on arm, puddle of sweat trickles out of navel, stock post-coital
stickiness and languor but SOMATIC: Female sexual tension 0.20 (vaguely
unsatisfied). SUBLIMINAL: Female orgasm 0.05, feel of feathers stroking
places that can't be reached.

GIRL

I...of course.

LONG TWO SHOT as HAZLIK stretches and yawns hugely, smiles at GIRL
and says goodbye with casual wave. CAMERA FOLLOWS as he returns to
party. He passes several other couples making love, but of course pays no
attention, except to exchange spoken greeting with one man.

CUT TO: LONG SHOT, party interior. SMELL: Dope and tobacco smoke,
incense, crowd odor very slight, alcohol and coffee. There are about sixty
people standing and sitting around in small groups. HAZLIK enters through
inconspicuous automatic door, walks toward bar. SOMATIC: Thirst, nervous
energy. SUBLIMINAL: Male sexual tension 0.05.

HAZLIK

TO BARTENDER

Double wine punch, ice.

MEDIUM TWO SHOT as CELIA approaches HAZLIK's back. ADRENALINE:
0.10, SUBLIMINAL: Feel of hands squeezing HAZLIK's throat.

CELIA

Having a good time, darling?

HAZLIK

TURNS

Ah, Celia. Darling. Yes, a wonderful time.

CELIA

TO BARTENDER (OFF)

Cold bhang, please... Thank you.

CELIA moves in very close to HAZLIK, smiles.

CELIA

OVER GLASS, VENOMOUS WHISPER

You old goat...that...*child!*

HAZLIK

ARTIFICIAL SMILE. SUBLIMINAL: Buggery, violent rape.

I didn't know you'd had experience with goats, too, darling.

CELIA

Only you, my dear.

Tense silence for several seconds. TASTE: Cold bhang, spiced wine. SOMATIC: Dope 0.05. ADRENALINE down and OUT.

HAZLIK

SOFTENING SLIGHTLY

She was something special to you?

CELIA gulps half of her drink and looks away from HAZLIK, abstracted. SOMATIC: Dope 0.10.

CELIA

Once.

SUBLIMINAL: Fear spectrum slowly UP to SOMATIC: Stomach tightens, ADRENALINE: 0.20 as HAZLIK remembers CELIA's reputation.

HAZLIK

SLOWLY

I'm sorry. I really am...there was no way I could have known.

CELIA

LOOKING AT HIM STRANGELY

No.

CELIA walks away as HAZLIK studies his drink. SOMATIC: Fear spectrum fade DOWN and slowly OUT. HAZLIK walks off in other direction. CAMERA FOLLOWS for a short distance. HAZLIK idly stops to watch a dice game in progress on a table which is a large block of natural crystal. The three dice clatter down and come to a rest: fifteen. Mixed murmurs of approval and unhappiness. Money changes hands. SUBLIMINAL: Feel, smell of money. SOUND of money crinkling.

PLAYER

High up *sans* thirteen.

OTHER PLAYERS

Cover high.

Low middle.

High middle.

Low field.

PLAYER

Thirteen, somebody.

HAZLIK

How much?

PLAYER

One thou...oh, Hazlik. Good party. Why don't you wait for a field?

HAZLIK

Ah...luck is luck.

While HAZLIK takes wallet from cape pocket, MORENO approaches, comes up very close.

TIGHT TWO SHOT as MORENO speaks softly to HAZLIK. SMELL: Strong coffee on breath.

MORENO

WHISPERS

Hazlik. I have to talk to you.

HAZLIK hands single bill to PLAYER, turns back to MORENO.

                    HAZLIK

A LITTLE ANNOYED

    Can't it wait?

                    MORENO

    No. Not at all.

HAZLIK turns back on game as dice clatter. CAMERA FOLLOWS as he walks off with MORENO.

                    PLAYER (OFF)

    Fifteen *again!*

                    HAZLIK

AS THEY WALK

    Well?

                    MORENO

LOOKING AROUND

    One of your guests, um...(WHISPERS) have you met
    Fredrika's escort?

                    HAZLIK

EXPRESSIONLESS

Yes. Pleasant fellow.

MORENO

Can we go somewhere in private?

HAZLIK

SHRUGS

The outside balcony. Here.

They both step into a lift zone and float to the second floor.

SOMATIC: Stomach dropping reinforced by ADRENALINE: 0.10. HAZLIK
opens manual door and steps outside. MORENO follows.

LONG SHOT past HAZLIK as he goes to edge of balcony and looks out over
grounds. The full moon is up; acres of neat grass, landscaping, formal gardens.
SMELL: Flowers, grass. SOUND: Crickets, far-off jungle noises, MORENO's
footsteps as he comes to join HAZLIK.

TIGHT TWO SHOT on MORENO and HAZLIK.

MORENO

You keep the jungle away quite well.

HAZLIK

Yes. I wish I could pattern my life so. (SMILES) Fredrika?

INTERCUT CLOSE-UPS MORENO and HAZLIK.

MORENO

Her "George." He worked for me once. I had to discharge him.

HAZLIK

STILL GAZING OVER GROUNDS

For good reason, I'm sure.

MORENO

He killed a man.

HAZLIK laughs, a short bark, and looks at MORENO, wryly.

HAZLIK

You've never killed a man.

MORENO snorts and walks a short distance away. He talks into the night.

MORENO

I'm not talking about business. He killed this man for pleasure...

PAUSE. SUBLIMINAL: Spiders crawling through filth.

...after making love to him. I later found...(PAUSE) that he had done it before. Also to women.

HAZLIK

LIGHTLY

He seems a man well suited to his profession.

HAZLIK turns his back to the railing and studies the party below, through the glass doors. SOUND: Faint party noises.

HAZLIK

What has this to do with me?

MORENO

Everything and nothing. (TURNS) There *will* be murder here tonight. She wouldn't have brought...him...as a social ornament.

HAZLIK takes out a dopestick and has trouble waving it alight. TIGHT on HAZLIK as he blows the tip into flame and sucks. SOMATIC: Dope 0.40 then UNDER to 0.10.

HAZLIK

This is the most private of private property, on Earth. She will play her games and there will be no trouble, unless somebody wants to make trouble. With her, not many would.

MORENO

Don't you care who is going to die in your own house?

HAZLIK

I don't care to *know*. Not ahead of time.

MORENO

Not even if it's a friend, or someone you love? Not even if it is yourself?

HAZLIK turns around again, slowly, and throws dopestick over balcony edge. He watches the spark fall and die.

HAZLIK

Fredrika is bold. But she is not stupid. (PAUSES) Besides, how could *you* know who her...intended is?

MORENO

SHRUGS

I don't. But I have men here, too.

HAZLIK

COLDLY

Were they invited?

MORENO

Yes. You said to bring a friend. I brought a very good friend. So did Porfiry Esterbrook, and so did...

HAZLIK

I see. How many?

MORENO

Enough to isolate..."George" ...and ask him some questions.

HAZLIK

TO HIMSELF

> You aren't doing this for my sake. (ADDRESSES MORENO DIRECTLY, SHADE OF MENACE) Exactly what is going on?

MORENO

> That also may be one of those things that you don't wish to know.

MORENO sees HAZLIK's face and realizes he's gone a little too far. SOMATIC: Stomach tightening and ADRENALINE: 0.20.

MORENO

LONG PAUSE, SWALLOWS

> All right. A...a power struggle, so to speak. No—an extermination! (SPEAKING WITH PASSION FOR THE FIRST TIME) The old bitch has got to go! Our lives are... too complicated, too uncertain. Get rid of her, and—

HAZLIK

> I believe she has been useful to me in the past. You've probably used her services, too. One never remembers, of course.

MORENO

ANGRY

> No. Never.

HAZLIK

It certainly was convenient to your industry when Mlle. Legrange passed on.

MORENO

Yes. But I never would have hired that old hag to do it. It was a fortunate accident.

HAZLIK

LIGHT LAUGH, SOMEHOW EVIL

Our little world is full of accidents that turn out to favor one or the other of us. Fredrika is behind most of them.

MORENO

FACE SET

But not Mlle. Legrange.

HAZLIK

As you wish.

The two men stand in silence for twenty seconds. HAZLIK takes out a dopestick and then returns it to the pack.

HAZLIK

At any rate...you wish to enlist my aid, against Fredrika?

MORENO

Not directly. I'd like some guarantee that you won't interfere, though.

HAZLIK silent.

> Do you still have those, uh, small rooms...underneath the
> place?

HAZLIK

> The soundproofed conference rooms? Of course. Would you
> like one?

MORENO

> Yes! If we could get him...

HAZLIK

> I don't want to hear about it. Not until afterwards. And never,
> unless it directly concerns me.

MORENO

> Excellent. I'll tell—

HAZLIK

> Wait. I go first.

HAZLIK leaves. CUT TO: BIG CLOSE-UP of MORENO, smiling now.

FADE OUT to COMMERCIAL.

COMMERCIAL: One-minute Stiffener © spot

FADE IN: ESTABLISHING SHOT III: MEDIUM, GROUP SHOT of
FREDRIKA and GEORGE with several other people, talking. A white-coated
servant glides up to FREDRIKA and whispers something to her. She goes away

with him. GEORGE begins to follow, but THREE MEN pass between them.

BIG CLOSE-UP on right hand of FIRST MAN, who is holding a small ampoule.

TIGHT TWO SHOT of FIRST MAN and GEORGE as FIRST MAN squeezes ampoule and a jet of colorless fluid sprays into GEORGE's face. It is "come-along" gas. SMELL of ammonia, FEEL icy splash on face.

GEORGE reaches out with left "hand" but barely brushes man's arm. GEORGE gets a funny passive look, his hand drops back, and he stands still.

FIRST MAN

WHISPERING

Now, George, just follow us.

TIGHT GROUP SHOT of the THREE MEN herding GEORGE away. CAMERA FOLLOWS for a short distance.

CUT TO: MEDIUM TWO SHOT of FREDRIKA and SERVANT. She is arguing with him and doesn't notice GEORGE is headed the other way.

CUT TO: LONG SHOT of downstairs room as THREE MEN and GEORGE enter. The walls and ceiling are covered with a mossy substance; the soundproofing. There is a conference table in the center of the room. The chair at the end of the table has manacles attached to the arms. SMELL: Dry "chemical" odor of soundproofing. SUBLIMINAL: Feel scratchy dry moss, smell brimstone and rotting flesh. ADRENALINE: 0.10 and OUT.

CAMERA FOLLOWS FIRST MAN and GEORGE to the end of the table.

FIRST MAN

You sit here.

TIGHT ON FIRST MAN as he grips edge of table, wobbles. SOMATIC: Extreme nausea, fire in right arm.

                    SECOND MAN (OFF)

What's wrong?

                    FIRST MAN

I don't...know...he must have...gotten (CHOKING SOUND)

MEDIUM GROUP SHOT as FIRST MAN falls to floor, begins jerking around. SECOND MAN moves to help him, stops. Looks up at GEORGE, who is watching the whole thing with quiet interest.

                    SECOND MAN (TO GEORGE)

Did you do that?

                    GEORGE

INNOCENT SMILE

Yes. Nerve poison.

TIGHT ON FIRST MAN as he expires noisily, messily on floor. SMELL of vomit, SUBLIMINAL: Taste of vomit, extreme nausea, SOMATIC: White-out.

                    THIRD MAN

God.

                    SECOND MAN

SWALLOWS, TRYING TO STAY CALM

How did you do it?

GEORGE

I told you. Nerve poison.

THIRD MAN

Let's fasten him down and loosen him up.

SECOND MAN

So do it. The manacles.

THIRD MAN gives SECOND MAN a hard glance, goes cautiously to GEORGE. He stands just out of arm-reach.

THIRD MAN

Put your arms up on the arms of the chair.

GEORGE obeys without hesitation, but moving slowly. ADRENALINE: 0.15.

THIRD MAN

All right. Stay that way.

ADRENALINE: 0.25. GEORGE's hands are laying palm up on the chair arms. BIG CLOSE-UP as THIRD MAN turns right hand over and latches manacle (SOUND: Loud click and SUBLIMINAL: Metal tightness around wrist.) over wrist. He reaches for left hand and GEORGE closes hand over his. MICRO CLOSE-UP shows fingernail slitting flesh.

TIGHT TWO SHOT of GEORGE and THIRD MAN as THIRD MAN jerks his hand away.

THIRD MAN

Ouch! (TOUCHES CUT TO MOUTH) Some fingernails
this guy...(SHARP INTAKE OF BREATH) He...

BIG CLOSE-UP on THIRD MAN's face. ADRENALINE: 0.35.

SECOND MAN (OFF)

Sit down. Don't move—I'll get some atropine.

LONG GROUP SHOT: GEORGE watches passively as SECOND MAN runs
from room. THIRD MAN sits down cautiously. ADRENALINE: 0.40.

THIRD MAN

Will atropine work?

GEORGE

If he gets back in time.

ADRENALINE: 0.50 and OUT.

CUT TO: TIGHT GROUP SHOT of MORENO, HAZLIK and others sitting at
crystal table playing dice. SECOND MAN hurries up to MORENO, whispers.

MORENO

TO HAZLIK, ACROSS

Do you have any atropine in the place?

INTERCUT CLOSE-UPS, HAZLIK and MORENO

HAZLIK (COUNTING MONEY)

ANNOYED

What?

MORENO

Atropine! Uh...a drug overdose.

HAZLIK (TO SECOND MAN)

There might be some. Ask the butler.

HAZLIK (TO MORENO)

One of your men popping on duty?

MORENO

Not really...it's more, uh, concerned with what we discussed earlier.

HAZLIK

The woman?

MORENO

Her man, actually.

HAZLIK

STANDS CASUALLY

Let's go take a look.

CUT TO: LONG SHOT past MORENO and HAZLIK standing in door of conference room. THIRD MAN is sitting with his arms wrapped around himself, deathly pale. GEORGE is exactly as we left him: one wrist manacled, monumentally unconcerned with everything. Corpse of FIRST MAN has skin like marble, has gone into *rigor mortis*. (Note: ask State Correction Board whether we can get two young Terminals to play the parts of FIRST and THIRD MEN.)

ADRENALINE: 0.50, SOMATIC. SUBLIMINAL: Nausea and angina. SMELL: Vomit and feces.

THIRD MAN

Atr-...atropine?

HAZLIK

BRUSQUE

Maybe. Coming.

MORENO

What did he do? Protter said something about his hand.

THIRD MAN

I don't think it's a hand. It's a p-pross. Nerve, ah, nerve p-poison under the finger...nails...sharp...oh God—

THIRD MAN flops down on floor, rigid, and begins beating arm on floor. He jerks several times, vomits explosively and dies. SMELL: as before, UP and DOWN. Stinger of ADRENALINE: 0.80 and OUT. SUBLIMINAL: Drowning in filth.

MEDIUM TWO SHOT of HAZLIK and MORENO standing in door, staring. PROTTER (SECOND MAN) runs up to them from behind.

PROTTER

OUT OF BREATH

I've got the...oh.

SMELL down to strong SUBLIMINAL.

HAZLIK

Let me have that. (SPEAKS INTO BRACELET) Sandler. This
is the boss. Got some garbage to be taken out, in Conference
A. (LISTENS) That's right. (TURNS A MICRODIAL on the
bracelet) Johns, this is the boss. Get an interrogation team
down to Conference A, sooner. (LISTENS) Doesn't make too
much difference. Right.

TO NOBODY IN PARTICULAR

It had to come to this, sooner or later.

HAZLIK (TO MORENO)

You were right. We've allowed Fredrika too much.

MORENO

Yes. (TO PROTTER) You can go.

PROTTER shuffles, lost, down the hall and HAZLIK and MORENO stand
outside door and smoke. SOMATIC: Dope 0.25, SUBLIMINAL FADE to OUT.

Four men hustle up, with stretchers and a sanitizer. They go straight through
the door without saying a word to either man. High-pitched humming,
sanitizer SOUND. HAZLIK shouts over:

HAZLIK

Stay away from the man in the chair.

and then closes door. SOUND OUT abruptly.

HAZLIK sits down on floor; then MORENO does also. Soon the four men come back out, bearing the stretchers. Again, they show no sign of seeing the two.

HAZLIK

Just when everything was going so well. (PAUSE)

UNSENTIMENTALLY

Moreno, do you consider yourself a happy man?

MORENO

UNCOMFORTABLE

Well...I suppose so. I have all that I need...and I keep busy.

HAZLIK

LOOKING AT ATROPINE SYRETTE, FIDDLING WITH IT

Until a few weeks ago, I would never have called myself... happy...there was a strange—

WITH SUDDEN VEHEMENCE (ADRENALINE: 0.25)

—a *weight* on my soul, Moreno! An actual weight of, I don't know; sorrow, guilt...questioning whether I might not have been...different. (PAUSE) But one day; three weeks, a month ago, I woke up one morning and it was all gone, I was free.

That's when I decided to throw a party. (PAUSE) But now I feel it coming back.

SOUND of footsteps approaching; HAZLIK looks up.

                          HAZLIK

GETTING UP

    Ah, Johns. We have a little problem.

MEDIUM GROUP SHOT past HAZLIK and MORENO to the interrogation team: JOHNS and his two assistants, FRIEDMAN (male) and O'HARA (female).

                          JOHNS

    We'll do what we can, sir. Have you met O'Hara and Friedman?

                          HAZLIK

No, I haven't.

                          JOHNS

    They're very good.

                          HAZLIK

WITH A WAVE OF HIS HAND

    I trust your judgment in these things. Follow me.

All five enter the "conference" room. HAZLIK walks over to stand (not too near) by GEORGE.

HAZLIK

This man works for Fredrika Oblimov...George.

GEORGE

Yes?

HAZLIK

What sort of work do you do for Fredrika?

GEORGE

SMALL SMILE

I am her husband.

HAZLIK (TO MORENO)

What did they drug him with?

MORENO

If they followed my instructions, it was come-along gas.

HAZLIK

Makes sense. He doesn't really have to tell the truth, then. Not even to a direct order.

JOHNS

We can fix that, sir.

HAZLIK

IMPATIENTLY

Of course you can. But nothing so crude as dissolvers or triple-scop. I want to be able to return him to Fredrika no worse for wear, except for a lack of memory...of these proceedings. Can you do that?

JOHNS

DOUBTFUL

How soon would he have to be returned?

HAZLIK

No more than an hour.

JOHNS

I don't know...that lets out most of our drugs. We can keep him on come-along, of course, and he won't remember...but it won't make him talk.

O'HARA

Let me work on him.

JOHNS

All right.

O'HARA approaches GEORGE without caution.

HAZLIK

Watch out! His left hand's a pross. Nerve poison under the

fingernails.

> O'HARA (TO GEORGE)

SULTRY

Now, George. Is that right?

> GEORGE

LITTLE-BOY SMILE

Uh-huh.

> O'HARA

Now, George, turn your hand over, palm down, and don't touch me while I fasten your arm to the chair.

> GEORGE

All right.

O'HARA binds him without any trouble.

> O'HARA (TO HAZLIK)

Exactly what do you want to know?

> HAZLIK

He's here to kill somebody. You know about Fredrika's contracts? (SHE NODS) I want to find out who the victim is supposed to be—and who contracted for it, if *he* knows.

> O'HARA

SOFTLY

>George, who did you come here to kill?

GEORGE

SING-SONG

>I'm not...sup-posed...to tell.

O'HARA

>You can tell *me*, George. I'll keep it a secret.

GEORGE

PETULANT

>Huh-uh!

O'HARA

LOOKS UP

>Friedman. Bring the kit over.

HAZLIK

>No marks!

JOHNS

>Don't worry, sir. They're too good for that.

FRIEDMAN

CROSSING OVER

That's right, sir. Direct stimulation of the pain centers in the brain, the newest thing. Doesn't leave a sign.

O'HARA

Now this man is going to hurt you, George. I can't stop him from hurting you unless you tell me who you came here to kill, and why.

GEORGE

GIGGLES

He can't hurt me. Fredrika told me, nobody can hurt me if I don't want.

FRIEDMAN

Probably a simple hypnotic injunction.

SQUEEZES GEORGE'S EARLOBE BETWEEN FINGER AND THUMBNAIL

No reaction. Well...

FRIEDMAN opens up black case, brings out a small limp net of wire mesh. He shakes it out.

I think this will bypass it.

FRIEDMAN lays net over GEORGE's head and secures it with a chinstrap. He takes out a little box with a dial on it.

FRIEDMAN (TO O'HARA)

Ready?

O'HARA

LICKS LIPS, STARING AT GEORGE INTENTLY

Yes...

BIG CLOSE-UP of little box. FRIEDMAN turns dial to first setting. BIG CLOSE-UP on GEORGE's face. Beads of sweat break out on his forehead. SOMATIC SUBLIMINAL: Steel band tightening around chest.

DOLLY BACK to TIGHT TWO SHOT, faces of GEORGE and O'HARA. SOMATIC: Female sexual tension 0.20.

O'HARA

It hurts, doesn't it, George.

GEORGE

SMALL VOICE

Yes, it hurts.

O'HARA

Who are you going to kill?

GEORGE

CHILDISH DEFIANCE

That's for me to know and you to find out.

O'HARA glances at FRIEDMAN and he adjusts dial upward with audible click. HOLD SUBLIMINAL and ADD SUBLIMINAL: Little finger being pushed back to breaking point.

BIG CLOSE-UP on O'HARA's face, smiling. Sharp intake of breath from GEORGE (OFF).

> O'HARA

> Who are you going to kill?

> GEORGE

> Stop it. Make him stop it.

> O'HARA

> Who are you going to kill?

> GEORGE

> Make him stop.

> O'HARA

> MOVING EVEN CLOSER TO GEORGE, SMILING

> More.

HOLD SUBLIMINAL and ADD SUBLIMINAL: Knitting needle being pushed through thigh. GEORGE moans. SOMATIC: Female sexual tension 0.40. BIG CLOSE-UP on O'HARA, panting through her nose, teeth clenched.

> O'HARA

> Who are you going to kill?

GEORGE

I...can't...say.

O'HARA

More...

Click and HOLD SUBLIMINAL and ADD SUBLIMINAL: Extreme pressure on testicles. SOMATIC: Female sexual tension 0.75.

MEDIUM TWO SHOT of GEORGE and O'HARA. GEORGE has head thrown back, features contorted, screaming; O'HARA leaning over him, hands on his forearms, shouting into his face:

O'HARA

AT THE TOP OF HER LUNGS

Who are you going to kill who are you going to kill who are you going to kill?

HAZLIK (OFF)

WHISPERS

God.

FRIEDMAN

CALMLY, ACADEMICALLY

This level of pain is greater than that experienced by one who burns to death.

JOHNS

SLIGHTLY BOTHERED

You might as well try something else. This isn't going to work.

FRIEDMAN

You're probably right.

GEORGE's screams stop abruptly. SUBLIMINALS OUT.

O'HARA

Who are you going to kill who are you going to kill who are you?

O'HARA slips lithely off him and holds hand out to FRIEDMAN.

O'HARA

Quickly.

FRIEDMAN HANDS her a small ampoule. She grabs GEORGE by the hair—his head is lolling and he's whimpering like a child—and holds his head up while she crushes ampoule under his nose. Immediate SOMATIC: Male sexual tension 0.70, SMELL of full-strength Stiffener ©.

O'HARA

TEASING GROTESQUELY

I've got something you wa-ant.

GEORGE looks at her sickly and takes in ragged breath. SOMATIC: Male sexual tension 0.75.

GEORGE

HOARSELY

Come here.

O'HARA

Not until you tell me. Who did Fredrika order you to kill?

FULL BODY SHOT of O'HARA past GEORGE. O'HARA pulls shift over her head and, underneath, is wearing only a little wisp of bright material which clings wetly to her. She has a ripe young figure, shiny with perspiration. SOMATIC: Male sexual tension 0.85, painful erection.

O'HARA

Who-o-o?

GEORGE shakes his head violently, incapable of speech or not trusting himself. A little salvia has trickled out of the corner of his mouth. O'HARA approaches him and kneels, begins caressing the back of his hand with her breast. FEEL: Feather-light touch of breast on back of hand which is struggling to clutch but unable to turn over. SOMATIC: Male sexual tension 0.93. SMELL: Female, male musk.

O'HARA

Just one little name and I'll take care of you.

O'HARA stands and turns her back to GEORGE; slowly slides final garment down. SOMATIC: Male sexual tension 0.95.

O'HARA (FACING AWAY)

Just tell me, George.

GEORGE groans something intelligible. O'HARA turns and, in a quick smooth motion, mounts his hand and begins rubbing back and forth. FEEL: Slippery labia, unnaturally hot and wet. SMELL: Female musk UP. SOMATIC: Male sexual tension 0.99; unbearable, gut-wrenching frustration.

                              O'HARA
HUSKILY

        If you want...

                              GEORGE
SCREAMS

        Haz-lik! *Hazlik!*

FEEL, SMELL, SOMATIC all OUT. O'HARA slides off GEORGE and slips back into clothes. FEEL: Wetness on back of hand turning cold and sticky as HAZLIK crosses in blind fury. ADRENALINE: 0.75.

                              HAZLIK
BARELY CONTROLLED

        You are going to die...

TIGHT TWO SHOT: HAZLIK and GEORGE. HAZLIK has produced a shooter and is holding it at GEORGE's head. He lowers aim, pointing it at his groin.

        ...and it's up to you whether you die quickly or in great agony.

                              GEORGE

        Don't...don't kill...

HAZLIK

Who ordered the contract? Who wants me dead?

GEORGE

I don't know, she never tells me, please, *please* don't kill...

MORENO (OFF)

He's probably telling the truth, Hazlik.

HAZLIK thumbs safety on shooter; it begins to hum. ADRENALINE: Down to 0.50.

HAZLIK

You're right.

HAZLIK turns to face MORENO and drops shooter in tunic pocket. ADRENALINE: 0.35.

HAZLIK

Let's go talk to Fredrika.

JOHNS

Shall we kill him?

HAZLIK

Eventually.

TO O'HARA, LEERING

You may practice on him first. Don't worry about marks.

CUT TO: Main room again. Party going full swing, people laughing and chattering. FREDRIKA is seated near the bar, looking deadly. DOLLY in for TIGHT GROUP SHOT as HAZLIK and MORENO approach.

SOUND UNDER and HOLD ADRENALINE.

                          FREDRIKA

COLDLY, TO HAZLIK

     Where is my husband?

                          HAZLIK

     He's enjoying his own private party right now.

                          MORENO

     And being positively garrulous.

                          FREDRIKA

     Oh? I'm glad to hear that. I was afraid he wasn't having a very
     good time.

                          MORENO

HISSES

     He still—

                          HAZLIK

INTERRUPTING

He talked, Fredrika. I know he came here to kill me. *You* came here to kill me.

FREDRIKA

WHISPERS

You fool. Both of you, fools.

MORENO

No, dear, for a change you play the fool. This time you went too far.

FREDRIKA

VENOMOUS

If you kill me, an army will be at your door by dawn.

HAZLIK

By dawn, I will have an army here to meet them.

MORENO

Two armies.

HAZLIK

Perhaps, though, if you will tell me who contracted for my death...

FREDRIKA

You know I can't do that.

HAZLIK

This one time; this last time, you had better.

FREDRIKA

LOOKING AT MORENO

Alone.

HAZLIK

All right. (TO MORENO) You will excuse us?

MORENO makes exaggerated bow. FREDRIKA and HAZLIK leave wordlessly. MORENO watches them go and speaks softly into his bracelet.

CUT TO: TIGHT TWO SHOT of FREDRIKA and HAZLIK alone in a corridor. HAZLIK opens an ornate, old-fashioned manual door.

HAZLIK

WRYLY

My chambers.

LONG SHOT past HAZLIK and FREDRIKA to opulent bedroom; a fantasy of glass and velvet and silk. SUBLIMINAL: Feel of velvet and silk, sound of fine glass tinkling. Slight SMELL of dope. SOMATIC: Dope 0.08. A tall, beautiful girl sits naked on the couch by the bed, smoking dope and reading. Unruffled, she puts down the viewer and slips a housecoat over her shoulders; crosses to exit between HAZLIK and FREDRIKA.

HAZLIK

I'll call for you later. (MOTIONS TO FREDRIKA) Have a seat, dear.

HAZLIK crosses to a large bar and selects a fine decanter.

HAZLIK

Brandy?

FREDRIKA

Just a taste.

HAZLIK pours two small glasses of brandy, his back to FREDRIKA, watching her in a mirror. She doesn't move. He reaches in tunic pocket and takes out his shooter. SOUND: Soft hum; still activated. He crosses to FREDRIKA with shooter in right hand and drink in left.

HAZLIK

Distilled from the finest Antarean vintage.

FREDRIKA accepts, not looking at shooter, and takes a small sip.

FREDRIKA

It travels well.

HAZLIK returns to the bar and gets his glass, then sits on bed about two meters from FREDRIKA. He empties the glass in one swallow. TASTE and SMELL of fine brandy, SOMATIC: Liquor burning on its way down.

HAZLIK

Well?

FREDRIKA

The man who contracted for your death is one of my oldest and most valued customers.

HAZLIK

Was. As our friend pointed out, you are no longer in the business. (PAUSES) You may yet live, though.

FREDRIKA

LAUGHS SOFTLY

You can't allow me to live.

TAKES LONG SLOW SIP OF BRANDY

Neither can Moreno.

FREDRIKA reaches up and takes a long pin out of her hair. The hair falls in a soft white cascade around her shoulders. She was very beautiful once.

HAZLIK

RAISING SHOOTER

That pin is a weapon.

FREDRIKA

With proper knowledge, anything is a weapon. (PAUSES) Don't worry I won't throw it at you.

HAZLIK

More of your nerve poison?

FREDRIKA

Oh, you found out George's little secret? How many men did it take?

HAZLIK

Two. We have atropine now, though. (TAKES AMPOULE OUT OF HIS POCKET AND SHOWS IT TO HER) You might as well tell me who your customer was. If nothing else, I can promise you a pleasant death.

FREDRIKA

Having made a life-long study of the subject, I can assure you that there is no such thing as a pleasant death. Not even painless death is pleasant, not even for an eighty-year-old woman.

FREDRIKA stands and begins walking. For once, she looks as old as she is. CAMERA FOLLOWS as she talks, fiddling with the pin.

FREDRIKA

You don't recall the last time you contracted for my services.

HAZLIK (OFF)

Of course not.

FREDRIKA

It was a most unusual request. Also very difficult. But I

accepted the challenge.

HAZLIK (OFF)

So? You were paid well, no—

FREDRIKA

I wouldn't have risked it if it hadn't meant so much to you. I've always respected you, Theo; loved you in my own way.

ADRENALINE: 0.20. SUBLIMINAL: Rattlesnake coiling.

FREDRIKA

You were very disturbed, agitated. You had tried a multitude of other possible solutions before coming to me. None of them was satisfactory.

ADRENALINE: 0.40. SUBLIMINAL: Guillotine rising, rusty squeak.

HAZLIK (OFF)

What has this to do—

FREDRIKA

Patience. Old people do rattle on.

FREDRIKA stops walking a little more than an arm's length from HAZLIK. ADRENALINE: 0.50, SUBLIMINAL: Losing balance on edge of cliff.

FREDRIKA

You were afraid that your empire was going to crumble because of the weakness of one man.

FREDRIKA points pin at HAZLIK, as if for emphasis. ADRENALINE: 0.60. SUBLIMINAL: Tied to stake and flames licking at feet.

FREDRIKA

You arranged for that man to be killed. One month ago this night, you arranged it. Because he had just turned fifty and was sad and afraid and knew that his empire soon would be down around his ears, and was not strong enough to commit suicide, he—you, Theo, *you* hired me to be your instrument of suicide.

FREDRIKA rests point of pin lightly on HAZLIK's chest. ADRENALINE: 0.70, SUBLIMINAL: Falling in darkness.

HAZLIK

You're insane.

FREDRIKA

No, Theo. Your subconscious knows. Put down the shooter.

HAZLIK puts muzzle of shooter against FREDRIKA's abdomen. ADRENALINE: 0.85, HOLD SUBLIMINAL.

FREDRIKA

No difference.

FREDRIKA leans on the needle and, at the same instant, HAZLIK fires. FREDRIKA explodes, cut in two.

TOTAL SENSORY NULL as HAZLIK stares at pin, a couple of centimeters sticking into his chest. He drops the shooter into the confusion of gore all over the rug, and takes the atropine ampoule out of his pocket.

Then HAZLIK throws the ampoule away and shoves the pin the rest of the way into his chest.

ADRENALINE: 1.0.

SOMATIC: Male orgasm 1.0

SMELL, TASTE, FEEL, HEAR, SIGHT all UP with white noise TO: FULL SENSORY OVERLOAD.

FADE TO BLACK

CREDITS

COMMERCIAL

Introduction to the Twentieth Anniversary Edition of *Amusing Ourselves to Death* by Neil Postman

Andrew Postman

In 1985, media scholar and educator Neil Postman's (1931–2003) very famous commentary on television and society, *Amusing Ourselves to Death: Public Discourse in the Age of Show Business* (Viking Penguin, 1985), took television to task for its starkly negative impact on society. Postman made reference to Huxley's *Brave New World* as he attacked television and lamented how the medium degrades the social discourse and turns even important news into entertainment. In 2005, a twentieth-anniversary edition of the book was issued, and Postman's son, Andrew, wrote this important and perceptive introduction to the new edition, in which he asks college students and instructors for their reactions to reading the book and for their thoughts on the modern media and their effect on society today and on into the future.

Now this?

A book of social commentary...published twenty years ago? You're not busy enough writing emails, returning calls, downloading tunes, playing games (online, PlayStation, Game Boy), checking out websites, sending text messages, IM'ing, Tivoing, watching what you've Tivoed, browsing through magazines and newspapers, reading new books—now you've got to stop and read a book that first appeared in the last century, not to mention millennium? Come on—like, your outlook on today could seriously be rocked by this plain-spoken provocation about The World of 1985, a world yet to be infiltrated by the Internet, cell phones, PDAs, cable channels by the hundreds, DVDs, call-waiting, caller ID, blogs, flat-screens, HDTV, and iPods? Is it really plausible that this slim volume, with its once-urgent premonitions about the nuanced and deep-seated perils of television, could feel timely today, in the Age of Computers? Really, could this book about how TV is turning all public life (education, religion, politics, journalism) into entertainment; how the image is undermining other forms of communication, particularly the written word;

and how our bottomless appetite for TV will make content so abundantly available, context be damned, that we'll be overwhelmed by "information glut" until what is truly meaningful is lost and we no longer care what we've lost as long as we're being amused.... Can such a book possibly have relevance to you and The World of 2006 and beyond?

I think you've answered your own question.

I, too, think the answer is yes, but as Neil Postman's son, I'm biased. Where are we to find objective corroboration that reading *Amusing Ourselves to Death* in 2006, in a society that worships TV and technology as ours does, is nearly an act of defiance, one of those I-didn't-realize-it-was-dark-until-someone-flipped-the-switch encounters with an illuminating intellect?

Ask the Students

Let's not take the word of those who studied under my father at New York University, many of whom have gone on to teach in their own college (and occasionally high school) courses what he argues in these pages. These fine minds are, as my father's was, of a bygone era, a different media environment, and their biases may make them, as they made him, hostage of another time, perhaps incapable of seeing the present world as it is rather than as they'd like it to be. (One man's R-rated is another's PG-13.)

And just to make a clean slate of it, let's not rely, either, on the opinions of the numerous readers of the original edition of *Amusing Ourselves* (translated into a dozen languages, including German, Indonesian, Turkish, Danish, and, most recently, Chinese), so many of whom wrote to my father, or buttonholed him at public speaking events, to tell him how dead-on his argument was. Their support, while genuine, was expressed over the last two decades, so some of it might be outdated; we'll disregard the views of these teachers and students, businesspeople and artists, conservatives and liberals, atheists and churchgoers, and all those parents. (We'll also disregard Roger Waters, co-founder of the legendary band Pink Floyd, whose solo album, *Amused to Death*, was inspired by the book. Go, Dad.)

So whose opinion matters?

In re-reading this book to figure out what might be said about it twenty years later, I tried to think the way my father would, since he could no longer, nor could I ask him. He died in October 2003, at age seventy-two. Channeling him, I realized immediately who offers the best test of whether *Amusing Ourselves to Death* is still relevant.

College kids.

"Teachers are not considered good if they don't entertain their classes."

Today's 18-to-22-year-olds live in a vastly different media environment from the one that existed in 1985. Their relationship to TV differs. Back then, MTV was in its late infancy. Today, news scrolls and corner-of-the-screen promos and "reality" shows and infomercials and 900 channels are the norm. And TV no longer dominates the media landscape. "Screen time" also means hours spent in front of the computer, video monitor, cell phone and handheld. Multitasking is standard. Communities have been replaced by demographics. Silence has been replaced by background noise. It's a different world. (It's different for all of us, of course—children, young teens, parents, seniors—but college kids form an especially rich grouping, poised between innocence and sophistication, respect and irreverence.)

When today's students are assigned *Amusing Ourselves to Death*, almost none of them have heard of Neil Postman or been exposed to his ideas (he wrote over twenty books, on such subjects as education, language, childhood, and technology), suggesting that their views, besides being pertinent, are relatively uncorrupted.

I called several of my father's former students who are now teachers, and who teach *Amusing Ourselves to Death* in courses that examine some cross-section of ideas about TV, culture, computing, technology, mass media, communications, politics, journalism, education, religion, and language. I asked the teachers what their students thought of the book, particularly its timeliness. The teachers were kind enough to share many of their students' thoughts, from papers and class discussion.

"In the book [Postman] makes the point that there is no reflection time in the world anymore," wrote Jonathan. "When I go to a restaurant everyone's on their cell phone, talking or playing games. I have no ability to sit by myself and just think." Said Liz: "It's more relevant now. In class we asked if, now that there's cable, which there really wasn't when the book was written, are there channels that are not just about entertainment? We tried to find one to disprove his theory. One kid said the Weather Channel but another mentioned how they have all those shows on tornadoes and try to make weather fun. The only good example we came up with was C-SPAN, which no one watches."

Cara: "Teachers are not considered good if they don't entertain their classes." Ben (whose professor called him the "class skeptic," and who, when the book was assigned, groaned, "Why do we have to read this?"): "Postman says TV makes everything about the present—and there we were, criticizing the book because it wasn't published yesterday." Reginald: "This book is not just about TV." Sandra: "The book was absolutely on-target about the 2004 presidential election campaign and debates." One student pointed out that Arnold Schwarzenegger announced his candidacy for the California governorship on *The Tonight Show*.

Postman's And Now This...

Maria noted that the oversimplification and thinking "fragmentation" promoted by TV-watching may contribute to our Red State/Blue State polarization. Another noted the emergence of a new series of "bible magazines," whose cover format is modeled on teen magazines, with coverlines like "Top 10 Trips to Getting Closer to God"—"it's religion mimicking an MTV kind of world," said the student. Others wondered if the recent surge in children diagnosed with Attention Deficit Disorder was an indication of a need to be constantly stimulated.

Kaitlin switched her major to print journalism after reading the book. Andrea would recommend it to anyone concerned with media ethics. Mike said even those who won't agree with the book's arguments—as he did not—should still read it, to be provoked. Many students ("left wingers and right wingers both," said the professor) were especially taken with my father's "Now...this" idea: the phenomenon whereby the reporting of a horrific event—a rape or a 5-alarm fire or global warming, say—is followed immediately by the anchor's cheerfully exclaiming "Now...this," which segues into a story about Janet Jackson's exposed nipple, or a commercial for lite beer, creating a sequencing of information so random, so disparate in scale and value, as to be incoherent, even psychotic.

Another teacher remarked that students love how the book is told—by a writer who's at heart a storyteller. "And they love that he refers to books and people they've heard of," she said. Alison: "He doesn't dumb it down—

he makes allusions to great art and poetry. Yet it's impossible to lose track of his argument." Matt said that, ironically, "Postman proves you can be entertaining—and without a single picture."

Of her students' impressions, one teacher said, "He speaks to them without jargon, in a way in which they feel respected. They feel he's just having a conversation with them, but inspiring them to think at the same time. " Another professor noted that "kids come to the conclusion that TV is almost exclusively interested in presenting show business and sensationalism and in making money. Amazing as it seems, they had never realized that before."

It no doubt appears to you that, after all my grand talk of objectivity, I've stacked the deck in favor of the book's virtue. But that's honestly the overwhelming reaction—at least among a slice of Generation Y, a population segment that one can imagine has as many reasons not to like the book as to like it. One professor said that in a typical class of twenty-five students who read the book, twenty-three will write papers that either praise, or are animated by, its ideas; two will say the book was a stupid waste of time. A 92% rating? There's no one who expresses an idea—certainly no politician—who wouldn't take that number.

"A common critique was that he should have offered solutions."

Of course, students had criticisms of the book, too. Many didn't appreciate the assault on television—a companion to them, a source of pleasure and comfort—and felt as if they had to defend their culture. Some considered TV their parents' culture, not theirs—they are of the Internet—so the book's theses were less relevant. Some thought my father was anti-change, that he so exalted the virtues fostered by the written word and its culture, he was not open to acknowledging many of the positive social improvements TV had brought about, and what a democratic and leveling force it could be. Some disagreed with his assessment that TV is in complete charge: remote control, an abundance of channels, and VCRs and DVRs all enable you to "customize" your programming, even to skip commercials. A common critique was that he should have offered solutions; you can't put the toothpaste back in the tube, after all, so what now?

And there was this: Yeah, what he said in 1985 had come startlingly true, we had amused ourselves to death...so why read it?

One professor uses the book in conjunction with an experiment she calls an "e-media fast." For twenty-four hours, each student must refrain from electronic media. When she announces the assignment, she told me, 90% of the students shrug, thinking it's no big deal. But when they realize all the things they must give up for a whole day—cell phone, computer, Internet, TV, car radio, etc.—"they start to moan and groan." She tells them they can still read books. She acknowledges it will be a tough day, though for roughly eight of the twenty-four hours they'll be asleep. She says if they break the fast—if they answer the phone, say, or simply have to check email—they must begin from scratch.

They actually walk down the street to visit their friend.

"The papers I get back are amazing," says the professor. "They have titles like 'The Worst Day of My Life' or 'The Best Experience I Ever Had,' always extreme. I thought I was going to die, they'll write. I went to turn on the TV but if I did I realized, my God, I'd have to start all over again. Each student has his or her own weakness—for some it's TV, some the cell phone, some the Internet or their PDA. But no matter how much they hate abstaining, or how hard it is to hear the phone ring and not answer it, they take time to do things they haven't done in years.

They actually walk down the street to visit their friend. They have extended conversations. One wrote, I thought to do things I hadn't thought to do ever. The experience changes them. Some are so affected that they determine to fast on their own, one day a month. In that course I take them through the classics—from Plato and Aristotle through today—and years later when former students write or call to say hello the thing they remember is the media fast."

Like the media fast, *Amusing Ourselves* is a call to action. It is, in my father's words, "an inquiry...and a lamentation," yes, but it aspires to greater things. It is an exhortation to do something. It's a counterpunch to what my father thought daily TV news was: "inert, consisting of information that gives us something to talk about but cannot lead to any meaningful action." Dad was a lover of history, a champion for collective memory and what we now quaintly refer to as "civilizing influences," but he did not live in the past. His book urges us to claim a way to be more alert and engaged. My father's ideas are still here, he isn't, and it's time for those of a new generation to take the reins, natives of this brave new world who understand it better.

"'Change changed,' my father wrote."

Twenty years isn't what it used to be. Where once it stood for a single generation, now it seems to stand for three. Everything moves faster. "Change changed," my father wrote in another book. A lot has changed since this book appeared. News consumption among the young is way down. Network news and entertainment divisions are far more entwined, despite protests by the news divisions (mostly for their own benefit).

When Jon Stewart, host of Comedy Central's *The Daily Show*, goes on CNN's *Crossfire* to make this very point—that serious news and show business ought to be distinguishable, for the sake of public discourse and the republic—the hosts seem incapable even of understanding the words coming out of his mouth.

The sound bite is now more like a sound nibble, and it's rare, even petulant, to hear someone challenge its absurd insubstantiality; the question of how television affects us has receded into the background (Dad's words, not mine, from 1985). Fox News has established itself, and thrived. Corporate conglomeration is up, particularly among media companies. Our own media companies don't provide truly gruesome war images as part of the daily news, but then they didn't do so twenty years ago either (though forty years ago they did). The quality of graphics (i.e., the reality quotient) of computer and video games is way up.

Communities exist that didn't, thanks to the Internet, particularly to peer-to-peer computing. A new kind of collaborative creativity abounds, thanks to the "open source" movement, which gave us the Linux operating system. However, other communities are collapsing: far fewer people join clubs that meet regularly, fewer families eat dinner together, and people don't have friends over or know their neighbors the way they used to. More school administrators and politicians and business executives hanker to wire schools for computers, as if that is the key to improving American education.

Huxley, not Orwell

The number of hours the average American watches TV has remained steady, at about four-and-a-half hours a day, every day (by age sixty-five, a person will have spent twelve uninterrupted years in front of the TV). Childhood obesity is way up. Some things concern our children more than they used to, some not at all. Maybe there's more hope than there was, maybe less. Maybe the amount is a constant.

Substantive as this book is, it was predicated on a "hook": that one British writer (George Orwell) with a frightening vision of the future, a vision that many feared would come true, was mostly off-base, while another British writer (Aldous Huxley) with a frightening vision of the future, a vision less well-known and feared, was scarily on target. My father argued his point, persuasively, but it was a point for another time—the Age of Television. New technologies and media are in the ascendancy.

Fortunately—and this, more than anything, is what I think makes *Amusing Ourselves to Death* so emphatically relevant—my father asked such good questions that they can be asked of non-television things, of all sorts of transforming developments and events that have happened since 1985, and since his death, and of things still unformed, for generations to come (though "generations to come" may someday mean a span of three years). His questions can be asked about all technologies and media.

What happens to us when we become infatuated with and then seduced by them? Do they free us or imprison us? Do they improve or degrade democracy? Do they make our leaders more accountable or less so? Our system more transparent or less so? Do they make us better citizens or better consumers? Are the trade-offs worth it? If they're not worth it, yet we still can't stop ourselves from embracing the next new thing because that's just how we're wired, then what strategies can we devise to maintain control? Dignity? Meaning?

"It's a twenty-first century book published in the twentieth century."

My father was not a curmudgeon about all this, as some thought. It was never optimism he lacked; it was certainty. "We must be careful in praising or condemning because the future may hold surprises for us," he wrote. Nor did he fear TV (as some thought) across the board. Junk television was fine. "*The A-Team* and *Cheers* are no threat to our public health," he wrote. "*60 Minutes*, *Eyewitness News*, and *Sesame Street* are."

A student of Dad's, a teacher himself, says his own students are more responsive, not less, to *Amusing Ourselves* than they were five or ten years ago. "When the book first came out, it was ahead of its time, and some people didn't understand its reach," he says. "It's a twenty-first century book published in the twentieth century." In 1986, soon after the book was published and started to make ripples, Dad was on ABC's *Nightline*, discussing with Ted Koppel the effect TV can have on society if we let it control us, rather than vice versa. As I recall, at one juncture, to illustrate his point that our brief attention span and our appetite for feel-good content can short-circuit any meaningful discourse, Dad said, "For example, Ted, we're having an important discussion about the culture but in thirty seconds we'll have to break for a commercial to sell cars or toothpaste."

Mr. Koppel, one of the rare serious figures on network television, smiled wryly—or was it fatigue? "Actually, Dr. Postman," he said, "it's more like ten seconds."

There's still time.

Science fiction writer Kit Reed has published two dozen novels and short story collections and more than one hundred short stories in genre and mainstream magazines and anthologies. Longtime Resident Writer at Wesleyan University, Reed is known for her dystopian depictions of the future. In this excellent and disturbingly prescient story from 1967, she shows us a future where television offers just about everything the viewer could want. And more.

In the autumn of his sixteenth year Van fell in love with Missy Beaton on the television, and once he understood what was happening to him his life at home was not enough. It did not matter that his waking hours were filled with all the figures of his childhood; he lay in his cupboard and they still came to him at the appointed times. They were laughing, weeping or dancing, marking off the hours and half-hours as they always had, but Ma Prindle ceased to grip Van even though he had followed her from the beginning, and Cap'n Jack failed to amuse him even though he had laughed at Cap'n Jack before he even comprehended speech. The June Taylor Dancers delighted him no longer; the Pico Players were as nothing for he had waked one morning to find a change in his schedule; Uncle Stingo would not appear, said the announcer, and in the next moment there she was.

He was not sure what it was about her that arrested him, whether it was her lithe body in the pink tunic or the flashing toes of her black tap shoes or whether it was only the fact that she was young; he could not be sure what held him but she had danced into his life with a toss of her head and now Van felt the tongue of restlessness stirring inside him, moving up and down his bones. At first he tried to ignore it, drawing the covers about him and waiting doggedly for the other shows to come in their appointed order, but no matter how he tried he could not lay the restlessness, not even when he joined the family in front of the big set in the living room, watching the food commercials and waiting while Dad put the money in and breakfast came. He found he could not eat while Missy was dancing; he could not think and he did not want to talk and so he crawled back to his cupboard, pulling the curtains so he could be alone with the postcard set on the pillow beside him; alone he would commune with Missy Beaton. Then one morning she turned and winked and improbable as it was Van knew the wink was meant for him, he knew what he had to do. Damn the war, damn the census figures and the crush of bodies in the streets; he would say goodbye to his safe cupboard, his family, his pocket TV set. He would set his shoulders and burrow his way through the crowds, he would lay people right and left if he had to—he would go to her.

The worst wrench was parting with the television; it was an old one without any of the conveniences, he had found it in the back of a cupboard and no one knew he had it. If the truth be known, no one cared. The rest of the family lived around the big set in the parlor, going to the cupboards only to sleep. Sprawled in a morass of food wrappers and left-over purchases, they watched with their mouths open and coins at the ready, and if Missy Beaton offered anything they wanted then they would fall on the television, feeding it coins until the bell rang, and if she didn't, then there would be something else along in a minute, they never had to wait for long.

That particular day Missy Beaton was offering a hairstyle; if you bought the product you too could look like that. By the time Van passed the living room Sister was putting in a handful of coins and then one of the machines on the wall did something and Sister looked like that. In the ell his brother Louis was locked in mortal combat with the telephone; they were grappling because Louis was trying to call Uncle Ralph in California and the machine was after his money, all the money it could get. In the small room off the parlor the teaching machine ran on and on unattended; Van held his breath and scuttled past.

Of course the bell rang, somebody was trying to leave during learning hours; the bell rang and Van's mother wrenched herself away from the TV long enough to poke her head into the hallway. She said:

"Oh, it's you."

"Hi, Mom." They hadn't seen each other in several days.

"I thought you were in the cupboard."

"I was. I have to go out for a couple of minutes."

"Out? You can't go out. The streets are jammed."

"I have to see someone."

"Son, you can't be serious."

"I'm in love."

She snorted. "Don't be absurd. Come on, they're about to serve a frozen lunch."

"I don't *want* a frozen lunch." If he didn't hurry she was going to make a grab for him. "Don't you want grandchildren?"

"The census..." She looked frightened. "Van, think about the crush."

The door was stiff; it hadn't been used in several years. She was breathing heavily; her eyes glazed over and Van could read what she saw; the door opening a crack, and oozing through that crack a puddle, a stream, a tidal wave of humanity, bodies spilling one over the other, bloating and squeezing, overflowing their few precious rooms. She lunged, bellowing: YOU'LL RUIN EVERYTHING but she was in poor condition from so many years of just sitting around, consuming, and now he had the door open and now he was outside, slamming it shut before her fingers could close on him. He thought he heard her calling, Goodbye Forever as he stood against the door with his eyes shut, waiting for the crush. He hunched his shoulders and held his breath until his chest exploded. He had to open his eyes, understanding at last that there was no one in the hall. He had not been down the stairs since the family sealed itself in some eight years before and so he had to go slowly, so pained by waking muscles that he had to lie down in the vestibule. The building rose around him, tall and silent, but in the streets outside he heard or imagined he heard the unceasing rush of bodies being carried along like lemmings, with no sea in sight. Given his choice, he would have fled back up the stairs, banging on the door until the family let him in. But Missy was out there, he had to find her, and so in a minute he would open the door and launch himself, knowing exactly where he would go.

She would be at Central; the very thought gave him strength. Central towered over the city, he had seen it pictured a million times, and at Central was everything that mattered; the actors and singers and dancers all lived and worked there, so did the stars and announcers and the newscasters who followed television's roving eyes, reporting on the census, the wars, the ships which left weekly for the stars; at Central were the technicians and cameramen, the great red lights and many eyes of the vast television network which served that part of the world. At Central were the projectors which transmitted goods from Central stockpiles to a billion hands in a matter of seconds; from Central came the machines which collected coins from the nation's billion TV sets;

from Central came new packets of coins, they came from the set into the living room with the heartwarming regularity of an expected gift. Van cared little for the coins but he sensed the pulse, the heart of life itself at Central; for years he had thought about setting out for Central, for years he had been kept home only by the crush. But now he was in love with Missy and today she had winked at him; his mother would have laughed but to Van it seemed personably reasonable: if he could watch television then so could the great network's roving eye dart out—and light on him. So now he would open the door and hurl himself into the stream of humanity; he would lunge toward Central, which glowed on the horizon like a great green jewel. If he stumbled then he would stumble and if he fell so be it and if he died, then very well, at least he would have died on his way to something big.

He was frankly disappointed to open the door and find nobody there. The street was empty except for the cartons and wrappers which fell like soft rain from a thousand garbage chutes; the windows had all been boarded up against the crush and they looked out like so many blind eyes; the doors were boarded over too and the garbage chutes were the only openings on to the street. Van was distracted by a brilliant flash followed by a glare: a starship leaving; pressed close to his set, he had seen a thousand of them go, taking lottery winners to Mars and open worlds beyond. Over his head whined a rocket, going off to the war. This, at least, was as it should be. But the census, the empty streets... He would not dwell on it; instead he turned left, seeing at the end of the street's canyon the green throb of Central. He began to run.

It took longer than he thought. Lincoln walked twelve miles to school, anyone who watched the teaching machines knew that, but that was in olden times. Van had tried to keep in condition by pacing between his cupboard and the living room, but he could only run a few steps; he was exhausted by so much open space. He ought to go back and tell his parents it was all right to come out; they could walk for blocks without running into another living soul. It crossed his mind that life wasn't exactly as advertised; perhaps he should have sat down and thought about it but Missy had winked and now he was on his way to her.

He wasn't sure how he would handle it when he reached Central; maybe he would need a pass to get in; maybe the guards would try to head him off, suggesting a tour of the control room or the studio, but he wouldn't be diverted by meeting Ma Prindle or Uncle Stingo or Cap'n Jack, and he wouldn't stop for the Pico Players, not even if they offered to let him be on the show. He would find Missy's number in the directory and he would go to her room and if she wasn't there he would look for her in the rehearsal room and if she wasn't there he would go on to the studio, he would fight his way through her million fans; he would pull her off the air in mid-show if he had to. He would beg her to love him or marry him or whatever it was people used to do.

He would have, too, except that there was a steel grill over the big door at Central; the TVC emblems welded to the bars kept him from seeing inside. Well then he would wait, he would rest on the steps until somebody came along—maybe Jolly and the Dreamers, on their way back from one of their camera treks through the city, or the Pall Mall Minstrels, spilling out and down the steps, heading for the nearest bar; somebody would come by in a cab or a truck, a guard would open the steel doors and Van would ask his way inside.

Another starship took off; he could see the glare in the distance.

Several rockets whistled past; Van imagined them exploding, lighting up the distant war.

The sun got lower.

At twilight something clicked and Central's outer lights went on.

Van grew faint with hunger; as dark fell he hauled himself up, clinging to the embossed TVC, trying to look inside.

Nothing.

He might have given up for the day, he might even have gone home, but he was halted by a tiny, pervasive whir, the sound of a thousand small machines coming; as he watched, the first of them came around a corner. It trundled up the steps and nudged a sensitive plate in a wall Van took to be solid glass. A small passage opened and the machine went inside. The whir grew until it filled the air; the machine was followed by another and another until the streets streamed with them; they flowed along and up the steps, going into the building single file. Then one misfired, landing athwart the little entrance; Van set it right and then, wedging back the plate with one of his shoes, he joined the stream inside. In the tunnel, with a thousand machines in front of him and another thousand running up his heels, Van almost despaired. Then he was in the lobby and the lobby was full of light and sound; loudspeakers everywhere gave out the organ strains that introduced Ma Prindle and there, at the end of the lobby, there was Ma Prindle on a gigantic screen. He sat and watched until he felt better. By the time he pulled himself away, the last of the little machines had disappeared. He imagined he heard a cascade of coins, going from the machines into a distant maw.

He was struck by an uncanny silence; at home he had always been conscious of the others breathing, the friction of their bodies in their chairs. Yet here, in the heart and navel of the city he heard nothing but the metallic voice of Ma Prindle, magnified and coming at him from every wall. Uneasy, he roved the lobby, peering over the counter at the deserted information desk, tapping on a dozen different office doors. When the silence became too much to bear he threw himself down on a leather couch and fled into sleep. When he woke he was still alone and he would have given it all up, fleeing, except that Missy was beaming at him from the giant screen. He watched the swing of her hair, the intoxicating wink and when she spoke he answered back:

"I'll find you, Missy. I'll take you out of here."

Later that day he found one of the product storerooms; he watched in awe as food, clothes and drugs moved toward the transferral machines on conveyer belts, disappearing as they came under the golden rays. When, in his hunger he snatched a chocolate bar from out of the belts, a machine replaced it without missing a beat. He took another and another, gorging until he was able to stand without trembling. He finished off with a frozen pot pie, gnawing at it slowly, and then he set out again, walking with firmer step.

On the third day he found the studios and rehearsal rooms and he wandered the corridors, feasting on the photographs of Uncle Stingo and all the rest; made brave by their names on the doors, he began tapping, trying knobs until one opened finally and he was in a studio. He shrank for a minute, thinking he was interrupting a show; he thought wildly of waving in case he was on camera: Hi Mom; the others would be surprised when he came into view on the big TV set at home. Then the silence welled up and he opened his eyes to find a membrane of dust over everything; rats ran out of the ruined plush seats and a spider wove an intricate web between the teleprompter and the microphones. The cameras stood silent as giraffes at a taxidermist's and it reassured Van not at all that lights flickered here and there. Still the National Concert Orchestra performed somewhere; he could see it on all the monitors. He went into the control room and after considerable thought picked up the telephone. "Sorry, this line is..." He pushed another button. "The cir-cuits are busy, pul-leeze hang up and dial again..." "The number you have called has been dis-connect-ed..."

"Hello?"

Van's mouth flooded with saliva.

"I said, hello."

"—H-I. You."

"Welcome to Central, baby."

"M-Missy..."

"Not Missy. Name's Bert." The voice jiggled on the edge of gaiety; "Come on down here, baby, this is where everything is."

Van scrawled madly in the dust, trying to take down the directions. He was aware of a void; in a minute there would be a click and the voice would be gone forever. "Hey," he said. "Who are you?"

"Me?" The chuckle crackled in his ear. "Baby, I'm the man."

It took him half a day to find his way; once he rested and twice he broke into supply rooms, renewing his strength on macaroons. He went in a descending spiral, so that the halls grew shorter and the stairways down shorter and the doors on each landing fewer until at last he was in the pit or heart of Central, at a final door and he gathered himself in an orgy of fulfillment and hurled himself inside.

"Bert?"

"Hiya, baby." He swung his sneakers off the table and stood, creaky and slightly bowlegged in tight white jeans. He pushed back his straw hat, revealing a face blanched by age and yet hauntingly familiar.

The face began to waver. "You're just in time." Before Van could stop him, Bert burst into tears.

"Hey, Bert, don't...please don't..." Van knew it was rude, but he couldn't help squinting, trying to make out the face; he knew it... After a while he made himself look beyond to the control panel and the stacks or shelves which stretched beyond, towering on every side; he took them in, noting without comprehension that each shelf was equipped with a trolley or selector which whirred busily, moving along the endless rows of cans. "Look, I..." Bert was still sniffling and Van had to make him stop somehow. He said, "Where is everybody?"

"In there."

"Huh?"

"In the can. They're all in the can."

Just then the National Symphony finished and Bert did something at the controls; after a series of hums and clicks Missy Beaton came on, so close that Van must have called out her name.

He heard Bert, as if from a distance. "So that's it."

Then Bert looked at his watch. "Uh-oh. Rocket time." He pushed another button and as Van watched, Missy's image faded from the screen. The announcer's voice was young and firm: WE INTERRUPT THIS PROGRAM..." Then there was a shot of a rocket going off and then Missy Beaton came back, smiling her maddening smile, and Van watched until she took her last bow and danced out of sight.

"Take me to her."

Bert finished with his dials.

"I want to marry her."

"Her." Bert gestured at the screen. His eyes filmed. "Look, Missy isn't exactly... she isn't..." Bert squinted at him. "I take care of Missy now, and I... I..." He stooped, growing frailer as Van watched. "Good thing you came along." Oh-oh, census figures. Hang on a minute and I'll be right with you. My show's next," he said. "That'll give us some time to ourselves."

Bert put on the census figures and then he passed his hand over the control panel and on a far shelf a selector whirred. In the next second Uncle Stingo danced on to the screen, young and light-footed and natty in white. Uncle Stingo did a time step; Bert did a time step and Van cried out, "Wait, oh wait," but it was too late; Bert had him by the arm and they were going through the endless stacks of tapes and on the door at the far side was Missy Beaton's name and above it was her photograph; she beamed out, lithe and promising, aglow with youth and love.

Bert was tapping. "Missy? Missy, baby."

"In a minute, Bert."

Shuffle. Drag. Shuffle. Van wanted to turn away. Shuffle.

Missy opened the door.

The black tights flapped about her old bones and the pink tutu was bedraggled now but there was enough of the old expression in her face to keep Van from screaming; she smiled, bright and friendly, and because there was something engaging, almost sweet about her, he took her hand.

"H-how do you do."

"Hello, sweetie." She tilted her head in the old way, touching his arm with a hand like a leaf. "Isn't he nice, Bert. Isn't he *young*."

But Bert was looking at Van. "So you see how it is. We're the last."

Panic fluttered in Van's throat. "But the Pico Players, Cap'n Jack, all the rest..."

"All dead. All in the can."

"And the starships, and the census, and the war..."

Bert grinned foolishly. "All in the can."

Van shook his head. "I saw rockets going off."

"Oh yeah, that's Sam's department. Keeps him busy."

"I saw a starship go."

"Jimmy sends them. 'S how we got the streets cleared out."

"*No*." Van wheeled.

Bert's voice curled after him. "We just keep things going."

But Van was already on the run.

"*Some*body has to." Bert was after him now, panting hard.

But they were too old and slow to stop him and he tore out of Missy's grasp, racing down one aisle of shelves and then another, making false turns and doubling back; he ran, gasping, mumbling, trying speeches in his throat. Missy and Bert went the straight way, shuffling into the control area just as he stepped in front of the nearest camera, screaming into the boom microphone:

"Hi Mom, Hi Dad, Hi Louis, Sister, Marty and Jack. Hi everybody out there at home. Listen, world, it's all a big fake in here, it's all been over for years and they are giving you the same old stuff over and over, it all comes out of cans. They're making up the population crush, they're even making up the war. Look, you've got to come on down and *do* something...we've all got to start over, you've all got to help..."

Breathing defiance, he stood and waited with his back to the control panel. In a minute the nearest ones would come running; in a second all the phones would begin to ring. Bert didn't seem disturbed. He took Missy's hand and led her to a ruined leather couch. They chattered and giggled and Missy lost track of her cane and Bert scrambled after it and returned it; he presented it with a bow and she took it with a touching grin.

The Pico Players came on. The Saint Spree Singers came on. Bert brought sandwiches for him and Missy. He offered one to Van but Van refused it. He was still strung taut, waiting for the first ones to thunder into the hallways, waiting for his army to come.

"You'll do," Bert said kindly, breaking an intolerable silence.

On the screen a starship took off. Bert brushed by Van and pushed a button; two buzzes came from somewhere.

"That's Jimmy, down at his place," Bert said conversationally. A second ship went up. "Enterprise," Bert said. "That's what makes it all fun."

Outside were no footsteps. No phones rang.

Van drooped. "Where is everybody?"

"Home. Glued to the tube."

"But I just told them. I told them and I *told* them."

"They're happy. They don't care."

Missy touched his cheek, trying to explain. "Sweetie, the machines do everything."

"Watching and buying. It's *terrible.*"

Bert tossed his head. "Hell, baby, it keeps them off the streets."

"I like his manner," Missy said unexpectedly.

Bert stood off, appraising him. "I like the way you got off that announcement. I'll start training you right away... I haven't got too long."

Van shook his head, baffled. "All those people..." He took Bert by the shoulders. "What do you *get* out of it?" He looked around as if he expected to see a new shape in the studio. "Money? Power?"

"Somebody needs me." Bert touched Missy's hand. Then he drew himself up, saying proudly: "Hell, honey, don't you see it? I have a job."

Missy sat down, patting the seat beside her. "Come and have a sandwich."

"I've got to get out of here."

But Bert wasn't listening to Van. His eyes misted and he said, "When I kick off... Look... You *will* take good care of Missy, won't you?"

Van hesitated. Missy watched him from the couch; she was so shrunken that her feet didn't touch the floor; her hair flew like white plumage. Her hands trembled and her eyes were misted too. Still she managed to toss her head gaily and she gave Van a brave little wink.

"You don't have to worry about me."

But Van was coming forward. "It's OK, Missy." He bowed. "I'd be happy to."

"Good," said Bert. "Now let me show you how to run the board."

Excerpt From *Bug Jack Barron*
Norman Spinrad

Norman Spinrad has been a major figure in science fiction since the mid-1960s, when he began publishing a long list of successful novels and short stories. *Bug Jack Barron* is arguably his most famous novel and has been under option in Hollywood continuously since its first publication in 1969. The book, first serialized in the British science fiction magazine *New Worlds*, follows provocative, often angry, television host Jack Barron as he stumbles onto a conspiracy involving immortality treatments. In this excerpt, we see Barron at work during his television show. Television viewers will note a surprising resemblance to Spinrad's depiction of Barron's interviewing techniques and any number of cable news shows today, more than forty years after the publication of the novel.

Chapter 8

"Deathbed at go" the promptboard flashed, and Jack Barron, clocking Vince's smart-ass Sicilian-type grin, was sure Gelardi had to have Mafiosa blood in him somewhere even though he claimed to be strictly *Napolitan*. The promptboard flashed "45 Seconds," and Barron shuddered as the last seconds of the opening commercial reeled by—schtick was a bunch of diplomats relaxing around the old conference table with good old Acapulco Golds. Ain't as funny as it looks, he thought, vips run the world like they're stoned half the time anyway, and for the other half things are *worse*. Wonder what Bennie Howards would be like high? Well, maybe tonight all hundred million Brackett Count chilluns gonna see—they say adrenalin's like a psychedelic, and before I'm through tonight, Bennie's gonna go on an adrenalin bummer he won't believe.

Watching the commercial fade into his own face on the monitor, Barron felt a weird psychedelic flash go through him, the reality of the last week compressed into an instantaneous image flashed on the promptboard of his mind: Sitting in the studio chair, electronic feedback-circuitry connecting him with subsystems of power—Foundation power, S.I.C.-Democrat-Republican power, hundred million Brackett Count power—he was like the master transistor in a massive satellite network confluence circuit of power, gigantic input of others' power feeding into his head through vidphone circuits, none of it his, but all feeding through him, his to control by microcosmic adjustment; for one hour, 8–9 P.M. Eastern Standard Time, that power was de facto *his.*

He felt his subjective head-time speeding up, like an alien drug in his bloodstream, at the focus of forces far beyond him yet at his command as letters crawled across the promptboard an electric-dot message that seemed to take ten million years: "On the Air."

"And what's bugging you out there tonight?" Jack Barron asked, playing to the kinesthop-darkness shapes double-reflected (backdrop off desktop) in his eye hollows ominous with foreknowledge of the shape of the show to come. "What bugs you, bugs Jack Barron," he said, digging his own image on the monitor, eyes picking up flashes as never before. "And we'll soon see what happens when you bug Jack Barron. The number is Area Code 212, 969-6969, and we'll take our first call right...*now.*"

Now, he thought, making the vidphone connection, nitty-gritty time, Bennie-baby, better be good and ready, here it comes *now.* And the screen split down the middle; left half a pallid gray on gray image of a dough-faced middle-aged woman with deep lines of defeat-tension etched around her hollow-bagged eyes like dry kernels of mortal disaster, a hag-gray ghost begging her living-color image for alms from gods.

"This is *Bug Jack Barron,* and you're on the air, plugged into me, plugged into *one hundred million Americans* (drawing out the words for special audience of one, one hundred million, count 'em Bennie, 100,000,000) and this is your chance to let 'em all know what's bugging you and get some action, 'cause action's the name of the game when you bug Jack Barron. So let's hear it all, the right here right now live no time-delay nitty-gritty; what's bugging *you?*"

"My...my name is Dolores Pulaski," the woman said, "and I've been trying to talk to you for three weeks, Mr. Barron, but I know it's not your fault." (Vince gave her three-quarters screen, put Barron in upper righthand corner catbird-seat, living-color Crusader dwarfed by yawning gray need. Just the right touch, Barron thought.) "I'm calling for my father, Harold Lopat. He...he can't speak for himself." Her lips quivered on the edge of a sob.

Jesus Christ, Barron thought, hope Vince didn't feed me a crier, gotta underplay this schtick or I'll push Howards too far. "Take it easy, Mrs. Pulaski," he soothed, "you're talking to friends. We're all on your side."

"I'm sorry," the woman said, "it's just so hard to...." Her eyes frightened and furtive, her jaw hardened to numbness, the tension came across beautifully as she forced herself calm. "I'm calling from the Kennedy Hospital for Chronic Disease in Chicago. My father, he's been here ten weeks...die...die...he's got cancer, cancer of the stomach, and it's spread to the lym...*lymphatics,* and the doctors all say...we've had four specialists...He's dying! He's dying! They say they can't do anything. My father, Mr. Barron, My father...he's going to *die!*"

She began sobbing; then her face went off camera, and a huge pale hand obscured the vidphone image as she picked her vidphone up, turned its camera on the room. Trembling, disjointed, out of focus pieces of hospital room stumbled across the monitor screen: Walls, wilted flowers, transfusion stands, bed, blankets, the thousand deathhead's wrinkled ether-smell shriveled face of a ruined old man, and her voice—"Look! Look! Look at him!"

Jeez, Barron thought, pumping his screen-control foot-button even as Vince changed the monitor-mix to three-quarters Jack Barron the lower lefthand quadrant still a jumble of sliding images, old man's face fingers vased flower trays of needles bedpan—hideous gray montage of death by inches now muted at least, surrounded by full-color embracing image of concerned Big Brother Jack Barron, and Dolores Pulaski's screaming sobs were a far-away tinny unreality as Vince bled her audio and Barron's voice reestablished control.

"Take it easy, Mrs. Pulaski." Barron stopped just short of harshness. "We all want to help you, but you'll have to stay calm. Now put the vidphone down in front of you, and just try to remember you'll have all the time you need to say what you want to. And if you can't find the words, I'm here to help you. Try to relax. A hundred million Americans are on your side and *want* to understand."

The woman's face reappeared in the lower left quadrant, eyes dull, jaw slack, a spent, pale-flesh robot-image, and Barron knew he was back in control. After a little hair-tearing, she's got nothing left in her, you can make her say anything, she won't make more waves. And he foot-signaled Vince to give her three-quarters screen, her schtick to the next commercial, as long as she stayed tame.

"I'm sorry I had to be so short with you. Mrs. Pulaski," Barron said softly. "Believe me, we all understand how you must feel."

"I'm sorry too, Mr. Barron," she said in a loud stage whisper. (Vince, Barron

thought, on the ball as usual, turning up her volume.) "It's just that I feel so...
you know, helpless, and now when I can finally *do* something about it, it all
just came out, everything I've been holding in.... I don't know what to do, what
to say, but I've got to make everyone understand...."

Here it comes, Barron thought. Sitting on the edge of your sweaty little
seat, Bennie? Not yet, eh? Keep cool, Bennie-baby, 'cause now you get yours!

"Of course we all sympathize. Mrs. Pulaski, but I'm not quite sure what
anyone can do. If the doctors say...." Give, baby! Shit, don't make me fish for
it.

"The doctors say...they say there's no hope for my father. Surgery, radiation,
drugs—nothing can save him. My father's dying. Mr. Barron. They give him
only weeks. Within a month...within a month he'll be dead."

"I still don't see—"

"Dead!" she whispered. "In a few weeks, my father will be dead forever. Oh
he's a good man, Mr. Barron! He's got children and grandchildren who love
him, and he's worked hard for us all his life, and he loves us. He's as good a
man as anyone who ever lived! Why, *why* should he be dead and gone forever
while other men, *bad* men, Mr. Barron, men who've gotten rich on good men's
sweat, they can live forever just by buying their way into a Freezer with the
money they've stolen and cheated people like us to get? It's not fair, it's...*evil*.
A man like my father, and honest, kind man, works all his life for his family,
and when he dies he's buried and gone like he had never existed, while a man
like Benedict Howards holds...holds immortal lives in his filthy hands like he
was God..."

Dolores Pulaski blanched at the weight of the word that hung from her
lips. "I didn't mean...." she stammered. "I mean, forgive me, to mention a man
like that in the same sentence with God..."

Jeez, spare me the Hail Marys! Barron thought. "Of course you didn't," he
said, picturing Howards sweating somewhere in the bowels of his Colorado
Freezer with no place to hide. He tapped his right foot-button twice, signaling
Vince to give him a two-minute count to the next commercial as he paused,
casually kind, before continuing. "But tell me, Mrs. Pulaski, what are you
asking *me* to do?" he said, all earnest choir-boy innocence.

"Get my father a place in a Freezer!" Dolores Pulaski shot back. (Beautiful,
thought Barron. Couldn't be better if we were working from a script; you're
show biz all the way, Dolores Pulaski.)

"I'm afraid I don't swing much weight at the Foundation for Human Immortality," Barron said archly as Vince now split the screen evenly between them, "as I'm sure you'll remember if you saw the last show." The promptboard flashed "90 Seconds." (Don't fail me now, Mrs. Pulaski, come out with the right line and I make you a star.)

"I know that, Mr. Barron. It's that Benedict Howards...one man in the whole world who can save my father, and he sells immortality like the devil buys souls. God forgive me for saying it, but I mean it—like Satan! Who else but Satan and Benedict Howards are evil enough to put a price on a man's immortal life? Talk to him, Mr. Barron, show the world what he's like. Make him explain to poor people dying everywhere without a hope of living again how he can set a price on human life. And if he can't explain, I mean in front of millions of people, well, then he'll have to do something about my father, won't he? He can't afford to look like a monster in public. I mean, an important man like that...?" The promptboard flashed "60 Seconds."

"You've got a point, Mrs. Pulaski," Barron said, cutting her off quickly before too much more peasant shrewdness could come through. (Such a thing as *too* show biz, Dolores Pulaski—can't stand a straightman steps on *my* lines.)

Vince expanded his image to three-quarters screen, cut Dolores Pulaski to prefadeout inset, cut her audio too, and a good thing, the chick's getting a wee bit naked, Barron thought as the promptboard flashed "30 Seconds."

"Yeah, Mrs. Pulaski sure has a point, doesn't she?" Barron said, staring straight into the camera as his living-color image filled the monitor screen in extreme close-up, darkness-shadows, bruised sullen hollows framing his eyes. "If there's a reason to set a dollar value on a man's chance at immortality, there's sure as hell a reason to hear what it is, with all America watching, with a bill pending in Congress to make this monopoly on freezing into Federal law. And we'll get the answer from Mr. Benedict Howards right after this word from our sponsor—or a hundred million Americans will know the reason why."

What a lead-in! Barron thought as they rolled the commercial. Dolores Pulaski, you're beautiful, baby! So long as you don't flip out again while I'm playing chicken with Bennie....

He punched the intercom button on his number one vidphone. "Hey Vince," he said, "keep your finger on that audio dial. It's me and Bennie all the way from here on in. I want Mrs. Pulaski seen but not heard. Keep her audio down, unless I ask her a direct question. And if you gotta cut her off, then fade it—make it look like a bad vidphone connection not the old ax. Got Bennie on the line yet?"

Gelardi grinned from behind the control booth glass. "Been on the line for the last three minutes, and by now he's foaming at the mouth, Wants to talk to you right now, before you go back on the air. Still got 45 seconds...?"

"Tell him to get stuffed," Barron answered. "He'll have more time than he can handle to talk to me when he's on the air. And, baby, when I get my hooks into him, he won't be in any position to hang up."

Poor Bennie! Barron thought. Two strikes already. He's playing the master's game on the master's turf, and he's gibbering mad to boot. And as the promptboard flashed "30 Seconds," Barron suddenly realized that for the rest of the show he held Benedict Howards, the most powerful man in the United States, right there in his hot little hand, to play with like a cat plays with a wounded mouse. Can kill his Freezer Bill just for openers if I get that feeling; do him in all the way any time I want to close my fist just gotta twitch and he's had it, is all. Cat and mouse. And Luke and Morris out there now, wondering just what the hell game I'm playing...maybe theirs? It's what they're both hot for, ain't it—Jack Barron down on the Foundation with high-heeled hobnails and off to the races...? So hung on "Hail to the Chief" the poor bastards could never dream there could be *bigger* game in town....

"On the Air" the promptboard said.

Barron made the number two vidphone connection and Dolores Pulaski appeared in a small lower-right inset, with Howards seemingly glowering down from the upper left quadrant at her across the color image of larger-than-either-adversary Jack Barron. Groovy, Barron thought as he said, "This is *Bug Jack Barron*, and the man on the screen with me and Mrs. Pulaski is Mr. Benedict Howards himself, President, Chairman of the Board, and founder of the Foundation for Human Immortality. Mr. Howards, Mrs. Pulaski has—"

"I've been watching the show, *Mr. Barron*," Howards interrupted, and Barron could see him fighting for control, eyes hot in the cool and earnest mask of his face. (But he still can't keep from dripping acid, Barron thought gleefully.) "It's one of my favorites and I rarely miss it—it's sure long on excitement; you know how to create heat. Too bad you're so short in the light department."

Tsk, tsk! Watch it Bennie, your fly's open and your *id*'s hanging out, Barron thought as he smiled nastily into the camera. "That's my job after all, Mr. Howards," he said blandly. "I'm just here to turn the spotlight on things that need seeing, like...turning over a lot of wet rocks to see what crawls out. I'm not here to tell anyone anything; I just ask questions America thinks need answering. Enlightenment's gotta come from the other end of the vidphone, *your* end, Mr. Howards.

"So since you've been watching the show, let's not bore a hundred million Americans with repetition. Let's get right down to the nitty-gritty. There's a man dying in a hospital in Chicago—fact. There's one of your Freezers in Cicero, isn't there?—that's a hard fact too. Mrs. Pulaski and her family want a place for Mr. Lopat in that Freezer. If he isn't Frozen, he dies and never lives again. If he is Frozen, he's got the same chance at immortality as anyone else in a Freezer. You hold Harold Lopat's life in your hands, Mr. Howards, you say whether he lives or he dies. So you see, it all boils down to one simple question, Mr. Howards, and a hundred million Americans know that you and only you have the answer: Does Harold Lopat live or die?"

Howards' mouth snapped open, and time stopped for a beat; he seemed to think twice, and closed it. (Got you right on the knife-edge, Bennie—the Nero schtick: thumbs up, the cat lives, thumbs down, he dies. Thumbs down, you're a murderer in front of a hundred million people. Thumbs up, and you've opened the floodgates and the dam's busted for every deadbeat dying everywhere, people, Mr. Howards, people, is all, free Freeze for everyone on Emperor Howards.... Whatever you say next, Bennie, it's gotta be *wrong*.)

"Neither you nor Mrs. Pulaski understands the situation," Howards finally said. "I don't have the power to say who's to be Frozen and who isn't. Nobody does. It's sheer economics, just like who can afford a new Cadillac and who has to drive an old '81 Ford. Fifty thousand dollars or more must be assigned to the Foundation for every man Frozen. I assure you that if Mr. Lopat or his family have the requisite assets, he *will* be Frozen, if that's what they want."

"Mrs. Pulaski...?" Barron said, foot-signaling Gelardi to cut in her audio.

"Fifty thousand dollars!" Dolores Pulaski shouted. "A man like you doesn't know how much money that is—more than my husband makes in eight years, and he's got a wife and a family to support! Even with Medicare, the specialists, the extra doctors, aren't covered, and our savings, my father's and my husband's and my brother's, are all gone. Why don't you just make it a million dollars or a billion; what's the difference, when ordinary people can't afford it, what kind of filthy...." Her voice trailed off in crackles, fading simulated hisses as Gelardi cut her off.

"Seems to be a bug in Mrs. Pulaski's connection," Barron said as Vince rearranged the images, giving Howards' naked discomfort half the screen alongside him, Dolores Pulaski reduced to a tiny inset-creature looking on. "But I think she's made her point. Fifty thousand dollars is a hell of a lot of bread to hold onto, taxes and cost of living being what they are. You know, I knock down a pretty nice piece of change for this show, I probably make more money than ninety percent of the people in the country, and even I can't squirrel that kind of bread away. So when you set the price of a Freeze at fifty big ones you're really saying that ninety percent of all living Americans gonna be food for the worms when they die, while a few million fat cats get the chance to live forever. Hardly seems right that money can buy life. Maybe the people who're yelling for Public Freezers—"

"Commies!" shouted Howards. "Can't you see that? They're all Communists or dupes of the Reds. Look at the Soviet Union, look at Red China—they got any Freezer Programs *at all?* Of course not, because a Freezer Program can only be supported by a healthy free enterprise system. Socialized Freezing means no Freezing at all. The Commies would love—"

"But aren't you the best friend the Communists have in America?" Barron cut in, signaling for a commercial in three minutes.

"*You* calling *me* a Communist!" Howards said, forcing his face into a soundless parody of a laugh. "That's good. Barron, the whole country knows the kind of people *you've* been involved with."

"Let's skip the name-calling shall we? I didn't call you a Communist...just, shall we say, an unwitting dupe of the Reds? I mean, the fact that less than ten percent of the population—shall we say, the exploiters of the working class, as they put it—have a chance to live forever, while everyone else has to die and like it....is there a *better* argument against a pure capitalistic system that the Reds can dream up? Isn't your Foundation the best piece of propaganda the Reds have?"

"I'm sure your audience isn't swallowing that crap," Howards said (knowing it damn well is, Barron thought smugly). "Nevertheless, I'll try to explain it so that even *you* can understand it, *Mr.* Barron. Maintaining Freezers costs lots of money, and so does research on restoring and extending life. It costs billions each year, so much money that, for instance, the Soviet government simply can't afford it—and neither can the government of the United States. But an effort like ours must be financed somehow, and the only way is for the people who are Frozen to pay their own way. If the government tried to Freeze everyone who died, it'd go bankrupt, it'd cost tens of billions a year. The Foundation, by seeing to it that those who are Frozen pay for it, and pay for the research, at least keeps the dream of human immortality alive. It may not be perfect, but it's the only thing that can work. Surely a man of your...*vast intelligence* should be able to see *that*."

Five points for you, Bennie, Barron conceded. Thing is that the fucker's essentially *right*. Letting the few that are Frozen now feed the worms won't get anyone else into a Freezer, and if you got a thousand people dying for every slot open, well baby, that's where life's always been at—the winners win, and the losers lose. But you're too right for your own good, Bennie, muscle talks, and muscle's what you'll get from good old Jack Barron.

"Of course I understand the hard economic realities," Barron said as the promptboard flashed "2 Minutes." "I mean, sitting here, fat and healthy and thirty-eight years old. Dollars and sense and all that crap, on paper your Foundation looks real good. Yeah, I understand, Mr. Howards. But I wonder if I'd feel so damn philosophical if I were dying. Would you, Mr. Howards? How'd you like to die like Harold Lopat—broke, and the life leaking out of you drop by drop, while some cat in a two-hundred-and-fifty-dollar suit explains real logical-like how it's economically impractical to give you the chance to live again some day?"

To Barron's surprise, Howards seemed genuinely stricken: a mist of what seemed like sheer madness drifted behind his eyes, his jaw trembling, Howards muttered something unintelligible and then froze entirely. The basilisk himself turned to stone? Bennie Howards with an attack of conscience? Barron wondered. More likely something he ate. Well, it's an ill wind, he thought as the promptboard flashed "90 Seconds."

"What's the matter, Mr. Howards," Barron asked, "can't you identify with the situation? Okay, Mrs. Pulaski, let's give Mr. Howards some help. Please turn the camera of your vidphone on your father and hold it there."

Vince's right on the ball, Barron thought as Vince blew up Dolores Pulaski's small inset to virtually fill the entire monitor screen as the image danced fragments of walls, vase, ceiling, then became a huge close-up black and white newspaper photo-image of the wasted old man's face, a long rubber tube trailing from one nostril and taped to his forehead; the gray deathbed photo tilted at a crazy home-videotape angle, and made the closed blind eyes of Harold Lopat seem to stare down at the image of Benedict Howards in the lower left-quadrant like an avenging ghost of death looking down at a scuttling insect after kicking over a wet rock, as the promptboard flashed "60 Seconds."

And Jack Barron, in a once-in-a-blue-moon off-camera spectral-voice gambit, etched Howards' face into a mask of terror and fury with precise scalpel-words: "Look, Howards, you're looking at death. That's not $50,000 on your balance sheet, that's a human being, and he's dying. Go ahead, look at that face, look at the pain, look at the disease eating it up behind the mask. Only it's not a mask, Howards, it's a human being—a human life in the process of being snuffed out forever. We all come down to that in the end, don't we, Mr. Howards? You, and me, and Harold Lopat, all of us, sooner or later, fighting for just another breath, another moment of life before the Big Nothing closes in. And there, but for $50,000, go you or I. What's so holy about fifty grand that it buys a man's life? How much is $50,000 in pieces of silver, Mr. Howards? A thousand? Two thousand? Once a man's life was sold for thirty pieces of silver, Mr. Howards, just *thirty,* and *he* was Jesus Christ. How many lives you got in your Freezers worth more than His? You think any man's life is worth more money than was the life of Jesus Christ?"

And Gelardi filled the screen with the face of Benedict Howards, ghost-white in an extreme close-up that showed every razor nick, every pimple, network of coarse open pores, the eyes of a maddened trapped carnivore as Jack Barron's voice said, "And maybe we'll have some answers from Benedict Howards after this word from our sponsor."

Jesus H. himself on a bicycle! Barron thought gleefully as they rolled the commercial. Days like this, I scare *myself!*

"Oooh, does *he* want to talk to *you!*" Vince Gelardi's voice said over the intercom circuit the moment the commercial was rolling. "Sounds like he's down with hydrophobia." Barron saw Gelardi grin, give him the high sign, start the count with "90 Seconds" on the promptboard as Benedict Howards' face appeared on the tiny number two vidphone screen and his voice came on in the middle of a tirade:

"....to the fucking fishes! No one plays games like *that* with Benedict

Howards. You lay off me, you crazy bastard, or I'll have you off the air and in jail for libel before—"

"Fuck off, Howards!" Barron said. "And before you shoot your big mouth off again, just remember that this call goes through the control booth, it's not a private line. (He shot Howards a cool-it, we're-still-fencing, don't-spill-the-beans look.) You know where all this is at, and you've got about sixty seconds before we go on the air again to give me a reason to lay off—and I *don't* mean a lot of dumb threats. I don't like threats. Tell you just what's gonna happen in the next segment. I'm gonna tear you to pieces, is all, but I'm gonna leave just enough left so you can throw in the towel during the next commercial and save what's left of your ass. Unless you wanna be smart, meet my terms *now*—and we both know what those terms are."

"Don't threaten me, you goddamned clown!" Howards roared. "You lay off, or I'll just hang up, and when I get through with you, you won't be able to get a job cleaning cesspools in—"

"Go ahead, hang up," Barron said as the promptboard flashed "30 Seconds." "I've got five calls just like the first one—only seedier—lined up to fill the rest of the show. I don't need you on the air to do you in. One way or the other you're gonna learn it doesn't pay to screw around with me, 'cause unless you come around by the next commercial your Freezer Bill has had it, and your whole fucking Foundation will stink so bad you'll think Judas Iscariot was your press agent. How's that grab you, bigshot?"

"You filthy fuck—" And Gelardi cut Howards off just in time as the promptboard flashed "On the Air."

Jack Barron grinned at his own image filling the monitor—flesh-eyes digging phosphor-dot-eyes in adrenalin-feedback reaction—and he felt a strange light-headed exhilaration, a psychic erection. More than anticipation of the coming catbird-seat five-aces-in-the-hole poker game for the big chips with Howards blood humming behind his ears, Barron felt the primal sap rising, the hot berserker joy ghost of Berkeley Baby Bolshevik jugular thrill of the hunt, amplified by electronic satellite network hundred million Brackett Count living-color image-power shooting sparks out of his phosphor-dot eyes, and for the first time felt himself giving the show over to the gyroscope of his endocrine system and didn't know what would happen next. And didn't care.

Gelardi gave Howards a lower left-quadrant inquisition dock inset—Dolores Pulaski having finished her schtick—as Barron said: "Okay, we're back on the air, Mr. Howards, and we're gonna talk about your favorite subject for a change. Let's talk about money. How many...er, clients you figure you got in your Freezers?"

"There are over a million people already in Foundation Freezers," Howards answered (and Barron could sense him fighting for purchase, trying to anticipate the line of the jugular thrust he *knew* was coming). "So you see, Freezing is not really just for the few at all. A million human beings with hope for eternal life someday is quite a large—"

"You ain't just whistling Dixie," Barron interrupted. "A million's a nice round number. Let's continue with our little arithmetic lesson, shall we? How much would you say it costs to maintain one body in a cryogenic Freezer for one year?"

"It's impossible to come up with an average figure just like that," said Howards. "You've got to figure in the cost of preparation for Freezing, the cost of the Freezing itself, amortization on the Freezer facilities, the cost of replacing evaporated coolant, power to run the pumps, salaries, taxes, insurance..."

"Yeah, we know you run a real complicated show," Barron replied. "But let's take a generous average figure no one can say is stingy..." Lay the trap right, he thought. True figure can't be more than three thou per stiff per year, and he's gotta know it, so give him more than enough rope..."...Let's say $5,000 will cover it, five thou per client per year. Sound reasonable?—or am I way too high? I don't have much of a head for business, as my accountant keeps telling me every year around April fifteenth."

"I suppose that's about right," Howards admitted grudgingly, and Barron could see the fear showing through his eyes. (Scared shitless, eh, Bennie? 'Cause you don't see where all this is going, 'cause you know there's something happening and you don't know what it is, do you Mr. Jones?)

"And in order to be Frozen, you've gotta sign over a minimum of $50,000 in liquid assets to the Foundation in order to cover costs, right?"

"We've gone through all that," Howards muttered, obviously uncertain as to what was going to happen next.

"All rightie..." Barron drawled, foot-signaling to Vince to kill Howards' audio. He stared straight into the camera, tilted his head forward, picking up darkness-shadows reflected off the desk-arm of the chair from the kinesthop background in the hollows of his dead-end-kid innocent eyes, gave a little bemused inside-joke grin. "Okay, out there, we've got the figures, now let's all do a little arithmetic. Check me, out there, will you? I've got a lousy head for figures—at least the *numerical* kind. Lessee...multiply how many bodies in the Freezers by $50,000 per body... That comes to...ah...ten zeros and...why, that's fifty billion dollars, isn't that right folks? Foundation's got at least fifty billion bucks in assets. Now *there's* cigarette money! About half the defense budget of the United States, is all. Okay, students, now one more problem in multiplication—$5,000 for each body for a year times a million bodies in the Freezers...in nice round numbers it comes to...*five billion dollars*. Now, let's see—if I had fifty billion bucks to play around with I ought to be able to make—oh, say ten percent a year on it. Couldn't you, out there?—and wouldn't you like to try? That comes to...why, it's about five billion dollars, isn't it? What a coincidence! Same as Foundation expenses—one tenth, count it folks, ten percent of the Foundation's total assets. Boy, numbers are fun!"

Visualizing the path to the punchline, Barron signaled Gelardi to give him a two-minute count to the next commercial and to cut in Howards' audio.

"What the hell is this?" Howards snapped. "Who do you think you are, the Internal Revenue Service?"

"Patience, Mr. Howards, patience," Barron drawled with purposefully irritating slowness. "Jack Barron, great swami knows all, sees all, tells all. Now let's try some simple subtraction. Subtract five billion in expenses from five billion a year in interest on your assets. That leaves a big fat zero, doesn't it? That's exactly how much maintaining those million bodies in the Freezers cuts into that fifty billion bucks in assets you got squirreled away—*zero!* Not at all. How neat! And that's how you hold on to your nonprofit, tax-exempt status, isn't it? Expenses balance income. And that $50,000 each client chucks in— why, that's not nasty old income at all, is it? Technically it's not even yours, and that keeps the Income Tax boys' hot little hands out of your till. Boy, I'd like to borrow your accountant!"

"What're you gibbering about?" Howards said, with a totally unconvincing show of incomprehension.

"I'm gibbering about the small matter of fifty billion dollars," Barron told him as the promptboard flashed "60 Seconds." "Fifty billion dollars free and clear that you've got to play around with *above* Freezer expenses, a fifty-billion-dollar slush fund. Who do you think you're putting on, Howards? That's enough bread to provide a free Freeze for every man, woman, and child who dies every year in the United States, and in Canada too, for that matter, *isn't it?*

Fifty billion bucks sitting there, while Harold Lopat and millions like him die and are gone forever while you poormouth us! What *does* happen to that fifty billion, Howards? You must have mighty big holes in your pockets or else—"

"Research!" Howards croaked frantically. "Without research—"

Gelardi, anticipating even as Barron foot-signaled, flashed "30 Seconds" on the promptboard and cut his audio off.

"Research!" Barron mimicked, his image now filling the entire monitor screen, a mask of righteous indignation scowling into Brackett Audience Count estimated hundred million pairs of eyes.

"Yeah, sure, *research*, but research in *what*? Research in how to buy votes in Congress to get this cozy little set-up written into law? Research into how to own Governors and Senators and...who knows, maybe your very own Presidential candidate? I don't like to speak ill of the dead—the conveniently *permanent* dead—but you were awfully tight with a certain late Senator who was putting on a rather well-financed campaign for the Democratic Presidential nomination, weren't you? That come under '*research*' too? Fifty billion bucks worth of *research*—with people like Harold Lopat dying all around you every day. Research. Yeah, let's talk about research! And we'll have plenty of time to discuss fifty billion dollars' worth of scientific—or is it *political*—research after this word from our relatively impoverished sponsor."

As they rolled the final commercial Barron felt a weird manic exhilaration, knowing that he had set up a focus of forces which in the next few minutes could squash the fifty-billion-dollar Foundation for Human Immortality like a bug if Bennie proved dumb enough to not holler "Uncle." Fifty billion bucks! Never added it up before, Barron thought. What the fuck *is* he really doing with all that bread? Shit, he could buy the Congress, the President, and the Supreme Court out of petty cash, if it came down to it. Talk about big-league action! Bennie Howards is bigger than the whole fucking country!

Yeah, but right here right now no time-delay live, he's nothing but a punk I can dribble like a basketball. And what's that make me? Luke and Morris maybe not as crazy as they sound....?

He made the connection on the number two vidphone and Howards, his eyes now reptile-cold gimlets, stared up at him from the oh-so-tiny vidphone screen like a bug trapped in amber.

"All right, Barron," Howards said in a dead-flat, money-talk voice, "you've made your point. We've been playing your game, and we both know I'm no match for you at it. You hurt me, and you hurt me bad. Maybe you can do more damage to me than I thought possible, but I warn you, you play ball and get me out of this mess or I'll *really* finish you and quick. And don't con me, you know damn well I can do it. You keep this up, and you'll find out just how much muscle fifty billion dollars is—I'll use every penny of it, if I have to, to pound you to a pulp. You'll lose more than your show, I can have your tax returns for the last ten years investigated, sue you for libel and buy the judge, and that's just off the top of my head. Play ball, remember what you've got to lose—*and what you've got to gain.*"

And it brought Barron down like a bucket of ice water smack in the face. Sure, I can finish the hatchet-job, he thought, but good-bye *Bug Jack Barron*, and good-bye free Freeze, and Christ knows what else the bastard can do to me—kamikaze's the name of that game. An old Dylan lyric ran through his head:

> *"I wish I could give Brother Bill his big thrill;*
> *I would tie him in chains at the top of the hill,*
> *Then send out for some pillars and Cecil B. DeMille...."*

Yeah, I can do him in and he can do me in if we both want to do that Samson schtick. Bluff's the name of the *real* game.

And the promptboard told him he had sixty seconds to play his hand.

"Look Howards," he said, "we can do each other in, or play ball and cool it. *Your* choice, Bennie-baby. You know what I want, the straight poop plus that *other thing*. I don't change my mind—matter of principle. So maybe I'm bluffing, so call me on it, I dare. But before you do, ask yourself what you've got to gain by calling me that's worth the risk of losing what *you've* got to lose. I'm a dangerous lunatic, Howards, I'm not afraid of you. You *that* sure you're not afraid of me?"

Howards was silent for a long moment, bit his lip, then said, "All right, you win. It's all negotiable. You get me out of this, and we'll talk turkey on your terms. Good enough?"

The promptboard flashed "30 Seconds" for instant decision on the course of the rest of the show and all that was riding on it. As close to "Uncle" as you'll hear from Bennie, Barron knew. He'll say anything now to get off the hook, thinks he can maybe welch later, those fifty-billion-bucks Foundation aces, but he doesn't know all the aces I got—Luke and Morris' fun and games up my sleeve, enough to bluff him out for good, comes nitty-gritty time, no matter what he's holding. So okay Bennie, you get off the hook or anyway I don't give the *descabello*, leave your bod bleeding but alive.

"All right, Howards, things don't get any worse tonight, but don't expect to make any big points in the next ten minutes either. All I'm gonna do is make things kinda fuzzy in all those heads out there."

"But you've got me backed into a corner," Howards whined. "How you gonna get me out of this with a whole skin?"

"That's my line of evil, Bennie," Barron said. He flashed Howards an ironic man-in-control smirk. "What's the matter, Bennie, don't you trust me?"

And the promptboard flashed "On the Air," and Gelardi gave Howards the same lower left-quadrant inquisition seat as before.

"Now what were we talking about?" Barron said. (Gotta back off real gradual-like, and not too far.) "Ah, yes, *research*. Fifty billion dollars' worth of research. Since by some fancy sleight of hand the Foundation is tax-exempt, I think that the American people have a right to know just what kind of... *research* that money is being spent on. Now, we can always check this with the tax boys, Mr. Howards, so let's have the straight poop—just what *is* your annual research budget?"

"Somewhere between three and four billion dollars," Howards said. Barron foot-signaled Gelardi to give him a half-screen, ease him out of the hotseat.

"That's a far cry from fifty billion dollars, isn't it?" Barron said, but with the cutting edge eased out of his voice (come on schmuck, he telepathed, pick up on it, don't expect me to make your points for you). "What's the story on that fifty billion?"

Howards seemed to relax a bit, catching on that the lead was being passed over to him. "You've been tossing that figure around pretty freely," he said, "but you obviously don't understand what it represents. If you'd studied a Freeze Contract you'd know that the $50,000 per client is *not* a fee turned over free and clear to the Foundation. Upon clinical death, the total assets of the client go into a *trust-fund* administered by the Foundation for as long as the client is biologically and legally dead. But on revival all assets originally placed in the trust fund revert to the client, and only the interest and capital appreciation during the time the client is in the Freezer actually become the property of the foundation. So you see, that fifty billion dollars is simply not ours to spend. It certainly is an enormous amount of money, but the fact is that we must maintain *all of it* as a reserve against the day when we can revive our clients and return it to them. The fund works essentially the way a bank works—a bank can't go around spending its deposits, and we can't spend that fifty billion dollars. It's not really ours."

Can't make *me* look bad, Barron thought. Can't make it too easy; gotta back off slow. "But a chunk of capital that big grows awfully fast unless you're some kind of idiot or you're blowing it on the horses," he said. "And you've just admitted that all increases in the original capital *do* belong to the foundation, so you've gotta have billions in assets that *are* yours free and clear. What about that?"

Howards pounced quickly. (Now he's sees daylight! Barron thought.) "Quite true. But our expenses are enormous...something like five billion a year for maintenance, and that eats up all the interest on the original capital. So the four billion for research must come from profits on the investment of our *own* capital. After all, if we started spending *capital* on research we'd quickly go bankrupt."

Suddenly, almost unwillingly, Barron realized that Howards had handed him a weapon that could make the rest of the show look like a love-pat. Shit, he thought, Bennie's got a vested interest in keeping all those quick-Frozen stiffs dead! The day he can thaw 'em out and revive 'em he loses that fifty-billion-dollar trust fund. Hit him with *that* baby, and you'll stomp him into the ground! Why—Cool it! Cool it! he reminded himself. You're supposed to be pulling the lox out of the hole, not digging it deeper!

"So it all comes down to *research*," Barron said, reluctantly leading away from the jugular. "Four billion bucks is still one hell of a research budget, more than enough to hide...all kinds of interesting things. Suppose you explain what kind of research you're spending all that bread on?"

Howards shot him a dirty look.

Jeez, what you expect, Bennie? Barron thought. I still gotta look like kick-'em-in-the-ass Jack Barron, don't I?

"First off, you've got to understand that all those people in our Freezers are *dead*. Dead as anyone in a cemetery. All cryogenic freezing does is preserve the bodies from decay—those bodies are simply corpses. The problem of bringing a corpse back to life is enormous. I'm no scientist and neither are you, Barron, but you can imagine how much research and experimentation must be done before we can actually bring a dead man back to life—and it's all very expensive. And even then, cures must be developed for whatever killed the clients in the first place—and most of the time, it's old age. And that's the toughest nut of all to crack, a cure for aging, I mean, so you revive a ninety-year-old client, but if you haven't licked aging, he dies again almost immediately. See what we're up against? All this will cost billions a year for decades, maybe centuries. Man in my position's gotta take the long view, the real long view...." And for a moment, Howards' eyes seemed to be staring off into some unimaginable future.

And Barron got a flash: Could it be that the whole Freezer schtick's a shuck? Way to raise money for something else? Pie in the sky in the great bye and bye? The whole Freezer Program's useless unless they lick aging. (And how much is that free freeze *really* worth? Maybe I'm selling myself awful cheap...) But the way Bennie babbled in my office about living forever, *that* was no shuck, he was really zonked on it! Yeah, it all adds up—he doesn't want to lick the revival problem 'cause that'd cost him that fifty billion. But he's sure hot to live forever. Five'll get you ten the Foundation scientists are just pissing around with revival research, big bread's gotta be behind immortality research. And if *that* gets out, how many more suckers gonna spring for that fifty thou? Bennie-baby, we gonna have a long long talk. Let's see if we can hit a little nerve, he thought, what they call an exploratory operation, as the promptboard flashed "3 Minutes."

"Someday all men will live forever through the Foundation for Human Immortality," said Barron.

"What?" Howards grunted, his eyes snapping back into sharp focus like a man called back from a trance.

"Just quoting a Foundation slogan," Barron said. "Isn't that where it's really at? I mean all that bread spent on Freezing is money down a rathole unless it really leads to immorality, right? Some old coot signs over fifty thou so you can revive him a hundred years later so he can die again of old age in a year or two, that doesn't make much sense to me. The Freezer Program is a way to preserve a few people who die now so they can have immortality in the future, whenever you lick *that* one. I mean young cats like me, the country in general, main stake we've got in letting the Foundation do business is like that slogan of yours about *all* people living forever someday through the Foundation for Human Immortality, right? So either you're going hot-and-heavy on immortality research, or the whole thing's just a con. You follow me, Mr. Howards?"

"Wh...wh...why, of course we are!" Howards stammered, and his eyes went reptile-uptight cold. "It's called 'The Foundation for Human Immortality,' not 'The Freezing Foundation,' after all. Immortality is our goal and we're spending billions on it, and in fact..."

Howards hesitated as the promptboard flashed "2 Minutes." That hit a nerve, all right, Barron thought, but *which* nerve? Seemed like he was on the edge of blowing something he didn't want to...120 seconds to try to find out what.

"Well, it seems to me," said Barron, "that with you having tax-exempt status and by your own admission spending billions on immortality research and some of that bread being indirectly public money, you owe the American people a progress report. Just how is all this expensive research going?"

Howards shot him a look of pure poison. Lay off! his eyes screamed. "Foundation scientists are following many paths to immortality," Howards said slowly. (He must be watching the clock too, Barron realized.) "Some, of course, are more promising than others...Nevertheless, we feel that all possibilities should be explored...."

Barron tapped his left foot-button three times, and Vince gave him three-quarters of the screen, with Howards in the inquisition slot again, as the promptboard flashed "90 Seconds." "How about some specifics?" he asked. "Tell us what the most promising line of research seems to be, and how far along you are."

"I don't think it would be right to raise any false hopes this early," Howards said blandly, but Barron's teeth sensed something tense?—fearful?—threatening?—behind it. "Discussing specifics would be a mistake at this time...." But false hopes are your stock in trade, Barron thought. Why don't you want to give a nice sales spiel, Bennie...? Unless...

"You mean to tell me you've spent all those billions and you're right back where you started?" Barron snapped in a tone of cynical disbelief. "That can only mean one of two things: the so-called scientists you've got working for you are all quacks or idiots, or...or the money you've got budgeted for immortality research is going for something else—like pushing your Freezer Bill through Congress, like backing political campaigns..."

"That's a lie!" Howards shrieked, and suddenly he seemed back in that strange trance state. "You don't know what you're talking about! (The promptboard flashed "30 Seconds.") Progress *is* being made. More progress than anyone drea—" Howards shuddered, as if he had suddenly found himself blowing his cool, caught himself short.

Barron foot-signaled Gelardi to give him the full-screen windup. Something's going on here, he thought. Something bigger than...bigger than...? Anyway, too big to thrash out on the air. Good timing, as usual.

"Well that's about it, folks," he said, "we're out of time. Been quite an hour, eh? And if this whole thing's still bugging you, then next Wednesday night you just pick up that vidphone and dial Area Code 212, 969-6969, and we'll be off to the races again with another hour of *Bug Jack Barron*."

And they were rolling the wrap-up commercial, and he was off the air.

"He wants to—"

"No!" Jack Barron said even as Gelardi's voice spoke over the intercom circuit. "I don't talk to Howards now for no reasons under no conditions."

Gelardi made hair-pulling motions behind the glass wall of the control booth. "I've never heard any of your victims this pissed," he said. "You've gotta get this fruitcake off the line before he melts every circuit in the joint. Such language!"

Barron felt the old talked-out satisfying fatigue come over him as he got up out of the hotseat and thought, as usual, about going somewhere and picking up a chick and fucking her brains—and then, like a new burst of energy, he remembered. Them days is gone forever! Home to Sara, and Sara there! Changes, changes, and good ones for a change *this* time round.

"Come on, Jack, for chrissakes, cool Howards already!" Gelardi whined.

Who the fuck wants him cooled? Barron thought. Something happened during those last few minutes, I hit something real tender, and he almost spilled some mighty important beans—and not because he kept his cool. Let him stew a while. I want him hot and raving when we get down to nitty-gritty—and not witnesses, Vince, baby.

"Give him my home phone number," Barron said. "If that doesn't cool him, tell him to fuck off. In fact why don't you give him my number and tell him to fuck off anyway? Tell him...tell him Mohammed can damn well come to the mountain."

"But man, all we need is Howards—"

"Let me do the worrying, Vince. Boy Wonder Jack Barron's still in the catbird-seat."

As vip Bennie Howards will soon find out.

The Prize of Peril
Robert Sheckley

Robert Sheckley (1928–2005) was the author of fifteen novels, a dozen short story collections, and more than four hundred short stories. He was known for his absurdist wit and sharp satire, and his short fiction, in particular, found ready markets in some of the best magazines of his day. "The Prize of Peril" was published in 1958 in *The Magazine of Fantasy & Science Fiction* and later adapted into a French movie and a German made-for-television film. Predictive of reality television with its escalating threats as the episodes go by, the story shows what television contestants will risk in order to win whatever prize is offered and also takes an interesting look at television's manipulation of "reality" for the sake of ratings and profit.

Raeder lifted his head cautiously above the windowsill. He saw the fire escape, and below it a narrow alley. There was a weather-beaten baby carriage in the alley and three garbage cans. As he watched, a black-sleeved arm moved from behind the farthest can, with something shiny in its fist. Raeder ducked down. A bullet smashed through the window above his head and punctured the ceiling, showering him with plaster.

Now he knew about the alley. It was guarded, just like the door.

He lay at full length on the cracked linoleum, staring at the bullet hole in the ceiling, listening to the sounds outside the door. He was a tall man with bloodshot eyes and a two-day stubble. Grime and fatigue had etched lines into his face. Fear had touched his features, tightening a muscle here and twitching a nerve there. The results were startling. His face had character now, for it was reshaped by the expectation of death.

There was a gunman in the alley and two on the stairs. He was trapped. He was dead.

Sure, Raeder thought, he still moved and breathed; but that was only because of death's inefficiency. Death would take care of him in a few minutes. Death would poke holes in his face and body, artistically dab his clothes with blood, arrange his limbs in some grotesque position of the graveyard ballet...

Raeder bit his lip sharply. He wanted to live. There had to be a way.

He rolled onto his stomach and surveyed the dingy cold-water apartment into which the killers had driven him. It was a perfect little one-room coffin. It had a door, which was watched, and a fire escape, which was watched. And it had a tiny windowless bathroom.

He crawled to the bathroom and stood up. There was a ragged hole in the ceiling, almost four inches wide. If he could enlarge it, crawl through into the apartment above...

He heard a muffled thud. The killers were impatient. They were beginning to break down the door.

He studied the hole in the ceiling. No use even considering it. He could never enlarge it in time.

They were smashing against the door, grunting each time they struck. Soon the lock would tear out, or the hinges would pull out of the rotting wood. The door would go down, and the two blank-faced men would enter, dusting off their jackets....

But surely someone would help him! He took the tiny television set from his pocket. The picture was blurred, and he didn't bother to adjust it. The audio was clear and precise.

He listened to the well-modulated voice of Mike Terry addressing his vast audience.

"...terrible spot," Terry was saying. "Yes, folks, Jim Raeder is in a truly terrible predicament. He had been hiding, you'll remember, in a third-rate Broadway hotel under an assumed name. It seemed safe enough. But the bellhop recognized him, and gave that information to the Thompson gang."

The door creaked under repeated blows. Raeder clutched the little television set and listened.

"Jim Raeder just managed to escape from the hotel! Closely pursued, he entered a brownstone at one fifty-six West End Avenue. His intention was to go over the roofs. And it might have worked, folks, it just might have worked. But the roof door was locked. It looked like the end... But Raeder found that apartment seven was unoccupied and unlocked. He entered..."

Terry paused for emphasis, then cried:—"and now he's trapped there, trapped like a rat in a cage! The Thompson gang is breaking down the door! The fire escape is guarded! Our camera crew, situated in a nearby building, is giving you a close-up now. Look, folks, just look! Is there no hope for Jim Raeder?"

Is there no hope? Raeder silently echoed, perspiration pouring from him as he stood in the dark, stifling little bathroom, listening to the steady thud against the door.

"Wait a minute!" Mike Terry cried. *"Hang on, Jim Raeder, hang on a little longer. Perhaps there is hope! I have an urgent call from one of our viewers, a call on the Good Samaritan Line! Here's someone who thinks he can help you, Jim. Are you listening, Jim Raeder?"*

Raeder waited, and heard the hinges tearing out of rotten wood.

"Go right ahead, sir," said Mike Terry. *"What is your name, sir?"*

"Er—Felix Bartholemow."

"Don't be nervous, Mr. Bartholemow. Go right ahead."

"Well, okay. Mr. Raeder," said an old man's shaking voice, *"I used to live at one five six West End Avenue. Same apartment you're trapped in, Mr. Raeder— fact! Look, that bathroom has got a window, Mr. Raeder. It's been painted over, but it has got a—"*

Raeder pushed the television set into his pocket. He located the outlines of the window and kicked. Glass shattered, and daylight poured startling in. He cleared the jagged sill and quickly peered down.

Below was a long drop to a concrete courtyard.

The hinges tore free. He heard the door opening. Quickly Raeder climbed through the window, hung by his fingertips for a moment, and dropped.

The shock was stunning. Groggily he stood up. A face appeared at the bathroom window.

"Tough luck," said the man, leaning out and taking careful aim with a snub-nosed .38.

At that moment a smoke bomb exploded inside the bathroom.

The killer's shot went wide. He turned, cursing. More smoke bombs burst in the courtyard, obscuring Raeder's figure.

He could hear Mike Terry's frenzied voice over the TV set in his pocket. *"Now run for it!"* Terry was screaming. *"Run, Jim Raeder, run for your life. Run now, while the killers' eyes are filled with smoke. And thank Good Samaritan Sarah Winters, of three four one two Edgar Street, Brockton, Mass., for donating five smoke bombs and employing the services of a man to throw them!"*

In a quieter voice, Terry continued: "You've saved a man's life today, Mrs. Winters. Would you tell our audience how it—"

Raeder wasn't able to hear any more. He was running through the smoke-filled courtyard, past clotheslines, into the open street.

He walked down 63rd Street, slouching to minimize his height, staggering slightly from exertion, dizzy from lack of food and sleep.

"Hey, you!"

Raeder turned. A middle-aged woman was sitting on the steps of a brownstone, frowning at him.

"You're Raeder, aren't you? The one they're trying to kill?"

Raeder started to walk away.

"Come inside here, Raeder," the woman said.

Perhaps it was a trap. But Raeder knew that he had to depend upon the generosity and good-heartedness of the people. He was their representative, a projection of themselves, an average guy in trouble. Without them, he was lost. With them, nothing could harm him.

Trust in the people, Mike Terry had told him. They'll never let you down.

He followed the woman into her parlor. She told him to sit down and left the room, returning almost immediately with a plate of stew. She stood watching him while he ate, as one would watch an ape in the zoo eat peanuts.

Two children came out of the kitchen and stared at him. Three overalled men came out of the bedroom and focused a television camera on him. There was a big television set in the parlor. As he gulped his food, Raeder watched the image of Mike Terry, and listened to the man's strong, sincere, worried voice.

"*There he is, folks,*" Terry was saying. "*There's Jim Raeder now, eating his first square meal in two days. Our camera crews have really been working to cover this for you! Thanks, boys... Folks, Jim Raeder has been given a brief sanctuary by Mrs. Velma O'Dell, of three forty-three Sixty-Third Street. Thank you, Good Samaritan O'Dell! It's really wonderful how people from all walks of life have taken Jim Raeder to their hearts!*"

"You better hurry," Mrs. O'Dell said.

"Yes, ma'am," Raeder said.

"I don't want no gunplay in my apartment."

"I'm almost finished, ma'am."

One of the children asked, "Aren't they going to kill him?"

"Shut up," said Mrs. O'Dell.

"*Yes, Jim,*" chanted Mike Terry. "*you'd better hurry. Your killers aren't far behind. They aren't stupid men, Jim. Vicious, warped, insane—yes! But not stupid. They're following a trail of blood—blood from your torn hand, Jim!"*

Raeder hadn't realized until now that he'd cut his hand on the windowsill.

"Here, I'll bandage that," Mrs. O'Dell said. Raeder stood up and let her bandage his hand. Then she gave him a brown jacket and a gray slouch hat.

"My husband's stuff," she said.

"He has a disguise, folks!" Mike Terry cried delightedly. *"This is something new! A disguise! With seven hours to go until he's safe!"*

"Now get out of here," Mrs. O'Dell said.

"I'm going, ma'am," Raeder said. "Thanks."

"I think you're stupid," she said. "I think you're stupid to be involved in this."

"Yes, ma'am."

"It just isn't worth it."

Raeder thanked her and left. He walked to Broadway, caught a subway to 59th Street, then an uptown local to 86th. There he bought a newspaper and changed for the Manhasset through-express.

He glanced at his watch. He had six and a half hours to go.

The subway roared under Manhattan. Raeder dozed, his bandaged hand concealed under the newspaper, the hat pulled over his face. Had he been recognized yet? Had he shaken the Thompson gang? Or was someone telephoning them now?

Dreamily he wondered if he had escaped death, or was he still a cleverly animated corpse, moving around because of death's inefficiency? (My dear, death is so *laggard* these days! Jim Raeder walked about for hours after he died, and actually answered people's *questions* before he could be decently buried!)

Raeder's eyes snapped open. He had dreamed something...unpleasant. He couldn't remember what.

He closed his eyes again and remembered, with mild astonishment, a time when he had been in no trouble.

That was two years ago. He had been a big, pleasant young man working as a truck driver's helper. He had no talents. He was too modest to have dreams.

The tight-faced little truck driver had the dreams for him. "Why not try for a television show, Jim? I would if I had your looks. They like nice, average guys with nothing much on the ball. As contestants. Everybody likes guys like that. Why not look into it?"

So he had looked into it. The owner of the local television store had explained it further.

"You see, Jim, the public is sick of highly trained athletes with their trick reflexes and their professional courage. Who can feel for guys like that? Who can identify? People want to watch exciting things, sure, but not when some joker is making it his business for fifty thousand a year. That's why organized sports are in a slump. That's why the thrill shows are booming."

"I see," said Raeder.

"Six years ago, Jim, Congress passed the Voluntary Suicide Act. Those old senators talked a lot about free will and self-determinism at the time. But that's all crap. You know what the Act really means? It means that amateurs can risk their lives for the big loot, not just professionals. In the old days you had to be a professional boxer or footballer or hockey player if you wanted your brains beaten out legally for money. But now that opportunity is open to ordinary people like you, Jim."

"I see," Raeder said again.

"It's a marvelous opportunity. Take you. You're no better than anyone, Jim. Anything you can do, anyone can do. You're *average*. I think the thrill shows would go for you."

Raeder permitted himself to dream. Television shows looked like a sure road to riches for a pleasant young fellow with no particular talent or training. He wrote a letter to a show called *Hazard* and enclosed a photograph of himself.

Hazard was interested in him. The JBC network investigated, and found that he was average enough to satisfy the wariest viewer. His parentage and affiliations were checked. At last he was summoned to New York and interviewed by Mr. Moulian.

Moulian was dark and intense, and chewed gum as he talked. "You'll do," he snapped. "But not for *Hazard*. You'll appear on *Spills*. It's a half-hour daytime show on Channel Three."

"Gee," said Raeder.

"Don't thank me. There's a thousand dollars if you win or place second, and a consolation prize of a hundred dollars if you lose. But that's not important."

"No, sir."

"*Spills* is a *little* show. The JBC network uses it as a testing ground. First- and second-place winners on *Spills* move on to *Emergency*. The prizes are much bigger on *Emergency*."

"I know they are, sir."

"And if you do well on *Emergency*, there are the first-class thrill shows, like *Hazard* and *Underwater Perils*, with their nationwide coverage and enormous prizes. And then comes the really big time. How far you go is up to you."

"I'll do my best, sir," Raeder said.

Moulian stopped chewing gum for a moment and said, almost reverently, "You can do it, Jim. Just remember. You're *the people*, and *the people* can do anything."

The way he said it made Raeder feel momentarily sorry for Mr. Moulian, who was dark and frizzy-haired and pop-eyed, and was obviously not *the people*.

They shook hands. Then Raeder signed a paper absolving the JBC of all responsibility should he lose his life, limbs, or reason during the contest. And he signed another paper exercising his rights under the Voluntary Suicide Act. The law required this, and it was a mere formality.

In three weeks, he appeared on *Spills*.

The program followed the classic form of the automobile race. Untrained drivers climbed into powerful American and European competition cars and raced over a murderous twenty-mile course. Raeder was shaking with fear as he slid his big Maserati into the wrong gear and took off.

The race was a screaming, tire-burning nightmare. Raeder stayed back, letting the early leaders smash themselves up on the counterbanked hairpin turns. He crept into third place when a Jaguar in front of him swerved against an Alfa-Romeo, and the two cars roared into a plowed field. Raeder gunned for second place on the last three miles, but couldn't find passing room. An S-curve almost took him, but he fought the car back on the road, still holding third. Then the lead driver broke a crankshaft in the final fifty yards, and Jim ended in second place.

He was now a thousand dollars ahead. He received four fan letters, and a lady in Oshkosh sent him a pair of argyles. He was invited to appear on *Emergency*.

Unlike the others, *Emergency* was not a competition-type program. It stressed individual initiative. For the show, Raeder was knocked out with a non-habit-forming narcotic. He awoke in the cockpit of a small airplane, cruising on autopilot at ten thousand feet. His fuel gauge showed nearly empty. He had no parachute. He was supposed to land the plane.

Of course, he had never flown before.

He experimented gingerly with the controls, remembering that last week's participant had recovered consciousness in a submarine, had opened the wrong valve, and had drowned.

Thousands of viewers watched spellbound as this average man, a man just like themselves, struggled with the situation just as they would do. Jim Raeder was *them*. Anything he could do, they could do. He was representative of *the people*.

Raeder managed to bring the ship down in some semblance of a landing. He flipped over a few times, but his seat belt held. And the engine, contrary to expectation, did not burst into flames.

He staggered out with two broken ribs, three thousand dollars, and a chance, when he healed, to appear on *Torero*.

At last, a first-class thrill show! *Torero* paid ten thousand dollars. All you had to do was kill a black Miura bull with a sword, just like a real, trained matador.

The fight was held in Madrid, since bullfighting was still illegal in the United States. It was nationally televised.

Raeder had a good cuadrilla. They liked the big, slow-moving American. The picadors really leaned into their lances, trying to slow the bull for him. The banderilleros tried to run the beast off his feet before driving in their banderillas. And the second matador, a mournful man from Algeciras, almost broke the bull's neck with fancy cape-work.

But when all was said and done, it was Jim Raeder on the sand, a red muleta clumsily gripped in his left hand, a sword in his right, facing a ton of black, blood-streaked, wide-horned bull.

Someone was shouting, "Try for the lung, *hombre*. Don't be a hero, stick him in the lung." But Jim only knew what the technical advisor in New York had told him: Aim with the sword and go in over the horns.

Over he went. The sword bounced off bone, and the bull tossed him over its back. He stood up, miraculously ungouged, took another sword and went over the horns again with his eyes closed. The god who protects children and fools must have been watching, for the sword slid in like a needle through butter, and the bull looked startled, stared at him unbelievingly, and dropped like a deflated balloon.

They paid him ten thousand dollars, and his broken collarbone healed in practically no time. He received twenty-three fan letters, including a passionate invitation from a girl in Atlantic City, which he ignored. And they asked him if he wanted to appear on another show.

He had lost some of his innocence. He was now fully aware that he had been almost killed for pocket money. The big loot lay ahead. Now he wanted to be almost killed for something worthwhile.

So he appeared on *Underwater Perils*, sponsored by Fairlady's Soap. In face mask, respirator, weighted belt, flippers and knife, he slipped into the warm waters of the Caribbean with four other contestants, followed by a cage-protected camera crew. The idea was to locate and bring up a treasure which the sponsor had hidden there.

Mask diving isn't especially hazardous. But the sponsor had added some frills for public interest. The area was sown with giant clams, moray eels, sharks of several species, giant octopuses, poison coral, and other dangers of the deep.

It was a stirring contest. A man from Florida found the treasure in a deep crevice, but a moray eel found him. Another diver took the treasure, and a shark took him. The brilliant blue-green water became cloudy with blood, which photographed well on color TV. The treasure slipped to the bottom, and Raeder plunged after it, popping an eardrum in the process. He plucked it from the coral, jettisoned his weighted belt and made for the surface. Thirty feet from the top he had to fight another diver for the treasure.

They feinted back and forth with their knives. The man struck, slashing Raeder across the chest. But Raeder, with the self-possession of an old contestant, dropped his knife and tore the man's respirator out of his mouth.

That did it. Raeder surfaced and presented the treasure at the standby boat. It turned out to be a package of Fairlady's Soap—"The Greatest Treasure of All."

That netted him twenty-two thousand dollars in cash and prizes, and three hundred and eight fan letters, and an interesting proposition from a girl in Macon, which he seriously considered. He received free hospitalization for his knife slash and burst eardrum, and injections for coral infection.

But best of all, he was invited to appear on the biggest of the thrill shows. *The Prize of Peril*.

And that was when the real trouble began....

The subway came to a stop, jolting him out of his reverie. Raeder pushed back his hat and observed, across the aisle, a man staring at him and whispering to a stout woman. Had they recognized him?

He stood up as soon as the doors opened, and glanced at his watch. He had five hours to go.

At the Manhasset station, he stepped into a taxi and told the driver to take him to *New Salem.*

"New Salem?" the driver asked, looking at him in the rear-vision mirror.

"That's right."

The driver snapped on his radio. "Fare to New Salem. Yep, that's right. New Salem." They drove off. Raeder frowned, wondering if it had been a signal. It was perfectly usual for taxi drivers to report to their dispatchers, of course. But something about the man's voice...

"Let me off here," Raeder said.

He paid the driver and began walking down a narrow country road that curved through sparse woods. The trees were too small and too widely separated for shelter. Raeder walked on, looking for a place to hide.

There was a heavy truck approaching. He kept on walking, pulling his hat low on his forehead. But as the truck drew near, he heard a voice from the television set in his pocket. It cried, *"Watch out!"*

He flung himself into the ditch. The truck careened past, narrowly missing him, and screeched to a stop. The driver was shouting, "There he goes! Shoot, Harry, shoot!"

Bullets clipped leaves from the trees as Raeder sprinted into the woods.

"It's happened again!" Mike Terry was saying, his voice high-pitched with excitement. *"I'm afraid Jim Raeder let himself be lulled into a false sense of security. You can't do that, Jim! Not with your* life *at stake! Not with killers pursuing you! Be careful, Jim, you still have four and a half hours to go!"*

The driver was saying, "Claude, Harry, go around with the truck. We got him boxed."

"They've got you boxed, Jim Raeder!" Mike Terry cried. *"But they haven't got you yet! And you can thank Good Samaritan Susy Peters of twelve Elm Street, South Orange, New Jersey, for that warning shout just when the truck was bearing down on you. We'll have little Susy on stage in just a moment.... Look,*

folks, our studio helicopter has arrived on the scene. Now you can see Jim Raeder running, and the killers pursuing, surrounding him..."

Raeder ran through a hundred yards of woods and found himself on a concrete highway, with open woods beyond. One of the killers was trotting through the woods behind him. The truck had driven to a connecting road, and was now a mile away, coming toward him.

A car was approaching from the other direction. Raeder ran into the highway, waving frantically. The car came to a stop.

"Hurry!" cried the blond young woman driving it.

Raeder dived in. The woman made a U-turn on the highway. A bullet smashed through the windshield. She stamped on the accelerator, almost running down the lone killer who stood in the way.

The car surged away before the truck was within firing range.

Raeder leaned back and shut his eyes tightly. The woman concentrated on her driving, watching for the truck in her rear-vision mirror.

"*It's happened again!*" cried Mike Terry, his voice ecstatic. "*Jim Raeder has been plucked again from the jaws of death, thanks to Good Samaritan Janice Morrow of four three three Lexington Avenue, New York City. Did you ever see anything like it, folks? The way Miss Morrow drove through a fusillade of bullets and plucked Jim Raeder from the mouth of doom! Later we'll interview Miss Morrow and get her reactions. Now, while Jim Raeder speeds away—perhaps to safety, perhaps to further peril—we'll have a short announcement from our sponsor. Don't go away! Jim's got four hours and ten minutes until he's safe. Anything can happen!*"

"Okay," the girl said. "We're off the air now. Raeder, what in the hell is the matter with you?"

"Eh?" Raeder asked. The girl was in her early twenties. She looked efficient, attractive, untouchable. Raeder noticed that she had good features, a trim figure. And he noticed that she seemed angry.

"Miss," he said, "I don't know how to thank you for—"

"Talk straight," Janice Morrow said. "I'm no Good Samaritan. I'm employed by the JBC network."

"So the program had me rescued!"

"Cleverly reasoned," she said.

"But why?"

"Look, this is an expensive show, Raeder. We have to turn in a good performance. If our rating slips, we'll all be in the street selling candy apples. And you aren't cooperating."

"What? Why?"

"Because you're terrible," the girl said bitterly. "You're a flop, a fiasco. Are you trying to commit suicide? Haven't you learned *anything* about survival?"

"I'm doing the best I can."

"The Thompsons could have had you a dozen times by now. We told them to take it easy, stretch it out. But it's like shooting a clay pigeon six feet tall. The Thompsons are cooperating, but they can only fake so far. If I hadn't come along, they'd have had to kill you—air-time or not."

Raeder stared at her, wondering how such a pretty girl could talk that way. She glanced at him, then quickly looked back to the road.

"Don't give me that look!" she said. "*You* chose to risk your life for money, buster. And plenty of money! You knew the score. Don't act like some innocent little grocer who finds the nasty hoods are after him. That's a different plot."

"I know," Raeder said.

"If you can't live well, at least try to die well."

"You don't mean that," Raeder said.

"Don't be too sure... You've got three hours and forty minutes until the end of the show. If you can stay alive, fine. The boodle's yours. But if you can't, at least try to give them a run for the money."

Raeder nodded, staring intently at her.

"In a few moments we're back on the air. I develop engine trouble, let you off. The Thompsons go all out now. They kill you when and if they can, as soon as they can. Understand?"

"Yes," Raeder said. "If I make it, can I see you some time?"

She bit her lip angrily. "Are you trying to kid me?"

"No. I'd like to see you again. May I?"

She looked at him curiously. "I don't know. Forget it. We're almost on. I think your best bet is the woods to the right. Ready?"

"Yes. Where can I get in touch with you? Afterward, I mean."

"Oh, Raeder, you aren't paying attention. Go through the woods until you find a washed-out ravine. It isn't much, but it'll give you some cover."

"Where can I get in touch with you?" Raeder asked again.

"I'm in the Manhattan telephone book." She stopped the car. "Okay, Raeder, start running."

He opened the door.

"Wait." She leaned over and kissed him on the lips. "Good luck, you idiot. Call me if you make it."

And then he was on foot, running into the woods.

He ran through birch and pine, past an occasional split-level house with staring faces at the big picture window. Some occupant of those houses must have called the gang, for they were close behind him when he reached the washed-out little ravine. Those quiet, mannerly, law-abiding people didn't want him to escape, Raeder thought sadly. They wanted to see a killing. Or perhaps they wanted to see him *narrowly escape* a killing.

It came to the same thing, really.

He entered the ravine, burrowed into the thick underbrush and lay still. The Thompsons appeared on both ridges, moving slowly, watching for any movement. Raeder held his breath as they came parallel to him.

He heard the quick explosion of a revolver. But the killer had only shot a squirrel. It squirmed for a moment, then lay still.

Lying in the underbrush, Raeder heard the studio helicopter overhead. He wondered if any cameras were focused on him. It was possible. And if someone were watching, perhaps some Good Samaritan would help.

So looking upward, toward the helicopter, Raeder arranged his face in a reverent expression, clasped his hands and prayed. He prayed silently, for the audience didn't like religious ostentation. But his lips moved. That was every man's privilege.

And a real prayer was on his lips. Once, a lip-reader in the audience had detected a fugitive *pretending* to pray, but actually just reciting multiplication tables. No help for that man!

Raeder finished his prayer. Glancing at his watch, he saw that he had nearly two hours to go.

And he didn't want to die! It wasn't worth it, no matter how much they paid! He must have been crazy, absolutely insane to agree to such a thing....

But he knew that wasn't true. And he remembered just how sane he had been.

One week ago, he had been on the *Prize of Peril* stage, blinking in the spotlight, and Mike Terry had shaken his hand.

"Now, Mr. Raeder," Terry had said solemnly, "do you understand the rules of the game you are about to play?"

Raeder nodded.

"If you accept, Jim Raeder, you will be a *hunted man* for a week. *Killers* will follow you, Jim. *Trained* killers, men wanted by the law for other crimes, granted immunity for this single killing under the Voluntary Suicide Act. They will be trying to kill *you*, Jim. Do you understand?"

"I understand," Raeder said. He also understood the two hundred thousand dollars he would receive if he could live out the week.

"I ask you again, Jim Raeder. We force no man to play for stakes of death."

"I want to play," Raeder said.

Mike Terry turned to the audience. "Ladies and gentlemen, I have here a copy of an exhaustive psychological test which an impartial psychological testing firm made on Jim Raeder at our request. Copies will be sent to anyone who desires them for twenty-five cents to cover the cost of mailing. The test shows that Jim Raeder is sane, well-balanced, and fully responsible in every way." He turned to Raeder. "Do you still want to enter the contest, Jim?"

"Yes, I do."

"Very well!" cried Mike Terry. "Jim Raeder, meet your would-be killers!"

The Thompson gang moved on stage, booed by the audience.

"Look at them, folks," said Mike Terry, with undisguised contempt. "Just look at them! Antisocial, thoroughly vicious, completely amoral. These men have no code but the criminal's warped code, no honor but the honor of the cowardly hired killer. They are doomed men, doomed by our society, which will not sanction their activities for long, fated to an early and unglamorous death."

The audience shouted enthusiastically.

"What have you to say, Claude Thompson?" Terry asked.

Claude, the spokesman of the Thompsons, stepped up to the microphone. He was a thin, clean-shaved man, conservatively dressed.

"I figure," Claude Thompson said hoarsely, "I figure we're no worse than anybody. I mean, like soldiers in a war, *they* kill. And look at the graft in government, and the unions. Everybody's got their graft."

That was Thompson's tenuous code. But how quickly, with what precision, Mike Terry destroyed the killer's rationalizations! Terry's questions pierced straight to the filthy soul of the man.

At the end of the interview, Claude Thompson was perspiring, mopping

188 | FUTURE MEDIA

his face with a silk handkerchief and casting quick glances at his men.

Mike Terry put a hand on Raeder's shoulder. "Here is the man who has agreed to become your victim—if you can catch him."

"We'll catch him," Thompson said, his confidence returning.

"Don't be too sure," said Terry. "Jim Raeder has fought wild bulls—now he battles jackals. He's an average man. He's *the people*—who mean ultimate doom to you and your kind."

"We'll get him," Thompson said.

"And one thing more," Terry said, very softly. "Jim Raeder does not stand alone. The folks of America are for him. Good Samaritans from all corners of our great nation stand ready to assist him. Unarmed, defenseless, Jim Raeder can count on the aid and goodheartedness of *the people*, whose representative he is. So don't be too sure, Claude Thompson! The average men are for Jim Raeder—and there are a lot of average men!"

Raeder thought about it, lying motionless in the underbrush. Yes, *the people* had helped him. But they had helped the killers, too.

A tremor ran through him. He had chosen, he reminded himself. He alone was responsible. The psychological test had proved that.

And yet, how responsible were the psychologists who had given him the test? How responsible was Mike Terry for offering a poor man so much money? Society had woven the noose and put it around his neck, and he was hanging himself with it and calling it free will.

Whose fault?

"Aha!" someone cried.

Raeder looked up and saw a portly man standing near him. The man wore a loud tweed jacket. He had binoculars around his neck and a cane in his hand.

"Mister," Raeder whispered, "please don't tell—"

"Hi!" shouted the portly man, pointing at Raeder with his cane. "Here he is!"

A madman, thought Raeder. The damned fool must think he's playing Hare and Hounds.

"Right over here!" the man screamed.

Cursing, Raeder sprang to his feet and began running. He came out of the ravine and saw a white building in the distance. He turned toward it. Behind him he could still hear the man.

"That way, over there. Look, you fools, can't you see him yet?"

The killers were shooting again. Raeder ran, stumbling over uneven ground, past three children playing in a tree house.

"Here he is!" the children screamed. "Here he is!"

Raeder groaned and ran on. He reached the steps of the building and saw that it was a church.

As he opened the door, a bullet struck him behind the right kneecap.

He fell, and crawled inside the church.

The television set in his pocket was saying, *"What a finish, folks, what a finish! Raeder's been hit! He's been hit, folks, he's crawling now, he's in pain, but he hasn't given up! Not Jim Raeder!"*

Raeder lay in the aisle near the altar. He could hear a child's eager voice saying, "He went in there, Mr. Thompson. Hurry, you can still catch him!"

Wasn't a church considered a sanctuary? Raeder wondered.

Then the door was flung open, and Raeder realized that the custom was no longer observed. He gathered himself together and crawled past the altar, out of the back door of the church.

He was in an old graveyard. He crawled past crosses and stars, past slabs of marble and granite, past stone tombs and rude wooden markers. A bullet exploded on a tombstone near his head, showering him with fragments. He crawled to the edge of an open grave.

They had deceived him, he thought. All of those nice, average, normal people. Hadn't they said he was their representative? Hadn't they sworn to protect their own? But no, they loathed him. Why hadn't he seen it? Their hero was the cold, blank-eyed gunman, Thompson, Capone, Billy the Kid, Young Lochinvar, El Cid, Cuchulain, the man without human hopes or fears. They worshipped him, that dead, implacable, robot gunman, and lusted to feel his foot in their face.

Raeder tried to move, and slid helplessly into the open grave.

He lay on his back, looking at the blue sky. Presently a black silhouette loomed above him, blotting out the sky. Metal twinkled. The silhouette slowly took aim.

And Raeder gave up all hope forever.

"WAIT, THOMPSON!" roared the amplified voice of Mike Terry.

The revolver wavered.

"It is one second past five o'clock! The week is up! JIM RAEDER HAS WON!"

There was pandemonium of cheering from the studio audience.

The Thompson gang, gathered around the grave, looked sullen.

"He's won, friends, he's won!" Mike Terry cried. *"Look, look on your screen! The police have arrived, they're taking the Thompsons away from their victim— the victim they could not kill. And all this is thanks to you, Good Samaritans of America. Look folks, tender hands are lifting Jim Raeder from the open grave that was his final refuge. Good Samaritan Janice Morrow is there. Could this be the beginning of a romance? Jim seems to have fainted, friends, they're giving him a stimulant. He's won two hundred thousand dollars! Now we'll have a few words from Jim Raeder!"*

There was a short silence.

"That's odd," said Mike Terry. *"Folks, I'm afraid we can't hear from Jim just now. The doctors are examining him. Just one moment..."*

There was a silence. Mike Terry wiped his forehead and smiled.

"It's the strain, folks, the terrible strain. The doctor tells me... Well, folks, Jim Raeder is temporarily not himself. But it's only temporary! JBC is hiring the best psychiatrists and psychoanalysts in the country. We're going to do everything humanly possible for this gallant boy. And entirely at our own expense."

Mike Terry glanced at the studio clock. *"Well, it's about time to sign off, folks. Watch for the announcement of our next great thrill show. And don't worry, I'm sure that very soon we'll have Jim Raeder back with us."*

Mike Terry smiled, and winked at the audience. *"He's bound to get well, friends. After all, we're all pulling for him!"*

Sex, Death, and Machinery, or
How I Fell in Love with My Prosthesis
Allucquére Rosanne Stone

Allucquére Rosanne Stone is Associate Professor at the University of Texas at Austin, Senior Artist at the Banff Centre, Professor of New Media and Performance at the European Graduate School, Artist, Performer, Author, Critic, Public Intellectual, Transgender, Wife, Mother, Drive-By Theoretician, and Science Fiction Writer. Better known, of course, for her books and articles on new-media theory and as an artist of considerable reputation, Stone published several science fiction stories in the early 1970s in *Galaxy* magazine and in the *Magazine of Fantasy & Science Fiction*, two of the field's most famous publications. "Sex, Death and Machinery," from 1996, was the introduction to Stone's critical study for MIT Press, *The War of Desire and Technology at the Close of the Mechanical Age*. In this piece, she discusses the past and then-future of gaming, virtual reality, immersive environments, "Space War," and "Habitat," our sense of "presence." And her pair of boots.

It started this afternoon when I looked down at my boots. I was emerging from a stall in the women's room in my department. The university was closed for the holidays. The room was quite silent except for the distant rush of the air conditioning, imparting to the cramped institutional space the mechanical qualities of a submarine. I was idly adjusting my clothing, thinking of nothing in particular, when I happened to look down, and there they were: My boots. Two completely unremarkable boots. They were right where they belonged, on the ends of my legs. Presumably my feet were inside.

I felt a sudden thrill of terror.

Maybe, I suppose, the boots could have reminded me of some long-buried trauma, of the sort that Freudians believe leads to shoe fetishism. But my sudden fear was caused by something quite different. What was driving me was not the extraordinariness of the sight of my own boots, but the ordinariness of them. They were common as grass. In fact, I realized that I hadn't even thought about putting them on. They were *just there*. If you wanted to "get real ugly about it"—as they say in Austin—you might call it a moment of radical existential *Dasein,* in the same way you might say déjà vu again. I had become transparent to myself. Or rather, the *I* that I customarily express and that reflexively defines me through my chosen personal style had become part of the wallpaper.

This is hardly a serious problem for me. But I tend to see myself as an entity that has chosen to make its life career out of playing with identity. It sometimes seems as though everything in my past has been a kind of extended excuse for experiments with subject position and interaction. After all, what material is better to experiment with than one's self? Academically speaking, it's not exactly breaking new ground to say that any subject position is a mask. That's well and good, but still most people take some primary subject position for granted. When pressed, they may give lip service to the idea that perhaps even their current "root" persona is also a mask, but nobody really believes it. For all intents and purposes, your "root" persona is *you.* Take that one away, and there's nobody home.

Perhaps someone with training in drama already perceives this, but it was a revelation to me. In the social sciences, symbolic interactionists believe that the root persona is always a momentary expression of ongoing negotiations among a horde of subidentities, but this process is invisible both to the onlooker and to the persona within whom the negotiations are taking place. For me this has never been particularly true. My current *I* has been as palpably a mask to me as any of my other *I*'s have been. Perceiving that which is generally invisible as really a kind of capital has been more than a passing asset (as it were); it has been a continual education, a source of endless challenge, not to mention fear, and certainly not least, an ongoing celebration of the sacred nature of the universe of passing forms. It was for these reasons, then, that I found looking down rather complacently at my boots and not really seeing them to be so terrifying. Like an athlete who has begun to flub a long-polished series of moves, I began to wonder if I was losing my edge.

Going through life with this outlook has been a terrific asset in my chosen work, and the current rise in the number of people who engage in social interactions without ever meeting in the customary sense of the term—that is, engaging in social intercourse by means of communication technologies—has given me increasing opportunities to watch others try on their own alternative personae. And although most still see those personae as just that—alternatives to a customary "root" identity—there are some out at the margins who have always lived comfortably with the idea of floating identities, and inward from the margins there are a few who are beginning, just a bit, to question. What it is they are questioning is a good part of what this essay is about.

A bit of background may be appropriate here.

I have bad history: I am a person who fell in love with her own prostheses. Not once, but twice. Then I fell in love with somebody *else's* prosthesis.

The first time love struck was in 1950. I was hunkered down in the dark late at night, on my bed with the big iron bedstead on the second floor, listening absently to the crickets singing and helping a friend scratch around on the surface of a galena crystal that was part of a primitive radio. We were looking for one of the hot spots, places where the crystal had active sites that worked like diodes and could detect radio waves. There was nothing but silence for a long, long time, and then suddenly the earphones burst into life, and a whole new universe was raging in our heads—the ranting voice of Jean Shepherd, boiling into the atmosphere from the massive transmitter of WOR-AM, 50 kilowatts strong and only a few miles away. At that distance we could have heard the signal in our tooth fillings if we'd had any, but the transmitter might as well have been in Rangoon, for all the fragrant breath of exotic worlds it suggested. I was hooked. Hooked on technology. I could take a couple of coils of wire and a hunk of galena and send a whole part of myself out into the ether. An extension of my will, of my instrumentality...that's a prosthesis, all right.

The second time happened in 1955, while I was peering over the edge of a 24×24 recording console. As I stood on tiptoe, my nose just clearing the top of the console, from my age and vantage point the massive thing looked as wide as a football field. Knobs and switches from hell, all the way to the horizon... there was something about that vast forest of controls that suggested the same breath of exotic worlds that the simple coil of wire and the rickety crystal did. I was hooked again. Hooked on even bigger technology, on another extension of my instrumentality. I could create whole oceans of sound, universes of sound, could at last begin on my life's path of learning how to make people laugh, cry, and throw up in darkrooms. And I hadn't even heard it turned *on*.[1]

But the third time...

The third time was when Hawking came to town.

Stephen Hawking, the world-famous physicist, was giving a lecture at UC

Santa Cruz. The auditorium was jammed, and the overflow crowd was being accommodated outside on the lawn. The lawn looked like a medieval fair, with people sitting on blankets and towels, others standing or milling around, all ears cocked toward the loudspeakers that were broadcasting Hawking's address across the landscape.

If you haven't seen Stephen Hawking give a talk, let me give you a quick background. Hawking has amyotrophic lateral sclerosis, which makes it virtually impossible for him to move anything more than his fingers or to speak. A friendly computer engineer put together a nice little system for him, a program that displays a menu of words, a storage buffer, and a Votrax allophone generator—that is, an artificial speech device. He selects words and phrases, the word processor stores them until he forms a paragraph, and the Votrax says it. Or he calls up a prepared file, and the Votrax says that.

So I and a zillion other people are on the lawn, listening to Hawking's speech, when I get the idea that I don't want to be outside with the PA system— what I really want to do is sneak into the auditorium, so I can actually hear Hawking give the talk.

In practice this maneuver proves not too hard. The lecture is under way, security is light—after all, it's a *physicist,* dammit, not the UC Board of Regents, for which they would have had armed guards with two-way radios—so it doesn't take long for me to worm my way into the first row.

And there is Hawking. Sitting, as he always does, in his wheelchair, utterly motionless, except for his fingers on the joystick of the laptop; and on the floor to one side of him is the PA system microphone, nuzzling into the Votrax's tiny loudspeaker.

And a thing happens in my head. Exactly where, I say to myself, *is* Hawking? Am I any closer to him now than I was outside? Who is it doing the talking up there on stage? In an important sense, Hawking doesn't stop being Hawking at the edge of his visible body. There is the obvious physical Hawking, vividly outlined by the way our social conditioning teaches us to see a person as a person. But a serious part of Hawking extends into the box in his lap. In mirror image, a serious part of that silicon and plastic assemblage in his lap extends into him as well...not to mention the individual ways, displaced in time and space, in which discourses of medical technology and their physical accretions already permeate him and us. No box, no discourse; in the absence of the prosthetic, Hawking's intellect becomes a tree falling in the forest with nobody around to hear it. On the other hand, with the box his voice is auditory and simultaneously electric, in a radically different way from that of a person *speaking* into a microphone. Where *does* he stop? Where are his edges? The issues his person and his communication prostheses raise are boundary debates, borderland/*frontera* questions. Here at the close of the mechanical age, they are the things that occupy a lot of my attention.[2]

Flashback: I Was Idly Looking

I was idly looking out my window, taking a break from some nasty piece of academic writing, when up the dusty, rutted hill that constitutes my driveway and bastion against the world there abruptly rode, on a nasty little Suzuki Virago, a brusque, sharp-tongued person of questionable sexuality. Doffing her helmet, she revealed herself, both verbally and physically, as Valkyrie, a postoperative m/f transgender with dark hair and piercing black eyes who evinced a pronounced affinity for black leather. She announced that there were things we had to do and places we had to go, and before I could mutter "science fiction" we were off on her bike.[3]

Valkyrie proceeded to introduce me to a small community of women in the San Francisco Bay area. Women's collectives were not new to me; I had recently studied a group of women who ran a business, housed themselves under one roof, and lived their lives according to the principles of a canonically undefined but quite powerful idea known as lesbian separatism.[4] But the group to which my new friend now introduced me did not at all fit the model I had painstakingly learned to recognize. This collective ran a business, and the business was hetero phone sex...not something of which my other research community, immured in radical lesbian orthodoxy, would have approved.

I was instantly entranced, and also oddly repelled. After all, I had broken bread with one of the most episcopal of women's collectives for five years, and any deviation from group norms would have been punishable in fairly horrid ways. To imagine that hetero sex could be enjoyable, not to mention profitable, was playing into the hands of the gentiles, and even to spend time with a group that supported itself in such a manner (and even joked about it) could have had mortal consequences.

For reasons best described as kismet, the phone sex workers and I became good friends. We found each other endlessly fascinating. They were intrigued

196 | FUTURE MEDIA

by my odd history and by what I'd managed to make out of it. In turn, I was intrigued by the way they negotiated the minefields of ethics and personal integrity while maintaining a lifestyle that my other research community considered unthinkable.

After a while, we sorted out two main threads of our mutual attraction. From my point of view, the more I observed phone sex the more I realized I was observing very practical applications of data compression. Usually sex involves as many of the senses as possible. Taste, touch, smell, sight, hearing—and, for all I know, short-range psychic interactions—all work together to heighten the erotic sense. Consciously or unconsciously phone sex workers translate all the modalities of experience into audible form. In doing so they have reinvented the art of radio drama, complete down to its sound effects, including the fact that some sounds were best represented by *other* improbable sounds that they resembled only in certain iconic ways. On the radio, for example, the soundmen (they were always literally men) represented fire by crumpling cellophane, because to the audience it sounded *more like* fire than holding a microphone to a real fire did.

The sex workers did similar stuff. I made a little mental model out of this: The sex workers took an extremely complex, highly detailed set of behaviors, translated them into a single sense modality, then further boiled them down to a series of highly compressed tokens. They then squirted those tokens down a voice-grade phone line. At the other end of the line the recipient of all this effort added boiling water, so to speak, and reconstituted the tokens into a fully detailed set of images and interactions in multiple sensory modes.

Further, what was being sent back and forth over the wires wasn't just information, it was *bodies*. The majority of people assume that erotics implies bodies; a body is a part of the idea of erotic interaction and its concomitants, and the erotic sensibilities are mobilized and organized around the idea of a physical body which is the seat of the whole thing. The sex workers' descriptions were invariably and quite directly about physical bodies and what they were doing or what was being done to them.

Later I came to be troubled by this focus on bodies because of its relation to a remark of Elaine Scarry's. In a discussion of human experience in her book *The Body in Pain*, she says,

Pain and imagining are the "framing events" within whose boundaries all other perceptual, somatic, and emotional events occur; thus, between the two extremes can be mapped the whole terrain of the human psyche. (p. 165)

By that time I had stopped thinking of the collective as a group of sex workers and had begun to think of them in rather traditional anthropological terms as *my* sex workers. I had also moved on to a more complex mode of fieldwork known as participant observation, and I was getting an education I hadn't expected. Their experience of the world, their ethical sense, the ways they interpreted concepts like work and play were becoming part of my own experience. I began to think about how I could describe them in ways that would make sense to a casual reader. As I did so, Scarry's remark returned to intrigue me because of its peculiar relationship to the social groups I was studying. It seemed to me that the sex workers' experiential world was organized in a way that was almost at right angles to Scarry's description of the continuum of pain and imagining. The world of the sex workers and their clients, I observed, was not organized along a continuum of pain and imagination but rather within an experiential field in which *pleasure* and imagination were the important attractors.

Patently it is not difficult in these times to show how phone sex interactions take place within a field of power by means of which desire comes to have a particular shape and character. In the early days of phone sex that view would have been irrefutable, but things are changing rather fast in the phone sex business; more traditional hetero and hetero-modeled interactions may still get their kick from very old patterns of asymmetrical power, but there seems little doubt that the newer forums for phone sex (as well as other forms of technologically mediated human interaction) have made asymmetrical power relationships part of a much larger and more diverse erotic and experiential tool kit.

This diversity has obvious and interesting implications for critical studies, but it does not in any way imply that a hypothetical "new erotics," if that's what I'm describing, has escaped from the bottomless gravity well of the same power structures within which we find ourselves fixed in position, regardless of what our favorite position is. It does seem to mean, though, that a good many of the people I observe are aware of the effects of those structures, even though as of this writing I see little effort to alter or transcend them. There does appear to be a central and critical reason for this lack of effort, particularly in regard to erotics, and that is that none of the people I observe who *do* erotics—even those who play with different structures of power—have yet begun to speculate on how erotics really works.

There are other areas of inquiry which are organized around what might be called an epistemological Calvinism. A recent but fairly broad area of inquiry in the social sciences into the nature and character of human-computer interaction is known as the study of computer-supported cooperative work (CSCW). Part of the informing philosophy of this discipline is the idea that all human activity can be usefully interpreted as a kind of work, and that work is the quintessential defining human capacity. This, too, I think, misses some of the most important qualities of human-computer interaction just as it does when applied to broader elements of human experience. By this I mean that a significant part of the time that humans spend in developing interactional skills is devoted not to work but to what by common understanding would be called play. Definitions of what counts as play are many and varied, generally revolving around the idea of purposive activities that do not appear to be directly goal-oriented. "Goal orientation" is, of course, a problematic phrase. There is a fine body of research addressed to the topic of play versus work activities, but it doesn't appear to have had a deep effect on CSCW and its allied disciplines. From the standpoint of cultural criticism, the issue is not one of definitions of work or play, but of how the meanings of those terms are produced and maintained. Both work and play have culture-specific meanings and purposes, and I am conducting a quite culture-specific discussion when I talk about the primacy of play in human-computer interaction (HCI, or for our purposes just "interaction") as I do here.[5]

In order to clarify this point, let me mention that there are many definitions of interaction and many opinions about what interaction is for. As I write, large industry consortiums are finalizing their standards for what they call interactive multimedia platforms. These devices usually consist of a computer, color monitor, mouse, CD-ROM drive, sound car, and pair of speakers. This electronic instantiation of a particular definition freezes the conceptual framework of interaction in a form most suitable for commercial development—the user moves the cursor to the appropriate place and clicks the mouse, which causes something to happen—or what the interactivist

Michael Naimark would call, more pejoratively, poke-and-see technology. This definition of interaction has been in the wind for so long now that few researchers say much about it. It is possible to play within the constraints of such a system, but the potential for *interaction* is limited, because the machine can only respond to an on-off situation: that is, to the click of the mouse. Computer games offer a few more input modes, usually in the form of a joystick, which has two or three degrees of freedom, However, from the standpoint of kind and gentle instruction, what the game companies do with this greater potential is not very inspiring. Technologically speaking, Sega's *Sewer Shark* (1993), for example, was an amazing exercise in game design for its time, but it reinforced the feeling that interaction in a commercial frame is still a medium like television, in which the most advanced product of the technological genius of an entire species conveys Geraldo Rivera to millions of homes in breathtaking color

I don't want to make this a paradise-lost story, but the truth is that the definitions of interactivity used by the early researchers at MIT possessed a certain poignancy that seems to have become lost in the commercial translation. One of the best definitions was set forth by Andy Lippman, who described interaction as mutual and simultaneous activity on the part of both participants, usually working toward some goal—but, he added, not necessarily. Note that from the beginning of interaction research the idea of a common goal was already in question, and in that fact inheres interaction's vast ludic dimension.[6]

There are five corollaries to Lippman's definition. One is *mutual interruptibility*, which means that each participant must be able to interrupt the other, mutually and simultaneously. Interaction, therefore, implies conversation, a complex back-and-forth exchange, the goal of which may change as the conversation unfolds.

The second is *graceful degradation*, which means that answerable questions must be handled in a way that doesn't halt the conversation: "I'll come back to that in a minute," for example.

The third is *limited look-ahead*, which means that because both parties can be interrupted there is a limit to how much of the shape of the conversation can be anticipated by either party.

The fourth is *no-default*, which means that the conversation must not have a preplanned path; it must develop fully in the interaction.

The fifth, which applies more directly to immersive environments (in which the human participant is surrounded by the simulation of a world), is that the participants should have *the impression of an infinite database*. This principle means that an immersive interactional world should give the illusion of not being much more limiting in the choices it offers than an actual world would be. In a nonimmersive context, the machine should give the impression of having about as much knowledge of the world as you do, but not necessarily more. This limitation is intended to deal with the Spock phenomenon, in which more information is sometimes offered than is conversationally appropriate.

Thus interactivity implies two conscious agencies in conversation, playfully and spontaneously developing a mutual discourse, taking cues and suggestions from each other as they proceed.

In order to better draw this out let me briefly review the origins and uses of computers. Afterward I will return to the subject of play from a slightly different perspective.

The first devices that are usually called computers were built as part of a series of projects mandated by the military during World War II. For many years, computers were large and extremely costly. They were also cranky and prone to continual breakdown, which had to do with the primitive nature of their components. They required continual maintenance by highly skilled technicians. The factors of cost, unreliability, and the need for skilled and continual attention, not to mention the undeniable aura of power that surrounded the new machines like some heady smell, combined to keep computers available only to large corporations and government organizations. These entities came already equipped with their own ideas of efficiency, with the concepts of time and motion study then in vogue in industry (of which my colleagues have written at length), and of course with the cultural abstraction known as the work ethic perpetually running in the background. Even within the organizations themselves, access to the new machines was restricted to a technological elite which, though by no means monolithic in its view of technological achievement, had not had enough time to develop much of a sense, not to mention a sensibility, of the scope and potential of the new devices.

These factors combined to keep attention focused on the uses of computers as rather gross instrumentalities of human will—that is, as number crunches and databases. Computers could extend human abilities, physically and conceptually. That is, computers were tools, like crowbars and screwdrivers, except that they primarily extended the mind rather than the muscles. Even Vannevar Bush's astonishingly prophetic "As We May Think" (1949) treated computers as a kind of superswitch. In this frame of understanding, computers were prosthetic in the specific sense of the Greek term *prosthenos*—extension. Computers assisted or augmented human intelligence and capabilities in much the same way that a machine or even another human being would; that is, as separate, discrete agencies or tools that occupied physical or conceptual spaces separate from those of the human.

It seems significant that the epistemic evolution that appeared to be gradually but inexorably making its way across Western cultures also manifested itself in a number of unexpected and quite unpredictable ways in cultural milieus far removed from the context of the Enlightenment and after. A pertinent though perhaps startling (and perhaps offensive) example is the aesthetics and philosophy of bullfighting. Prior to the schismatic work of the torero Juan Belmonte in the 1940s and 1950s, the physical area in which bullfighting took place was divided into spaces of signification called "territories of the bull" and "territories of the torero." When designing his choreography for the bullring, Belmonte raised the heretical argument that since the human possessed the only agency in the arena, territory of the bull was a polite but fictional concept; all territories were territories of the torero. The choreographic movements Belmonte developed as a result of this argument transformed the character of bullfighting. The abstraction I call attention to here is the breakdown of boundaries between two systems of agency and how that transformation affects the play of power within a field of social action. In dance, Martha Graham articulated a similar revision of shared spaces of action, but somewhat closer to the center of what might be called traditional Western culture. Graham's relocating the center of agency to a hypothesized center of the body redefined the quality of contact that was possible between two agents. Susan Foster's theoretical and practical work on dance discusses these points in considerable detail.

All this changed in the 1960s, but the change was largely invisible both physically and conceptually. Deleuze and Guattari and Manuel De Landa and the eerie concept of the machine phylum would not arrive on the scene for some thirty years. In 1962, the young hackers at Project MAC, deep in the bowels of MIT, made hardly a ripple in corporate arenas with their invention of a peculiarly engrossing computational diversion that they called *Space War.*[7] This first computer game was still firmly identified with the military, even down to its name and playing style, but in that moment something quite new and (dare I say it) completely different had happened to the idea of computation. Still, it would not be until the 1970s that two kids in a garage in Mountain View, California, rather than a corporate giant like Sperry Rand or IBM or a government entity like the Bureau of Vital Statistics, would knock the props out from under the idea of computation-as-tool for all time.

Let me return to the discussion of work versus play once again, from the standpoint of computation and instrumentality. Viewing computers as calculatory devices that assist or mediate human work seems to be part of a Kuhnian paradigm that consists of two main elements. The first is a primary *human work ethic;* the second is a particularized view of *computers as tools.* The emergence of the work ethic has been the subject of innumerable essays, but the view of computers as tools has been so totally pervasive among those with the power to determine meaning in such forums as school policy and corporate ethics that only recently has the idea begun to be seriously challenged. The paradigm of computers as tools burst into existence, more or less, out of the Allied victory in World War II (although the Nazis were working on their own computers). A paradigm of computers as something other than number crunchers does not have a similar launching platform, but the signs of such an imminent upheaval are perspicuous. Let me provide an example.

One of the most perceptive scholars currently studying the emergent computer societies is the anthropologist Barbara Joans. She describes the community of cyberspace workers as composed of two groups that she calls Creative Outlaw Visionaries and Law and Order Practitioners. One group has the visions; the other group knows how to build stuff and get it sold. One group fools around with terminology and designs fantastic stuff; the other group gets things done and keeps the wheels turning. They talk to each other, if they talk to each other, across a vast conceptual gulf. These groups are invisible to each other, I think, because one is operating out of the older paradigm of computers as tools and the other out of the newer paradigm of computers as something else. Instead of carrying on an established work ethic, the beliefs and practices of the cultures I observe incorporate a *play* ethic— not to displace the corporate agendas that produce their paychecks, but to complexify them. This play ethic is manifest in many of the communities and situations I study. It is visible in the northern California Forth community, a group of radical programmers who have adopted for their own an unusual and controversial programming language; in the CommuniTree community, an early text-based virtual discussion group that adopted such mottos as "If you meet the electronic avatar on the road, laserblast Hir"; and in the Atari Research Lab, where a group of hackers created an artificial person who became real enough to become pro tem lab director. The people who play at these technosocial games do not do so out of any specific transformative agenda, but they have seized upon advantages afforded by differences of skill, education, and income to make space for play in the very belly of the monster that is the communication industry.

This production and insertion of a play ethic like a mutation into the corporate genome is a specifically situated activity, one that is only possible for workers of a certain type and at a certain job level. In specific, it is only possible to the communities who are perhaps best described as hackers—mostly young (although the demographic changes as the first- and second-generation hackers age), mostly educated (although the field is rife with exceptions, perhaps indicating the incapability of U.S. public schools to deal with talented individuals), mostly white (and exceptions are quite rare in the United States), and mostly male (although a truly egregious exception is part of this study). They create and use a broad variety of technological prosthetics to manifest a different view of the purpose of communication technology, and their continual and casual association with the cutting edge of that technology has molded them and their machines separately and jointly—in novel and promising ways. In particular, because they are thoroughly accustomed to engaging in nontrivial social interactions through the use of their computers—social interactions in which they change and are changed, in which commitments are made, kept, and broken, in which they may engage in intellectual discussions, arguments, and even sex—they view computers not only as tools but also as *arenas for social experience*.

The result is a multiple view of the state of the art in communication technology. When addressing the question of what's new about networking, it's possible to give at least two answers. Let's stick with two for now.

Answer 1: Nothing
The tools of networking are essentially the same as they have been since the

telephone, which was the first electronic network prosthesis. Computers are engines of calculation, and their output is used for quantitative analysis. Inside the little box is information. I recently had a discussion with a colleague in which he maintained that there was nothing new about virtual reality. "When you sit and read a book," he said, "you create characters and action in your head. That's the same things as VR, without all the electronics." Missing the point, of course, but understandably.

Answer 2: Everything

Computers are arenas for social experience and dramatic interaction, a type of media more like public theater, and their output is used for qualitative interaction, dialogue, and conversation. Inside the little box are *other people*.

In order for this second answer to be true, we have to rethink some assumptions about presence. Presence is currently a word that means many different things to many different people. One meaning is the sense that we are direct witnesses to something or that we ourselves are being directly apprehended. This is what we might call the straightforward meaning, the one used by many sober virtual reality researchers. Another meaning is related to agency, to the proximity of intentionality. The changes that the concept of presence is currently undergoing are embedded in much larger shifts in cultural beliefs and practices. These include repeated transgressions of the traditional concept of the body's physical envelope and of the locus of human agency. This phenomenon shows itself in such variegated forms as the appearance and growth of the modern primitive movement, and the astonishing fascination of a portion of the population with prosthetic implants. Simultaneously new companies spring up to develop and manufacture wearable and eventually implantable computers. The film *Tetsuo, the Iron Man* appears, with its disturbingly florid intermingling of biology and technology. William Gibson's cyberspace and Neal Stephenson's Metaverse are both science-fiction inflections of inhabitable virtual worlds. A slow process of belief and acceptance, perhaps most clearly instantiated in the process of cultural acclimatization to the telephone, accompanied by the issues of warranting and authentication raised by the interjection into human social life of a technological object that acts as a channel or representative for absent human agencies.

In studying issues of presence, warranting, and agency, the work of theorists of dramatic interaction vis-à-vis computation, of which Brenda Laurel is an outstanding example, is invaluable. Many of the interesting debates involved in my research would not have been possible without the arguments Laurel presents in *Computers as Theatre* and elsewhere.

My first organized piece of research in the field of virtual systems involved studying a group of phone sex workers in the early 1980s. In this study I was doing two things. On one hand, I was beginning to develop some of the ideas I set forth here and, on the other, also discovering in microcosm the fascinating interplays among communication technology, the human body, and the uses of pleasure. If I were to frame some of the questions that occurred to me during that time, they might be these: How are bodies represented through technology? How is desire constructed through representation? What is the relationship of the body to self-awareness? What is the role of play in an emergent paradigm of human-computer interaction? And overall: What is happening to sociality and desire at the close of the mechanical age?

If I'm going to give in to the temptation to periodize—which I do again and again, through frequently with tongue in cheek—then I might as well take the period that follows the mechanical age and call it the virtual age. By the virtual age I don't mean the hype of virtual reality technology, which is certainly interesting enough in its own ways. Rather, I refer to the gradual change that has come over the relationship between sense of self and the body, and the relationship between individual and group, during a particular span of time. I characterize this relationship as virtual because the accustomed grounding of social interaction in the physical facticity of human bodies is changing. Partly this change seems good, and partly it seems bad. There are palpable advantages to the virtual mode in relation to the ways that the structure of cities and expectations of travel have changed with the advent of the telephone, the rise of large corporations, the invention and marketing of inexpensive tract housing, the development of the shopping mall, the commercial development and exploitation of electronic mass media, the development of the personal computer, the greening of large-scale information networks (which can be co-opted for social interaction), and the increasing miniaturization of electronic components (eventually perhaps to be extended to mechanical devices, that is, Drexler and others). There are equally palpable disadvantages to each of these deep changes in our lives. I don't want this perhaps too-familiar list to be read as either extolling or condemnation. They are the manifestations, as well as causative agents, of the social changes, ruptures, and reorganizations that they accompany. In the course of this essay I sometimes organize the manifestation of these developments as a progressus, an ensemble of events that had a beginning and that leads in a particular direction. In doing so, I nod in the direction of Deleuze and Guattari, Paul Virilio, and Manuel De Landa.[8] But I am large; I contain multitudes. At other times the story is not at all meant to be teleological, because I don't foresee the telos toward which it tends. I may make some suggestions in that regard, but they are suggestions only and do not arise from any prophetic vision. I try to leave the prophetic side of things to my academic betters in the same line of work.

In the process of articulating the gradual unfolding of the cultural and technological foundations for virtual systems, I call on the work of scholars in a number of disciplines. One factor that bears importantly on the emergence of virtual systems is a change in the character of public space and the development and articulation of particular kinds of private space. I discuss this change in the context of portions of the social world of Elizabethan England with the help of the useful and important work of Francis Barker. In her study *The Tremulous Private Body*, Barker discusses from the point of view of textuality the creation of new social spaces; of particular relevance to our concerns here is a new and progressively ramified division of social space from a predominantly public space to a congeries of spaces increasingly privatized.[9] Barker uses the physicality of this new privatized space as a link to the metaphoricality of symbolic and psychological private space that is both elicited by and is mutually supportive of its physical concomitant. In this regard the development of separate interior spaces within small dwellings—changes in philosophies of architecture and in methods of carpentry—is crucial.

The relationship of these changes to the changing concepts of interior and exterior space that enable and support the character of virtual systems is complex. In regard to the emergence of the concepts of the interiorized cultural and epistemic individual, which we are by now used to calling the sovereign subject and to seeing as perhaps the most egregious product of the Enlightenment, this too bears a complex relationship to the changes in social and architectural space within which it is embedded. In his study *Segmented Worlds and Self*, Yi-Fu Tuan calls attention to these changes in the context of studies of architecture and subjectivity. Over time, Tuan shows, we can trace the emergence of an increasing social and epistemic privatization that leads to the idea of the individual, for better or worse, as we understand it today. The development of a palpable awareness of self can be followed through the changes by means of which it is produced, beginning in the Middle Ages when information first begins to accumulate—the increasing number of family and self-portraits; the increasing popularity of mirrors; the development of autobiographical elements in literature; the evolution of seating from benches to chairs; the concept of the child as a stage in development; the ramification of multiple rooms in small dwellings; the elaboration of a theater of interiority in drama and the arts; and, most recently, psychoanalysis.

The development of a sense of individuality seems to be accompanied by a corresponding withdrawal of portions of a person's attention and energy from the public arena and their nourishment and concentration within the new arena of social action called the self. In the discourses with which we are perhaps most familiar, the self appears to be a constant, unchanging, the stable product of a moment in Western history. This seems a rather episcopal view of something that is not only better described as a process but that is also palpably in continual flux. Yet our institutions continue to be based on a fixed notion of what a self is—a local notion, a culturally delimited notion that inhabits the larger cultural infections of the mass media. It seems clear enough that the self continues to change, in fact has changed, beyond the snapshots we have of it that were taken within the last hundred years or so. The trends toward interiority and perhaps more important toward textuality that Barker reported still continue with increasing speed.

Further, they are abetted by concomitant developments in communication technology. Just as textual technologies—cheap paper, the typewriter, printing—accompanied new discourse networks and social formations, so electronic communication technologies—radio, television, computer networks—accompany the discourse networks and social formations now coming into being. These technologies, discourse networks, and social formations continue the trend toward increasing awareness of a sense of self; toward increasing physical isolation of individuals in Western and Western-influenced societies; and toward displacement of shared physical space, both public and private, by textuality and prosthetic communication—in brief, the constellation of events that define the close of the mechanical age and the unfolding or revealing of what, for lack of a better term, we might call the virtual age.

About Method

In regard to the term *virtual age*, I want it clear that when I talk about *ages*, *closes*, and *dawns*, it is not without being aware of what these words mean. I am grappling with the forms of historicization, and seeking—if frequently not finding—different ways to tell these stories. Pasted to one corner of my monitor screen I have a card that says,

NO CAUSES
NO EFFECTS
MUTUAL EMERGENCE

which is also an extreme position. Death and furniture, as Malcolm Ashmore said: If somebody whacks me in the head, I could rightly attribute my headache to their intervention. Larger phenomena are, of course, tricky. I don't think I can show with any assurance what "caused" the Atari Lab, but I can tell a few of the stories that surround its coming into being, each one of which is situated in a web of stories of its own. If I could walk the walk as well as talk the talk, there would be no "ages" or "dawns" in this essay, and eventually, given time, I hope to produce a different account in which the events I discuss here are more deeply situated in their context...and vice versa.

My chosen method of representation for this attempt—a kind of adventure narrative interspersed with forays into theory—developed out of earlier work in which I mentioned that my hypothesized ideal method would be a cross between Sharon Traweek's *Beamtimes and Lifetimes* and Leo Tolstoy's *War and Peace*.[10] This piece/*peace* is a sally in that direction. It is thoroughly experimental and subject to recall for factory modification at any time. I feel that it is only through the process of trying out various forms of representation, some experimental and some not, that I can properly grapple with the formidable challenge of finding viable pathways into academic discourse in the time of cultural studies. ("In the time of..." There I've done it again.)

Rather than presenting a succession of chapters explicating a common theme, I have tried to organize the work as a set of provocations whose central ideas remain more or less unstated—hovering, as I would like to imagine them, in the background. In this effort, my idealized stance as a novelist is the motivating concept. That is my *preferred, ideal* method; however, in the interests of avoiding some possibly unfortunate debates I have cheated and provided a theoretical section as well, and more explanation than I would have liked. I am still trying to move toward a methodology that Donna Haraway recently called cat's cradle. In other work I have mentioned that I prefer to thread these discourses and hold them in productive tension rather than allowing them to collapse in to a univocal account, and cat's cradle describes this move perfectly. Haraway has added to my experimental statement the missing piece of community, of passing the accounts from hand to hand, perhaps turning them in different ways and threading them in new configurations, being ever mindful that we tell our stories within webs of power that distort them; and of course the important thing about a cat's cradle is that you can never let it collapse.

On Content

Although other accounts of cyberspace communities and the people who construct them are now appearing, it is possible that readers of this essay may not yet have encountered them; therefore, I include a few here. In any account of the advent of ludic interactive technology the MIT Media Lab occupies a central role as nurturer of almost all of the first generation of "reality hackers," and its founder, Nicholas Negroponte, continues to be seen as an individual with both tremendous foresight and stupendous abilities to attract capital and power.

When the first generation of young technokids left MIT in 1987 for the physical world I eschewing for now the slippery tem *real*), many of them moved directly to a brand-new research lab financed by the Atari Corporation in California. The Atari Lab was headed by Alan Kay, who might have been compared to Negroponte in his ability to understand and navigate structures of power. It included among its staff the largest percentage of women in any laboratory up to that time and for a long time afterward, and this fact appears to have been due to Negroponte's influence both at the MIT Media Lab and on Alan Kay. The high attrition rates among women staff members that plagued most research labs did not affect the Media Lab in its early days. It appears that Negroponte's encouragement, his even-handedness, and possibly his personal charm helped keep a cadre of bright young women in the lab long enough for Kay to hire them. Negroponte himself moved in a web of events that enabled and constrained his choices, including his secure and prestigious directorship of *Le Grand Experiment,* the modestly named World Center for Research in Computation, just opened in Paris. The fortunes of the Atari Lab, unlike the Media Lab or the World Center, were tied to the continued success of a single company, and the glory days of Atari passed their peak shortly after its lab started work. But the days of success for both the Xerox Palo Alto Research Center and the World Center ended within a few months of the sudden fall of Atari, thus ending one of the most interesting and perhaps most promising periods in prosthetic communication research.

A "golden window" of financial support, theoretical encouragement, free imagination, and peer camaraderie was open at Atari for perhaps two years, perhaps no longer than six months, depending upon which events seem important. But in that brief period the young researchers performed astonishing feats. The thrust of their work was toward issues of presence not in terms of an hypothecated "human-machine" interface, but in *situated* technologies that addressed such issues as gender and ethnicity. The impact of this work was largely lost on Atari, because of a hidden misunderstanding among Kay, the researchers, and Atari management about the purpose of the lab. This miscommunication didn't become visible until later, and consequently the young researchers' work remained to bear fruit at other research organizations at later times. When Warner sold Atari to the notorious Tramiel brothers, known in Silicon Valley for their bloodthirsty approach to entrepreneurism, the lab in its original form was doomed.[11] Its research group, composed of brilliant young men and an unusually high proportion of brilliant young women, suddenly found themselves on the street. As they scattered, they founded the first generation of companies directly associated with the development of what would come to be called virtual reality technology. The Atari Lab remains both emblematic of and the best example of a singular moment in the emergence of a constellation of ideas concerning what research in communication prosthetics and agency should be.

Already in California were several groups of computer engineers who saw computer technology as a transformative force for society McLuhan-like, they believed that the technology itself was already producing deep changes in consciousness, but that belief would not stop them from hurrying things along. They developed programs to make dial-up bulletin boards into social forums within which certain people with access to computers and modems could quickly form new kinds of communities unrestricted by barriers of distance or, perhaps more significantly, of physical appearance. (They were not unrestricted by other means—such as ethnicity, class, income, and fluency in the English language.) Wide dissemination of the telephone numbers of these early virtual communities led to unexpected clashes as different and mutually incomprehensible cultures faced off within the electronic environment. As the survivors built new communities out of the ashes of the old, they unconsciously built much older Western theories of social life into their systems...such as defensive countermeasures, surveillance, and control. This might be called the Great Wall moment in the history of virtual systems, in retrospect a rather primitive beginning, but more sophisticated techniques were not long in arriving.

Working in tandem with the early researchers were a few people who were directly concerned with designing and implementing environments for virtual social interaction. They designed their environments as games. The earliest of these were the multiple-user dungeons, or MUDs. The MUDs were direct descendants of a species of role-playing game known as Dungeons and Dragons, and they later changed (or rather attempted to change) the full name of their environments to multiple-user *domains* in an effort to attain a modicum of respectability.

The concept of MUDs was taken up as a research tool at the Xerox Corporation's Palo Alto Research Campus (PARC), where anthropologists have for a number of years observed social interactions within structured virtual environments with an eye toward eventual uses in the workplace. But the best known of the descendants of text-based MUDs was designed at Lucasfilm as a pay-per-minute virtual game. Players entered *Habitat* via modem in the same way they would access any of the on-line services such as America Online or CompuServe. Once inside, they met other players, engaged in treasure hunts, apprehended (or became) criminals, published newspapers, married, divorced, and in general replicated in the virtual environment many of the pleasures and annoyances of life in the physical world. But the experiment never quite caught on in the United States. Almost unknown here, *Habitat* was acquired by Fujitsu, a Japanese company, and moved to a mainframe in Tokyo. There it became extremely successful, and attracted approximately 1.5 million inhabitants—an astonishing number even in light of Lucasfilm's ambitious predictions for their American version.[12]

Habitat is a useful early example of how economies evolve in virtual spaces, in particular because sex work is a common form of employment in the simulation. Since Chip Morningstar and Randall Farmer—*Habitat's* designers—were running nine months behind on the code's ship date, they didn't have time to provide ways for inhabitants to assume any of the vanilla sexual positions. For example, there is no code to describe characters lying on top of each other, and a fortiori dog positions are unknown.[13] Thus in order to engage in sex in *Habitat* people must be inventive, and so they have been. Also, because Fujitsu keeps good records, it is possible to get some idea of how gender works in the space. An item of particular interest to me is that at any given time approximately 15 percent of the *Habitat* population is actively engaging in cross-dressing or cross-gender behavior.

A subset of multiple-user domains consists of multiple-play, games set in virtual environments. The earliest of these was a multiple user environment called RBT, for Reality Built for Two, constructed at VPL Research in Palo Alto by one of the best-known of the first-generation virtual hackers, Jaron Lanier. Lanier's trademark dreadlocks became widely recognized in the world's business community when his picture (or, more correctly, an engraving of his face—*WSJ* never uses photographs) appeared on the front page of the *Wall Street Journal* on January 23, 1990. Lanier's steamy hyperbole on the subject of virtual reality is legendary in the virtual communities, and if his entry into the world of international finance did not precisely signal the arrival of the young virtuality industry, at least it indicated that industry's vigor and sent a message that it should be taken seriously. In 1991, VPL was acquired by Thomson CSF. Thomson, which VPL modestly described in its investors' brochure as a "French electronics firm," is the largest defense contractor in Europe and was a major embarrassment to the largely Greenpeace-oriented VPI. Thomson's subsequent gutting of VPI in 1992 is by now well known.

Currently there is only one other player in the high-stakes field of virtual games entrepreneurship. That is John Waldern of W Industries, in Leicester, England. The informing philosophy behind W's games is the essential attraction of exotic total-immersion visual environments coupled with the proven thrill of bang-bang-shoot-'em-up action. While this use of the technology holds all the thrill for me of chopping up Abel Gance's *Napoleon* to insert commercials for television viewing, there is no question that arcade games will represent a significant drive behind technological innovation in virtual-worlds equipment for the public sector. In addition there also seems no question that a significant proportion of young people will spend a significant and increasing proportion of their waking hours playing computer-based games in one form or another, and so far the implications of this trend have yet to be fully addressed in academic forums. A major obstacle appears to be the feeling on the part of many academics that computer games are beneath serious notice, a situation perhaps best characterized as holding our cocktail party in a house that is already ablaze. Within a short time, the number of hours that a broad segment of children will spend playing computer-based games will exceed the number of hours that they spend watching television. It is entirely possible that computer-based games will turn out to be the major acknowledged source of socialization *and* education in industrialized societies before the 1990s have run their course.[14]

While the current generation of multiple-player games would seem to have no particular redeeming virtue, their designers are among the fiercest of the techno entrepreneurs. In addition, of all the possible commercial uses bruited about for virtual-worlds equipment, multiple-player games are the only commercial application that is currently returning a profit. Clearly they speak to some deep desires on the part of a significant number of consumers. Thus there will inevitably be more of them.

It is impossible to study the emergence of virtual systems without acknowledging the overwhelming influence exerted upon the entire field of virtual technologies research by the military. The earliest large-scale virtual environments were built for military purposes by engineers who were working for military organizations: Ivan Sutherland, who began his research in three-dimensional displays in 1966, became director of the Information Processing Techniques Office at the Defense Advanced Research Projects Agency (DARPA); Tom Furness, who started the "Supercockpit" project for the U.S. Air Force in 1965, became chief of the Visual Display System Branch, Human Engineering Division of the Armstrong Aerospace Research Laboratory at Wright-Patterson Air Force Base; Scott Fisher and Mike McGreevy did a good deal of their work at NASA Ames in the late 1980s.

Sooner or later we can trace any funding back to government sources; if we include MIT, which has always been heavily funded by military budgets, there is almost no one working in the field today whose original research is not or was not funded by military money. Still, some of the early and influential researchers were not directly involved with government funding. Myron Krueger is more of an artist than scientist; Jaron Lanier worked in the video game industry and wanted to become a composer; Fred Brooks is head of the computer science department at the University of North Carolina at Chapel Hill; Brenda Laurel took her M.F.A. at Ohio State in acting and directing, and later earned a Ph.D. in theater criticism. For better or worse, my focus in this essay is not on the military or even particularly on government; any number of my colleagues have done a far better and much more thorough job of studying military and government involvement in research and technological development than I could possibly do. In particularly, Bruce Sterling's account of the U.S. military's networked environmental battle simulation SIMNET is eminently worth reading (although it may be hard to find, since it appeared in the now-scarce first issue of *Wired* magazine).

Several critical events in the development of virtual systems theory do not seem to me to fit comfortably into a narrative description of the emergence of the technology of virtual systems. The first documented account of a virtual cross-dresser, for example—a person who caused considerable consternation and some misery among the women in the virtual community that he frequented—requires a different sort of description from that accorded the first tree-structured bulletin board. It is difficult to look back over such a brief period to 1985 and realize how naive most inhabitants of the virtual communities were at the time "Julie Graham" was giving her sensitive and helpful, albeit unquestionably deceptive, advice to unhappy women on the nets. From the first documented instance to 1992, when at any given time 15 percent of the population of *Habitat* (or, by one estimate, 150,000 people) was engaged in cross-gendered behavior, represents a span of seven years.

The trial of a man who was accused of raping a woman with multiple personalities by seducing one of her personae is important to this work. The trial became something of a spectacle, recalling in new surroundings the old power to fascinate that still inheres in freaks and monsters, the power of near-legibility; it raised issues of multiplicity and continuity, of what constitutes a single identity in social and legal terms. The trial itself and the media circus that surrounded it were similar in useful ways to the landmark suit brought by the Mashpee Wampanoag Tribal Council, Inc., against the town of Mashpee, on Cape Code, which James Clifford reported in his marvelous paper "Identity in Mashpee."

In his study Clifford identified three assumptions that he felt compromised the Mashpees' case against the government. He described these as (1) the idea of cultural wholeness and structure, (2) the hierarchical distinction between oral and literate forms of knowledge, and (3) the narrative continuity of history and identity. I found that Clifford's three points constituted a provocative background for the trial then under way in Oshkosh, Wisconsin, even in light of the fact that it was just such issues that the attorneys and judge in the Oshkosh case hoped would *not* intrude into an already complex debate.

I use the Oshkosh trial here to constitute a parallel narrative thread to my account of events in Silicon Valley in the 1970s and 1980s, and as a specimen of one kind of public response to a visible transgression of cultural norms of unitary subjectivity. That is, it is not simply the spectacle of difference in operation, but a voice from the shadows—a reflection of deeper conflicts and negotiations regarding the physical and conscious expression of a drive for closure, which is one of Western culture's most important ways of making meaning. Joseph Campbell refers to the social emergence of the drive for culture as the *yoke of individuality*. There is nothing ontological about this idea. What I call the drive for closure is itself an emergent manifestation of the interactions of complex events and forces. At this point I become daunted by complexity. Maybe I'm talking about what Foucault calls power, and maybe not; whatever it is, it is damnably hard to describe. Samuel Delany once described power as something like a thin mist in a valley, which is all but invisible when one is in it, and which only becomes visible when one can look back on it from a height or a distance.[15] Delany said it in the context of a work of fiction, which is a mode of representation with which I have great sympathy; and how to say just that in an academic context is for me a serious preoccupation.

Development of self-awareness takes place in a field that is already contoured by that invisible and impalpable structure called power. And while there is still plenty of mystery about how the self manages to emerge under these circumstances, there is an even deeper mystery about how self and power mutually constitute each other. A particle physics approach to psychology: We see selves, and we see power, and we talk about how they exchange forces in terms of discrete quantities or thoroughly muzzy qualities; but at bottom there are still problems in representing this exchange in satisfying terms. Describing the sort of entities that could move easily through such a field and produce satisfying accounts is a concrete example of Haraway's Three Aspects of Representation, as discussed *passim* in her preface to *Coyote's Sisters* (Tokyo: Routledge, 1999).[16] For those who have not yet received their copies of *Coyote's Sisters*, of course the three aspects are these: refuse closure; insist upon situation; and seek multiplicity.

I hope to reconsider the disparate accounts I have presented and attempt to point out their correspondences and divergences *without* trying to produce an overarching theoretical framework that appears to encompass them all. In so doing I am performing the activity for which I was trained and which embroiled me in such mischegas in the Science Studies Program at San Diego: attempting to hold these various discourses in productive tension without allowing them to collapse into a univocal account. My game is for the reader—that's you—to perform your own synthesis, if synthesis is your game.

I treat the strategy I have just outlined as a challenge—the challenge of how to best convey information to an imagined "reader." This could come under a broader heading along with a constellation of issues generally identified as part of what is sometimes referred to as a crisis of representation in the social sciences. How best to convey a complex description of a culture whose chief activity is complex description? Here it is useful to keep in mind that while I am attempting to describe cultures of sorts, even though they do not fit many of the customary definitions of cultures,[17] it is necessary to embed other information that is equally important and that becomes something else if it is extracted from the context of cultural quasi-description.

The choice among the three or perhaps four representational methods that would best serve the purposes here would be quite difficult. If I had to narrow the field to two, the choice would be between the method that Ursula Le Guin employed with such excellent results in *Always Coming Home*, and I hope that her success with it will rub off on me in the future. The first part of the book would consist of parallel narrative threads interspersed with descriptions of artifacts, information on cultural byways, "tribal" songs and poetry, and some interpretation of "tribal" philosophy and epistemology by members of the "tribe." I would have left it at that but for what I feel are certain academic constraints, and consequently the second section would consist of my own theoretical interpretations of what is going on. The other possible choice, as I indicated earlier, would be a cross between Traweek's *Beamtimes and Lifetimes* and Tolstoy's *War and Peace*. Those who do not have much truck with anthropology of emergent or perhaps phantasmic cultures may find their purpose better served by ignoring these remarks.

Finally I do something that for lack of a better description might be called implications and consequences. Where does this stuff lead? What kind of world are these folks bringing into being? Or, perhaps to take up the questions raised by Deleuze, Guattari, and De Landa, what kind of system is using them to become realized? To address this question I frame my last few words in the context of a discussion with my daughter, who is eleven years old as of this writing and who is still trying to figure out just what it is that I do. And at the very end, my favorite person puts in an appearance—Anne Rice's fictional antihero the Vampire Lestat, who has mysteriously acquired a Ph.D. in anthropology. In the context of a work on cultural theory, Lestat may have a few pithy things to say about vision between the worlds.

NOTES

1. This is the first instance of the collapse of fiction and fact (whatever that is), narrativization and description, that the style of this essay implies. Being a novelist at heart causes me to create krasis narratives, and it's hard to know to what depth I need to explicate them. Consequently let's try treating these two descriptive paragraphs as exemplary, to an extent that I will not carry on into the rest of the text. Both events are emblematic rather than specific. The bedroom is a combination of bedrooms from at least four different locales, including the young Kal-el's room on the farm in *Superman I*. There was no friend present; for reasons of my own I wanted to decenter the moment of discovery. Peering over a 24 × 24 console would have been impossible in 1955, since the state of the art was three-track recording, and at any rate I was too tall to have my nose at that level; the scene combines visits to various control rooms beginning in the late 1940s and extending into the 1970s, and when I was a preteen to pilgrimages to the transmitter of WOR itself, which, with its black bakelite monoliths and glowing 1920s-style power meters, resembled most closely some science-fiction author's depiction of mighty forces coiled to spring. There was little doubt in my mind that much of the early cinematic depictions of technology as mysterious and inexplicable power, as exemplified in *Metropolis*, came from the movie set designers' own visits to the few instantiations of technology at work that yet existed—that is, the control rooms of the few radio stations that maintained remote transmitter sites. These were invariably located far from populated areas, usually in swamps, thus specifically invoking the motif of lonely isolation in spooky circumstances.

2. All of this, of course, is about the interplay among communications technology, prosthetic community, the human body, and the uses of pleasure.

3. For some reason this sort of thing—having someone barge into my humdrum life and drag me off on some adventure—keeps happening, and I have gotten more good story material in such fashion than I like to admit.

4. This is perhaps the most egregious point of convergence of the two theses I have been

pursuing. A more detailed description and analysis of the oddly interdependent issues of lesbian separatism and transgender can be found in my "other" book, *The Gaze of the Vampire: Tales from the Edges of Identity*.

5. My use of the world *talk* to refer to writing and reading is both playful and a considered position. Part of the work of this essay is to play in the boundaries between speech and writing as I discuss the play I observe in electronically prostheticized human interaction. A typical example is a letter waiting in my e-mail box that begins, "Good to read from you."

6. Lippman had been developing these ideas in discussions at the MIT Media Lab over a period of time beginning in the early 1980s, but they were perhaps best captured by Stewart Brand in his recounting of talks with Lippman in *The Media Lab: Inventing the Future at MIT* (1987).

7. The invention of *Space War* is variously dated. Laurel (1991) puts it at 1962.

8. In particular I am referring to Deleuze and Guattari's discussions of deterritorialization and multiplicity in *Anti-Oedipus* (1983) and *A Thousand Plateaus* (1987), Virilio in *The Aesthetics of Disappearance* (1991a) and *The Light of Speed* (1991b), and Manuel De Landa in *War in the Age of Intelligent Machines* (1991).

9. I refer to Barker as "she" here without really being sure what s/he is. Some colleagues have assured me that Barker is a woman. Others claim that because of the spelling of the first name, Barker must be a man. Certainly this is something that should have been cleared up before publication, but I rather enjoy the confusion and the debates thus precipitated.

10. At the time I was first thrashing this out I had recently read Bruno Latour's *The Pasteurization of France* (1988) in its French incarnation, *Les Microbes: Guerere et paix suivi les irreductions*. As I struggled to regain whatever fluency in French I may have previously possessed, I completely missed Latour's pun on Tolstoy in the title of the book. It must have stuck around in the background.

11. Few of these adjectives, like *bloodthirsty* and *infamous,* are accidental, and I am fully aware of their tendentious character. These stories are experimental, and part of the experiment is to see how much (if any) of what I might term "dangerous" story forms can be recuperated into a different discourse without contaminating it (another deliberate word choice). The events at the Atari Lab are emblematic of what happened when the first generation of graduates—bright, dedicated, and to an extent thrillingly conscious of the liberatory potential of their creations—hit the buzz saw of commodification and then the street.

12. There are wide variations in the estimates of *Habitat*'s actual population, even within Fujitsu. The actual figure is probably lower, but how much lower is uncertain.

13. Morningstar and Farmer maintain that it never occurred to them that the characters might want to have sex; they were too preoccupied with just getting characters to look reasonably right and to be able to walk around. It is also possible that Lucasfilm might have frowned on the idea, had it arisen at the time. It is not clear whether Fujitsu would have exercised the same scruples, nor that it would have made much difference vis-à-vis sexual activity within the simulation.

14. My use of the term *computer-based* is already becoming an anachronism, because the meanings of culturally defined objects such as television, telephone, cable, and comput-

ers, and the boundaries between them, are already in hot debate and increasing flux. Nicholas Negroponte had already pointed out in the late 1970s that there would soon come a time when there might be more MIPS (a measure of processor speed) in kitchen appliances than in the objects commonly called computers. This development prefigures, in part at least, the cultural redefinition, now under way, of these objects. It is partly driven by economics and partly by the effect of ubiquitous technology (technology so familiar as to be culturally invisible) on engineers' interpretations of the boundaries of their specialties, as well as ubiquitous technology's effect on the cultural paradigm of biological-machine binarism. An exhilarating and problematic time.

15. In Samuel R. Delany, *Tales of Nevèrÿon* (New York: Bantam Books, 1979).

16. I want to emphasize that this sort of thing, that is, quoting from nonexistent work, is meant in a wholly humorous way. However, the case in point had its beginnings in a real and somewhat bizarre event. When I first came to the History of Consciousness program at the University of California at Santa Cruz, I had several dreams in which I was reading scholarly papers written by Haraway. Later, while writing a critique of some aspect of scientific research I absentmindedly quoted from one of the papers I'd dreamed about, confusing it in my fevered brain with a "real" Haraway paper. Some time later, while trying to attribute page and line, I realized that the paper I'd cited was in physical terms nonexistent, The quote itself, however, whatever its true source in my memory, was exactly apt and productively useful. I mentioned this to Haraway, who jokingly requested coauthorship if I ever wrote out the papers I'd dreamed I read. In retrospect this was a rather novel instantiation of the mentoring relationship, neatly avoiding problems of age and experience, while evincing several of the advantages of virtuality as well as a considerable amount of tribality. Virtual mentoring, or shamanistic training? In regard to the quote, Haraway actually said, "Refuse closure and insist upon situation"; I have interpolated "Seek multiplicity."

17. I left this sentence in because it's fun. When I first wrote it, I had a lot of convincing to do, and a lot of forums to legitimize. Now academic panels on "virtual community" pop up like mushrooms, but times have changed so fast that the sentence makes me chuckle.

Baby, You Were Great
Kate Wilhelm

Kate Wilhelm is the award-winning author of numerous science fiction and fantasy novels and short stories, including the famous *Where Late the Sweet Birds Sang* and "The Girl Who Fell into the Sky," among others. She is also the author of the successful Barbara Holloway and of the Constance and Charlie series of mystery novels. She and her husband Damon Knight (1922–2002) helped establish the famous Clarion Writers' Workshop and the Milford Writers' Workshop and so influenced hundreds of successful writers in the science fiction genre. "Baby, You Were Great," a Nebula nominee in 1967, is Wilhelm's take on virtual reality, immersive environments, the sense of "presence," and the price that is paid for that kind of entertainment.

John Lewisohn thought that if one more door slammed, or one more bell rang, or one more voice asked if he was all right, his head would explode. Leaving his laboratories he walked through the carpeted hall to the elevator that slid wide to admit him noiselessly, was lowered, gently, two floors, where there were more carpeted halls. The door he shoved open bore a neat sign, AUDITIONING STUDIO. Inside he was waved on through the reception room by three girls who knew better than to speak to him unless he spoke first. They were surprised to see him; it was his first visit there in seven or eight months. The inner room where he stopped was darkened, at first glance appearing empty, revealing another occupant only after his eyes had time to adjust to the dim lighting.

John sat in the chair next to Herb Javits, still without speaking. Herb was wearing the helmet and gazing at a wide screen that was actually a one-way glass panel permitting him to view the audition going on in the adjacent room. John lowered a second helmet to his head. It fit snugly and immediately made contact with the eight prepared spots on his skull. As soon as he turned it on, the helmet itself was forgotten.

A girl had entered the other room. She was breathtakingly lovely, a long-legged honey blonde with slanting green eyes and apricot skin. The room was furnished as a sitting room with two couches, some chairs, end tables and a coffee table, all tasteful and lifeless. Like an ad in a furniture-trade publication. The girl stopped at the doorway and John felt her indecision heavily tempered with nervousness and fear. Outwardly she appeared poised and expectant, her smooth face betraying none of the emotions. She took a hesitant step toward the couch, and a wire showed trailing behind her. It was attached to her head. At the same time a second door opened. A young man ran inside, slamming the door behind him; he looked wild and frantic. The girl registered surprise, mounting nervousness; she felt behind her for the door handle, found it and tried to open the door again. It was locked, John could hear nothing that was being said in the room; he only felt the girl's reaction to the unexpected interruption. The wild-eyed man was approaching her, his hands slashing through the air, his eyes darting glances all about them constantly. Suddenly he pounced on her and pulled her to him, kissing her face and neck roughly. She seemed paralyzed with fear for several seconds, then there was something else, a bland nothing kind of feeling that accompanied boredom sometimes, or too complete self-assurance. As the man's hands fastened on her blouse in the back and ripped it, she threw her arms about him, her face showing passion that was not felt anywhere in her mind or in her blood.

"Cut!" Herb Javits said quietly.

The man stepped back from the girl and left her without a word. She looked about blankly, her blouse torn, hanging about her hips, one shoulder strap gone. She was very beautiful. The audition manager entered, followed by a dresser with a gown that he threw about her shoulders. She looked startled; waves of anger mounted to fury as she was drawn from the room, leaving it empty. The two watching men removed their helmets.

"Fourth one so far," Herb grunted. "Sixteen yesterday; twenty the day before...all nothing." He gave John a curious look. "What's got you stirred out of your lab?"

"Anne's had it this time," John said. "She's been on the phone all night and all morning.

"What now?"

"Those damn sharks! I told you that was too much on top of the airplane crash last week. She can't take much more of it."

"Hold it a minute, Johnny," Herb said. "Let's finish off the next three girls and then talk." He pressed a button on the arm of his chair and the room beyond the screen took their attention again.

This time the girl was slightly less beautiful, shorter, a dimply sort of brunette with laughing blue eyes and an upturned nose. John liked her. He adjusted his helmet and felt with her.

She was excited; the audition always excited them. There was some fear and nervousness, not too much. Curious about how the audition would go, probably. The wild young man ran into the room, and her face paled. Nothing else changed. Her nervousness increased, not uncomfortably. When he grabbed her, the only emotion she registered was the nervousness.

"Cut," Herb said.

The next girl was brunette, with gorgeously elongated legs. She was very cool, a real professional. Her mobile face reflected the range of emotions to be expected as the scene played through again, but nothing inside her was touched. She was a million miles away from it all.

The next one caught John with a slam. She entered the room slowly, looking about with curiosity, nervous, as they all were. She was younger than the other girls had been, less poised. She had pale-gold hair piled in an elaborate mound of waves on top of her head. Her eyes were brown, her skin nicely tanned. When the man entered, her emotion changed quickly to fear, and then to terror. John didn't know when he closed his eyes. He was the girl, filled with unspeakable terror; his heart pounded, adrenalin pumped into his system; he wanted to scream but could not. From the dim unreachable depths of his psyche, there was came something else, in waves, so mixed with terror that the two merged and became one emotion that pulsed and throbbed and demanded. With a jerk he opened his eyes and stared at the window. The girl had been thrown down to one of the couches, and the man was kneeling on the floor beside her, his hands playing over her bare body, his face pressed against her skin.

"Cut!" Herb said. His voice was shaken. "Hire her," he said. The man rose, glanced at the girl, sobbing now, and then quickly bent over and kissed her cheek. Her sobs increased. Her golden hair was down, framing her face; she looked like a child. John tore off the helmet. He was perspiring.

Herb got up, turned on the lights in the room, and the window blanked out, blending with the wall, making it invisible. He didn't look at John. When he wiped his face, his hand was shaking. He rammed it in his pocket.

"When did you start auditions like that?" John asked, after a few moments of silence.

"Couple of months ago. I told you about it. Hell, we had to, Johnny. That's the six hundred nineteenth girl we've tried out! Six hundred nineteen! All phonies but one! Dead from the neck up. Do you have any idea how long it was taking us to find that out? Hours for each one. Now it's a matter of minutes."

John Lewisohn sighed. He knew. He had suggested it, actually, when he had said, "Find a basic anxiety situation for the test." He hadn't wanted to know what Herb had come up with. He said, "Okay, but she's only a kid. What about her parents, legal rights, all that?"

"We'll fix it. Don't worry. What about Anne?"

"She's called me five times since yesterday. The sharks were too much. She wants to see us, both of us, this afternoon."

"You're kidding! I can't leave her here now!"

"Nope. Kidding I'm not. She says no plug up if we don't show. She'll take pills and sleep until we get there."

"Good Lord! She wouldn't dare!"

"I've booked seats. We take off at 12:35." They stared at one another silently for another moment, then Herb shrugged. He was a short man, not heavy but solid. John was over six feet, muscular, with a temper that he knew he had to control. Others suspected that when he did let it go, there would be bodies lying around afterward, but he controlled it.

Once it had been a physical act, an effort of body and will to master that temper; now it was done so automatically that he couldn't recall occasions when it even threatened to flare any more.

"Look, Johnny, when we see Anne, let me handle it, right?" Herb said. "I'll make it short."

"What are you going to do?"

"Give her an earful. If she's going to start pulling temperament on me, I'll slap her down so hard she'll bounce a week." He grinned happily. "She's had it all her way up to now. She knew there wasn't a replacement if she got bitchy. Let her try it now. Just let her try." Herb was pacing back and forth with quick, jerky steps.

John realized with a shock that he hated the stocky, red-faced man. The feeling was new, it was almost as if he could taste the hatred he felt, and the taste was unfamiliar and pleasant.

Herb stopped pacing and stared at him for a moment. "Why'd she call you?

Why does she want you down, too? She knows you're not mixed up with this end of it."

"She knows I'm a full partner, anyway," John said.

"Yeah, but that's not it." Herb's face twisted in a grin. "She thinks you're not still hot for her, doesn't she? She knows you tumbled once, in the beginning, when you were working on her, getting the gimmick working right." The grin reflected no humor then. "Is she right, Johnny, baby? Is that it?"

"We made a deal," John said coldly. "You run your end, I run mine. She wants me along because she doesn't trust you, or believe anything you tell her any more. She wants a witness."

"Yeah, Johnny. But you be sure you remember our agreement." Suddenly Herb laughed. "You know what it was like, Johnny, seeing you and her? Like a flame trying to snuggle up to an icicle."

At three-thirty they were in Anne's suite in the Skyline Hotel in Grand Bahama. Herb had a reservation to fly back to New York on the 6 P.M. flight. Anne would not be off until four, so they made themselves comfortable in her rooms and waited. Herb turned her screen on, offered a helmet to John, who shook his head, and they both seated themselves. John watched the screen for several minutes; then he, too, put on a helmet.

Anne was looking at the waves far out at sea where they were long, green, undulating; then she brought her gaze in closer, to the blue-green and quick seas, and finally in to where they stumbled on the sand bars, breaking into foam that looked solid enough to walk on. She was peaceful, swaying with the motion of the boat, the sun hot on her back, the fishing rod heavy in her hands. It was like being an indolent animal at peace with its world, at home in the world, being one with it. After a few seconds she put down the rod and turned, looking at a tall smiling man in swimming trunks. He held out his hand and she took it. They entered the cabin of the boat, where drinks were waiting. Her mood of serenity and happiness ended abruptly, to be replaced by shocked disbelief and a start of fear.

"What the hell...?" John muttered, adjusting the audio. You seldom needed audio when Anne was on.

"...Captain Brothers had to let them go. After all, they've done nothing yet..." the man was saying soberly.

"But why do you think they'll try to rob me?"

"Who else is here with a million dollars worth of jewels?"

John turned it off and said to Herb, "You're a fool! You can't get away with something like that!"

Herb stood up and crossed the room to stand before a window wall that was open to the stretch of glistening blue ocean beyond the brilliant white beaches. "You know what every woman wants? To own something worth stealing." He chuckled, a low throaty sound that was without mirth. "Among other things, that is. They want to be roughed up once or twice, and forced to kneel....Our new psychologist is pretty good, you know? Hasn't steered us wrong yet. Anne might kick some, but it'll go over great."

"She won't stand for an actual robbery." Louder, emphasizing it, he added, "I won't stand for that."

"We can dub it," Herb said. "That's all we need, Johnny, plant the idea, and then dub the rest."

John stared at his back. He wanted to believe that. He needed to believe it. His voice showed no trace of emotion when he said, "It didn't start like this, Herb. What happened?"

Herb turned then. His face was dark against the glare of light behind him. "Okay, Johnny, it didn't start like this. Things accelerate, that's all. You thought of a gimmick, and the way we planned it, it sounded great, but it didn't last. We gave them the feeling of gambling, of learning to ski, of automobile racing, everything we could dream of, and it wasn't enough. How many times can you take the first ski jump of your life? After a while you want new thrills, you know? For you it's been great, hasn't it? You bought yourself a shining new lab and pulled the cover over you and it. You bought yourself time and equipment, and when things didn't go right you could toss it out and start over, and nobody gave a damn. Think of what it's been like for me, kid! I gotta keep coming up with something new, something that'll give Anne a jolt and, through her, all those nice little people who aren't even alive unless they're plugged in. You think it's been easy? Anne was a green kid. For her everything was new and exciting, but it isn't like that now, boy. You better believe it is *not* like that now. You know what she told me last month? She's sick and tired of men. Our little hot-box Annie! Tired of men!"

John crossed to him and pulled him around. "Why didn't you tell me?"

"Why, Johnny? What would you have done that I didn't do? *I* looked harder for the right guy for her. What would you do for a new thrill for her? I worked for them, kid. Right from the start you said for me to leave you alone.

Okay. I left you alone. You ever read any of the memos I sent? You initialed them, kiddo. Everything that's been done, we both signed. Don't give me any of that why-didn't-I-tell-you stuff. It won't work!" His face was ugly red and vein bulged in his neck. John wondered if he had high blood pressure, if he would die of a stroke during one of his flash rages.

John left him at the window. He had read the memos, Herb knew he had. Herb was right; all he had wanted was to be left alone. It had been his idea; after twelve years of work in a laboratory on prototypes he had shown his... gimmick...to Herb Javits. Herb was one of the biggest producers on television then; now he was the biggest producer in the world.

The gimmick was fairly simple. A person fitted with electrodes in his brain could transmit his emotions, which in turn could be broadcast and picked up by the helmets to be felt by the audience. No words or thoughts went out, only basic emotions...fear, love, anger, hatred...That, tied in with a camera showing what the person saw, with a voice dubbed in, and you were the person having the experience, with one important difference, you could turn it off if it got to be too much. The "actor" couldn't. A simple gimmick. You didn't really need the camera and the soundtrack; many users never turned them on at all, but let their own imagination fill in to fit the emotional broadcast.

The helmets were not sold, only rented after a short, easy fitting session. Rent of one dollar a month was collected on the first of the month, and there were over thirty-seven million subscribers, Herb had bought his own network after the second month when the demand for more hours barred him from regular television. From a one-hour weekly show, it had gone to one hour nightly, and now it was on the air eight hours a day live, with another eight hours of taped programming.

What had started out as A DAY IN THE LIFE OF ANNE BEAUMONT was now a life in the life of Anne Beaumont, and the audience was insatiable.

Anne came in then, surrounded by the throng of hangers-on that mobbed her daily—hairdressers, masseurs, fitters, script men...She looked tired. She waved the crowd out when she saw John and Herb were there. "Hello, John," she said, "Herb."

"Anne, baby, you're looking great!" Herb said. He took her in his arms and kissed her solidly. She stood still, her hands at her sides.

She was tall, very slender, with wheat-colored hair and gray eyes. Her cheekbones were wide and high, her mouth firm and almost too large. Against her deep red-gold sun-tan her teeth looked whiter than John remembered them. Although too firm and strong ever to be thought of as pretty, she was a very beautiful woman. After Herb released her, she turned to John, hesitated only a moment, and then extended a slim, sun-browned hand. It was cool and dry in his.

"How have you been John? It's been a long time."

He was very glad she didn't kiss him or call him darling. She smiled only slightly and gently removed her hand from his. He moved to the bar as she turned to Herb.

"I'm through, Herb," she said. Her voice was too quiet. She accepted a whiskey sour from John, but kept her gaze on Herb.

"What's the matter, honey? I was just watching you, baby. You were great today, like always. You've still got it, kid. It's coming through like always."

"What about this robbery? You must be out of your mind...."

"Yeah, that. Listen, Anne baby. I swear to you I don't know a thing about it. Laughton must have been telling you the straight good on that. You know we agreed that the rest of this week you just have a good time, remember? That comes over too, baby. When you have a good time and relax, thirty-seven million people are enjoying life and relaxing. That's good. They can't be stimulated all the time. They like the variety...." Wordlessly John held out a glass, Scotch and water. Herb took it without looking.

Anne was watching him coldly. Suddenly she laughed. It was cynical, bitter sound. "You're not a damn fool, Herb. Don't try to act like one." She sipped her drink again, continuing to stare at him over the rim of the glass. "I am warning you, if anyone shows here to rob me, I'm going to treat him like a real burglar. I bought a gun after today's broadcast, and I learned how to shoot when I was only nine or ten. I still know how. I'll kill him, Herb, whoever it is."

"Baby," Herb started, but she cut him short.

"And this is my last week. As of Saturday, I'm through."

"You can't do that, Anne," Herb said. John watched him closely, searching for a sign of weakness, anything; he saw nothing. Herb exuded confidence. "Look around, Anne, at this room, your clothes, everything...You are the richest woman in the world, having the time of your life, able to go anywhere, do anything..."

"While the whole world watches..."

"So what? It doesn't stop you, does it?" Herb started to pace, his steps jerky and quick. "You knew that when you signed the contract. You're a rare girl, Anne, beautiful, emotional, intelligent. Think of all those women who've got nothing but you. If you quit them, what do they do? Die? They might, you know. For the first time in their lives they are able to feel like they're living. You're giving them what no one ever did before, what was only hinted at in books and films in the old days. Suddenly they knew what it feels like to face excitement, to experience love, to feel contented and peaceful. Think of them, Anne, empty, with nothing in their lives but you, what you're able to give them. Thirty-seven million drabs, Anne, who never felt anything but boredom and frustration until you gave them life. What do they have? Work, kids, bills. You've given them the world, baby! Without you they wouldn't even want to live anymore."

She wasn't listening. Almost dreamily she said, "I talked to my lawyers, Herb, and the contract is meaningless. You've already broken it countless times by insisting on adding to the original agreement. I agreed to learn a lot of new things so they could feel them with me. I did. My God! I've climbed mountains, hunted lions, learned to ski and water ski, but now you want me to die a little bit each week....that airplane crash, not bad, just enough to terrify me. Then the sharks. I really do think it was having sharks brought in when I was skiing that did it, Herb. You see, you will kill me. It will happen, and you won't be able to top it, Herb. Not ever."

There was a hard, waiting silence following her words. "No!" John shouted, soundlessly, the words not leaving his mouth. He was looking at Herb. He had stopped pacing when she started to talk. Something flicked across his face, surprise, fear, something not readily identifiable. Then his face went completely blank and he raised his glass and finished the Scotch and water, replacing the glass on the bar. When he turned again, he was smiling with disbelief.

"What's really bugging you, Anne? There have been plants before. You knew about them. Those lions didn't just happen by, you know. And the avalanche needed a nudge from someone. You know that. What else is bugging you?"

"I'm in love, Herb. I want out now before you manage to kill me." Herb waved that aside impatiently.

"Have you ever watched your own show, Anne?" She shook her head. "I thought not. So you wouldn't know about the expansion that took place last month, after we planted that new transmitter in your head. Johnny boy here's been busy, Anne. You know these scientist types, never satisfied, always improving, changing. Where's the camera, Anne? Do you ever know where it is any more? Have you even seen a camera in the past couple of weeks, or a recorder of any sort? You have not, and you won't again. You're on now, honey." His voice was quite low, amused almost. "In fact the only time you aren't on is when you're sleeping. I know you're in love; I know who he is; I know how he makes you feel; I even know how much money he makes per week. I should know, Anne baby, I pay him." He had come closer to her with each word, finishing with his face only inches from hers. He didn't have a chance to duck the flashing slap that jerked his head around, and before either of them realized it, he had hit her back. Anne fell back to the chair, too stunned to speak for a moment.

The silence grew, became something ugly and heavy, as if words were being born and dying without utterance because they were too brutal for the human spirit to bear. There was a spot of blood on Herb's mouth where her diamond ring had cut him. He touched it and looked at his finger. "It's all being taped now, honey, even this," he said. He returned to the bar, turning his back on her.

There was a large red print on her cheek. Her gray eyes had turned black with rage; she didn't take her gaze from him.

"Honey, relax," Herb said as after a moment, his voice soft and easy again. "It won't make any difference to you, in what you do, or anything like that. You know we can't use most of the stuff, but it gives the editors a bigger variety to pick from. It was getting to the point where most of the interesting stuff was going on after you were off. Like buying the gun. That's great stuff there, baby. You weren't blanketing a single thing, and it'll all come through like pure gold." He finished mixing his drink, tasted it, and then swallowed most of it. "How many women have to go out and buy a gun to protect themselves? Think of them all, feeling that gun, feeling the things you felt when you picked it up, looked at it...."

"How long have you been tuning in all the time?" she asked. John felt a stirring along his spine, a tingle of excitement. He knew what was going out over the miniature transmitter, the rising crests of emotion she was feeling. Only a trace of them showed on her smooth face, but the raging interior torment was being recorded faithfully. Her quiet voice and quiet body were lies; only the tapes never lied.

Herb felt it too, a storm behind her quietude. He put his glass down and went to her, kneeling by the chair, taking her hand in both of his. "Anne, please, don't be that angry with me. I was desperate for new material. When Johnny got this last wrinkle out, and we knew we could record around the clock, we had to try it, and it wouldn't have been any good if you had known. That's no way to test anything. You knew we were planting the transmitter..."

"How long?"

"Not quite a month."

"And Stuart? He's one of your men? He is transmitting also? You hired him to...to make love to me? Is that right?"

Herb nodded. She pulled her hand free and averted her face, not willing to see him any longer. He got up then and went to the window. "But what difference does it make?" he shouted. "If I introduced the two of you at a party, you wouldn't think anything of it. What difference if I did it this way? I knew you'd like each other. He's bright, like you, likes the same sort of things you do. Comes from a poor family, like yours...Everything said you'd get along..."

"Oh, yes," she said almost absently. "We get along." She was feeling in her hair, her fingers searching for the scars.

"It's all healed by now," John said. She looked at him as if she had forgotten he was there.

"I'll find a surgeon," she said, standing up, her fingers white on her glass. "A brain surgeon..."

"It's a new process," John said slowly. "It would be dangerous to go in after them..."

She looked at him for a long time. "Dangerous?"

He nodded.

"You could take it back out..."

He remembered the beginning, how he had quieted her fear of the electrodes and the wires. Her fear was that of a child for the unknown and the unknowable. Time and again he had proven to her that she could trust him, that he wouldn't lie to her. He hadn't lied to her, then. There was the same trust in her eyes, the same unshakable faith. She would believe him. She would accept without question whatever he said. Herb had called him an icicle, but that was wrong. An icicle would have melted in her fires. More like a stalactite, shaped by centuries of civilization, layer by layer he had been formed until he had forgotten how to bend, forgotten how to find release for the stirrings he felt somewhere in the hollow, rigid core of himself. She had tried and, frustrated, she had turned from him, hurt, but unable not to trust one she had loved. Now she waited. He could free her, and lose her again, this time irrevocably. Or he could hold her as long as she lived.

Her lovely gray eyes were shadowed with fear and the trust that he had given to her. Slowly he shook his head.

"I can't," he said. "No one can."

"I see," she murmured, the black filling her eyes. "I'd die, wouldn't I? Then you'd have a lovely sequence, wouldn't you, Herb? "She swung around, away from John. "You'd have to fake the story line, of course, but you are so good at that. An accident, emergency brain surgery needed, everything I feel going out to the poor little drabs who never will have brain surgery done. It's very good," she said admiringly. Her eyes were very black. "In fact, anything I do from now on, you'll use, won't you? If I kill you, that will simply be material for your editors to pick over. Trial, prison, very dramatic.... On the other hand, if I kill myself..."

John felt chilled; a cold, hard weight seemed to be filling him. Herb laughed. "The story line will be something like this," he said. "Anne has fallen in love with a stranger, deeply, sincerely in love with him. Everyone knows how deep that love is; they've all felt it, too, you know. She finds him raping a child, a lovely little girl in her early teens. Stuart tells her they're through. He loves the little nymph. In a passion she kills herself. You are broadcasting a real storm of passion, right now, aren't you, honey? Never mind, when I run through this scene, I'll find out." She hurled her glass at him, ice cubes and orange sections leaving a trail across the room. Herb ducked, grinning.

"That's awfully good, baby. Corny, but after all, they can't get too much corn, can they? They'll love it, after they get over the shock of losing you. And they will get over it, you know. They always do. Wonder if it's true about what happens to someone experiencing a violent death?" Anne's teeth bit down on her lip, and slowly she sat down again, her eyes closed tight. Herb watched her for a moment, then said, even more cheerfully, "We've got the kid already. If you give them a death, you've got to give them a new life. Finish one with a bang. Start one with a bang. We'll name the kid Cindy, a real Cinderella story after that. They'll love her, too."

Anne opened her eyes, black dulled now; she was so tight with tension that John felt his own muscles contract and become taut. He wondered if he would be able to stand the tape she was transmitting. A wave of excitement swept him and he knew he would play it all, feel it all, the incredibly contained rage, fear, the horror of giving a death to them to gloat over, and finally, anguish. He would know them all. Watching Anne, he wished she would break then, with him there. She didn't. She stood up stiffly, her back rigid, a muscle hard and ridged in her jaw. Her voice was flat when she said, "Stuart is due in half an hour. I have to dress." She left them without looking back.

Herb winked at John and motioned toward the door. "Want to take me to the plane, kid?" In the cab he said, "Stick close to her for a couple of days, Johnny. There might be an even bigger reaction later when she really understands just how hooked she is." He chuckled again. "By God! It's a good thing she trusts you, Johnny, boy!"

As they waited in the chrome-and-marble terminal for the liner to unload its passengers, John said, "Do you think she'll be any good after this?"

"She can't help herself. She's too life oriented to deliberately choose to die. She's like a jungle inside, raw, wild, untouched by that smooth layer of civilization she shows on the outside. It's a thin layer, kid, real thin. She'll fight to stay alive. She'll become more wary, more alert to danger, more excited and exciting...She'll really go to pieces when he touches her tonight. She's primed real good. Might even have to do some editing, tone it down a little." His voice was very happy. "He touches her where she lives, and she reacts. A real wild one. She's one; the new kid's one; Stuart...They're few and a far apart, Johnny. It's up to us to find them. God knows we're going to need all of them we can get." His face became thoughtful and withdrawn. "You know, that really wasn't such a bad idea of mine about rape and the kid. Who ever dreamed we'd get that kind of a reaction from her? With the right sort of buildup..." He had to run to catch his plane.

John hurried back to the hotel, to be near Anne if she needed him. He hoped she would leave him alone. His fingers shook as he turned on his screen; suddenly he had a clear memory of the child who had wept, and he hoped Stuart would hurt Anne just a little. The tremor in his fingers increased; Stuart was on from six until twelve, and he already had missed almost an hour of the show. He adjusted the helmet and sank back into a deep chair. He left the audio off, letting his own words form, letting his own thoughts fill in the spaces.

Anne was leaning toward him, sparkling champagne raised to her lips, her eyes large and soft. She was speaking, talking to him, John, calling him by name. He felt a tingle start somewhere deep inside him, and his glance was lowered to rest on her tanned hand in his, sending electricity through him. Her hand trembled when he ran his fingers up her palm, to her wrist where a blue vein throbbed. The slight throb became a pounding that grew, and when he looked again into her eyes, they were dark and very deep. They danced and he felt her body against his, yielding, pleading. The room darkened and she was an outline against the window, her gown floating down about her. The darkness grew denser, or he closed his eyes, and this time when her body pressed against his, there was nothing between them, and the pounding was everywhere.

In the deep chair, with the helmet on his head, John's hands clenched, opened, clenched, again and again.

Rock On
Pat Cadigan

Pat Cadigan is an award-winning science fiction writer known for her early work as one of the creators of the cyberpunk movement of the 1980s and, later, for more than a dozen novels or short story collections and dozens more short stories in anthologies and magazines. "Rock On" first appeared in the anthology *Light Years and Dark* (Berkley, 1985) and was reprinted in the famous *Mirrorshades* anthology edited by Bruce Sterling, who notes in his introduction to that book that cyberpunk stories are notable for their "visionary intensity," exemplified by Cadigan's melding of an immersive high-tech future and the dark undercurrents of rock and roll.

Rain woke me. I thought, shit, here I am, Lady Rain-in-the-Face, because that's where it was hitting, right in the old face. Sat up and saw I was still on Newbury Street. See beautiful downtown Boston. Was Newbury Street downtown? In the middle of the night, did it matter? No, it did not. And not a soul in sight. Like everybody said, let's get Gina drunk and while she's passed out, we'll all move to Vermont. Do I love New England? A great place to live, but you wouldn't want to visit here.

I smeared my hair out of my eyes and wondered if anyone was looking for me now. Hey, anybody shy a forty-year-old rock 'n' roll sinner?

I scuttled into the doorway of one of those quaint old buildings where there was a shop with the entrance below ground level. A little awning kept the rain off but pissed water down in a maddening beat. Wrung the water out of my wrap pants and my hair and just sat being damp. Cold too, I guess, but didn't feel that so much.

Sat a long time with my chin on my knees: you know, it made me feel like a kid again. When I started nodding my head, I began to pick up on something. Just primal but I tap into that amazing well. Man-O-War, if you could see me now. By the time the blueboys found me, I was rocking pretty good.

And that was the punchline. I'd never tried to get up and leave, but if I had, I'd have found I was locked into place in a sticky field. Made to catch the b&e

kids in the act until the blueboys could get around to coming out and getting them. I'd been sitting in a trap and digging it. The story of my life.

They were nice to me. Led me, read me, dried me out. Fined me a hundred, sent me on my way in time for breakfast.

Awful time to see and be seen, righteous awful. For the first three hours after you get up, people can tell whether you've got a broken heart or not. The solution is, either you get up *real* early so your camouflage is in place by the time everybody else is out, or you don't go to bed. Don't go to bed ought to work all the time, but it doesn't. Sometimes when you don't go to bed, people can see whether you've got a broken heart all day long. I schlepped it, searching for an uncrowded breakfast bar and not looking at anyone who was looking at me. But I had this urge to stop random pedestrians and say, Yeah, yeah, it's true, but it was rock 'n' roll broke my poor old heart, not a person, don't cry for me or I'll pop your chocks.

I went around and up and down and all over until I found Tremont Street. It had been the pounder with that group from the Detroit Crater—the name was gone but the malady lingered on—anyway, him; he'd been the one told me Tremont had the best breakfast bars in the world, especially when you were coming off a bottle drunk you couldn't remember.

When the c'muters cleared out some, I found a space at a Greek hole in the wall. We shut down 10:30 A.M. sharp, get the hell out when you're done, counter service only, take it or shake it. I like a place with Attitude. I folded a seat down and asked for coffee and a feta cheese omelet. Came with home fries from the home fries mountain in a corner of the grill (no microwave *garbazhe*, hoo-ray). They shot my retinas before they even brought me coffee, and while I was pouring the cream, they checked my credit. Was that badass? It was badass. Did I care? I did not. No waste, no machines when a human could do it, and real food, none of this edible polyester that slips clear through you so you can stay looking like a famine victim, my deah.

They came in when I was half finished with the omelet. Went all night by the look and sound of them, but I didn't check their faces for broken hearts. Made me nervous but I thought, well, they're tired; who's going to notice this old lady? Nobody.

Wrong again. I became visible to them right after they got their retinas shot. Seventeen-year-old boy with tattooed cheeks and a forked tongue leaned forward and hissed like a snake.

"Sssssssinner."

The other four with him perked right up. "Where?" "Whose?" "In here?"

"Rock 'n' roll sssssssinner."

The lady identified me. She bore much resemblance to nobody at all, and if she had a heart it wasn't even sprained a little. With a sinner, she was probably Madame Magnifica. "Gina," she said, with all confidence.

My left eye tic'd. Oh, please. Feta cheese on my knees. What the hell, I thought, I'll nod, they'll nod, I'll eat, I'll go. And then somebody whispered the word, *reward*.

I dropped my fork and ran.

Safe enough, I figured. Were they all going to chase me before they got their Greek breakfasts? No, they were not. They sent the lady after me.

She was much the younger, and she tackled me in the middle of a crosswalk when the light changed. A car hopped over us, its undercarriage just ruffling the top of her hard copper hair.

"Just come back and finish your omelet. Or we'll buy you another."

"No."

She yanked me up and pulled me out of the street. "Come on." People were staring, but Tremont's full of theaters. You see that here, live theater; you can still get it. She put a bring-along on my wrist and brought me along, back to the breakfast bar, where they'd sold the rest of my omelet at a discount to a bum. The lady and her group made room for me among themselves and brought me another cup of coffee.

"How can you eat and drink with a forked tongue?" I asked Tattooed Cheeks. He showed me. A little appliance underneath, like a *zipper*. The Featherweight to the left of the big boy on the lady's other side leaned over and frowned at me.

"Give us one good reason why we shouldn't turn you in for Man-O-War's reward."

I shook my head. "I'm through. This sinner's been absolved."

"You're legally bound by contract," said the lady. "But we could c'noodle something. Buy Man-O-War out, sue on your behalf for nonfulfillment. We're Misbegotten. Oley." She pointed at herself. "Pidge." That was the silent type next to her. "Percy." The big boy. "Krait." Mr. Tongue. "Gus." Featherweight. "We'll take care of you."

I shook my head again. "If you're going to turn me in, turn me in and collect. The credit ought to buy you the best sinner ever there was."

"We can be good to you."

"I don't have it anymore. It's gone. All my rock 'n' roll sins have been forgiven."

"Untrue," said the big boy. Automatically, I started to picture on him and shut it down hard. "Man-O-War would have thrown you out if it were gone. You wouldn't have to run."

"I didn't want to tell him. Leave me alone. I just want to go and sin no more, see? Play with yourselves, I'm not helping." I grabbed the counter with both hands and held on. So what were they going to do, pop me one and carry me off?

As a matter of fact, they did.

In the beginning, I thought, and the echo effect was stupendous. *In the beginning...the beginning...the beginning....*

In the beginning, the sinner was not human. I know because I'm old enough to remember.

They were all there, little more than phantoms. Misbegotten. Where do they get those names? I'm old enough to remember. Oingo-Boingo and Bow-Wow-Wow. Forty, did I say? Oooh, just a little past, a little close to a lot. Old rockers never die, they just keep rocking on. I never saw The Who; Moon was dead before I was born. But I remember, barely old enough to stand, rocking in my mother's arms while thousands screamed and clapped and danced in their seats. *Start me up...if you start me up. I'll never stop...*763 Strings did a rendition for elevator and dentist's office, I remember that, too. And that wasn't the worst of it.

They hung on the memories, pulling more from me, turning me inside out. Are *you experienced?* On a record of my father's because he'd died too, before my parents even met, and nobody else ever dared ask that question. *Are you experienced?...Well, I am.*

(Well, *I* am.)

Five against one and I couldn't push them away. Only, can you call it rape when you know you're going to like it? Well, if I couldn't get away, then I'd give them the ride of their lives. *Jerkin' Crocus didn't kill me but she sure came near....*

The big boy faded in first, big and wild and too much badass to him. I reached out, held him tight, showing him. The beat from the night in the rain, I gave it to him, fed it to his heart and made him live it. Then came the lady, putting down the bass theme. She jittered, but mostly in the right places.

Now the Krait, and he was slithering around the sound, in and out. Never mind the tattooed cheeks, he wasn't just flash for the fools. He knew; you wouldn't have thought it, but he knew.

Featherweight and the silent type, melody and first harmony. Bad. Featherweight was a disaster, didn't know where to go or what to do when he got there, but he was pitching ahead like the S.S. *Suicide*.

Christ. If they had to rape me, couldn't they have provided someone upright? The other four kept on, refusing to lose it, and I would have to make the best of it for all of us. Derivative, unoriginal—Featherweight did not rock. It was a crime, but all I could do was take them and shake them. Rock gods in the hands of an angry sinner.

They were never better. Small change getting a glimpse of what it was like to be big bucks. Hadn't been for Featherweight, they might have gotten all the way there. More groups now than ever there was, all of them sure that if they just got the right sinner with them, they'd rock the moon down out of the sky.

We maybe vibrated it a little before we were done. Poor old Featherweight.

I gave them better than they deserved, and they knew that too. So when I begged out, they showed me respect at last and went. Their techies were gentle with me, taking the plugs from my head, my poor old throbbing abused brokenhearted sinning head, and covered up the sockets. I had to sleep and they let me. I hear the man say, "That's a take, righteously. We'll rush it into distribution. Where in *hell* did you find that sinner?"

"Synthesizer," I muttered, already asleep. "The actual word, my boy, is synthesizer."

Crazy old dreams, I was back with Man-O-War in the big CA, leaving him again, and it was mostly as it happened, but you know dreams. His living room was half outdoors, half indoors, the walls all busted out. You know dreams; I didn't think it was strange.

Man-O-War was mostly undressed, like he'd forgotten to finish. Oh, that *never* happened. Man-O-War forget a sequin or a bead? He loved to act it out, just like the Krait.

"No more," I was saying, and he was saying, "But you don't know anything else, you shitting?" Nobody in the big CA kids, they all shit; loose juice.

"Your contract goes another two and I get the option, I always get the option. And you love it, Gina, you know that, you're no good without it."

And then it was flashback time and I was in the pod with all my sockets plugged, rocking Man-O-War through the wires, giving him the meat and bone that made him Man-O-War and the machines picking it up, sound and vision, so all the tube babies all around the world could play it on their screens whenever they wanted. Forget the road, forget the shows, too much trouble, and it wasn't like the tapes, not as exciting, even with the biggest FX, lasers, spaceships, explosions, no good. And the tapes weren't as good as the stuff in the head, rock 'n' roll visions straight from the brain. No hours of setup and hours more doctoring in the lab. But you had to get everyone in the group dreaming the same way. You needed a synthesis, and for that you got a synthesizer, not the old kind, the musical instrument, but something—somebody—to channel your group through, to bump up their tube-fed little souls, to rock them and roll them the way they couldn't do themselves. And anyone could be a rock 'n' roll hero then. Anyone!

In the end, they didn't have to play instruments unless they really wanted to, and why bother? Let the synthesizer take their imaginings and boost them up to Mount Olympus.

Synthesizer. Synner. Sinner.

Not just anyone can do that, sin for rock 'n' roll. I can.

But it's not the same as jumping all night to some bar band nobody knows yet...Man-O-War and his blown-out living room came back, and he said, "You rocked the walls right out of my house. I'll never let you go."

And I said, "I'm gone."

Then I was out, going fast at first because I thought he'd be hot behind me. But I must have lost him and then somebody grabbed my ankle.

Featherweight had a tray, he was Mr. Nursie-Angel-of-Mercy. Nudged the foot of the bed with his knee, and it sat me up slow. She rises from the grave, you can't keep a good sinner down.

"Here." He set the tray over my lap, pulled up a chair. Some kind of thick soup in a bowl he'd given me, with veg wafers to break up and put in. "Thought you'd want something soft and easy." He put his left foot up on his right leg and had a good look at it. "I *never* been rocked like that before."

"You don't have it, no matter who rocks you ever in this world. Cut and run, go into management. The *big* Big Money's in management."

He snacked on his thumbnail. "Can you always tell?"

"If the Stones came back tomorrow, you couldn't even tap your toes."

"What if you took my place?"

"I'm a sinner, not a clown. You can't sin and do the dance. It's been tried."

"*You* could do it. If anyone could."

"No."

His stringy cornsilk fell over his face and he tossed it back. "Eat your soup. They want to go again shortly."

"No." I touched my lower lip, thickened to sausage size. "I won't sin for Man-O-War and I won't sin for you. You want to pop me one again, go to. Shake a socket loose, give me aphasia."

So he left and came back with a whole bunch of them, techies and do-kids, and they poured the soup down my throat and gave me a poke and carried me out to the pod so I could make Misbegotten this year's firestorm.

I knew as soon as the first tape got out, Man-O-War would pick up the scent. They were already starting the machine to get me away from him. And they kept me good in the room—where their old sinner had done penance, the lady told me. Their sinner came to see me, too. I thought, poison dripping from his fangs, death threats. But he was just a guy about my age with a lot of hair to hide his sockets (I never bothered, didn't care if they showed). Just came to pay his respects, how'd I ever learn to rock the way I did?

Fool.

They kept me good in the room. Drunks when I wanted them and a poke to get sober again, a poke for vitamins, a poke to lose the bad dreams. Poke, poke, pig in a poke. I had tracks like the old B&O, and they didn't even know what I meant by that. They lost Featherweight, got themselves someone a little more righteous, someone who could go with it and work out, sixteen-year-old snip girl with a face like a praying mantis. But she rocked and they rocked and we all rocked until Man-O-War came to take me home.

Strutted into my room in full plumage with his hair all fanned out (hiding the sockets) and said, "Did you want to press charges, Gina darling?"

Well, they fought it out over my bed. When Misbegotten said I was theirs now, Man-O-War smiled and said, "Yeah, and I bought *you*. You're *all mine* now, you *and* your sinner. My sinner." That was truth. Man-O-War had his conglomerate start to buy Misbegotten right after the first tape came out.

Deal all done by the time we'd finished the third one, and they never knew. Conglomerates buy and sell all the time. Everybody was in trouble but Man-O-War. And me, he said. He made them all leave and sat down on my bed to re-lay claim to me.

"Gina." Ever see honey poured over the edge of a sawtooth blade? Ever hear it? He couldn't sing without hurting someone bad and he couldn't dance, but inside, he rocked. If I rocked him.

"I don't want to be a sinner, not for you or anyone."

"It'll all look different when I get you back to Cee-Ay."

"I want to go to a cheesy bar and boogie my brains till they leak out the sockets."

"No more, darling. That was why you came here, wasn't it? But all the bars are gone and all the bands. Last call was years ago; it's all up here now. All up here." He tapped his temple. "You're an old lady, no matter how much I spend keeping your bod young. And don't I give you everything? And didn't you say I had it?"

"It's not the same. It wasn't meant to be put on a tube for people to *watch*."

"But it's not as though rock 'n' roll is dead, lover."

"You're killing it."

"Not me. You're trying to bury it alive. But I'll keep you going for a long, long time."

"I'll get away again. You'll either rock 'n' roll on your own or give it up, but you won't be taking it out of me any more. This ain't my way, it ain't my time. Like the man said, 'I don't love today.'"

Man-O-War grinned. "And like the other man said, 'Rock 'n' roll never forgets.'"

He called in his do-kids and took me home.

Feel the Zaz
James Patrick Kelly

James Patrick Kelly is one of just two writers to have work included in this book on the fiction and nonfiction sides of the coin. Kelly, an award-winning novelist and short story writer, won the Nebula Award for his novella *Burn*, and the Hugo Award twice for his famous novelettes "Think Like a Dinosaur" and "Ten to the Sixteenth to One." "Feel the Zaz" first appeared in the June 2000 issue of *Asimov's Science Fiction* magazine and was nominated for several of the field's major awards. The story speculates about an immersive, interactive, multiuser future where the stars come out to play, and two women—or one—find their own kind of success in the midst of a poignant struggle.

> *Everyone wants to be Cary Grant. I want to be Cary Grant.*
> —Cary Grant

click

"Accepting for Vanity Mode is Dylan McDonough, artistic director of *Starscape*."

Dylan was stunned. For a few ticks he couldn't move, couldn't hear, or even see the audience which filled the virtual Colosseum. It had happened just as Vanity had planned. Then Bug pounded him on the back. "Go on. Go get it!" He could see that Letty was crying.

Dylan brought his avatar off the stone bench into sheets of cold applause. The designers had re-created the Colosseum in all its marble and gilt glory for this year's Websters. Fifty thousand avatars watched in disappointment as Dylan played his avatar through the virtual crowd to pick up Vanity's award. He knew the zaz was plummeting. Everyone had been hoping to see what Vanity Mode looked like, or at least how she would present when she wasn't doubling. Nobody cared what Dylan McDonough looked like. The Academy crowd would be clicking out by the dozens, the general audience by the millions. Of course, it would have been impossible for most people to tell the difference. The avatars in the audience were still clapping; their smiling faces beamed up at him as he passed. But the Vnet was where Dylan made his living. He could sense unattended avatars going flat, losing their edges.

He accepted the Webster from Lillian Citrus, who had her avatar presenting with a tree viper curled into her décolletage. "Wow," he said. The word came out as a croak. Back at the studio, he bumped his voice fx from delight to elation, although it was grief that caught in his throat. He held the little golden monitor at arm's length, saw the reflection of his face twist across its polished surface. This was all that she had ever wanted, and she wasn't here to enjoy it. "On behalf of Vanity Mode and *Starscape*," he said, "I'd like to thank the Academy for this award." He set the Webster for Best Double of 2038 on the podium. "I have a brief statement to read." His avatar took out a piece of paper. "When we're done here this evening, I would ask that you click to *Starscape*, where we will launch a biography sim to coincide with this great honor which you have bestowed on us. We have tried to tell Vanity Mode's story on it. I regret to inform you that it will mark her final appearance on our site."

The unattended avatars in the audience seemed puzzled at this, but nothing more. Only those who were live with their users registered shock. Dylan's avatar unfolded the virtual paper slowly, to give people time to click in. The paper was blank, but he, Letty, and Bug had spent weeks scripting the speech, now open on the desktop from which he controlled his avatar. While he waited, Dylan wondered if what he was feeling was a surge in the zaz. Two years ago, that would have worried him. Back then, he was quite certain that zaz was nothing but click count divided by attention quotient. It was something you measured afterward, not what you felt in the moment, like laughter or applause.

"Vanity Mode," he read, "was a true star, as eternal as any of those she brought back to life on *Starscape*."

Vanity had said once that great zaz was like being kissed by an entire country. He remembered thinking she was crazy.

click

The day he met Vanity Mode, Dylan had taken Roman Barone to lunch. The pitch had not gone well. Barone let Dylan buy him a plate of *penne all'arrabbiata* and a glass of Chianti and listened politely while Dylan described everything he was doing to turn *Starscape* around. *Roman's Nose* was one of the most influential guides on the net—a million clickthroughs a day. If *Nose* recommended *Starscape*, they would have to kick Barone back half a percent of their gross and it would be worth every nickel. Barone had delivered over eight million clicks to Dylan McDonough's last winner, *Duck Brings The Lunch*. But that had been six years ago—an eternity.

"Sure, your zaz isn't that bad for a boomer site," he said, "but the numbers are so skewed. What did you say you're getting from the under thirties?"

"They'll come, if only to see what their grandparents are talking about. And once they click in, we've got them. Because people love having Elvis as their best friend. It's the names, Roman. Say them and you can hear the magic. Marilyn, Bogie, Groucho, Ali, John Lennon, Michael Jordan, Fats Waller, JFK...."

"Hey, I'm almost fifty and *I* barely remember these people. And my kids don't give a damn about Michael Jordan. If they know him at all, it's as that fat old jack who owns Nike. Frankly, I was shocked when I'd heard you'd bought a dusty little site like *Starscape*. What were you thinking?"

"It was all I could afford after the divorce."

"I'm sorry to hear that." Barone pushed some cold *penne* across his plate and then set his fork down. "But that doesn't change the demographics, Dylan: boomers aren't exactly a growth segment of the population. Besides, all the research says your tech makes them uncomfortable. You think millions of retirees are going to start using airflexes? Hell, no. The boomers don't get virtuality. Some of them still don't get *computers*. If they want dead stars, they go to dead media."

"But Roman...."

"Look at the time." Barone stood. "And I've got a two o'clock meeting. Sounds as if you've been working hard, Dylan."

"We all have. It's because we believe in what we're doing, Roman."

"Always a plus." His expression was smooth as glass. "Appreciate the lunch." They shook hands.

Dylan considered debasing himself completely, begging for the link, but decided against it. "I know our zaz is going to spike any day now," he said. "How about if I message you then?"

"Sure." Barone's snort was no doubt meant as a laugh. "People message me all the time."

click

Dylan had been trying to relaunch *Starscape* on the cheap; so far it was just him and Bug and Letty. They had four rooms of flop space in the partly abandoned Meadowbrook Office Park. Building Number Two was a mirror-glass dinosaur from the late 1970s. Many of the seals in the window wall had failed, so their view of the interstate was distorted by the little fog banks that had been trapped for decades between panes of glass. The HVAC was old and too expensive to run, so the landlord usually didn't. Letty hung sheets over the windows in the summer and ran a couple of monitor heaters in the winter. But Building Number Two had electricity and working toilets and an ultrawide connection to the net. If *Starscape* clicked big, nobody would care whether the carpet in Dylan's office was raveling.

click

"Honeys," Dylan called as he opened the door. "I'm home." He was determined not to let them see how worried he was.

There was no answer. He followed the screech of twisting steel and the crash of a concrete avalanche to the theater. On the dome, Bug and Letty were running a Manhattan sim that he had never seen before. He could see Letty's long hands dance in front of her as she used the airflex to play her avatar, an eighty-foot-tall Barbara Walters, through the ruin she had just made of Rockefeller Center. Dylan couldn't immediately pick out Bug's avatar, but then he didn't know what to look for.

"Bug, what is this?" He got no answer. "Letty?"

"It's Bug's new demo," Letty said, "and I already told him you wouldn't like it." She peeled back part of the roof of the Radio City Music Hall. "So where would you be if you were Cary Grant?"

"I don't know," said Dylan. "Empire State Building?"

"Nah." She dropped the roof section onto 50th Street. "Been there."

He watched, bemused, as Letty sent Barbara Walters on an uptown rampage. "Um, Bug?" he said. "I'm not sure I want users playing the stars. And why is she stomping taxis?"

"Bug isn't talking today," said Letty. "He's having a mood."

"I am not!" snapped Bug. "We've got Stalin, Darth Vader, and Mick Jagger riding around town." Bug was a short, volatile, twenty-eight-year-old, who favored dark clothes and black humor. He slouched, scowling at the dome with arms folded. "Free ten minutes in the sim if you squash one of them."

"This is a party site," said Dylan, "not *Dirty Work IV*. It's not supposed to be about racking up a high score." He had plucked Bug from combat sim hell and was still trying to curb his twitch response.

"Give it a chance, Dylan. We never show any bodies and it bumps the attention quotient two point six. Hey, it's satire."

"Satire is what closes Saturday night." Dylan tried to hide his annoyance. The demo was obviously a waste of their time. The idea was give users the illusion of meeting the old celebrities, not to wear them like silly costumes. He wished Bug would stick to programming; content had never been his strength. But clearly Bug *was* having a mood, which meant that Dylan would have to pretend to consider his demo. "And Stalin is too dusty. You want someone people will know."

"You're in Lincoln Center," said Letty. She was a slender woman with sparkled hair and skin the color of milk. She moved with a dancer's precision; Barbara Walters clumped up Broadway like a grain elevator with legs.

"No! It's so obvious, Letty." Bug sighed. "I could paste in Lee Harvey Oswald," he said to Dylan.

"I was thinking more O. J. Simpson. So are you in this sim, Bug, or just peeping?"

"I'm Cary Grant and I'm hiding," Bug said. "Go seek is the point."

"*You're* Cary Grant?" said Dylan.

Bug had yet to look away from the dome. "We've got to get some action going, Letty. Try the Upper West Side."

"Cary Grant, Cary Grant," muttered Letty. "This is way too obscure, Bug. I don't know anything about Cary *blinking* Grant."

"He was in a bunch of Hitchcocks," said Dylan. "If finding Bug is the point, what's the payoff?"

"Oh, just the sex default," said Bug. "If she figures out my hiding place, the avatars screw." He leaned toward her. "Although I'm kind of losing interest."

"We're playing it totally softcore," said Letty. "Something like a kiss, maybe a bare shoulder, then cut to shadows on the wall." She spun Barbara Walters across Broadway to mash a taxi into yellow roadkill.

"Yeah, violence and sex, only very tasteful." Bug yawned. "Do me a favor, would you, and head uptown. Way-*way*-uptown."

Dylan put a hand on Bug's shoulder, trying to divert him from the sim. "When did you find the time to write a Barbara Walters AI?"

"I didn't." Bug glanced at him briefly and then focussed again on the dome. "She's just an image and bunch of movement routines lifted from fossil video." Bug was not good at eye contact. "That's the beauty of letting the users play the stars. No biography scan, no AI. So we cut programming costs and can start adding lots more celebrities to the cast."

Dylan shook his head. "Who's going to pay to watch Joe Modem pretend he's Cary Grant?"

"I told you he wouldn't like it," said Letty.

"Joe Modem will pay to pretend he's Cary Grant." Bug hunched his shoulders as if to ward off a blow. "And thousands of other Joes and Janes will pay. Letty, tell him how much fun we're having."

"It may be fun," said Dylan carefully, "but is it *Starscape*? Your sim is like producing a play and then picking the actors out of the audience."

"Excuse me, gentlemen," said Letty, "but would you mind taking this somewhere else? I'm in the middle of a session here and I'm losing major attention quotient."

"I told you when you bought this blinking site that the AI engine was no damn good." Bug's voice was icy. "It's a waste of money to write dodgy code for every celebrity on the site—money that we don't have. But if we let the users…"

Their deskbot interrupted. "Excuse me, pal, but we're going to have to ice this party for a while." It spoke in Humphrey Bogart's clipped voice.

"What is it, Bogie?" said Dylan.

"Could be nothing but a hill of beans. See, maybe I'm just software, but you hired me to do a job and I can't do it with one hand tied behind my back, now can I? Seems we got a visitor at the back door, a dame. Flesh and blood. Only I don't know why she's here and that bothers me. Makes me wonder if we've got some kind of security problem here. So who's been holding out?"

click

Dylan felt a momentary crinkle of panic. *Starscape* had been bleeding money over the past month. He'd spread $373,000 over five different cards, but had been careful not to overload any of them. The utilities and hardware payments were paid through next week. If Meadowbrook wanted money, they'd just reprogram the locks. Otherwise, no one knew *Starscape*'s bricks-and-mortar address.

"Anyone order a pizza?" Bug's grin was forced. They all knew how close to the edge *Starscape* was.

"ID her," said Dylan.

"You want a flat ID or deep?" said the deskbot.

"Flat."

"Flat will cost you twenty bucks."

"Authorized," he said.

click

"'Kay, she's got a name: Elizabeth Lee Corazon. And she's got a driver's license which gives us a date of birth of 4-11-02, which makes her thirty-four. Her Social Security number is 049-38-3829, eyes brown, height five-seven, weight a hundred thirty eight pounds. She lives at 43A Spring Street, Bedford...."

"Who does she work for?" asked Dylan.

"Appears she's out of work," said the deskbot. "Fact is, she's seventeen months into unemployment. Medical disability."

"What's the matter with her?"

"Med records are deep and deep will cost you, my friend."

"Well, at least she isn't here to turn out the lights," said Bug. "But why did she come to the back door?"

"Nobody is turning off anything, okay?" Dylan glared at them. "Got that?"

"Easy, boss," said Letty. "Bug's having the mood today. You can have yours tomorrow."

"Go find out what she wants while we finish here." Bug waved him away. "Maybe she's selling girl scout cookies."

"I'll have some trefoils," said Letty absently, as she rejoined the sack of Manhattan, already in progress.

click

As soon as Dylan saw their visitor through the wire mesh window of the back door, he thought he understood everything important about her. She was a stocky woman with broad, flattened features. Her brown hair did not quite cover the ears, which were big as fists. She stared back at him unabashedly, her eyes narrow and slanted, eyelids puffy. Her face seemed oddly childlike. If he had not known she was thirty-four, he might have guessed she was a teenager. She wore black jeans and a baggy adshirt on which a cartoon dolphin kept leaping out of a pitcher of Budweiser. She gave him a slow smile and mouthed the words *Open up*. He had never known anyone with Down syndrome—there weren't many left—but he believed he could handle her.

"I'm a double," she said as the door swung away. "And if you're *Starscape*, you need me."

"What?" Dylan was taken aback by her voice. It was as sultry as a silk pillowcase. "I'm afraid there's been a misunderstanding."

"This is *Starscape*, right? The site with all the oldie celebrities? *Live the glamour*?"

"I'm not sure I know what you're talking about, Ms...?"

"Are you the one who writes those tags?" She stepped through the door and surveyed the loading dock from the entryway, head bobbing with excitement. "*Touch the legend*. Hey, we're just clicking for fun, mister, not buying a new Rolex." She moved awkwardly, like someone who would knock things over.

Dylan felt his cheeks start to burn. First the bungled lunch with Barone, then Bug's slugnut demo, and now this crazy woman. "There's no *Starscape* here, this is...ah...Grant Associates. We do market analysis for non-profits. I'm afraid you've got the wrong address, Ms...."

"Mode. My name is Vanity Mode."

"Mode?" He blocked her from coming any farther into the building.

"What's the matter, am I going too fast for you?" She put her hands together as if clapping, but didn't make any noise. "Maybe if I speak to your boss?"

"But I am...." He realized then that she must have had one of those new CAT implants where they scooped out a chunk of cerebellum and replaced it with a computer grown from embryonic stem cells. The IQ improvement rate had just recently nudged over fifty percent. "This is my company."

"Then that would make you Dylan McDonough," she said and then let herself fall against him. "Oh, sorry." Her breasts nudged his chest and her legs tangled with his. He gave way with a mutter of astonishment, uncertain whether the contact was calculated or merely clumsy.

"Sorry," she said again, catching herself up and then escaping past him into the empty loading dock. "So Dylan, the idea of *Starscape* is delicious but the site is cold oatmeal. Your celebrities talk like computers in rubber suits. Take your Judy Garland—not half bipolar enough. You want a Jim Carrey so needy he'd swallow a goldfish for a laugh. Your problem is that nobody's wounded."

Dylan had been about to ask this creature how she had gotten his name but changed his mind. "And you do wounded? I mean, when you're doubling."

She extended her arms and bowed. "They don't come much more wounded than me."

click

Dylan knew there was no way he could afford to replace all *Starscape's* celebrity AIs with human doubles. Still, it hadn't occurred to him that the tags might be overblown. "Where would you hide if you were Cary Grant?" he said.

"Ah-ha!" she said, and nodded at least three too many times. "The old trick question trick." Then she went up on tiptoes beside the dumpster and peered in.

"No, not here. Say you were in New York City." When Dylan looked at her, the flat, empty face, the way she slouched, how she almost clapped her hands when she laughed at her own wisecracks, he was lulled into believing she was slow, even if she did have a Computer Aided Thinking implant.

"Doesn't matter where." She thought it over; he could see the tip of her tongue between her lips. "Cary Grant doesn't hide. He might duck into the next room or make a quick getaway but he knows he can't hide because he's Cary Grant. The camera will always find him."

"Really?" He was impressed despite himself. "And how would you know that?"

"Because I was born in the wrong century, Dylan, not to mention in the wrong body." Her head bobbed. "I should've been my grandmother. She was a special assistant to Vincente Minnelli when he worked at MGM. She once ate Louis B. Mayer's French toast by accident."

"There are more than just movie stars at *Starscape*."

"Oh, so now this is *Starscape*." She reached into the dumpster to snag an empty bag of Curry Snaps. "I can see why you'd want to keep this dump a secret." She folded it in quarters and stuffed it into the pocket of her jeans. "Well, Dylan, I've got Michael Jordan's rookie card and a home run ball that Ted Williams plunked into the bleachers at Fenway and a blue campaign button that says, 'I want Roosevelt again,' and Norman Mailer's ego pickled in alcohol—a joke, that's a joke." She clapped gleefully for herself. "I think the Hot Five was Louis Armstrong's best band and that *Rubber Soul* was the

Beatles' best album, so let's start over, shall we?" She pirouetted across the loading dock to him like Julie Andrews in *The Sound of Music*, except that she stumbled twice. She offered her hand. Her fingers were short and thick; the nails worried to the quick. "I'm Vanity Mode and you're Dylan McDonough and—ta-*da*—this is our historic first meeting, so enjoy it."

click

Reluctantly, he shook her hand. Her skin was blood hot; he wondered if she were sick.

"Here's the script the way I read it," she said. "First you take me on the tour, then we draw up a contract and then I make you famous."

He let her hand drop. "Ms. Mode, I'm afraid you just don't understand."

"What do you mean, I don't understand?" Her face flushed. "Don't think that just because I look like me that I'm *s-s-stu*pid." The voice was no longer a purr; it was as if her tongue had swollen until it was too big to get words around. "I *understand,* mister. Don't-don't-don't you think I'm *stupid.*" He realized that her steamy manner of speaking was a kind of mask, and that the mask had just slipped.

"It's just that I'm very busy."

"Right," she said, "so busy that mister answers the backy door his *own*self?"

"Are you all right?"

She closed her eyes; her lips moved but she made no sound. He thought she might be counting to ten or maybe saying a prayer. When she opened them, she smiled and was Vanity Mode again.

"Look Dylan," she said, "the zaz for *Starscape* is what? Twenty-three? Twenty-five? You should be doing eighty."

"How do you know that?" He squelched his alarm. Yesterday's zaz had been twenty-two-point-eight, down three-tenths from Wednesday's. He wondered if Bug or Letty might be selling him out. "Not that those numbers are right, Ms. Mode," he said, "but our zaz is proprietary information."

"Oh, I don't know it exactly." She smoothed her hands against the tee shirt. "I just...I *feel* it."

"You feel it?" He couldn't believe he was still talking to her. "And do you feel the times tables too? The stock market?"

She drew herself up. "I'm not like other people, in case you haven't noticed."

"This has gone far enough, Ms. Mode..."

"Vanity."

"Vanity, because even if I wanted to hire you, I can't afford to pay a double."

"You can't afford not to."

"We have a budget, a very tight budget." Dylan thought of the hundred dollar bill he had dropped on the table at lunch. "There's no money in it for doubling."

"But you're Dylan McDonough. You must have made a package at *Duck*. And what about *Stinger*?" Her voice slipped again. "Mister don't tell right. What ha-ha-happened to you?"

It was a question that had nagged at Dylan for the last two years but he was suddenly angry at this Down syndrome lunatic for asking it. "What happened to me is none of your blinking business."

"Sorry, mister."

"No, I'm sorry to be such a disappointment to *you*, Vanity. I'll try to do better in the future." He had made some bad guesses, had some bad luck and now he didn't know exactly what he was doing anymore. Instead of making his life happen, he often found himself watching as life happened to him—like this little fiasco.

"Mister, I-I-I...."

Dylan backed to the loading dock door. "Just so you know, *Duck Brings the Lunch* was pretty much over by '31. And I only owned two percent of *Stinger*. The fact is, if I could afford a double, I wouldn't be working out of this dump, as you so aptly put it." He opened the door. "So anyway, it's been nice meeting you."

This time she shut her eyes so tight that he could see her lids twitch. Her head lolled back. Dylan knew he ought to push her out of the building while she was helpless, but he couldn't bring himself to it. He realized he was in the presence of two different people. The thick, awkward, retarded woman before him was Elizabeth Lee Corazon, who looked as if she were about to fall apart. Except that Vanity Mode was trying to hold her together with steely ambition and wisecracks and a voice like liquid sex.

click

"Okay," she said, "okay, okay, okay." She shivered and then smiled at him as if nothing had happened. "Okay, we go with a rewrite. More drama when the heroine starts from nothing. So: I don't need to be paid, Dylan, not yet anyway.

You'll know when it's time." She waved airily at the open door. "Why don't you shut that? You're letting the flies in."

He didn't move. "I can call the police if you want."

"Good idea. Call the cops, the fire department, the Marines, and the starship *Enterprise*. How long will it take to pry me out of here, poor little retard that I am? A couple of hours? Give me half an hour. I'll double anyone you're running on *Starscape*. A cold reading. If you're not interested, Mr. McDonough, I'll walk out of here and you can get back to whatever it is you're so busy not doing."

Dylan hadn't known just how desperate the lunch with Barone had left him; he was actually thinking of giving Vanity Mode a chance. But it was not only desperation that was making him reconsider. Dylan was ashamed of letting her make him angry and then snapping at her. He wasn't Bug; it wasn't his style to show feelings.

"How long have you had the CAT implant?" he said.

"Eighteen months, but what's that got to do with anything?"

"I'm just wondering if they've worked all the kinks out of it. Or did Elizabeth Ann Corazon always have the manners of a police siren?"

She became very still—no twitching, no head bobbing. "You leave her out of this."

Dylan shook his head. "Lady, you're her, okay? We IDed you at the door. Call yourself whatever you want, but keep the multiple personalities to yourself."

Vanity flicked her fingers dismissively. "She's just along for the ride."

The coldness of the gesture decided him. "You know," he said, "at least one of us is crazy." He leaned against the door and it shut.

"At least." Seeing that she had won, Vanity Mode giggled and clapped.

click

"Grant's Tomb!" Letty's shriek carried from the theater, through the computer room all the way to the loading dock. "You're in Grant's *blinking* Tomb?" The floor reverberated with the muffled thud of granite blocks being hurled onto Riverside Drive. If Bug answered her, Dylan could not hear him.

"Who's that?" said Vanity.

"Our engineer, Letty." He rubbed the back of his neck. "I don't know why I'm doing this."

"To get rid of me, remember?"

"Half an hour." He tapped his datacuff to start the timer. "The chime is your exit cue."

"You know what they say. Every exit is an entrance someplace else."

"They say a lot of things." He brushed past her. "Come on then." He didn't look back, although he could hear her following him over the hum of the computer room. He paused at the door to the theater to watch Letty and Bug play the end of the new sim.

"I told you, I get the joke already." Letty gave Bug a friendly poke in the shoulder. "Now how do I lose it?"

On the screens, Cary Grant and a resized Barbara Walters were leaning against the rail of the *Titanic*. They gazed back at the Manhattan skyline silhouetted in a golden twilight. Barbara Walters nuzzled Cary Grant's shoulder.

"I've always been scared of women," said Cary Grant, "but I got over it."

Vanity came up behind Dylan but did not show herself to Letty and Bug. "It's all wrong," she whispered. "They open their mouths and spoil the illusion. That's why you need a double to play your stars. Someone who knows what she's doing."

"We have software for that," said Dylan.

"I'm better than software."

Cary Grant picked a Lucky from a cigarette case and let it dangle from his lips. He held the case out to Barbara Walters but she shook her head. The silver lighter lit on the first snap. Wisps of blue smoke caressed the famous cleft chin. There was a glow on Barbara Walters's face which was not entirely a lighting fx.

"Another mistake," said Vanity. "He doesn't offer her the cigarette. People used to say that Grant played hard to get, but that wasn't it. He *was* hard to get. Which is why everyone wanted him."

The lights in the theater came up. "How do you like the smoking porn, Dylan?" called Bug.

"Hot," said Dylan.

"And I finally nailed Jagger on Broadway and 96th," said Letty. "Is that your Girl Scout?"

click

"Letty, Bug," said Dylan, "this is..."

"Ta-*da!*" Vanity swept through the doorway and did two perfect pirouettes with arms outstretched. "Lettys and Gentlebugs, I give you the one, the only... *Vanity Mode!*" She clapped vigorously for herself, gave a curtain-call bow and, beaming, held up both hands as if to quiet applause. "Thank you, thanks, thanks so much, no, you're too kind."

They stared at her as if she had three heads.

"I know what you're all thinking," she said, "but seeing is definitely not believing."

"It's okay," said Dylan. "At least, I think it's okay. Vanity is..."

She rushed to place her forefinger to his lips. "No, no, don't be telling on me, Dylan. Letty, what are we using to control avatars?"

Letty shot Dylan an inquiring glance. He nodded. "Series 40 Airflex." She said, and tapped the CPU on her belt. "We've also got a couple of Sony discreets. And you can always run them off the console—but what's this about, Dylan?"

"The console would be best," said Vanity. "Bug, suppose I wanted to modify one of your characters on the fly, play her like an avatar."

"She's carrying a concealed weapon, is that it?" Bug said. "We're all hostages?"

"I've got this under control, Bug. Tell her."

Bug did not seem convinced. "Well, the easiest way is to go in through the doubling interrupt."

"So you *can* double on *Starscape.*"

"We can," said Bug, "but we don't. Not yet, anyway. But the original programmers thought the code would be more robust if they included doubling in the initial design rather than kludge it later."

"Vanity doubles," said Dylan. "She's going to give us a brief demonstration of what we're missing."

Vanity twisted his wrist toward her and checked the datacuff. "About twenty-three minutes brief. Hey, who do you have to screw to get some help around here?"

"Nobody but yourself." Bug turned his back to her and got busy doing nothing at the rack of unused airflexes.

"Bug, *enough*," said Dylan. "Letty, would you take her to the workshop, get her up to speed on the console."

"In twenty minutes?" Letty said. "I've spent two months massaging the console, there are at least a hundred macros...."

"That's okay, Letty." She winked at Dylan. "I'm a quick study."

Bug waited until they left before he exploded. "Jesus *blinking* Christ, Dylan."

"I know, pal—a piece of work. And she's got to have a pretty extreme CAT implant. You should've heard her out on the loading dock."

"Sure they didn't put it in backwards? Who the hell is she?"

"Bug, we're going to find out." Dylan pulled an airflex from the rack. "I should probably just bounce her out of here but I've got this hunch." He snugged the headband to his temple. "I feel like what *Starscape* needs just now is to get run over by a random variable." He bent over and fastened the ankle and wrist straps. "Maybe she's it."

Bug studied him. "It didn't happen with Barone, did it?"

"I don't think so." Dylan fitted the nose clips into his nostrils. "No."

"We're screwed, aren't we?"

He plugged the peripherals into his CPU and shrugged. "Let's just say that we could use a fairy godmother."

click

"I don't believe her." Letty rejoined them in the theater. "She's running the console like she built it herself."

"She's a quick study," said Bug sarcastically. "CAT power." He tapped a finger to his temple, then twirled it.

"Nobody is that fast." The theater dome began to darken and Letty jammed her peripherals into the CPU of her airflex. "Even with a CAT implant," she muttered.

"What's your pleasure?" Vanity's disembodied voice came at them from every direction. "Anybody, in any sim you've got."

"Bug?" said Dylan.

"I'm supposed to care?"

"Let her choose," called Letty.

"Is that all right with you, Dylan?" Vanity asked.

"Sure," Dylan said. "Whatever takes eighteen minutes."

click

On the dome the three of them were seated in the dining car at a table set for four. The silver gleamed on the white linen tablecloth. Letty and Dylan sat facing Bug and an empty chair. The walls were teak and mahogany inlaid with marquetry; the lights were garlands of bronze-work oak leaves. Out of the windows on their side of the car, Dylan caught a glimpse of the Danube as the train raced through the twilight toward the Czechoslovak border. The sommelier, dressed in a tight, black jacket and knickers with white stockings, filled their glasses with Veuve Clicquot. Dylan brought the glass to his mouth to get the benefit of the olfactors. He watched bubbles drift lazily through the champagne and pop like dreams. They tickled his nose. The wheels of the Orient Express sang along the rails.

"Kind of a slow starter." Bug squirmed in his chair. "Needs more action!" he called after the sommelier.

Katherine Hepburn hurried out of the drawing room. Dylan was surprised that Vanity had chosen to double the older Hepburn; she looked to be in her sixties. Her wild gray hair had been tamed into a bun. The face was drawn, which made her cheekbones even more astonishing; the tremor was scarcely noticeable.

"Thank goodness I've found you," said Katherine Hepburn. "Your friend, Bug—is it Bug? He was on the floor. I think he may be, he may be dead."

"I'm not dead." Bug raised his forefinger wearily. "I'm right here."

She settled beside him, cocked her head to one side and then another. "Why, so you are." She touched his arm. "Nevertheless, there's a body in the smoking room. In the next car, Mr. Bug, you must go and see for yourself."

Letty shook open her napkin and brought it to her mouth so that Bug wouldn't see her laughing.

"It's Bug," he grumbled, pushing back from the table. "Just plain Bug." The train swayed as he stood and he caught himself on the back of Katherine Hepburn's chair. "What's so funny?"

"Oh, do hurry," said Katherine Hepburn. "Bug."

After he was gone, she looked from Dylan to Letty and back again. "What?"

Dylan chuckled. "Nothing."

"Did I say something wrong?"

"No," said Letty. "It's just that you got to him—and in record time too."

"Is that good or bad?" Katherine Hepburn gave them a nervous little smile. She was wearing a heather gray pants suit and a black turtleneck. She slipped a hand into the pocket of the double-breasted jacket and pulled out a man's gold watch. "At least an hour until we arrive in Bratislava. Do you think we should alert the conductor about what's happened?"

Bug looked bemused as he reentered the dining car. Both of him did. Behind the Bug dressed in black plytex followed another Bug in a white tuxedo, his bow tie askew and hair mussed.

"So it was you," said Katharine Hepburn. "I knew it was. I'm glad you're all right."

"Bug?" Letty goggled at the resplendent Bug Two. "Bug, you look like a million bucks."

Bug One glared at her.

"Well, I feel like eight cents," said Bug Two. He touched the back of his head gingerly. "Somebody hit me when I wasn't looking." He stopped in front of Katharine Hepburn. "That wouldn't have been you, would it?"

She looked up at him in perfect astonishment. "Why I assure you, Bug, that I did no such thing."

"What are you trying to prove?" said Bug One. "You're supposed to be doubling stars, not us. Close him."

"Close...close who?" The corners of Katharine Hepburn's mouth turned down. "I'm not sure what you mean."

Dylan didn't think it was very fair of Bug to break verisimilitude but before he could object, Bug Two grabbed a fistful of Bug One's shirt. "Maybe what needs closing is your mouth."

"Oh, great plotting." Bug One went slack in his twin's grip. "As soon as things get boring, have a fistfight break out."

Letty shot out of her chair and wormed between them, facing Bug Two. Reluctantly, he let Bug One go. "Now, Bug, haven't you had enough excitement for one night?" She pressed up against him as she straightened his bow tie.

"I don't know," said Bug Two. "Have I?"

She laughed. The engineer sounded the horn as the train skirted a dark Austrian village.

"Do be a help," said Katharine Hepburn to Dylan, "and get another chair for Bug here."

"Don't bother," said Bug Two. "Letty, how long has it been since someone asked you to dance?"

"You can't dance on a moving train," Bug One said.

"Too long," said Letty.

"The land flattens out." Katharine Hepburn beamed at them; her teeth were so big they were scary. "The tracks are straight as an arrow."

"There's a Victrola in the drawing room." Bug Two made as if to brush his fingers through her hair, but hesitated at the last moment.

Letty leaned into his hand. "What are we waiting for?"

"Letty, no!" said Bug One, but she paid no attention. He sank onto his chair and watched as they threaded their way through the dining car. His expression was grim. In the dome, Letty walked straight to the rack, picked up a discreet, set the helmet on her head, and went through the door. On the dome, she paused to glance back at Bug before she left. It was a look that would have set fires in a monsoon.

"Wow," said Dylan.

Katharine Hepburn tucked a stray curl of hair back into her bun. "They make a nice couple, don't you think? You young people need to dance more, if you ask me. You all work too hard. There's more to life than sitting at your desks, worrying yourselves to shreds about deadlines and spreadsheets and all that. The world was made for us to enjoy—as we are made to enjoy each other. A little romance wouldn't hurt you, Bug, or you either, Dylan."

"Romance is easy," growled Bug. "Now show us hard, something with grit."

"Bug, this is a party site...." began Dylan.

click

The bus smelled of sandalwood and pot and sweat. Most of the seats had been ripped out and replaced with homemade furniture: beds and benches, a hi-fi system on a shaky table. Even though all the windows were open, it was sledgehammer hot, hot as sin, kick-the-dog hot. The bus was pulled over by the side of the highway and the hood was up. The view out of every window shimmered; saguaros put their arms up as if in surrender to the heat.

"Looks like the Magic Bus has broken down," said Dylan. "This gritty enough for you?"

Bug didn't reply. He was lying on a dirty mattress, staring up at the ceiling, which had been debauched with paint. It was as if Chagall had popped a Dali pill—bright shape and strange line melting, melting into rude oranges and reds, vulgar yellows, deranged blues—Mondrian with motion sickness.

The hood slammed and a thin, gawky man in mechanic's coveralls got on the bus. He acknowledged them with a nod. "We go about our daily lives understanding almost nothing about the world," said Stephen Hawking, in a computer synthesized voice. "The second law of thermodynamics tells us that all machines will ultimately break down, and that it makes no difference whether the machine is the universe or a 1948 International school bus." He swung into the driver's seat and turned the key in the ignition. The motor coughed and started.

"It was a loose hose," Stephen Hawking said, over the engine noise. "Thank God it is still possible to increase order locally." He leaned toward the open door and called to a shadow still baking just outside. "Are you on the bus or not?"

Janis Joplin tripped in the stepwell and sprawled onto the bus. As she fell she twisted to protect the open quart of Southern Comfort she was carrying. A few drops spilled onto her hand; she cackled and licked them up. "Man, I am *wasted.*" She was wearing a low cut red silk blouse that had sweat stains under the armpits.

"Aristotle believed in a preferred state of rest," said Stephen Hawking, "which any body would take up if it were not driven by some force or impulse."

"Far out." She grabbed the support beam, pulled herself up and held the bottle out to him. "Have some force, force to be reckoned with, man."

"No, thank you," said Stephen Hawking. "I am driving."

"How 'bout you two?" She aimed the bottle at Dylan and Bug and followed it down the aisle. Stephen Hawking crunched the bus into first gear and pulled back onto the highway.

"Not for me," said Dylan.

"Hey, I know you." Janis Joplin swayed next to him and he could smell the bitter fruit of her breath. "Or someone jus' like you. You're one of those uptight sonsabitches can never say what you're thinking. Or feeling. Feelings can't be wrong, feelings are what we're made of. Feelings are what we're composed of and exist of and live for, s'far as I'm concerned." She shook her head and her long hair danced in the swelter blowing at fifty-three miles an hour through the windows. "I think that kind of freedom is beautiful."

"Maybe you should sing." Dylan knew that some people liked watching celebrities veer out of control, so *Starscape* had a couple of sims which targeted that peculiar market niche. Humoring drunks, however, was not his idea of fun—even if they were famous. "Why don't you sing?"

"No way." She sniffed. "You think I just go ahead and sing for any jackoff who asks?" She took a hit off the bottle. "For me it's like...singing is like sex. Better than sex, sometimes. Why don't you ask me if I want to fuck?" She cackled. "I might actually say yes to that." The bus jounced through a rut and Janis Joplin staggered. She caught herself on the corner of Bug's mattress and noticed him as if for the first time. "You look kind of down, man. Something bugging you?"

"Okay," he said.

"Okay?" She puzzled over this for a few seconds, her lips moving. "Okay, what?"

"Okay, you're good."

"Damn straight I'm good." She cackled again. "Hell, I'm good and a half." She drifted over to the hi-fi; Dylan could hear her humming to herself as she sorted through a stack of LPs.

"Enough, okay?" Bug grunted and rolled off the mattress. "Sure, she's exactly what we need, except we'd have to hire at least thirty of her and we can't even afford this one. And she's crazy."

Janis Joplin put the record on the turntable. "Hey Bug," she said, turning from the hi-fi, "how do you get your mouth around all those words? Come on, dance with me." She opened her arms to him and cocked her hip. "You might get lucky, man."

"Get away from me."

"Okay, okay." She reached over and lowered the tone arm onto the record. "I see how it is with you."

"What do you mean?"

Janis Joplin sighed as the needle scratched across the lead-in groove and then her hair fell out and melted into the shag carpet on the floor. Her ears bloomed like dark flowers and her skin deepened to a midnight blue-black. She grew a guitar. By the time she started to play she was Robert Johnson.

"I went to the crossroad," sang Robert Johnson, "fell down on my knees." He gazed through Dylan as if his skull were clear as a fishbowl and his brain were a guppy.

"What's this about, Dylan?" said Bug. "What's going on here?"

"I don't know, Bug, I'm just..."

"You don't know—that's the problem. At first I thought I was mad at her for wasting our time, but it's you, Dylan. What the hell are you doing? Making it up as you go along?"

"What's wrong with that?" asked Dylan.

"It is impossible to predict a definite outcome no matter how rigorously you define the starting conditions," said Stephen Hawking. "We can only predict a number of different possible outcomes and tell how likely each of these is to occur."

Bug shook his head in disgust. "You want to play this session out, go ahead. But as far as I'm concerned, it's game over." On the dome, his avatar disappeared from the sim with an impolite *plop*.

"Didn't nobody seem to know me," sang Robert Johnson, "everybody pass me by."

Stephen Hawking pulled the bus off the road. "I believe this is your stop."

In the dome, Bug had already stripped off his airflex.

"Bug, wait!"

"For what, Dylan?" He stopped. "Tell me what I'm supposed to wait for." Bug gave him a two count before he spun away and stalked through the door.

Dylan thought about aborting the sim and going after Bug, except outside the bus window the landscape had gone impossibly blue and lush. The trees had indigo trunks and cerulean leaves, the clouds were bright as a robin's egg. It was his favorite of all their sims, the only one that could still make him feel like a little boy again. How had she known?

Stephen Hawking pushed an upright metal rod away from him and a complicated mechanism opened the creaking door of the bus. "Before one begins to theorize," he said, "it is helpful to examine all assumptions."

Dylan ducked down the passageway and stepped off into the sapphire afternoon light.

click

Vanity was waiting for him on a bench by a hut that looked like two scoops of blue ice cream. The Yellow Brick Road sliced through the cornflower fields of Munchkin Land to the distant gates of the Emerald City. But this was not the same woman who had come to the loading dock of Building Two of the Meadowbrook Office Park. Elizabeth Lee Corazon had been transfigured by *Starscape*'s image processors: the ugly duckling had gotten the swan upgrade. The virtual Vanity Mode presented with a fairy tale face and the body of a sylph. She wore a white blouse and a gingham dress and the ruby slippers.

"Time's almost up," she said as she rose to greet him. "So, Scarecrow, think of the adventures we could have together."

"Bug was right," he said. "You're good."

"Why is he so angry?"

"Just having a mood." He gestured and they sat together on the bench. "There's a programmer for you."

"He's angry at both of us."

"At me," said Dylan, "because of you."

She sighed and three Munchkins tumbled out of the blue hut.

"He's wrong, you know," said the first, hands thrust deep into the pockets of his pantaloons.

"I'm all you'll need." The second one tugged at his striped vest, which had ridden up over his paunch.

"I can multitask at least a hundred individual sessions simultaneously." The third thrust out his bearded chin and rocked from one foot to the other.

"Enough fx, Vanity," said Dylan. "Let's just talk, okay?"

The three little men turned as one and marched back through the door of the hut, muttering disconsolately.

"I can run even more sessions," Vanity said, "if you let me modify the console."

"And you'll work for nothing?"

"Let's just say that I'll agree to defer my compensation." She slid closer and laid her hand flat against the slats of the bench, her fingers just brushing his thigh. "I'll collect, Dylan." His olfactors picked up her sunshine scent. It made him think of his mother gathering in laundry from the clothesline. "Don't think I won't."

Dylan shivered; he could feel her gathering him in like a sheet. "Why do you want this so much?"

"Because I know exactly what you're trying to do here." Vanity Mode gazed off at the Emerald City for few moments, her eyes bright, then Elizabeth Ann Corazon finished her thought. "Feel it, feel it in my belly. At night I dream it right in my head, mister. All the pretty pretties. This where I belong."

Dylan was taken aback. "In Oz?"

"No, mister." She giggled. "No, no, no, *Starscape*."

"Elizabeth," he said gently, "who is Vanity?"

"My always dream." She caressed a fold of the gingham dress. "Always."

"And you let her take control?"

"Don't you talk to her," snapped Vanity. "Leave her alone!" Her pretty face flushed with anger.

"You drifted off and there she was." Dylan shrugged. "She sounded happy to be here."

"I'm here, Dylan," she said, "and *I'm* the one who is happy."

"You still haven't told me why."

She spoke without hesitation. "It's like your tag, *live the glamour*. You've made a world where everything is beautiful. *Touch the legend*. The myth is the message."

"You think Janis is beautiful?"

"Of course, she's the most beautiful of all. She absolutely owns the beautiful loser script."

On certain nights, if Dylan snooted more Placidil than was good for him and then squinted and held his breath, he could see the *Starscape* Vanity was talking about. But eventually he had to breathe or die. "You ever hear of Roman Barone?"

"Sure, he's *Roman's Nose*."

"I had lunch with him today. Pitched the site." Dylan looked away from her toward the Emerald City. "I don't think I got the link."

"So?"

"He says that the site is too dusty and our zaz is too skewed."

"Well, if that's what he says, tell him to shove his big fat nose up his ass."

It irked Dylan that she believed in *Starscape* more than he did. Her faith felt like another weight he had to carry when he was already staggering. He might use her talents but had no use for her illusions. "Barone says the only people who care about the old stars are boomers and, even though they've got money, they die by the busload every day. And they hate the hardware; the airflex makes them self-conscious. They never learned to fit reality and virtuality into their heads at the same time. Hell, some of them didn't even have televisions when they were kids, much less computers."

She dismissed Barone with the toss of her head. "He's wrong."

"If he's not, *Starscape* will go 404 by the end of the year."

"Well, I'm no boomer and I love the site, Dylan." She frowned. "What *are* the demographics on your zaz?"

He shook his head. "The last fix was six months ago. Fifty-and-older was almost eighty percent of all clicks; twenty-five to fifty was less than sixteen. But we've pulled back almost half of the sims since then and redesigned or replaced them. Now you can play croquet with Muhammad Ali, bake cookies with Gertrude Stein, or take John Wayne's philosophy course—but all we get is the raw zaz. We can't afford another demographic fix."

"Your thirty-somethings have gone way up since then. Believe it."

"That's one of your feelings? Like the way you feel the zaz?"

A horn honked and around the bend of the Yellow Brick Road came a gray 1939 DeSoto Custom Club Coupe. It was an elephant of car, with wide running boards and flaring fenders; the tiny windshield made it look nearsighted. Cary Grant braked to a stop in front them. His elbow hung out the driver's side window.

"Listen chum," he said, "why don't you stop sticking pins into her? She's not going to pop."

Dylan's datacuff began to chime. Vanity's thirty minutes were up.

"I know this girl," Cary Grant continued. "She can take a lot worse than anything you can dish out."

"Sorry everyone, but that's all the time we have for today," said Vanity. She crossed in front of the DeSoto, opened the passenger door and climbed in. Cary Grant ignored her, watching Dylan as if he were a Nazi spy.

Vanity waved. "See you next time."

click

Dylan felt the perceptual wrench that came from being dumped suddenly from virtuality. His heart pounded. Afterimages ghosted across the blank white expanse of the dome. The world did a quarter spin and then locked in. The theater was empty.

"Where is everyone?" he said. "Bogie?"

"Letty's in the kitchen," said the deskbot. "Bug took a powder."

"He left the building?"

"Headed for parts unknown."

"And Vanity?"

"She's still in the workshop, in session with Letty. Boss, I don't trust that dame."

On his way to the workshop, he passed Letty in *Starscape*'s kitchen, actually just a storage room with a sink knocked in. A little refrigerator hummed in the corner; on top of it was the microwave oven in which Dylan cooked most of his meals. Letty was sitting upright at the table, still wearing the discreet, muttering into the microphone. Although the visor covered her eyes, her posture and the set of her mouth indicated that she was investing serious attention quotient in the session.

"Letty?" he said.

"Hmm," she said absently. "Later."

The workshop was Bug's warren. An antique red barber chair faced a vidwall on which at least thirty different windows were open. Some were filled with code hieroglyphics, some were wire frames of new sim objects. There were livecams of the surf at Redondo Beach, Dawn Zoftiggle's bedroom, and a clerk's-eye-view of the 7-Eleven on the Nevski Prospekt in St. Petersburg. A few were action loops of monsters rampaging through inner cities: Kong in New York, Gojiro in Tokyo, and the Giant Behemoth in London.

Vanity Mode was sitting on the barber chair with the console on her lap. She twirled the chair around to face him. She was, of course, her lumpy self. "Deal?" She held out her hand.

"Are you and Letty still playing?"

"We danced. Then I stopped doubling Bug and now we're talking." She acknowledged his look of surprise with a bow. "I told you I can run a hundred sessions."

"And function in real time?"

"A session is a session." She continued to hold her hand out to him. "Virtual or real makes no difference."

"Are we in a session? Is that what this is?"

"Reality is session A1A." Her head lolled. "Always on top."

"And who are you doubling now?"

She laughed. "Why Vanity Mode, of course. But you're right, Dylan. Maybe I need to turn down the volume a touch, especially if we're going to be working together. So, deal?"

"If you're free, you're hired." Dylan crossed the room and shook her hand. "Do you know where Bug went?"

All the screens consolidated. Bug's avatar stared balefully out at them. "I'm not here so go away and don't touch anything," it said.

"When will you be back?" asked Dylan.

"Can't say. I left without telling me."

"Well, when you come back, ask yourself to step into my office."

The avatar turned its back to them. The message was stitched across the shoulders of its black leather jacket.

DYLAN WANTS TO SEE YOU ASAP.

LOOKS LIKE HE'S HIRED BLINKY.

click

After the bankruptcy, Dylan had decided to simplify his life. He had tried to convince himself that his problem was that he'd been distracted by the glittery side effects of his early success. Losing track of what mattered had cost him *Stinger* and Julie and the house in Woodstock and a large slice of self-respect. Of course, the banks had been eager to help him adjust his lifestyle to his new circumstances, which was why his office was spare and more than a little shabby. Bogie was a state-of-the-art *Assistencia* deskbot but Dylan had him mounted on an old gray Steelcase that had been left behind when Building Number Two of the Meadowbrook Office Park had been shut down. There were a couple of mismatched plaid chairs that would have gone begging at a country yard sale and a musty foldout couch where he had been sleeping for the past two weeks. Dylan was glad he had left the door to the executive washroom closed. He didn't want Vanity to see his suits hanging in the shower. About the only reminder he kept that he had ever been anyone was the Webster he had won for *Stinger*.

It was what Vanity saw first—possibly the only thing she saw in his office. She goggled as if it were the Holy Grail. "Can I?"

From the look on her face, he wasn't sure whether she wanted to handle the Webster or fall down and worship it.

"Help yourself." He stepped behind his desk. "Messages, Bogie?"

"Just a couple," said the deskbot.

"It's heavy," said Vanity. She cradled it in her arms and rocked it back and forth like a newborn.

"I've found that the longer you have one, the more it weighs. From who, Bogie?"

"First is a guy by the name of Creditworks-dot-com," said the deskbot.

"Delete it," said Dylan.

"I want one," she said, nodding excitedly. "I've always wanted one."

"Make me an offer."

"No, one of my own." She laughed. "Tell me about the night you won it. What did it feel like?"

Dylan didn't know what it felt like to win a Webster. The day of the ceremony there had been the champagne reception at two, moodfood at the Blackburns followed by early dinner at Maxx's, where they had drunk two thousand dollars' worth of Haut-Brion. At some point he had met Kyle in a bathroom for a snoot of Placidil. When he woke up the next morning, the damn thing had been on the nightstand. "It felt great," he said. "I'll never forget it as long as I live."

"Then there's Roman at Nose-dot-com," said Bogie. "Ever heard of him?"

Dylan felt the hair on the back of his neck prickle. "Wow." He laughed uncertainly. "Play it."

click

Roman Barone was sitting on a leather couch the size of Long Island. He looked like a little kid in it. He had taken his suit coat off and unsnapped the top snap of his shirt; he was wearing an airflex with the headband pulled up. The windows behind him appeared to be real; he had a view of a pond nestled in a grove of white pines.

"Dylan, this is Roman. First of all, you want something, you message me yourself from now on, understand? I find incoming in my mailbox about a half an hour ago from Vanity someone—the address is in your shop. Sounds like a blinking alias. Second of all, I don't like to reward sitemasters for going deep ID on me. You want to waste your money snooping my personal life, fine. But just because you know where I lived in 1996 doesn't mean you know what I'm going to put on *Nose* tomorrow. I realize this kind of crap goes on, but if you want to play that game, you need to be a hell of a lot more..."

Dylan stabbed at the pause icon. "What the hell did you do?"

"I don't know yet," said Vanity. "I haven't heard what the man has to say." She set the Webster back in its place. "You'd already blown the link, Dylan."

He sank back onto his chair as Barone finished.

"...subtle next time. But here's the real reason I'm messaging you. I don't remember the episode where Homer became a veterinarian. Did you make that up? If you did, your sim is brilliant. If not, I want the reference. Let me know either way."

The desktop went blank.

click

"Wow," said Dylan. "I don't believe it."

"He was born in 1987," said Vanity. "*The Simpsons* were just about the only show that kids and their parents watched together in the '90s. When I went deep on him, I found out that he put a fan site up on Geocities in 1999 called *Duff Beer Showcase*. It 404ed in '01. You had a Simpson's sim up already; I just doubled all the characters and sent him a taste."

"How much did the ID cost?"

"Not much. I made some lucky guesses."

"About time someone had some luck around here." Dylan waved the dictation processor on. "Reply to last message." He hesitated, then pressed the pause icon again. "What am I going to say to him?"

"The truth. The sim is original to us and he should've found it himself. Call his bluff. He's probably never even clicked *Starscape* before."

Bug stuck his head in the door. "You want to see me, Dylan? Because if you don't, I need to see you." He didn't acknowledge Vanity.

"In a minute, Bug. Vanity, you think that's *all* I should say? Seems kind of curt."

"Hey Bug," said Vanity. "Sorry about..."

He ducked out of the doorway before she could finish.

"Don't pay any attention to him," Dylan said. "Like I said, he's having a mood. What else for Barone?"

"Well, you might ask if he's visited our Super Bowl sim yet. His father taught Phys Ed and was football coach at North High in Denver. I can do a John Elway that could fool even his kids."

Dylan nodded and then came around the desk. "Look Vanity, I'm feeling a little gun-shy about this. You're absolutely right: I blew the contact and you saved it. So do me a favor—you message him back." He gestured for her to sit in his chair. "Use my name. Whatever you think will work is fine with me. Meanwhile, I'll pour some honey on our friend, Bug."

"You'd better," she said. "He hates me."

"Now, now, you're just an acquired taste." He patted her arm. "I'll give him some incentive to make the acquisition."

click

Dylan found Bug and Letty in the workshop, studying the vidwall. Half a dozen windows were scrolling old news feeds. The one in the middle opened onto a turn-of-the-century-sitcom with the sound turned down. A man with big eyes sat in a dentist's chair while a woman with big breasts flossed his teeth.

Dylan put his arm around Bug's shoulder. "She said she'd work for free so I told her she could stay. You're not going to give her a hard time, are you Bug?"

Letty shot Bug a warning glance; he shook his head.

"And the first thing she does is get Barone to take another look at the site. I'd say that's a pretty good day's work." Dylan gave Bug a friendly shake. "*Roman's Nose*, people. Our stock options might actually be worth something."

Bug didn't react. Dylan glanced at Letty; she was made of stone. On the sitcom, a woman in a lab coat was talking to the patient in the chair. The woman had beautiful silver hair and she was very pregnant. "What? Talk to me, Letty."

Bug cleared his throat. "You ever hear of Baby X?"

Dylan frowned. "Let's see, it was something about a lawsuit. And the mom was on TV."

"Elizabeth Ann Corazon is Baby X," said Bug. "While you were in a session with her, I stepped out and paid for a deep ID. My own money, Dylan. Her mother was Beth Ann Lewis. She was in that sitcom *Big Mouth*." He nodded at the center window. "She played the other dentist. So Beth Ann is in her first hit show at age forty-six and she gets pregnant, only she's not married. The father isn't in the picture but Beth Ann still really wants the baby. She's very careful, has the amniocentesis and when the tests come back, everything looks just fine, so she elects to carry the pregnancy to term. It's a kind of minor news story; they even write the pregnancy into the show."

Vanity burst into the room. "You were brilliant, Dylan. I don't know how Barone can pass..." When she saw the screens, she stopped. "Okay, okay, I suppose we have to go through this." She worried at her lower lip. "But just once, all right? How much have you got?"

"On April 11, 2002," said Bug. "Beth Ann gives birth to a baby girl."

"Ta-*da*." Vanity curtsied, her thick fingers holding the hem of her adshirt as if it were a dress. "A star is born."

"You want to tell the rest?" asked Bug.

"No, you go ahead." She was somber, unlike herself. "Maybe your script has the happy ending."

Bug shook his head. "I don't know that much more. Apparently the delivery is a disaster and Beth Ann ends up having a hysterectomy. And of course there was a major screwup at the lab because the baby was..."

"Defective," said Vanity. "I believe the word is defective."

"Anyway," continued Bug, "the jury finds gross negligence."

"Right," said Dylan. "We studied this in Bioethics. Baby X was the test case of the Uniform Conception and Gestation Act—the first successful wrongful birth suit."

"The jury awards Beth Ann sixty-three million dollars, which the judge reduces to twenty million. But as soon as the judgment is final, Beth Ann gives Baby X up. She is adopted by Raul and Marisa Corazon, which is where I picked up into the thread. But that's as deep as I got."

click

They waited. Vanity stood with her eyes shut, as if she were listening to someone giving her advice. Then she nodded several times and approached the wall. "In some ways, my birth mother was very kind." She touched the window where her mother was having dinner at a restaurant with a man who had a parrot on his shoulder. "She put the entire settlement in trust for me; not only what I got, but her punitive damages too. The trustees weren't to contact me or my adoptive family until my twenty-first birthday to ensure that I had a normal childhood. And because I was no longer the child of a celebrity, I didn't have to watch myself growing up ugly on the net."

Vanity turned to the three of them, leaning back against the windows that displayed the bare facts of her life. "But the Corazons were not the best choice the adoption agency could have made. They didn't abuse me or anything, but I figure they adopted me mostly to get the monthly support checks from the DSS. We never went out and I never made any friends. I spent most of my first twenty-one years in front of the TV, watching cable. We had one of the first vidwalls; Mommy Marisa liked to put four or five shows up at once. She was addicted to the old movies on AMC and Turner Classics and NostalgiaWorks; it was her mother who worked for Vincente Minnelli."

"And your birth mother did nothing?" asked Dylan.

Bug shook his head. "Anonymous adoption."

"That didn't stop *you* from buying a deep ID."

"Oh shut up," said Letty harshly. "Let her finish."

"Everything changed when I turned twenty-one. Mommy Marisa and Daddy Raul were shocked when they found out about the trust. All of a sudden they were so nice to me, everyone was. But I didn't understand any of it until after I had the CAT implant eighteen—no, seventeen months ago. I was a different person, you see. I wasn't just smarter, I was *me*."

"It must have been hard," said Letty.

Vanity smiled. "I made some mistakes. One of the first things I did after I got out of the hospital was go see my real mother. I wanted to thank her, you know. My real really...really truly ruly." She began to shake her head violently from side to side. "Bad Lizzy," she said with a moan. "Bad." *Shake.* "Bad." *Shake.*

"What's wrong with her?" said Bug

"Elizabeth," Dylan said. "It's okay."

"Bad." Vanity swallowed. "It bad for both of us. Her career pretty much ended because of me. People just didn't understand why she gave me up. She told me that, at the time, she figured that there were lots and lots of women who could mother me, and that she knew she wasn't one of them. That's why she'd had the tests done, she said. She knew exactly what she could do and what she couldn't. I was something she just couldn't do." She faced the vidwall. On the *Big Mouth* window, the receptionist was spearing green olives out of the jar with a dental pick. Vanity turned the show off. "So that's my big secret and you'd better keep it. Otherwise snoops like Bug here will go deep on poor Elizabeth Ann Corazon and hurt some people who just want to be left the hell alone."

"Tell Dylan the rest," said Letty. "Unless you want me to? Bug knows already."

"Oh, *that*." She flicked her middle finger off her thumb. "I don't mind. It's part of the terms of employment, even though you're not paying me. But then I don't need to get paid—in fact, I would have been willing to pay *you*. So don't strain any muscles patting yourself on the back, Dylan."

She sat in Bug's barber chair. Her hands curled over the keypads he'd had custom built into the arms and she started typing. She closed all the windows on the vidwall. Bug shifted uncomfortably.

"So Letty and I sat down and had a heart to heart after I stopped doubling Bug. No offense, but there's only so much Bug a girl can take, even if he does tango. All I was looking for was an ally, but I feel like maybe I made a friend. Anyway, I showed her some Down family pictures. You see, there aren't as many of us as there used to be. Almost all of us get prevented, so people kind of forget how we work."

click

She opened window after window of brain scans, some twenty in all. "Positron emissions don't necessarily show our good side, but there you go." She strode back to the vidwall and pointed to the top row. "Now this line, that's you folks—five pictures over time, birth to death. You lose a few cells, what the hell, you've got plenty to spare—it's still a pretty picture." She clapped silently. "Now compare the next two lines. This one is an Alzheimer's patient over time and here's a typical Down syndrome. Notice the similarities. By thirty-five, here..." She pointed to a scan in the middle of the Down line, "...we all start to develop brain lesions and neuritic plaques that look a lot like these folks up here in Alzheimer's land. In fact, lots of us do get full blown Alzheimer's, in which case we go down about twice as fast as the rest of the population. And even if we don't...well, put it this way. People with Down syndrome don't usually live to collect Social Security." She giggled. "Fifty is a pretty good life. Any questions so far?"

Dylan had his arms folded tight, hugging himself to ward off her scary good humor. Bug and Letty looked equally disturbed. None of them said a word.

"Come on, cheer up." She shook her finger at them and grinned. "You'd think this was *your* life. Now this last line belongs to one Elizabeth Ann Corazon. This shot here was taken when she was thirty," she pointed to the fourth window, "... and as you can see, things are getting kind of hollowed out." She rapped her fist against the side of her head.

"My God, Vanity," said Dylan.

She made a sound like a game show buzzer. "I'm sorry, but your response must be in the form of a question. Now all the experts agree that she's got early onset Alzheimer's. Insofar, as she can understand this, she's pretty depressed. Her doctors explain that she's not a particularly good candidate for a CAT implant since she has the life expectancy of a gerbil. But never underestimate the power of strategic investment. All of a sudden there are plans for the Raul and Marisa Corazon Wing of the Leahy Clinic and we come to the last window.

You see this darker blob? That's the very latest Computer Aided Thinking device, a half pound of artificial neurotissue developed from embryonic stem cells. That, my friends, is where Vanity Mode lives." Her head lolled and she smiled. "For now."

click

The night after the awards ceremony, they brought Vanity her Webster. Even though it was only on the other side of the reflecting pool, Dylan, Bug, and Letty rode out to the mausoleum site in a limo. According to *NewsMelt*, more than ten thousand people had unplugged from the Vnet to gather at *Starscape's* corporate campus. Dylan had arranged for police from six neighboring towns to assist in crowd control. The nets were there in force; with the lights of all the livecams, it was bright enough to grow corn.

Vanity had never had any doubts about what she wanted to leave behind. The lurid bio sim they had concocted on *Starscape* was obviously a joke; even the most gullible of the gullible would find it hard to believe that she was the love child of Prince Andrew and Julia Roberts or that she developed Cherry Budweiser for Anheuser-Busch or that she had stowed away on the Third Mars Expedition. The only true-to-life scene in it was our first meeting and even in that we took out everything about Elizabeth and her sitcom mom, CAT implants, and Down syndrome. Her bio sim protected the secrets of the late Elizabeth Ann Corazon, but Vanity Mode needed to make a lasting gesture to her public. She wanted a place where fans could come to remember: her Eternal Flame, her Graceland.

Vanity had specified the design of her mausoleum and had spared no expense in building it, although no one but Dylan, Bug, and Letty had known of its true nature. It was a fifteen-meter marble square; rising from its center was a Doric column atop which stood the life-sized figure of a woman. Her arms outstretched, she was caught in mid-pirouette. Her skirts flew out from her body. Her hair, a wild tangle, obscured her face. Her greatest hits were all there, carved in bas-relief on the marble base. Virginia Woolf, Bela Lugosi, Larry Bird, Ginger Rogers, Harpo Marx, Spiderman, Jane Goodall, Louis B. Mayer, Sandy Koufax, Grace Slick, Rod Serling, George Gershwin, Sherlock Holmes, and Billie Jean King stared up in silent approval of Vanity Mode's eternally frozen dance.

She had even left a place for the Webster. Dylan carried it up the temporary steps to the top of the pedestal. He pulled the plastic sheathing from the trophy pad, set the Webster into the griprite, which had aircured almost before he could straighten up. The composition of the sculpture was completed. But Vanity Mode's script was not yet finished.

click

Dylan   There was something I'd never really understood about Vanity Mode until after Elizabeth Ann Corazon died. Elizabeth had always wanted to be Vanity, but Vanity was afraid of being Elizabeth. Elizabeth was a creature of flesh and bone, slow and weak and all too mortal. Vanity was information racing at the speed of light; since she had no fixed material form, her death did not necessarily follow from that of Elizabeth. She could live—no, she could *exist*—in one computer as well as another. It may be that the best part of that strange twinned woman died with Elizabeth. Information can't long to love and be loved. It can neither aspire nor dream. At least, I don't think it can.

/SFX/   STARSCAPE FANFARE, UNDER...

Dylan   But if properly stored, information is, for all practical purposes, immortal.

Male Host   Welcome to *Starscape*, the interactive celebrity site. Come visit with your favorite stars of the twentieth century.

Female Host   Gone but never forgotten.

Male Host   Live the glamour.

Female Host   Touch the legend.

Dylan   It's me, Dylan.

/SFX/	STARSCAPE FANFARE CUTS OUT

/SFX/	STARSCAPE MENU CHORD

Male Host Please choose a simulation from the following menu.

/SFX/	KEYBOARD CLICKS

Female Host That simulation is password accessible only. Please enter or say your password now.

Dylan Zaz.

Male Host You have selected (*pause*) *Heaven.*

/SFX/	HEAVEN AMBIANCE, UNDER...

Vanity Dylan, I'm over here.
    (beat)
We did it! Ta-da!

Dylan We did.

Vanity I saw it all, monitored the unveiling on all the news-sites. We were everywhere. For maybe ten minutes, we *were* the net.
    (beat)
You're not happy. Come to bed, darling.

Dylan I'm fine, just tired.

/SFX/	BEDSPRINGS CREAK

Vanity Give us a kiss.
    (beat)
What's the matter?

Dylan   I feel strange. Something's changed.

Vanity   But this is our sim. And I'm just the same as I always was.

Dylan   Are you? Well, maybe it's me then. Listen, when you were watching the unveiling, did you feel it?

Vanity   Feel what?

Dylan   I don't know. Maybe I'm kidding myself, but after I set the Webster on the tomb, I turned around and the lights of the livecams blinded me...and I felt them, millions, maybe billions watching me, lots of them crying, some holding one another, some disgusted with me and some angry and it was so much bigger than I was...oh, I can't describe it, except that you were right, Vanity. I could actually feel it.
    (beat)
I could feel the zaz.

/SFX/   APPLAUSE MORPHS TO RAPID SCENE CHANGE CLICKS, WHICH FADE TO SILENCE

END

Dude, We're Gonna Be Jedi!
Henry Jenkins

Media scholar Henry Jenkins is Provost Professor of Communication, Journalism, and Cinematic Arts at the USC Annenberg School for Communication. Prior to moving to USC, Jenkins was Peter de Florez Professor in the Humanities and Director of MIT's Comparative Media Studies graduate-degree program from 1993–2009. Jenkins has been at the forefront of understanding the effects of participatory media—from print to film to new media—on society, politics, and culture. His research often focuses on fan communities, and in this excerpt from his book *Rethinking Media Change* (MIT Press, 2003), he offers a look at one very probable future for the movie industry as digital equipment makes inexpensive but high-quality production and distribution of movies possible and where (in this case) *Star Wars* fans are no longer limited in their amateur filmmaking to local audiences but can realistically reach a global audience.

> *"For me the great hope is now that 8mm video recorders are coming out, people who normally wouldn't make movies are going to be making them. And that one day a little fat girl in Ohio is going be the new Mozart and make a beautiful film with her father's camcorder. For once the so-called professionalism about movies will be destroyed and it will really become an art form."*
>
> —Francis Ford Coppola

> *"Maru pays homage to* Star Wars *and is intended to demonstrate to everyone who spent their entire childhood dreaming of wielding a light saber that inspired personal visions can now be realized using tools that are readily available to all of us.* Maru *was made using a camcorder and a PC with a budget of about \$500.... Technology and the new media facilitate the articulation and exchange of ideas in ways never before imagined, and we hope that others will harness the power of these tools as we have in order to share their dreams with the world."*
>
> —amateur filmmakers Adam Dorr, Erik Benson,
> Hien Nguyen, Jon Jones

George Lucas in Love, perhaps the best known of the *Star Wars* parodies, depicts the future media mastermind as a singularly clueless USC film student who can't quite come up with a good idea for his production assignment, despite the fact that he inhabits a realm rich with narrative possibilities. His stoner roommate emerges from behind the hood of his dressing gown and lectures Lucas on "this giant cosmic force, an energy field created by all living things." His sinister next-door neighbor, an archrival, dresses all in black and breathes with an asthmatic wheeze as he proclaims, "My script is complete. Soon I will rule the entertainment universe." As Lucas races to class, he encounters a brash young friend, who brags about his souped-up sports car, and his furry-faced sidekick, who growls when he hits his head on the hood while trying to do some basic repairs. His professor, a smallish man, babbles cryptic advice, but all this adds up to little until Lucas meets and falls madly for a beautiful young woman with buns on both sides of her head. Alas, the romance leads to naught, as he eventually discovers that she is his long-lost sister.

George Lucas in Love is, of course, a spoof of *Shakespeare in Love* as well as a tribute from one generation of USC film students to another. As co-director Joseph Levy, a 24-year-old recent graduate from Lucas's alma mater, explained, "Lucas is definitely the god of USC.... We shot our screening-room scene in the George Lucas Instructional Building—which we're sitting in right now. Lucas is incredibly supportive of student filmmakers and developing their careers and providing facilities for them to be caught up to technology." Yet what makes this film so endearing is the way that it pulls Lucas down to the same level of countless other amateur filmmakers and, in so doing, helps blur the line between the fantastical realm of space opera ("A long, long time ago in a galaxy far, far away") and the familiar realm of everyday life (the world of stoner roommates, snotty neighbors, and incomprehensible professors). Its protagonist is hapless in love, clueless at filmmaking, yet somehow he manages to pull it all together and produce one of the top-grossing motion pictures of all time. *George Lucas in Love* offers us a portrait of the artist as a young geek.

One might contrast this rather down-to-earth representation of Lucas—the auteur as amateur—with the way fan filmmaker Evan Mather's Web site constructs the amateur as an emergent auteur. Along one column of the site can be found a filmography, listing all of Mather's productions going back to high school, as well as a listing of the various newspapers, magazines, Web sites, and television and radio stations that have covered his work—*La Republica*, *Le Monde*, the *New York Times*, *Wired*, *Entertainment Weekly*, CNN, NPR, and so forth. Another sidebar provides up to the moment information about his works in progress. Elsewhere, you can see news of the various film-festival screenings of his films and whatever awards they have won. A tongue-in-cheek manifesto outlines his views on digital filmmaking: "...*no dialogue...no narration...soundtrack must be monaural...length of credits may not exceed 1/20 the length of the film...nonverbal human or animal utterances are permitted... nonsense sounds whilst permitted are discouraged...all credits and captions must be in both English and French whilst the type size of the French title may be no greater in height than 1/3 the height of the English....*" More than nineteen digital films are featured with photographs, descriptions, and links that enable you to download them in multiple formats. Another link allows you to call up a PDF file reproducing a glossy full-color, professionally designed brochure documenting the making of his most recent work, *Les Pantless Menace*, which includes close-ups of various props and settings, reproductions of stills, score sheets, and storyboards and detailed explanations of how he was able to do the special effects, soundtrack, and editing for the film. We learn, for example, that some of the dialogue was taken directly from Commtech chips that were embedded within Hasbro *Star Wars* toys. A biography provides some background: "Evan Mather spent much of his childhood running around south Louisiana with an eight-millimeter silent camera staging hitchhikings and assorted buggery.... As a landscape architect, Mr. Mather spends his days designing a variety of urban and park environments in the Seattle area. By night, Mr. Mather explores the realm of digital cinema and is the renowned creator of short films which fuse traditional hand drawn and stop motion animation techniques with the flexibility and realism of computer generated special effects."

The self-promotional aspects of Mather's site are far from unique. The Force.Net Fan Theater, for example, offers amateur directors a chance to offer their own commentary on the production and thematic ambitions of their movies. The creators of *When Senators Attack IV*, for example, give "comprehensive scene-by-scene commentary" on their film: "Over the next ninety pages or so, you'll receive an insight into what we were thinking when we made a particular shot, what methods we used, explanations to some of the more puzzling scenes, and anything else that comes to mind." Such materials often constitute a conscious parodying of the tendency of recent DVD releases to include alternative scenes, cut footage, storyboards, and director's commentary. Many of the Web sites provide information about fan films under production or may even include preliminary footage, storyboards, and trailers for films that may never be completed. Almost all the amateur filmmakers have developed their own posters and advertising images for their productions, taking advantage of new Pagemaker and Photoshop software packages that make it easy to manipulate and rearrange images using the home computer. In many cases, the fan filmmakers often produce elaborate trailers, complete with advertising catchphrases.

Some of these materials serve useful functions within amateur film culture. The "Making-of" articles that are found on so many of the fan Web sites enable the sharing of technical advice; trading such information helps improve the overall quality of work within the community. The trailers also respond to the specific challenges of the Web as a distribution channel: it can take hours to download relatively long digital movies, and, as a consequence, the shorter, lower resolution trailers (often distributed in a streaming video format) allow would-be viewers a chance to glimpse the work and determine whether it is worth the effort. Yet these mechanisms of self-promotion move beyond what would be required to support a functional network for amateur-film distribution, suggesting that the fans, too, have come to understand that the art of "high-concept" filmmaking (and the franchise system it supports) depends as much on the art of advertising and marketing as on the art of storytelling.

Many of the fans, after all, got their first glimpses of footage from *The Phantom Menace* by downloading the much-publicized trailer. In many cases, fan parodies of the trailer started to appear in the months during which fans were eagerly awaiting a chance to see the film itself. In some early examples, fans simply redubbed the original trailer with alternative soundtracks; in other cases, they remade the trailer shot by shot. For example, downloading the trailer inspired Ayaz Asif to produce a parody employing characters taken from *South Park*. When an acquaintance, Ted Bracewell, sent him a wallpaper he had drawn depicting *South Park* characters in *Star Wars* garb, the two decided to collaborate, resulting in a quickly made trailer for *Park Wars: The Little Menace*, then for a more elaborately made "special edition," and then for a series of other shorts based on the *Star Wars* versions of the

South Park characters. The production received such media interest, including an interview with Asif during a Sci-Fi Channel documentary, that the young filmmakers were ultimately invited to air it on Comedy Central, the same network that produces Trey Parker and Matt Stone's series.

Trailervision.com pushes fan cinema's fascination with the trailer format to its logical extreme, releasing a trailer each Monday for a nonexistent film. In some cases, these trailers spoof commercial films that hit the theaters that same week, including *The Jar Jar Binks Project, I Know What You'll Want to Do Next Summer, The Wimp Club, Scam 3*, and *American Booty*. These spoof trailers are, in some senses, the perfect genre for the current state of digital cinema—short, pithy, reflecting the amateur filmmaker's self-conscious relationship to commercial media, and recognizable by a mass audience who can be assumed to be familiar with the material that inspired them. These spoof trailers enable amateur and aspiring filmmakers to surf the publicity generated by a current release and thus to get media coverage (as was the case with a surprising number of the *Star Wars* spoofs) or to draw audiences already worked up about the commercial product.

All this publicity surrounding the *Star Wars* parodies serves as a reminder of one of the most distinctive qualities of these amateur films—the fact that they are so public. Mather, for example, reports, "Since I started keeping track in February 1998, this site has been visited by over a half-million people from all seven continents, including such faraway places as Antarctica, Iran, San Marino...and Canada." The idea that amateur filmmakers could develop such a global following runs counter to the historical marginalization of grassroots media production.

In her book *Reel Families: A Social History of Amateur Film*, Patricia R. Zimmermann offers a compelling history of amateur filmmaking in the United States, examining the intersection between nonprofessional film production and the Hollywood entertainment system. As Zimmermann notes, a variety of critics and theorists, including Harry Potamkin in the 1920s, Maya Deren in the 1950s, Jonas Mekas and George Kuchar in the 1960s, and Hans Magnus Enzensberger in the 1970s, had identified a radical potential in broadening popular access to the cinematic apparatus, fostering a new public consciousness about how media images are constructed and opening a space for alternative experimentation and personal expression outside the industrial context of the studio system. Amateur film production emerged alongside the first moving pictures. Tom Gunning has argued that the Lumière Brothers' shorts were best understood within a context of amateur photography in France, while Zimmermann points to the ways that amateur theater movements in the United States, as well as a prevailing entrepreneurial spirit, provided a base of support of amateur filmmaking efforts in the 1910s. However, the amateur film has remained, first and foremost, the "home movie," in several senses of the term: first, amateur films were exhibited primarily in private (and most often, domestic) spaces lacking any viable channel of distribution to a larger public; second, amateur films were most often documentaries of domestic and family life rather than attempts to make fictional or avant-garde films; and third, amateur films were perceived to be technically flawed and of marginal interest beyond the immediate family. Jokes and cartoons about the painfulness of being subjected to someone else's home movies are pervasive in our culture and represent a devaluing of the potential for an amateur cinema movement. Zimmermann cites a range of different critical appraisals that stress the artlessness and spontaneity of amateur film in contrast with the technical polish and aesthetic sophistication of commercial films. She concludes, "[Amateur film] was gradually squeezed into the nuclear family. Technical standards, aesthetic norms, socialization pressures and political goals derailed its cultural construction into a privatized, almost silly, hobby." Writing in the early 1990s, Zimmermann saw little reason to believe that the camcorder and the VCR would significantly alter this situation, suggesting that the medium's technical limitations made it hard for amateurs to edit their films and that the only public means of exhibition were controlled by commercial media makers (as in such programs as *America's Funniest Home Videos*).

Digital filmmaking alters many of the conditions that Zimmermann felt had led to the marginalization of previous amateur filmmaking efforts—the Web provides an exhibition outlet that moves amateur filmmaking from private into public space; digital editing is far simpler than editing Super-8 or video and thus opens up a space for amateur artists to more directly reshape their material; and the home PC has even enabled the amateur filmmaker to directly mimic the special effects associated with Hollywood blockbusters, such as *Star Wars*. As a consequence, digital cinema constitutes a new chapter in the complex history of interactions between amateur filmmakers and the commercial media. These films remain amateur, in the sense that they are made on low budgets, produced and distributed in noncommercial contexts, and generated by nonprofessional filmmakers (albeit often by people who want entry into the professional sphere), yet many of the other classic markers of amateur film production have disappeared. No longer home movies, these films are public movies—public in that, from the start, they are intended for audiences beyond the filmmakers' immediate circles of friends and acquaintances; public in their content, which involves the reworking of personal concerns into the shared cultural framework provided by popular mythologies; and public in their aesthetic focus on existing in dialogue with the commercial cinema (rather than existing outside the Hollywood system altogether).

Digital filmmakers tackled the challenge of making *Star Wars* movies for many different reasons. *Kid Wars* director Dana Smith is a fourteen-year-old who had recently acquired a camcorder and decided to stage scenes from *Star Wars* involving his younger brother and his friends, who armed themselves for battle with squirt guns and Nerf weapons. *The Jedi Who Loved Me* was shot by the members of a wedding party and intended as a tribute to the bride and groom, who were *Star Wars* fans. Some films—such as *Macbeth*—were school projects. Two high school students—Bienvenido Concepcion and Don Fitz-Roy—shot the film, which creatively blurs the lines between Lucas and Shakespeare, for their high school advanced-placement English class. They staged lightsaber battles down the school hallway, though the principal was concerned about potential damage to lockers; the *Millennium Falcon* lifted off from the gym, though they had to composite it over the cheerleaders who were rehearsing the day they shot that particular sequence. Still other films emerged as collective projects for various *Star Wars* fan clubs. *Boba Fett: Bounty Trail*, for example, was filmed for a competition hosted by a Melbourne, Australia, Lucasfilm convention. Each cast member made his or her own costumes, building on previous experience with science-fiction masquerades and costume contests. The film's stiffest competition came from *Dark Redemption*, a production of the Sydney fan community, which featured a lightsaber-waving female protagonist, Mara Jade. The filmmakers' personal motives for making such films are of secondary interest, however, once they are distributed on the Web. If such films are attracting worldwide interest, it is not because we all care whether Bienvenido Concepcion and Don Fitz-Roy made a good grade on their Shakespeare assignment; we are unlikely to know any of the members of the wedding party who made *The Jedi Who*

Loved Me. Rather, what motivates far-away viewers to watch such films is our shared investments in the *Star Wars* universe. These amateur filmmakers have reframed their personal experiences or interests within the context of a popular-culture mythology that is known around the world.

In a very tangible sense, digital filmmakers have blurred the line between amateur and professional, with films made for miniscule budgets duplicating special effects that cost a small fortune to generate only a decade earlier. Amateur filmmakers can make podracers skim along the surface of the ocean or landspeeders scatter dust as they zoom across the desert. They can make laser beams shoot out of ships and explode things before our eyes. Several fans tried their hands at duplicating Jar Jar's character animation and inserting him into their own movies with varying degrees of success. (One filmmaker spoofed the defects of his own work, having Jar-Jar explain that he took on a different accent for his part in Lucas's movie and suggesting that he had recently undergone a nose job.) The lightsaber battle, however, has become the gold standard of amateur filmmaking, with almost every filmmaker compelled to demonstrate his or her ability to achieve this particular effect. Many of the *Star Wars* shorts, in fact, consist of little more than lightsaber battles staged in suburban rec rooms and basements, in empty lots, in the hallways of local schools, inside shopping malls, or, more exotically, against the backdrop of medieval ruins (shot during vacations).

As amateur filmmakers are quick to note, Lucas and Steven Spielberg both made Super-8 fiction films as teenagers and saw this experience as a major influence on their subsequent work. Although these films have not been made available to the general public, some of them have been discussed in detail in various biographies and magazine profiles. These "movie brat" filmmakers have been quick to embrace the potentials of digital filmmaking, not simply as a means of lowering production costs for their own films but also as a training ground for new talent. Lucas, for example, told *Wired* magazine, "Some of the special effects that we redid for *Star Wars* were done on a Macintosh, on a laptop, in a couple of hours.... I could have very easily shot the Young Indy TV series on Hi-8.... So you can get a Hi-8 camera for a few thousand bucks, more for the software and the computer—for less than $10,000 you have a movie studio. There's nothing to stop you from doing something provocative and significant in that medium." Elsewhere, he has paid tribute to several of the fan filmmakers, including Kevin Rubio (the director of *Troops*) and Joe Nussbaum (the director of *George Lucas in Love*).

Lucas's rhetoric about the potentials of digital filmmaking seems to have captured the imaginations of amateur filmmakers, and they are struggling to confront the master on his own ground, to use digital cinema to create a far more vivid version of their childhood fantasies. As Clay Kronke, a Texas A&M University undergraduate who made *The New World*, explains, "This film has been a labor of love. A venture into a new medium.... I've always loved lightsabers and the mythos of the Jedi and after getting my hands on some software that would allow me to actually become what I had once only admired at a distance, a vague idea soon started becoming a reality.... Dude, we're gonna be Jedi." Kronke openly celebrates the fact that he made the film on a $26.79 budget, with most of the props and costumes part of his preexisting collection of *Star Wars* paraphernalia; that the biggest problem he faced on the set was that the plastic lightsabers kept breaking after they clashed together too often; and that those sound effects he wasn't able to borrow from a *Phantom Menace* PC game were "foleyed around my apartment, including the sound of a coat hanger against a metal flashlight, my microwave door, and myself falling on the floor several times."

The amateur's pride in recreating professional-quality special effects always seems to compete with a recognition of the enormous gap between his or her own productions and the big-budget Hollywood film the amateur is mimicking. Scholars and critics writing about third-world filmmaking have productively described those films as an "imperfect cinema," noting the ways that filmmakers have had to deal with low budgets and limited access to high-tech production facilities, making it impossible to compete with Hollywood on its own terms. Instead, these filmmakers have made a virtue out of their limitations, often spoofing or parodying Hollywood genre conventions and stylistic norms through films that are intentionally crude or ragged in style. The abruptness in editing, the roughness of camera movement, the grittiness of film stock, and the unevenness of lighting have become markers of authenticity, a kind of direct challenge to the polished look of a big-budget screen production. These amateur filmmakers have also recognized and made their peace with the fact that digital cinema is, in some senses, an "imperfect cinema," with the small and grainy images a poor substitute for the larger-than-life qualities of Lucas's original films when projected on a big screen with Dolby Surround Sound. The trailer for the *Battle of the Bedroom* promises "lots of dodgy special effects," while the team that made *When Senators Attack* chose to call themselves Ultracheese, Ltd. In some cases, the films are truly slapdash, relishing their sloppy special effects, embarrassing delivery, and salvage-store costumes. *The Throne Room*, for example, brags that it was shot and edited in only thirty minutes, and it shows. Two hammy adolescents cut up in home-movie footage clearly shot in their living room and inserted into the Throne Room sequence from *A New Hope* to suggest their flirtation with Princess Leia. In others, the productions are quite polished, but the filmmakers still take pleasure in showing the seams. Setting its story "a long, long time ago in a galaxy far cheaper than this one," Keri Llewellyn's technically accomplished *Star Wars* reproduces the assault on the Death Star, using origami-folded paper TIE fighters and a basketball painted white as a stand-in for the Death Star. As the Death Star bursts into flames, we hear a loud boink as the elastic string holding it in space snaps, and it falls out of the frame.

If the third-world filmmakers saw "imperfect cinema" as the basis for an implicit, and often very explicit, critique of the ideologies and market forces behind the Hollywood blockbuster and saw their parodies of American genre films as helping "destroy the very toys of mystification," no such radical goal governs the production of these amateur films. They have, indeed, turned toward parody as the most effective genre for negotiating between these competing desires to reproduce, not to destroy, the special effects at the heart of the contemporary blockbuster and to acknowledge their own amateur status. Yet their parody is almost always affectionate and rarely attempts to make an explicit political statement.

A notable exception may be *Tie-Tanic*, which directly references the huge corporate apparatus behind *Star Wars'* success and calls into question the franchising of contemporary popular culture. The filmmaker, John Bunt, redubbed a sequence from the original *Star Wars* film depicting a conference between Darth Vader, Grand Moff Tarkin, and other Imperial forces so that it now represents a Lucasfilm marketing meeting, as corporate executives plot to rob consumers of their entertainment dollars. During a period of "nostalgic consumption," the *Star Wars* trilogy has regained its bid to be the highest grossing box-office success of all time but remains potentially vulnerable to challenge while the producers are nervously awaiting the completion of the prequels. The slow deployment of trailers can only hold the audience's attention for so long in an environment of competing blockbusters. Although the studio executives are convinced that "talking pigs will hold the mouse-lovers in mind," the real point of vulnerability are teenage girls: "If the Rebels arouse sympathy and pathos in adolescent girls, it is possible—however unlikely—that they might find a market and exploit it." Darth Vader warns them that "the ability to control the medium for twenty years is insignificant next to the power of a good chick flick," only to be dismissed with, "Don't try to frighten us with your demographic ways, Lord Vader." Yet Grand Moff Tarkin heeds his advice and dispatches him to deal with all challenges to this market segment. In a spectacular finale, which mixes footage, sometimes within the same composite image, from *Star Wars* and *Titanic*, Vader's stormtroopers and TIE fighters open fire on the luxury liner. In several remarkable shots, we see R2D2, C-3PO, and a flaming Ewok among the terrified passengers flying from the sinking ship and watch a TIE fighter swoop down and blow up one of the escaping lifeboats. Rarely has the cutthroat competition between media conglomerates been depicted with such vivid and witty images! Yet, such an overt—and still pretty tame—critique of market forces is the exception rather than the rule.

More often, these amateur filmmakers see themselves as actively promoting media texts that they admire. For example, *Shadows of the Empire* is an unauthorized fan-made adaptation of Steve Perry's commercial *Star Wars* novel. Perry's original novel explored events that occurred between the end of *Empire Strikes Back* and the opening moments of *Return of the Jedi. Shadows of the Empire* has proven especially popular with *Star Wars* fans because it pays significant attention to the bounty hunter, Boba Fett, a character relatively marginal to the original films but central to the fan culture. Frustrated that this novel had never been adapted to the screen, fan filmmakers Jeff Hendrich and Bob Branch created their own serialization of the story: "We pooled every *Star Wars* action figure and toy that we could beg, borrow or steal to make up the cast of the film. The occasional special guest toy stands in for the characters we just couldn't find and as extras in the crowd scenes." Though the adaptation was unauthorized, it nevertheless follows the logic of the franchise system itself.

The Qui-Gon Show aptly suggests the blurring between professional and fan efforts that occurs in this context. The script emerged as part of AtomFilms. com's "Makin' Wookie" competition, a commercially sponsored contest that attracted more than 300 amateur and semiprofessional entries, including such promising titles as *Mos Angeles*, *The Real World—Tatooine*, *Springer Wars*, *Star Wars: Close Encounters*, and *Wookie Nights*. AtomFilms then provided budgets for several of the more acclaimed fan filmmakers, including Jason Wishnow and Evan Mather, to produce shorts based on Robert Fyvolent's contest-winning script. As with *The Qui-Gon Show*, many of the films have been distributed through the new commercial sites devoted to digital cinema and, in several notable cases, have been released on commercial video.

Even in the absence of such direct commercial connections, the mass marketing of *Star Wars* inadvertently provided many of the resources needed to support these productions. Amateur filmmakers often make use of commercially available costumes and props, sample music from the soundtrack album and sounds of *Star Wars* videos or computer games, and draw advice on special-effects techniques from television documentaries and mass-market magazines. For example, the makers of *Duel* describes the sources for their soundtrack: "We sampled most of the lightsaber sounds from the *Empire Strikes Back* special edition laserdisc, and a few from *A New Hope*. *Jedi* was mostly useless to us, as the lightsaber battles in the film are always accompanied by music. The kicking sounds are really punch sounds from *Raiders of the Lost Ark*, and there's one sound—hideous running across the sand—that we got from *Lawrence of Arabia*. Music, of course, comes from the *Phantom Menace* soundtrack." By contrast, some filmmakers made use of images from the films themselves but added soundtracks from other sources. *Stooge Wars*, for example, juxtaposes footage of Darth Vader and the stormtroopers with sounds and dialogue sampled from *I'll Never Heil Again*, a Three Stooges short that features Moe as Hitler.

More broadly, the availability of these various ancillary products has encouraged these filmmakers, since childhood, to construct their own fantasies within the *Star Wars* universe. As one fan critic explains, "Odds are if you were a kid in the seventies, you probably fought in schoolyards over who would play Han, lost a Wookie action figure in your backyard, and dreamed of firing that last shot on the Death Star. And probably your daydreams and conversations weren't about William Wallace, Robin Hood, or Odysseus, but, instead, lightsaber battles, frozen men, and forgotten fathers. In other words, we talked about our legend." Lucasfilm and Kenner may have initially understood the *Star Wars* action figures as commodities, but their cultural effects go much deeper. The action figures provided this generation with some of their earliest avatars, encouraging them to assume the role of a Jedi Knight or an intergalactic bounty hunter and enabling them to physically manipulate the characters and props to construct their own stories. Fans, for example, note that the Boba Fett action figure, far more than the character's small role in the trilogy, helped make this character a favorite among digital filmmakers. The fans, as children, had fleshed out Boba Fett's intentionally murky character, giving him (or her) a personality, motives, goals, and conflicts, which helped inspire the plots of a number of the amateur movies.

Not surprisingly, a significant number of filmmakers in their late teens and early twenties have turned toward those action figures as resources for their first production efforts. *Toy Wars* producers Aaron Halon and Jason VandenBerghe have launched an ambitious plan to produce a shot-by-shot remake of *Star Wars: A New Hope* cast entirely with action figures. Other filmmakers mix and match action figures from multiple fictional universes to create new works. For example, *Battle of the Bedroom* (Scott Middlebrook) teams Princess Leia and *Tomb Raider*'s Lara Croft against the Imperial stormtroopers in a battle that rocks a suburban home to its foundation. The *Enterprise* arrives with a well-timed message of peace, provoking combatants on both sides to open fire and blast the Federation starship out of the skies. Other filmmakers have made films using the Lego *Star Wars* construction kits, though these materials have proven less flexible in their movements and thus narrow the range of narrative options. To date, most Lego movies have been short lightsaber battles. The Lego blocks, however, have proven to be extremely useful for building sets and other props.

These action-figure movies require constant resourcefulness on the part of the amateur filmmakers. Damon Wellner and Sebastian O'Brien, two self-proclaimed "action-figure nerds" from Cambridge, Massachusetts, formed Probot Productions with the goal of "making toys as alive as they seemed in childhood." Probot has made several action-figure movies, including the forty-minute long *Star Wars* epic, *Prequel: Revenge of the Snaggletooth* (which they bill as "homage to the franchise that redefined Movie Merchandi$ing") and *Aliens 5* ("In space, no one can hear you playing with toys."). The Probot Web site offers this explanation of their production process: "The first thing you need to know about Probot Productions is that we're broke. We spend all our $$$ on toys. This leaves a very small budget for special effects, so we literally have to work with what we can find in the garbage. You may be surprised at what you can create with a video camera and some simple household items.... If you have seen *Aliens 5*, you may remember Ripley and Bishop running down the computer-generated hallways of the spaceship.... This effect was done simply by placing the camera directly in front of a TV, having one person holding the action figures up in front of the screen and another person playing the *Alien vs. Predator* video game. Any *Doom*-type 3-D environment game would work for this effect. It works so well because the video game is a "virtual-set," a HUGE 3-D environment in which you can easily shoot from any angle, and even mock complex camera movements. And video-game graphics are just getting better and better!... We used a lot of pyrotechnics in the film and had a fire extinguisher on the set at all times.... We used pump-action hairspray (not aerosol!!) and a lighter to create our flame-thrower effect. Please don't burn your house down making your movie.... For sets we used a breadbox, a ventilation tube from a dryer, cardboard boxes, a discarded piece from a vending machine, and milk crates. Large Styrofoam pieces from stereo component boxes work very well to create spaceshiplike environments!" Despite such primitive working conditions, Probot has been able to mimic the original film's lightsaber battles, space weaponry, and holographic images.

No digital filmmaker has pushed the aesthetics of the action figure as far as Evan Mather. Mather's films, such as *Godzilla Versus Disco Lando*, *Kung-fu Kenobi's Big Adventure*, and *Quentin Tarantino's Star Wars*, represent a no-holds-barred romp through contemporary popular culture. The rock-'em sock-'em action of *Kung-Fu Kenobi's Big Adventure* takes place against the backdrop of settings sampled from the film, drawn by hand, or built from Lego blocks, with the eclectic and evocative soundtrack borrowed from Neil Diamond, *Mission: Impossible*, *Pee-Wee's Big Adventure*, and *A Charlie Brown Christmas*. Dialogue in Mather's movies is often sampled from the original films or elsewhere in popular culture. *Disco Lando* puts the moves on everyone from Admiral Ackbar to Jabba's blue-skinned dancing girl, and all his pick-up lines come from the soundtrack of *The Empire Strikes Back*. Mace Windu "gets medieval" on the Jedi Council, delivering Samuel L. Jackson's lines from *Pulp Fiction*, before shooting up the place. The camera focuses on the bald head of a dying Darth Vader as he gasps "Rosebud." Rebels and stormtroopers battle it out on the snowy landscape of Hoth while cheery yuletide music plays in the background.

Literary critic Lois Rostow Kuznets has discussed the recurrent motif of toys coming to life across several centuries of children's literature, noting that such stories provide a variety of functions for their readers and authors: "Toy characters embody the secrets of the night: they inhabit a secret, sexual, sensual world, one that exists in closed toy shops, under Christmas trees, and behind the doors of dollhouses—and those of our parents' bedrooms. This is an uncanny (in Freudian terms) world of adult mysteries and domestic intrigue. It can be marginal, liminal, potentially carnival world." Mather and the other action-figure filmmakers explore the secrets of the night, blurring the boundaries between different fictional universes, playfully transgressing the family values of the original *Star Wars* films, to encourage our carnival-esque play with their molded plastic protagonists. The humor is often scatological. Yoda eats too many Banta Beans and farts repeatedly in Obi-Wan's face. A naked Barbie spews green vomit into a commode. Mather's characters belch, fart, and barf with total abandon, as they punch, kick, and pummel each other with little or no provocation. *Disco Lando* climaxes with a bloody fistfight between Godzilla and the Virgin Mary. And Mather loves to insinuate tabloid-style secret lives for the various characters. Obi-Wan wakes up in bed snuggling with Lobot. Luke Skywalker enjoys dressing in Princess Leia's skimpy slave-girl costume. As for Leia, Mather shows her smooching with her brother, Luke, and then pulls back to show a whole lineup of panting aliens waiting their turn for the princess.

Apart from their anarchic humor and rapid-fire pace, Mather's films stand out because of their visual sophistication. In some cases, Mather deftly pastiches the visual styles of contemporary filmmakers, especially Tarantino. Moreover, Mather's own frenetic style has become increasingly distinguished across the body of his works, constantly experimenting with different forms of animation, flashing or masked images, and dynamic camera movements. Mather has made a virtue of his materials, using the plastic qualities of the action figures to justify a movement into a brightly colored and totally surreal mise-en-scène.

Yet, if the action-figure filmmakers have developed an aesthetic based on their appropriation of materials from the mainstream media, then the mainstream media has been quick to imitate that aesthetic. Nickelodeon's *Action League Now*, for example, has a regular cast of characters consisting of mismatched dolls and mutilated action figures. In some cases, their faces have been melted or mangled through inappropriate play. One protagonist has no clothes. They come in various size scales, suggesting the collision of different narrative universes that characterizes children's action-figure play. Recurring gags involve the smashing of brittle characters or dogs gnawing on and mutilating the protagonists, situations all too common in domestic play. MTV's *Celebrity Death Match* creates its action figures using claymation, staging World Wrestling Federation-style bouts between various celebrities, some likely (Monica Lewinsky against Hillary Clinton), some simply bizarre (the rock star formerly known as Prince against Prince Charles). Screenwriter/Director Steve Oedekerk (*Ace Ventura 2, The Nutty Professor, Patch Adams*) produced *ThumbWars* using thumbs, dressed in elaborate costumes, as his primary performers and then digitally added facial features and expressions. UPN aired the decisively low-tech and low-humor result the week the *Star Wars* prequel opened in the theaters. It is in the context of such unlikely cult television productions that it becomes plausible to see the creation of a high-quality fan film for Web distribution as a "tryout" for gaining access into the media industries.

We are witnessing the emergence of an elaborate feedback loop between the emerging "DIY" aesthetics of participatory culture and the mainstream industry. The Web represents a site of experimentation and innovation, where amateurs test the waters, developing new practices and themes and generating materials that may well attract cult followings on their own terms. The most commercially viable of those practices are then absorbed into the mainstream media: directly, through the hiring of new talent or the development of television, video, or big-screen works based on those materials; or indirectly, through a second-order imitation of the same aesthetic and thematic qualities. In return, the mainstream-media materials may provide inspiration for subsequent amateur efforts, which, in turn, push popular culture in new directions. In such a world, fan works can no longer be understood as simply derivative of mainstream materials but must be understood as being open themselves to appropriation and reworking by the media industries.

This process is aptly illustrated by considering the work of such popular artists as Kevin Smith, Quentin Tarantino, Mike Judge, Matt Groening, and Kevin Williamson, whose films and television series reflect this mainstreaming of fan aesthetics and politics. Their works often deal explicitly with the process of forming one's own mythology using images borrowed from the mass media. One of the protagonists of *Pulp Fiction*, for example, decides at the end that he wants to "wander the earth," like Kane in television's *Kung Fu*. *Reservoir Dogs* opens with a five-minute discussion of the erotic connotations of Madonna's "Like a Virgin," defining the characters first and foremost through their relationships to popular culture. Characters in *Chasing Amy* engage in animated debates and speculations about the sexuality of the various teens in the *Archie* comics, while *Dazed and Confused* opens with the scene of high school students trying to recall as many different episodes of *Gilligan's Island* as they can, before one of the women offers a devastating critique of how the series builds upon the iconography of male pornography. Kevin Smith's films make recurring in-joke references to *Star Wars*, including a debate about the ethical obligations of the independent contractors who worked on the Death Star (*Clerks*), a comic episode when Silent Bob becomes convinced that he can actually perform Jedi mind tricks (*Mall Rats*), and a long rant about the "blackness" of Darth Vader (*Chasing Amy*); Smith devotes an entire issue of his *Clerks* comic book to various characters' attempts to corner the market on collectible *Star Wars* action figures.

The protagonist of Williamsons's television series *Dawson's Creek* decorates his room with posters for Steven Spielberg films, routinely discusses and critiques classic and contemporary films with the other characters on the series, and draws inspiration from them for the creation of his own videos. Tarantino's whole aesthetic seems to have emerged from his formative experiences working at a video store. In such an environment, older and newer films are more or less equally accessible; some movie is always playing on the monitor and providing a background for everyday interactions. These video-store experiences encourage a somewhat scrambled but aesthetically productive relationship to film history. Tarantino, Smith, Williamson, and their contemporaries make films that attract the interests of other video-store habitués, much as earlier generations of filmmakers—the French New Wave or the American Movie Brats—made movies for other cineastes. Much as the cineaste filmmakers set scenes in movie theatres or made whole movies centering around their protagonists' obsessions with the filmgoing experience, these newer filmmakers frequently cast video-store clerks as protagonists (*Clerks*, *Scream*), celebrating their expertise about genre conventions or their insightful speculations about popular films. This video-store aesthetic mixes and matches elements from different genres, different artistic movements, and different periods with absolute abandon. Tarantino's tendency toward quotation runs riot in the famous Jack Rabbit Slim's restaurant sequence in *Pulp Fiction*, where the service personnel are impersonating iconic figures of the 1950s and the menu uses comedy teams to designate different shake flavors. As the John Travolta character explains, "It's like a wax museum with a pulse," a phrase that might describe Tarantino's whole approach to filmmaking. Even his casting decisions, such as the use of *Medium Cool*'s Robert Forster and blaxploitation star Pam Grier in *Jackie Brown*, constitute quotations and appropriations from earlier film classics.

Not surprisingly, the works of these "video-store filmmakers" have been deeply influential on the emerging generation of amateur digital filmmakers— almost as influential, in fact, as *Star Wars* itself. Jeff Allen, a 27-year-old "HTML monkey" for an Atlanta-based Internet company, for example, made *Trooperclerks*, a spoof of the trailer for *Clerks*, which deals with the drab routine confronted by the stormtroopers who work in convenience stores and video-rental outlets on board the Death Star. The short spoof, which was immediately embraced and promoted by Kevin Smith's View Askew, was later followed by a half-hour animated film based on the same premise, made in response to the news that *Clerks* was being adapted into an animated network series. Allen's focus on *Clerks* came only after he considered and rejected the thought of doing a *Star Wars* parody based on Tarantino's *Reservoir Dogs*. Similarly, Allen Smith heads a team that is producing a feature-length animated film, *Pulp Phantom*, which offers a scene-by-scene spoof of *Pulp Fiction*, recast with characters from *Star Wars*. At writing, the team has produced more than ten episodes for the Web, taking the story up to the point where paid assassin Darth Maul races the overdosing Princess Amidala to the home of drug dealer Han Solo, frantic lest he get into trouble with her jealous gangland husband, Darth Vader. In a particularly inspired bit of casting, Jar Jar Binks plays the geeky college student whom, in a still-anticipated installment, Maul accidentally blows away in the back of Boba Fett's vehicle. "Fan boy" filmmakers, such as Smith and Tarantino, are thus inspiring the efforts of the next generation of amateur filmmakers, who are, in turn, developing cult followings that may ultimately gain them access to the commercial mainstream. The *Pulp Phantom* Web site, for example, includes a mechanism where loyal fans can receive e-mail each time a new installment of the series gets posted.

This cyclical process has only accelerated since the box-office success of *The Blair Witch Project*, which presented itself as an amateur digital film (albeit one that got commercial distribution and challenged *The Phantom Menace* at the box office in the summer of 1999) and built public interest through its sophisticated use of the Web. *The Blair Witch Project*, in turn, has inspired countless Web-based amateur parodies (including *The Jar Jar Binks Project* and *The Wicked Witch Project*) and has sparked increased public and industry interest in the search for subsequent amateurs who can break into the mainstream, while the bigger budget sequel to *The Blair Witch Project* takes as its central image the explosion of amateur filmmakers who have come to Burkittsville, Maryland, in hopes of making their own documentaries on the mysterious deaths.

CONCLUSION

"I personally find the opportunity to explore this new form of entertainment and creative expression both stimulating and liberating. While much of what we have learned throughout our careers will apply, I am also certain that new and unusual aesthetic values will quickly evolve—shaped by the medium itself, the public and the creative collaborations which this company will encourage."

—Ron Howard

"Just as MTV introduced a new entertainment forum for music videos, we think this new enterprise will offer a new form of entertainment for the rapidly growing population of Internet users. POP.com has the capability not only to offer a variety of entertainment options, but to tap into an as-yet-undiscovered talent pool that is as global as the Internet itself."

—Jeffrey Katzenberg

What is the future of digital cinema? One position sees digital cinema as an extension of avant-garde filmmaking practices, opening a new space for formal experimentation and alternative cultural politics and offering experimental artists access to a broader public than can be attracted to screenings of their works at film festivals, museums, or university classes. Another position, represented by the founders of Pop.com (see above), sees the digital cinema as a potential new site for commercial developments, an extension of the logic of media convergence, a kind of MTV for the 21st century. In this vision, established filmmakers, such as Steven Spielberg or Tim Burton, can produce shorter and riskier works; emerging talents can develop their production skills; and works may move fluidly back and forth between the Web, television, film, and computer games. Interestingly, both groups want to tap into the hipness of "DIY" culture, promoting their particular visions of the future of digital cinema in terms of democratic participation and amateur self-expression, pinning their hopes, as Coppola suggests, on the prospect that a "little fat girl" from the Midwest will become the "Mozart" of digital filmmaking. Both visions have inherent limitations: the "low-res" movement's appeals to avant-garde aesthetics, its language of manifestos, and its focus on film-festival screenings may well prove as elitist as the earlier film movements it seeks to supplant, while the new commercial version of the digital cinema may reinscribe the same cultural gatekeepers who have narrowed the potential diversity of network television or Hollywood cinema.

The *Star Wars* fan films discussed here represent a potentially important third space between the two. Shaped by the intersection between contemporary trends toward media convergence and participatory culture, these fan films are hybrid by nature—neither fully commercial nor fully alternative, existing as part of a grassroots dialogue with mass culture. We are witnessing the transformation of amateur film culture from a focus on home movies toward a focus on public movies, from a focus on local audiences toward a focus on a potential global audience, from a focus on mastering the technology toward a focus on mastering the mechanisms for publicity and promotion, and from a focus on self-documentation toward a focus on an aesthetics based on appropriation, parody, and the dialogic. Coppola's "little fat girl" has found a way to talk back to the dominant media culture, to express herself not simply within an idiolect but within a shared language constructed through the powerful images and narratives that constitute contemporary popular culture. She will find ways to tap into the mythology of *Star Wars* and use it as a resource for the production of her own stories, stories that are broadly accessible to a popular audience and that, in turn, inspire others to create their own works, much as Lucas created *Star Wars* through the clever appropriation and transformation of various popular culture influences (ranging from Laurel and Hardy to *Battleship Yamato* and *The Hidden Fortress*).

This third space will survive, however, only if we maintain a vigorous and effective defense of the principle of "fair use"; only if we recognize the rights of consumers to participate fully, actively, and creatively within their own culture; and only if we hold in check the desires of the culture industries to tighten their control over their own intellectual properties in response to the economic opportunities posed by an era of media convergence. At the moment, we are on a collusion course between a new economic and legal culture that encourages monopoly power over cultural mythologies and new technologies that empower consumers to archive, annotate, appropriate, and recirculate media images. The recent legal disputes around Napster represent only a skirmish in what is likely to be a decades-long war over intellectual property, a war that will determine not simply the future direction of digital cinema but the nature of creative expression in the 21st century.

From Women and Technology to Gendered Technoscience
Judy Wajcman

Sociologist Judy Wajcman has held posts at the London School of Economics, the University of Warwick Business School, the Australian National University, and elsewhere. She is currently a Visiting Fellow at All Souls College, Oxford, and a Visiting Professor at London Business School. Her research has focused on technological and social change, and she is best-known for her landmark study of the gendered character of technology and technological change. In this essay, she notes that Internet and communications technology has a relationship with gender and that young women, in particular, experience themselves differently in relationship to this technology than did previous generations. For the future, Wajcman looks to the renegotiation of gender power relations as communications technology continues to grow and to change.

Introduction

Feminist theories of gender and technology have come a long way over the last two decades. While much early second-wave feminism generated a fatalism that emphasized the role of technology in reproducing patriarchy, during the 1990s cyberfeminist writers celebrated digital technologies as inherently liberatory for women. In recent years feminist scholars have produced an important body of work, bridging the gap between technophobia and technophilia. Much of it has developed in tandem with the burgeoning field of science and technology studies. The resulting literature is generally more critical of technoscience while at the same time aware of its potential to open up new gender dynamics. Current approaches focus on the mutual shaping of gender and technology, where neither gender nor technology is taken to be pre-existing, nor is the relationship between them immutable. Such a co-construction approach provides a compelling critique of popular arguments and social theories that were and still are characterized by technological determinism. Rather than technology per se being credited as the main agent of change, feminist politics is recognized as the key to gender equality.

This article provides an overview of the various approaches to conceptualizing the link between gender and technology, both past and present. In turning to this task, I should emphasize that feminist discussions have always taken diverse and overlapping forms. While standard histories of feminist thought tend to present liberal, socialist and radical feminisms, for example, as distinct perspectives, in reality there were always interconnections and they certainly did not develop as independent strands or in a simple chronological order. For our purposes here, I present the different streams rather schematically in order to highlight their contrasting perspectives.

The early groundwork

A core concern of the women's movement since its inception has been women's limited access to scientific and technical institutions and professions. Many national and international studies have identified the structural barriers to women's participation, looking at sex discrimination in employment and the kind of socialization and education that girls receive which have channelled them away from studying mathematics and science (Rossiter 1982; Keller 1985; Harding 1996). Sex stereotyping in schools has been exposed, particularly the processes by which girls and boys are channelled into different subjects in secondary and tertiary education, and the link between education and the segregated labour market. Explaining the under-representation of women in science education, laboratories and scientific publications, research has highlighted the construction and character of femininity encouraged by our culture.

For liberal feminism in the 1970s and 1980s, the solution was posed in terms of getting more women to enter science and technology—seeing the issue as one of equal access to education and employment. Rather than questioning technoscience itself, it was generally assumed that science is intrinsically open, concerned with unbiased and objective research. The issue was framed in terms of the uses and abuses to which a fundamentally (gender) neutral science and technology has been put by men. Feminist writing in this vein focused on gender stereotypes and customary expectations, and denied the existence of sex differences between women and men. If girls were given the right opportunities and encouragement they could easily become scientists and engineers. Remedying the gender deficit was seen as a problem that could be overcome by a combination of different socialization processes and equal opportunity policies.

The strengths and limitations of equal employment opportunity policies have been much debated over the intervening decades (Bacchi 1996). What is beyond doubt, however, is the extent and intransigence of women's marginalization from scientific and technical pursuits. Feminists at that time pointed out that the liberal feminist tradition located the problem in women (their socialization, their aspirations and values) and did not ask the broader questions of whether and in what way technoscience and its institutions could be reshaped to accommodate women. Women were being asked to exchange major aspects of their gender identity for a masculine version without prescribing a similar "degendering" process for men.

Such critiques emphasized that in addition to gender structures, the culture of technology is important in making it a male domain. Technologies have a masculine image, not only because they are dominated by men but because they incorporate symbols, metaphors and values that have masculine connotations. Women's reluctance "to enter" is to do with the sex-stereotyped association of technology as an activity appropriate for men. As with science, the very language of technology, its symbolism, is masculine. It is not simply a question of acquiring skills, because these skills are embedded in a culture of masculinity that is largely conterminous with the culture of technology. Both at school and at the workplace this culture is incompatible with femininity. Therefore, to enter this world, to learn its language, women have first to forsake their femininity.

While liberal feminism conceived of the problem as one of equality of access and opportunity, socialist and radical feminisms analysed the gendered nature of technoscientific knowledge and culture, and put the spotlight on artefacts themselves. The social factors that shape different technologies came under scrutiny, especially the way technology reflects gender divisions and inequalities. The problem was not only men's monopoly of technology, but also the way gender is embedded in technology itself. In other words, feminist analyses of technology were shifting beyond the approach of 'women and technology' to examine the very processes whereby technology is developed and used, as well as those whereby gender is constituted. This approach took two broad directions: one influenced by radical feminism, the other identified with socialist feminism.

An important precept of radical and cultural feminism is that Western technology, like science, is deeply implicated in the masculine project of the domination and control of women and nature. These feminisms emphasize gender difference and celebrate what they see as specifically feminine, such as women's greater humanism, pacifism, nurturance and spiritual development. The idea that what was "specifically feminine" was socially produced was abandoned and notions of ineradicable difference flourished. This approach has been particularly influential in relation to the technologies of human biological reproduction (Corea *et al.* 1985; Spallone & Steinberg 1987). It is fuelled by the perception that the processes of pregnancy and childbirth were directed and controlled by ever more sophisticated and intrusive technologies. Radical feminists' strong opposition to the development of the new reproductive technologies such as IVF during the 1980s reflected fears of patriarchal exploitation of women's bodies. There was a call for new technology to be based on female rather than male values.

These approaches took the debate regarding gender and technology beyond the use/abuse model, focusing on the political qualities of technology. Where liberal feminism saw power in terms of relations between individual people, radical feminism emphasized the way in which gender power relations were embedded more deeply within science and technology. They were also a forceful assertion of women's interests and needs as being different from men's and highlighted the way in which women are not always well served by current technologies. However, in representing women as inherently nurturing and pacifist, they also perpetuated a tendency to gender essentialism. The historical and cultural specificity of our modern understanding of women as being radically other than men was overlooked. Too often the result was a pessimistic portrayal of women uniformly as victims of patriarchal technoscience.

While women's bodies and sexuality were the focus of radical feminism, socialist feminism concentrated on the machinery of production. It was widely believed that microelectronic technology would have a negative impact on women's work, and this led to a pronounced anti-technology stance. There were fears that computerization of office work, for example, would lead to deskilling, with jobs fragmented into routine and standardized tasks subject to the control of the machine. Influenced by Marxist analyses of technological change resulting from class conflict, feminist researchers revealed how the capitalist division of labour intersected with sexual divisions. A crucial historical perspective was brought to bear on the analysis of men's monopoly of technology. Extensive research on manufacturing and engineering demonstrated that women's exclusion from technology was as a consequence of the male domination of skilled trades that developed during the industrial revolution (Cockburn 1983; Milkman 1987; Bradley 1989). Craft workers, typically seen as the defenders of working-class interests in disputes over technical change, resisted the entry of women to skilled technical jobs in order to protect their own conditions. Industrial technology from its origins thus reflected men's designs, and is a defining feature of masculinity.

Socialist feminist frameworks, then, saw masculinity as embedded in the machinery itself, highlighting the role of technology as a key source of male power (Cockburn 1985; McNeil 1987; Webster 1989; Wajcman 1991). Instead of treating artefacts as neutral or value-free, social relations (including gender relations) are materialized in tools and techniques. Technology was seen as socially shaped, but shaped by men to the exclusion of women. While this literature did reflect an understanding of the historical variability and plurality of the categories of "women" and "technology," it was nevertheless pessimistic about the possibilities of redesigning technologies for gender equality. The proclivity of technological developments to entrench gender hierarchies was emphasized rather than the prospects they afford for change. In short, not enough attention was paid to women's agency. And it is precisely this rather negative register that provoked a reaction from a new generation of feminist scholars.

Contemporary approaches

Feminist approaches of the 1990s and today are much more positive about the possibilities of ICTs to empower women and transform gender relations (Kemp & Squires 1998; Green & Adam 1999; Kirkup et al. 2000). Indeed, early concerns about women being left out of the communications revolution, victims of the digital divide, now seem exaggerated. A proliferation of mobile phones, the Internet and cyber-cafés are providing new opportunities and outlets for women, particularly those in highly industrialized countries who are better placed to take advantage of these technologies. While the early adopters of the Internet and mobile phone were predominantly men, studies in recent years have found narrowing gender differences in adoption rates.

For example, while male ownership of mobile telephony is still higher across Western Europe, the gaps are not very wide, and in the United States women now slightly exceed men in mobile phone ownership (Castells *et al.* 2007, pp. 41–44). Certainly in wealthier countries, where diffusion levels are high, the gender gap is disappearing.

Given the dramatic changes in the ownership and use of digital technologies, many postmodern cyberfeminists enthusiastically embrace Web-based technologies. A common argument in this literature is that the virtuality of cyberspace and the Internet spelt the end of the embodied basis for sex difference (Millar 1998; Plant 1998). According to Sadie Plant (1998), for example, digital technologies facilitate the blurring of boundaries between humans and machines, and between male and female, enabling their users to choose their disguises and assume alternative identities. Industrial technology may have had a patriarchal character but digital technologies, based on brain rather than brawn, on networks rather than hierarchy, herald a new relationship between women and machines. Writers such as Plant are interested in revalorizing the feminine, bringing woman's radical alterity, her difference, into being. For them, the Internet and cyberspace are seen as feminine media, providing the technological basis for a new form of society that is potentially liberating for women. According to this view, women, rather than men, are uniquely suited to life in the digital age.

Perhaps the optimism of this postmodern literature is best summed up by Donna Haraway (1985, 1997), who urges us to embrace the positive potential of science and technology. She is sharply critical of those who reject technoscience in favour of a return to a mythical unpolluted natural state. Famously, and provocatively, she prefers to be a "cyborg"—a hybrid of organism and machine parts—rather than an ecofeminist "goddess." She notes the great power of science and technology to create new meanings and new entities, to make new worlds. She positively revels in the very difficulty of predicting what technology's effects will be and warns against any purist rejection of the "unnatural," hybrid entities produced by biotechnology. Genetic engineering, reproductive technology and the advent of virtual reality are all seen as fundamentally challenging traditional notions of gender identity. As such, they mark a transformation in the relationship between women and technology.

In looking forward to what ICTs and biotechnologies may make possible, such writers elaborate a new feminist "imaginary" different from the "material reality" of the existing technological order. Haraway's ground-breaking work has been particularly influential among feminist technoscience (STS) scholars and she epitomizes the challenge to second-wave feminism's tendency to portray women as victims. Instead, women's agency and capacity for empowerment are stressed. Young women in particular are orienting and experiencing themselves differently in relation to new media technologies, compared with previous generations. Developments in digital technologies do call for some radical rethinking both of the processes of technological innovation and of their impact on the culture and practices of everyday life.

However, uncritical enthusiasm for everything digital has exposed post-modern literature to charges of technological determinism—albeit of a celebratory rather than pessimistic bent. In common with other proponents of the progressive impact of information and biotechnologies, cyberfeminists insist on distinguishing new technologies from more established ones and downplay any continuities between them. While women have been actively engaged in constructing hybrid, transgendered identities through their consumption of new media (for example, diary writing on web logs is a popular activity among young women), the possibility and the fluidity of gender discourse in the virtual world is constrained by the material world.

Consider for a moment the hype about *Second Life*, an online virtual world with over one million registrations (http://www.secondlife.com). It is a sophisticated 3D space designed for adult "residents" who can imaginatively create avatars, homes and entire lifestyles using in-world currency. It is widely seen as promoting anti-establishment values, yet it has become a major source of virtual pornography, apparently well suited to those with a taste for sadomasochistic forms of sex (Bardzell & Bardzell 2006). Such fantasy cyberworlds, then, are not necessarily comfortable cultural environments for women to inhabit. To move forward, we need to continue to refine our understanding of the relationship between ICTs and gender, so that we do not treat technology as either inherently patriarchal or unambiguously liberating.

Technofeminism: combining feminist and technology studies

Over the last two decades, feminist writing within the field of science and technology studies (STS) has theorized the relationship between gender and technology as one of mutual shaping. A shared idea in this tradition is that technological innovation is itself shaped by the social circumstances within which it takes place. Crucially, the notion that technology is simply the product of rational technical imperatives has been dislodged. Objects and artefacts are no longer seen as separate from society, but as part of the social fabric that holds society together; they are never merely technical or social. Rather, the broad social shaping or constructivist approach treats technology as a sociotechnical product—a seamless web or network combining artefacts, people, organizations, cultural meanings and knowledge (Bijker *et al.* 1987; Law & Hassard 1999; MacKenzie & Wajcman 1999). It follows that technological change is a contingent and heterogeneous process in which technology and society are mutually constituted.

In terms of gender and ICTs, feminist STS scholarship has explored the effects of gender power relations on design and innovation, as well as the impact of technological change on the sexes. In common with European research, my own technofeminist approach conceives of technology as both a source and a consequence of gender relations (Berg 1996; Faulkner 2001; Oudshoorn *et al.* 2004; Wajcman 2004). In other words, gender relations can be thought of as materialized in technology, and gendered identities and discourses as produced simultaneously with technologies. Several empirical studies have demonstrated that the marginalization of women from the technological community has a profound influence on the design, technical content and use of artefacts (Lie 2003; Lerman *et al.* 2003; Oudshoorn 1994, 2003).

Importantly, this co-production of gender and technology does not end with the innovation and design process. Feminist research has been at the forefront of moves to deconstruct the designer/user divide, and that between production and consumption, emphasizing the connectedness of all phases of technological development (Cockburn & Ormrod 1993). This is an important move, as standard STS case studies focus on the groups or networks that actively seek to influence the direction of technological developments. Women's systematic absence from these sites of observable conflict is not often understood to indicate the mobilization of gender interests. For feminists, women's absence from particular sociotechnical networks is as telling as the presence of other actors, and even a condition of that presence. This points to the need to examine the ways in which the gendering of technology affects the entire life trajectory of an artefact. Integrating detailed studies of design, manufacture, marketing, purchase and consumption allows a range of social and cultural factors, including gender, to become apparent. For this reason, technofeminist approaches stress that gendering involves several dimensions, involving material, discursive and social elements. It is precisely this intricate interweaving of artefacts, culture and gendered identities in technoscientific practice that helps to explain why this link has proved so durable.

So far, I have been stressing how embedded gender relations are in the design, meaning and use of ICTs. However, STS scholarship increasingly recognizes that the social meanings of technology are contingently stabilized and contestable, that the fate of a technology depends on many social factors that cannot simply be read off fixed sets of power arrangements. Introducing terms like "interpretative flexibility" and "domestication" helps to capture the idea that the particular affordances of a technology are not given and predictable (Pinch & Bijker 1987; Haddon 2004). The interpretation, reading and making sense of technologies are constant features of everyday life. Feminist theorists are now much more aware of both the contradictory effects of ICTs on women and the different meanings the same artefact might have for different groups of women. Indeed, the concept of gender itself is now understood as a performance or social achievement, constructed in interaction. It is the product of a moving relational process, emerging from collective and individual acts of interpretation. As a result, the twin pitfalls of technological determinism and gender essentialism are much less in evidence.

The relationship between gender and ICTs, then, is not immutably fixed. While the design process is decisive, technologies also yield unintended consequences and unanticipated possibilities. ICTs are sociotechnical or sociomaterial configurations that exhibit different degrees of determination and contingency at different moments in their relationship. The capacity of women users to produce new, advantageous readings of artefacts is dependent on their broader economic and social circumstances. For example, a young woman in the West experiences her silver cell phone as a liberating extension of her body. For her mother, it may primarily be a tool to keep track of her daughter. For women working as traders in Bangladesh, the mobile phone provides the means to run businesses selling communication services to other women. There is enormous variability in gendering by place, nationality, class, race, ethnicity, sexuality and generation and thus women's experience of ICTs will be diverse.

The recent development of postcolonial technoscience brings the global dynamics in and around science and technology to the fore (Anderson 2002; McNeil 2005). It highlights the fact that too often STS studies, including feminist contributions, have lacked or marginalized global perspectives. The focus of the field has been predominantly Eurocentric and North American. By challenging the universalism of Western science and technology, this literature serves as a reminder of the wider context and conditions of living in the South. In doing so, it also reveals the social relations of production that underpin consumption of ICTs. To continue with the example above, as material objects mobile phones are mass-produced in factories. Like other electronic devices, such as laptops, they require the scarce mineral Coltan, the delivery of which feeds into military conflicts in Central Africa, and thus has very specific consequences for women. Feminist frameworks are increasingly attuned to these relations of production and consumption, and their implications for global inequalities.

Conclusion

The literature on gender and technology has grown to become a broad and diverse field. It foregrounds the need to investigate the ways in which women's identities, needs and priorities are being reconfigured together with digital technologies. This opens up fresh possibilities for studies that are more attuned to how different groups of women users creatively respond to and assimilate numerous ICTs in diverse real-world locations.

Despite women's massive consumption of new media, however, the reality of women working in the ICT industries is less changed than might have been expected (Gill 2002; Perrons 2003; Whitehouse 2006). For all the hyperbole about the network society, it has not led to women's full integration into its design. The Internet does not automatically transform every user into an active producer, and every worker into a creative subject. The potential for empowerment offered by ICTs will largely be realized by those groups with technical knowledge who understand the workings of the machine. Acquisition of this know-how will become ever more critical, and gender imbalance in technical expertise ever more telling.

The central premise of feminist technoscience is that people and artefacts co-evolve: the materiality of technology affords or inhibits the doing of particular gender power relations. Crucially, such a perspective redefines the problem of the exclusion of groups of people from technological domains and activities. Whereas policy-makers and researchers explain the problem in terms of the deficiency of users, such as women, technofeminism exposes how the concrete practices of design and innovation lead to the absence of specific users.

There is increasing recognition that the development of effective ICTs requires detailed knowledge of the sites and practices in and through which the new technologies will literally be made to work (Suchman 2007). While it is impossible to specify in advance the desirable design characteristics of artefacts and information systems that would guarantee more inclusiveness, it is imperative that women are involved throughout the processes and practices of shaping technological innovation. This may not necessarily result in technologies that are friendly to both women and men, as women programmers for example may adopt a "gender script," but it is a starting point. Drawing more women into design—the configuration of artefacts—is not only an equal employment opportunities issue but is also crucially about how the world we live in is designed, and for whom.

There is ample scope for more empirical research on the gender relations of ICTs. Just as gender relations are transforming, so ICTs themselves are changing and evolving over time. This will be ever more so as computing becomes ubiquitous, with digital devices increasingly embedded into everyday things and objects, part of our taken-for-granted environment and even of ourselves. A focus on studying sociotechnical networks or systems, instead of singular technologies, will then be increasingly necessary. ICTs are much more complex and flexible than the technologies that preoccupied earlier generations of feminist scholars. We require more nuanced research that captures the increasingly complex intertwining of gender and technoscience as an ongoing process of mutual shaping over time and across multiple sites. It is important that, for all the diversity of feminist voices, this reflect our shared concern with the hierarchical divisions marking relations between men and women. We live in a technological culture, a society that is constituted by science and technology, and so the politics of technology is integral to the renegotiation of gender power relations.

References

Anderson, W. (2002) "Introduction: postcolonial technoscience," *Social Studies of Science*, vol. 32, nos 5–6, pp. 643–658.

Bacchi, C. (1996) *The Politics of Affirmative Action*, Sage, London.

Bardzell, S. & Bardzell, J. (2006) "Sex—interface—aesthetics: the docile avatars and embodied pixels of *Second Life* BDSM," [Online] Available at: http://www.ics.uci.edu/johannab/sexual.interactions.2006/chi2006.sex.PAPERS.htm (9 May 2007).

Berg, A. (1996) *Digital Feminism*, Norwegian University of Science and Technology, Trondheim.

Bijker, W., Hughes, T. & Pinch, T. (eds) (1987) *The Social Construction of Technological Systems*, MIT Press, Cambridge, MA.

Bradley, H. (1989) *Men's Work, Women's Work*, Polity Press, Cambridge.

Castells, M., Fernandez-Ardevol, M., Qui, J. & Sey, A. (2007) *Mobile Communication and Society: A Global Perspective*, MIT Press, Cambridge, MA.

Cockburn, C. (1983) *Brothers: Male Dominance and Technological Change*, Pluto Press, London.

Cockburn, C. (1985) *Machinery of Dominance: Women, Men and Technical Know-How*, Pluto Press, London.

Cockburn, C. & Ormrod, S. (1993) *Gender and Technology in the Making*, Sage, London.

Corea, G., Klein, R. D., Hanmer, J., Holmes, H. B., Hoskins, B., Kishwar, M. *et al.* (1985) *Man-Made Women: How New Reproductive Technologies Affect Women*, Hutchinson, London.

Faulker, W. (2001) "The technology question in feminism: a view from feminist technology studies," *Women's Studies International Forum*, vol. 24, no. 1, pp. 79–95.

Gill, R. (2002) "Cool, creative and egalitarian? exploring gender in project-based new media work in Europe," *Information, Communication & Society*, vol. 5, no.1, pp. 70–89.

Green, E. & Adam, A. (eds) (1999) "Editorial comment," *Information, Communication & Society*, vol. 2, no. 4, pp. v–vii.

Haddon, L. (2004) *Information and Communication Technologies in Everyday Life*, Berg, Oxford.

Haraway, D. (1985) "A manifesto for cyborgs: science, technology, and socialist feminism in the 1980's," *Socialist Review*, vol. 80, no. 15, pp. 65–108.

Haraway, D. (1997) *Modest_Witness@Second_Millennium: FemaleMan©_Meets_On-comouse™*, New York, Routledge.

Harding, S. (1996) *The Science Question in Feminism*, Cornell University Press, New York.

Keller, E. Fox (1985) *Reflections on Gender and Science*, Yale University Press, New Haven, CT.

Kemp, S. & Squires, J. (eds) (1998) *Feminisms: An Oxford Reader*, Oxford University Press, Oxford.

Kirkup, G., Janes, L., Woodward, K. & Hovenden, F. (2000) *The Gendered Cyborg: A Reader*, Routledge, London.

Law, J. & Hassard, J. (eds) (1999) *Actor-Network Theory and After*, Blackwell, Oxford.

Lerman, N. E., Oldenziel, R. & Mohun, A. P. (eds) (2003) *Gender and Technology: A Reader*, Johns Hopkins University Press, Baltimore, MD.

Lie, M. (ed.) (2003) *He, She and IT Revisited: New Perspectives on Gender in the Information Society*, Gyldendal Akademisk, Oslo.

MacKenzie, D. & Wajcman, J. (1999) *The Social Shaping of Technology*, 2nd edn, Open University Press, Milton Keynes.

McNeil, M. (ed.) (1987) *Gender and Expertise*, Free Association Books, London.

McNeil, M. (2005) "Introduction: Postcolonial technoscience," *Science as Culture*, vol. 14, no. 2, pp. 105–112.

Milkman, R. (1987) *Gender at Work: The Dynamics of Job Segregation during World War II*, University of Illinois Press, Urbana.

Millar, M. (1998) *Cracking the Gender Code: Who Rules the Wired World?*, Second Story Press, Toronto.

Oudshoorn, N. (1994) *Beyond the Natural Body: An Archaeology of Sex Hormones*, Routledge, London.

Oudshoorn, N. (2003) *The Male Pill: A Biography of a Technology in the Making*, Duke University Press, Durham, NC.

Oudshoorn, N., Rommes, E. & Stienstra, M. (2004) "Configuring the user as everybody: gender and cultures of design in information and communication technologies," *Science, Technology & Human Values*, vol. 29, no. 1, pp. 30–64.

Perrons, D. (2003) "The new economy and the work-ife balance: conceptual explorations and a case study of new media," *Gender, Work & Organization*, vol. 10, no.1, pp. 65–93.

Pinch, T. & Bijker, W. (1987) "The social construction of facts and artifacts: or how the sociology of science and the sociology of technology might benefit each other," in *The Social Construction of Technological Systems*, eds W. Bijker, T. Hughes & T. Pinch, MIT Press, Cambridge, MA.

Plant, S. (1998) *Zeros and Ones: Digital Women + the New Technoculture*, Fourth Estate, London.

Rossiter, M. (1982) *Women Scientists in America*, Johns Hopkins Press, Baltimore, MD.

Spallone, P. & Steinberg, D. (eds) (1987) *Made to Order: The Myth of Reproductive and Genetic Engineering*, Pergamon Press, Oxford.

Suchman, L. (2007) *Human-Machine Reconfigurations: Plans and Situated Actions*, 2nd edn, Cambridge University Press, Cambridge.

Wajcman, J. (1991) *Feminism Confronts Technology*, Polity Press, Cambridge.

Wajcman, J. (2004) *TechnoFeminism*, Polity Press, Cambridge.

Webster, J. (1989) *Office Automation: The Labour Process and Women's Work in Britain*, Wheatsheaf, Hemel Hempstead.

Whitehouse, G. (2006) "Women, careers and information technology: an introduction," *Labour & Industry*, vol. 16, no. 3, pp. 1–6.

The Girl Who Was Plugged In

James Tiptree, Jr.

James Tiptree, Jr., was the pen name for writer Alice B. Sheldon (1915–1987), one of the most honored and critically praised science fiction writers of the 1970s and 1980s, winning Hugo, Nebula, World Fantasy, and Locus awards, among others, during that period. Sheldon, who had worked as an intelligence analyst during World War II, took the male pseudonym at the start of her science fiction career and maintained it successfully until the late 1970s, when her real name, and her gender, became known—much to the surprise of a number of writers, editors, and critics who had known "James Tiptree, Jr.," was a pseudonym but assumed the writer was male. The Girl Who Was Plugged In won the Hugo Award for best novella of 1974, and in the story Tiptree explores issues of beauty and celebrity, gender, power, sexuality, and deeply immersive virtual reality. The story is often discussed as a precursor to the cyberpunk subgenre in science fiction.

Listen, zombie. Believe me. What I could tell you—you with your silly hands leaking sweat on your growth-stocks portfolio. One-ten lousy hacks of AT&T on twenty-point margin and you think you're Evel Knievel. AT&T? You doubleknit dummy, how I'd love to show you something.

Look, dead daddy, I'd say. See for instance that rotten girl?

In the crowd over there, that one gaping at her gods. One rotten girl in the city of the future (That's what I said.) Watch.

She's jammed among bodies, craning and peering with her soul yearning out of her eyeballs. Love! Oo-ooh, love them! Her gods are coming out of a store called Body East. Three youngbloods, larking along loverly. Dressed like simple street-people but...smashing. See their great eyes swivel above their nosefilters, their hands lift shyly, their inhumanly tender lips melt? The crowd moans. Love! This whole boiling megacity, this whole fun future world loves its gods.

You don't believe gods, dad? Wait. Whatever turns you on, there's a god in the future for you, custom-made. Listen to this mob. "I touched his foot! Ow-oow, I TOUCHED Him!"

Even the people in the GTX tower up there love the gods—in their own way and for their own reasons.

The funky girl on the street, she just loves. Grooving on their beautiful lives, their mysterioso problems. No one ever told her about mortals who love a god and end up as a tree or a sighing sound. In a million years it'd never occur to her that her gods might love her back.

She's squashed against the wall now as the godlings come by. They move in a clear space. A holocam bobs above, but its shadow never falls on them. The store display-screens are magically clear of bodies as the gods glance in and a beggar underfoot is suddenly alone. They give him a token. "Aaaaah!" goes the crowd.

Now one of them flashes some wild new kind of timer and they all trot to catch a shuttle, just like people. The shuttle stops for them—more magic. The crowd sighs, closing back. The gods are gone.

(In a room far from—but not unconnected to—the GTX tower a molecular flipflop closes too, and three account tapes spin.)

Our girl is still stuck by the wall while guards and holocam equipment pull away. The adoration's fading from her face. That's good, because now you can see she's the ugly of the world. A tall monument to pituitary dystrophy. No surgeon would touch her. When she smiles, her jaw—it's half purple—almost bites her left eye out. She's also quite young, but who could care?

The crowd is pushing her along now, treating you to glimpses of her jumbled torso, her mismatched legs. At the corner she strains to send one last fond spasm after the godlings' shuttle. Then her face reverts to its usual expression of dim pain and she lurches onto the moving walkway, stumbling into people. The walkway junctions with another. She crosses, trips and collides with the casualty rail. Finally she comes out into a little bare place called a park. The sportshow is working, a basketball game in three-di is going on right overhead. But all she does is squeeze onto a bench and huddle there while a ghostly free-throw goes by her ear.

After that nothing at all happens except a few furtive hand-mouth gestures which don't even interest her bench mates. But you're curious about the city? So ordinary after all, in the FUTURE?

Ah, there's plenty to swing with here—and it's not all that *far* in the future, dad. But pass up the sci-fi stuff for now, like for instance the holovision technology that's put TV and radio in museums. Or the worldwide carrier field bouncing down from satellites, controlling communication and transport

314 | FUTURE MEDIA

systems all over the globe. That was a spin-off from asteroid mining, pass it by. We're watching that girl.

I'll give you just one goodie. Maybe you noticed on the sportshow or the streets? No commercials. No ads.

That's right. NO ADS. An eyeballer for you.

Look around. Not a billboard, sign, slogan, jingle, sky-write, blurb, sublimflash, in this whole fun world. Brand names? Only in those ticky little peep-screens on the stores, and you could hardly call that advertising. How does that finger you?

Think about it. That girl is still sitting there.

She's parked right under the base of the GTX tower, as a matter of fact. Look way up and you can see the sparkles from the bubble on top, up there among the domes of godland. Inside that bubble is a boardroom. Neat bronze shield on the door: Global Transmissions Corporation—not that that means anything.

I happen to know there are six people in that room. Five of them technically male, and the sixth isn't easily thought of as a mother. They are absolutely unremarkable. Those faces were seen once at their nuptials and will show again in their obituaries and impress nobody either time. If you're looking for the secret Big Blue Meanies of the world, forget it. I know. Zen, do I know! Flesh? Power? Glory? You'd horrify them.

What *they* do like up there is to have things orderly, especially their communications. You could say they've dedicated their lives to that, to freeing the world from garble. Their nightmares are about hemorrhages of information; channels screwed up, plans misimplemented, garble creeping in. Their gigantic wealth only worries them, it keeps opening new vistas of disorder. Luxury? They wear what their tailors put on them, eat what their cooks serve them. See that old boy there—his name is Isham—he's sipping water and frowning as he listens to a databall. The water was prescribed by his medistaff. It tastes awful. The databall also contains a disquieting message about his son, Paul.

But it's time to go back down, far below to our girl. Look!

She's toppled over sprawling on the ground.

A tepid commotion ensues among the bystanders. The consensus is she's dead, which she disproves by bubbling a little. And presently she's taken away by one of the superb ambulances of the future, which are a real improvement over ours when one happens to be around.

At the local bellevue the usual things are done by the usual team of clowns aided by a saintly mop-pusher. Our girl revives enough to answer the questionnaire without which you can't die, even in the future. Finally she's cast up, a pumped-out hulk on a cot in the long, dim ward.

Again nothing happens for a while except that her eyes leak a little from the understandable disappointment of finding herself still alive.

But somewhere one GTX computer has been tickling another, and toward midnight something does happen. First comes an attendant who pulls screens around her. Then a man in a business doublet comes daintily down the ward. He motions the attendant to strip off the sheet and go.

The groggy girl-brute heaves up, big hands clutching at bodyparts you'd pay not to see.

"Burke? P. Burke, is that your name?"

"Y-yes." Croak. "Are you...policeman?"

"No. They'll be along shortly, I expect. Public suicide's a felony."

"...I'm sorry."

He has a 'corder in his hand. "No family, right?"

"No."

"You're seventeen. One year city college. What did you study?"

"La—languages."

"H'mm. Say something."

Unintelligible rasp.

He studies her. Seen close, he's not so elegant. Errand-boy type.

"Why did you try to kill yourself?"

She stares at him with dead-rat dignity, hauling up the gray sheet. Give him a point, he doesn't ask twice.

"Tell me, did you see Breath this afternoon?"

Dead as she nearly is, that ghastly love-look wells up. Breath is the three young gods, a loser's cult. Give the man another point, he interprets her expression.

"How would you like to meet them?"

The girl's eyes bug out grotesquely.

"I have a job for someone like you. It's hard work. If you did well you'd be meeting Breath and stars like that all the time."

Is he insane? She's deciding she really did die.

"But it means you never see anybody you know again. Never, *ever*. You will be legally dead. Even the police won't know. Do you want to try?"

It all has to be repeated while her great jaw slowly sets. *Show me the fire I walk through.* Finally P. Burke's prints are in his 'corder, the man holding up the big rancid girl-body without a sign of distaste. It makes you wonder what else he does.

And then—THE MAGIC. Sudden silent trot of litterbearers tucking P. Burke into something quite different from a bellevue stretcher, the oiled slide into the daddy of all luxury ambulances—real flowers in that holder!—and the long jarless rush to nowhere. Nowhere is warm and gleaming and kind with nurses. (Where did you hear that money can't buy genuine kindness?) And clean clouds folding P. Burke into bewildered sleep.

...Sleep which merges into feedings and washings and more sleeps, into drowsy moments of afternoon where midnight should be, and gentle businesslike voices and friendly (but very few) faces, and endless painless hyposprays and peculiar numbnesses. And later comes the steadying rhythm of days and nights, and a quickening which P. Burke doesn't identify as health, but only knows that the fungus place in her armpit is gone. And then she's up and following those few new faces with growing trust, first tottering, then walking strongly, all better now, clumping down the short hall to the tests, tests, tests, and the other things.

And here is our girl, looking—

If possible, worse than before. (You thought this was Cinderella transistorized?)

The disimprovement in her looks comes from the electrode jacks peeping out of her sparse hair, and there are other meldings of flesh and metal. On the other hand, that collar and spinal plate are really an asset; you won't miss seeing that neck.

P. Burke is ready for training in her new job.

The training takes place in her suite and is exactly what you'd call a charm course. How to walk, sit, eat, speak, blow her nose, how to stumble, to urinate, to hiccup—DELICIOUSLY. How to make each nose-blow or shrug delightfully, subtly, different from any ever spooled before. As the man said, it's hard work.

But P. Burke proves apt. Somewhere in that horrible body is a gazelle, a houri, who would have been buried forever without this crazy chance. See the ugly duckling go!

Only it isn't precisely P. Burke who's stepping, laughing, shaking out her shining hair. How could it be? P. Burke is doing it all right, but she's doing it through something. The something is to all appearances a live girl. (You were warned, this is the FUTURE.)

When they first open the big cryocase and show her her new body, she says just one word. Staring, gulping, "How?"

Simple, really. Watch P. Burke in her sack and scuffs stump down the hall beside Joe, the man who supervises the technical part of her training. Joe doesn't mind P. Burke's looks, he hasn't noticed them. To Joe, system matrices are beautiful.

They go into a dim room containing a huge cabinet like a one-man sauna and a console for Joe. The room has a glass wall that's all dark now. And just for your information, the whole shebang is five hundred feet underground near what used to be Carbondale, Pa.

Joe opens the sauna cabinet like a big clamshell standing on end with a lot of funny business inside. Our girl shucks her shift and walks into it bare, totally unembarrassed. *Eager.* She settles in face-forward, butting jacks into sockets. Joe closes it carefully onto her humpback. Clunk. She can't see in there or hear or move. She hates this minute. But how she loves what comes next!

Joe's at his console, and the lights on the other side of the glass wall come up. A room is on the other side, all fluff and kicky bits, a girly bedroom. In the bed is a small mound of silk with a rope of yellow hair hanging out.

The sheet stirs and gets whammed back flat.

Sitting up in the bed is the darlingest girl child you've EVER seen. She quivers—porno for angels. She sticks both her little arms straight up, flips her hair, looks around full of sleepy pazazz. Then she can't resist rubbing her hands down over her minibreasts and belly. Because, you see, it's the god-awful P. Burke who is sitting there hugging her perfect girl-body, looking at you out of delighted eyes.

Then the kitten hops out of bed and crashes flat on the floor.

From the sauna in the dim room comes a strangled noise. P. Burke, trying to rub her wired-up elbow, is suddenly smothered in *two* bodies, electrodes jerking in her flesh. Joe juggles inputs, crooning into his mike. The flurry passes; it's all right.

In the lighted room the elf gets up, casts a cute glare at the glass wall, and goes into a transparent cubicle. A bathroom, what else? She's a live girl, and live girls have to go to the bathroom after a night's sleep even if their brains are in a sauna cabinet in the next room. And P. Burke isn't in that cabinet, she's in the bathroom. Perfectly simple, if you have the glue for that closed training circuit that's letting her run her neural system by remote control.

Now let's get one thing clear. P. Burke does not *feel* her brain is in the sauna room, she feels she's in that sweet little body. When you wash your hands, do you feel the water is running on your brain? Of course not. You feel the water on your hand, although the "feeling" is actually a potential-pattern flickering over the electrochemical jelly between your ears. And it's delivered there via the long circuits from your hands. Just so, P. Burke's brain in the cabinet feels the water on her hands in the bathroom. The fact that the signals have jumped across space on the way in makes no difference at all. If you want the jargon, it's known as eccentric projection or sensory reference and you've done it all your life. Clear?

Time to leave the honeypot to her toilet training—she's made a booboo with the toothbrush, because P. Burke can't get used to what she sees in the mirror—

But wait, you say. Where did that girl-body come from?

P. Burke asks that too, dragging out the words.

"They grow 'em," Joe tells her. He couldn't care less about the flesh department. "PDs. Placental decanters. Modified embryos, see? Fit the control implants in later. Without a Remote Operator it's just a vegetable. Look at the feet—no callus at all." (He knows because they told him.)

"Oh...oh, she's incredible...."

"Yeah, a neat job. Want to try walking-talking mode today? You're coming on fast."

And she is. Joe's reports and the reports from the nurse and the doctor and style man go to a bushy man upstairs who is some kind of medical cybertech but mostly a project administrator. His reports in turn go—to the GTX boardroom? Certainly not, did you think this is *a big* thing? His reports just go up. The point is, they're green, very green. P. Burke promises well.

So the bushy man—Dr. Tesla—has procedures to initiate. The little kitten's dossier in the Central Data Bank, for instance. Purely routine. And the phase-in schedule which will put her on the scene. This is simple: a small exposure in an off-network holoshow.

Next he has to line out the event which will fund and target her. That takes budget meetings, clearances, coordinations. The Burke project begins to recruit and grow. And there's the messy business of the name, which always gives Dr. Tesla an acute pain in the bush.

The name comes out weird, when it's suddenly discovered that Burke's "P." stands for "Philadelphia." Philadelphia? The astrologer grooves on it. Joe thinks it would help identification. The semantics girl references *brotherly love, Liberty Bell, main line, low teratogenesis,* blah-blah. Nicknames Philly? Pala? Pooty? Delphi? Is it good, bad? Finally "Delphi" is gingerly declared goodo. ("Burke" is replaced by something nobody remembers.)

Coming along now. We're at the official checkout down in the underground suite, which is as far as the training circuits reach. The bushy Dr. Tesla is there, braced by two budgetary types and a quiet fatherly man whom he handles like hot plasma.

Joe swings the door wide and she steps shyly in.

Their little Delphi, fifteen and flawless.

Tesla introduces her around. She's child-solemn, a beautiful baby to whom something so wonderful has happened you can feel the tingles. She doesn't smile, she... brims. That brimming joy is all that shows of P. Burke, the forgotten hulk in the sauna next door. But P. Burke doesn't know she's alive—it's Delphi who lives, every warm inch of her.

One of the budget types lets go a libidinous snuffle and freezes. The fatherly man, whose name is Mr. Cantle, clears his throat.

"Well, young lady, are you ready to go to work?"

"Yes, sir," gravely from the elf.

"We'll see. Has anybody told you what you're going to do for us?"

"No, sir." Joe and Tesla exhale quietly.

"Good." He eyes her, probing for the blind brain in the room next door.

"Do you know what *advertising* is?"

He's talking dirty, hitting to shock. Delphi's *eyes* widen and her little chin goes up. Joe is in ecstasy at the complex expressions P. Burke is getting through. Mr. Cantle waits.

"It's, well, it's when they used to tell people to buy things." She swallows. "It's not allowed."

"That's right." Mr. Cantle leans back, grave. "Advertising as it used to be is against the law. *A display other than the legitimate use of the product, intended to promote its sale.* In former times every manufacturer was free to tout his wares any way, place, or time he could afford. All the media and most of the landscape was taken up with extravagant competing displays. The thing became uneconomic. The public rebelled. Since the so-called Huckster Act sellers have been restrained to, I quote, displays in or on the product itself, visible during its legitimate use or in on-premise sales." Mr. Cantle leans forward. "Now tell me, Delphi, why do people buy one product rather than another?"

"Well..." Enchanting puzzlement from Delphi. "They, um, they see them and like them, or they hear about them from somebody?" (Touch of P. Burke there; she didn't say, from a friend.)

"Partly. Why did *you* buy your particular body-lift?"

"I never had a body-lift, sir."

Mr. Cantle frowns; what gutters do they drag for these Remotes?

"Well, what brand of water do you drink?"

"Just what was in the faucet, sir," says Delphi humbly. "I—I did try to boil it—"

"Good god." He scowls; Tesla stiffens. "Well, what did you boil it in? A cooker?"

The shining yellow head nods.

"What *brand* of cooker did you buy?"

"I didn't buy it, sir," says frightened P. Burke through Delphi's lips. "But—I know the best kind! Ananga has a Burnbabi. I saw the name when she—"

"Exactly!" Cantle's fatherly beam comes back strong; the Burnbabi account is a strong one, too. "You saw Ananga using one so you thought it must be good, eh? And it is good, or a great human being like Ananga wouldn't be using it. Absolutely right. And now, Delphi, you know what you're going to be doing for us. You're going to show some products. Doesn't sound very hard, does it?"

"Oh, no, sir..." Baffled child's stare; Joe gloats.

"And you must never, *never* tell anyone what you're doing." Cantle's eyes bore for the brain behind this seductive child.

"You're wondering why we ask you to do this, naturally. There's a very serious reason. All those products people use, foods and healthaids and cookers and cleaners and clothes and cars—they're all made by *people*. Somebody put in years of hard work designing and making them. A man comes up with a fine new idea for a better product. He has to get a factory and machinery, and hire workmen. Now. What happens if people have no way of hearing about his product? Word of mouth is far too slow and unreliable. Nobody might ever stumble onto his new product or find out how good it was, right? And then he and all the people who worked for him—they'd go bankrupt, right? So, Delphi, there has to be *some way* that large numbers of people can get a look at a good new product, right? How? By letting people see you using it. You're giving that man a chance."

Delphi's little head is nodding in happy relief.

"Yes, Sir, I do see now—but sir, it seems so sensible, why don't they let you—"

Cantle smiles sadly.

"It's an overreaction, my dear. History goes by swings. People overreact and pass harsh unrealistic laws which attempt to stamp out an essential social process. When this happens, the people who understand have to carry on as best they can until the pendulum swings back." He sighs. "The Huckster Laws are bad, inhuman laws, Delphi, despite their good intent. If they were strictly observed they would wreak havoc. Our economy, our society, would be cruelly destroyed. We'd be back in caves!" His inner fire is showing; if the Huckster Laws were strictly enforced he'd be back punching a databank.

"It's our duty, Delphi. Our solemn social duty. We are not breaking the law. You will be using the product. But people wouldn't understand, if they knew. They would become upset just as you did. So you must be very, very careful not to mention any of this to anybody."

(And somebody will be very, very carefully monitoring Delphi's speech circuits.)

"Now we're all straight, aren't we? Little Delphi here"—he is speaking to the invisible creature next door—"little Delphi is going to live a wonderful, exciting life. She's going to be a girl people watch. And she's going to be using fine products people will be glad to know about and helping the good people who make them. Yours will be a genuine social contribution." He keys up his pitch; the creature in there must be older.

Delphi digests this with ravishing gravity.

"But sir, how do I—?"

"Don't worry about a thing. You'll have people behind you whose job it is to select the most worthy products for you to use. Your job is just to do as they say. They'll show you what outfits to wear to parties, what suncars and viewers to buy, and so on. That's all you have to do."

Parties—clothes—suncars! Delphi's pink mouth opens. In P. Burke's starved seventeen-year-old head the ethics of product sponsorship float far away.

"Now tell me in your own words what your job is, Delphi."

"Yes, Sir. I—I'm to go to parties and buy things and use them as they tell me, to help the people who work in factories."

"And what did I say was so important?"

"Oh—I shouldn't let anybody know, about the things."

"Right." Mr. Cantle has another paragraph he uses when the subject shows, well, immaturity. But he can sense only eagerness here. Good. He doesn't really enjoy the other speech.

"It's a lucky girl who can have all the fun she wants while doing good for others, isn't it?" He beams around. There's a prompt shuffling of chairs. Clearly this one is go.

Joe leads her out, grinning. The poor fool thinks they're admiring her coordination.

It's out into the world for Delphi now, and at this point the up-channels get used. On the administrative side account schedules are opened, subprojects activated. On the technical side the reserved bandwidth is cleared. (That carrier field, remember?) A new name is waiting for Delphi, a name she'll never hear. It's a long string of binaries which have been quietly cycling in a GTX tank ever since a certain Beautiful Person didn't wake up.

The name winks out of cycle, dances from pulses into modulations of modulations, whizzes through phasing, and shoots into a giga-band beam racing up to a synchronous satellite poised over Guatemala. From there the beam pours twenty thousand miles back to Earth again, forming an all-pervasive field of structured energics supplying tuned demand-points all over the CanAm quadrant.

With that field, if you have the right credit rating, you can sit at a GTX console and operate an ore-extractor in Brazil. Or—if you have some simple credentials like being able to walk on water—you could shoot a spool into the network holocam shows running day and night in every home and dorm and rec site. Or you could create a continentwide traffic jam. Is it any wonder GTX guards those inputs like a sacred trust?

Delphi's "name" appears as a tiny analyzable nonredundancy in the flux, and she'd be very proud if she knew about it. It would strike P. Burke as magic; P. Burke never even understood robotcars. But Delphi is in no sense a robot.

Call her a waldo if you must. The fact is she's just a girl, a real-live girl with her brain in an unusual place. A simple real-time on-line system with plenty of bit-rate—even as you and you.

The point of all this hardware, which isn't very much hardware in this society, is so Delphi can walk out of that underground suite, a mobile demand-point draining an omnipresent fieldform. And she does—eighty-nine pounds of tender girl flesh and blood with a few metallic components, stepping out into the sunlight to be taken to her new life. A girl, with everything going for her including a meditech escort. Walking lovely, stopping to widen her eyes at the big antennae system overhead.

The mere fact that something called P. Burke is left behind down underground has no bearing at all. P. Burke is totally unselfaware and happy as a clam in its shell. (Her bed has been moved into the waldo cabinet room now.) And P. Burke isn't in the cabinet; P. Burke is climbing out of an airvan in a fabulous Colorado beef preserve, and her name is Delphi. Delphi is looking at live Charolais steers and live cottonwoods and aspens gold against the blue smog and stepping over live grass to be welcomed by the reserve super's wife.

The super's wife is looking forward to a visit from Delphi and her friends, and by a happy coincidence there's a holocam outfit here doing a piece for the nature nuts.

You could write the script yourself now, while Delphi learns a few rules about structural interferences and how to handle the tiny time lag which results from the new forty-thousand-mile parenthesis in her nervous system. That's right—the people with the leased holocam rig naturally find the gold aspen shadows look a lot better on Delphi's flank than they do on a steer. And Delphi's face improves the mountains too, when you can see them. But the nature freaks aren't quite as joyful as you'd expect.

"See you in Barcelona, kitten," the headman says sourly as they pack up.

"Barcelona?" echoes Delphi with that charming little subliminal lag. She sees where his hand is and steps back. "Cool, it's not her fault," another man says wearily. He knocks back his grizzled hair. "Maybe they'll leave in some of the gut."

Delphi watches them go off to load the spools on the GTX transport for processing. Her hand roves over the breast the man had touched. Back under Carbondale, P. Burke has discovered something new about her Delphi-body.

About the difference between Delphi and her own grim carcass.

She's always known Delphi has almost no sense of taste or smell. They explained about that: only so much bandwidth. You don't have to taste a suncar, do you? And the slight overall dimness of Delphi's sense of touch—she's familiar with that, too. Fabrics that would prickle P. Burke's own hide feel like a cool plastic film to Delphi.

But the blank spots. It took her a while to notice them. Delphi doesn't have much privacy; investments of her size don't. So she's slow about discovering there's certain definite places where her beastly P. Burke body *feels* things that Delphi's dainty flesh does not. H'mm! Channel space again, she thinks—and forgets it in the pure bliss of being Delphi.

You ask how a girl could forget a thing like that? Look. P. Burke is about as far as you can get from the concept *girl*. She's a female, yes—but for her, sex is a four-letter word spelled P-A-I-N. She isn't quite a virgin. You don't want the details; she'd been about twelve and the freak lovers were bombed blind. When they came down, they threw her out with a small hole in her anatomy and a mortal one elsewhere. She dragged off to buy her first and last shot, and she can still hear the clerk's incredulous guffaws.

Do you see why Delphi grins, stretching her delicious little numb body in the sun she faintly feels? Beams, saying, "Please, I'm ready now."

Ready for what? For Barcelona like the sour man said, where his nature-thing is now making it strong in the amateur section of the Festival. A winner! Like he also said, a lot of strip mines and dead fish have been scrubbed, but who cares with Delphi's darling face so visible?

So it's time for Delphi's face and her other delectabilities to show on Barcelona's Playa Nueva. Which means switching her channel to the EurAf synchsat.

They ship her at night so the nanosecond transfer isn't even noticed by that insignificant part of Delphi that lives five hundred feet under Carbondale, so excited the nurse has to make sure she eats. The circuit switches while Delphi "sleeps," that is, while P. Burke is out of the waldo cabinet. The next time she plugs in to open Delphi's eyes it's no different—do you notice which relay boards your phone calls go through?

And now for the event that turns the sugarcube from Colorado into the PRINCESS.

Literally true, he's a prince, or rather an Infante of an old Spanish line that got shined up in the Neomonarchy. He's also eighty-one, with a passion for birds—the kind you see in zoos. Now it suddenly turns out that he isn't poor at all. Quite the reverse; his old sister laughs in their tax lawyer's face and starts restoring the family hacienda while the Infante totters out to court Delphi. And little Delphi begins to live the life of the gods.

What do gods do? Well, everything beautiful. But (remember Mr. Cantle?) the main point is Things. Ever see a god empty-handed? You can't be a god without at least a magic girdle or an eight-legged horse. But in the old days some stone tablets or winged sandals or a chariot drawn by virgins would do a god for life. No more! Gods make it on novelty now. By Delphi's time the hunt for new god-gear is turning the earth and seas inside-out and sending frantic fingers to the stars. And what gods have, mortals desire.

So Delphi starts on a Euromarket shopping spree squired by her old Infante, thereby doing her bit to stave off social collapse.

Social what? Didn't you get it, when Mr. Cantle talked about a world where advertising is banned and fifteen billion consumers are glued to their holocam shows? One capricious self-powered god can wreck you.

Take the nose-filter massacre. Years, the industry sweated years to achieve an almost invisible enzymatic filter. So one day a couple of pop-gods show up wearing nose-filters like *big purple bats*. By the end of the week the world market is screaming for purple bats. Then it switched to bird-heads and skulls, but by the time the industry retooled the crazies had dropped bird-heads and gone to injection globes. Blood!

Multiply that by a million consumer industries, and you can see why it's economic to have a few controllable gods. Especially with the beautiful hunk of space R & D the Peace Department laid out for and which the taxpayers are only too glad to have taken off their hands by an outfit like GTX, which everybody knows is almost a public trust.

And so you—or rather, GTX—find a creature like P. Burke and give her Delphi. And Delphi helps keep things *orderly*, she does what you tell her to. Why? That's right, Mr. Cantle never finished his speech.

But here come the tests of Delphi's button-nose twinkling in the torrent of news and entertainment. And she's noticed. The feedback shows a flock of viewers turning up the amps when this country baby gets tangled in her new colloidal body-jewels. She registers at a couple of major scenes, too, and when the Infante gives her a suncar, little Delphi trying out suncars is a tiger. There's a solid response in high-credit country. Mr. Cantle is humming his happy tune as he cancels a Benelux subnet option to guest her on a nude cook-show called Wok Venus.

And now for the superposh old-world wedding! The hacienda has Moorish baths and six-foot silver candelabra and real black horses, and the Spanish Vatican blesses them. The final event is a grand gaucho ball with the old prince and his little Infanta on a bowered balcony. She's a spectacular doll of silver lace, wildly launching toy doves at her new friends whirling by below.

The Infante beams, twitches his old nose to the scent of her sweet excitement. His doctor has been very helpful. Surely now, after he has been so patient with the suncars and all the nonsense—

The child looks up at him, saying something incomprehensible about "breath." He makes out that she's complaining about the three singers she had begged for.

"They've changed!" she marvels. "Haven't they changed? They're so dreary. I'm so happy now!"

And Delphi falls fainting against a gothic vargueno.

Her American duenna rushes up, calls help. Delphi's eyes are open, but Delphi isn't there. The duenna pokes among Delphi's hair, slaps her. The old prince grimaces. He has no idea what she is beyond an excellent solution to his tax problems, but he had been a falconer in his youth. There comes to his mind the small pinioned birds which were flung up to stimulate the hawks. He pockets the veined claw to which he had promised certain indulgences and departs to design his new aviary.

And Delphi also departs with her retinue to the Infante's newly discovered yacht. The trouble isn't serious. It's only that five thousand miles away and five hundred feet down P. Burke has been doing it too well.

They've always known she has terrific aptitude. Joe says he never saw a Remote take over so fast. No disorientations, no rejections. The psychomed talks about self-alienation. She's going into Delphi like a salmon to the sea.

She isn't eating or sleeping, they can't keep her out of the body-cabinet to get her blood moving, there are necroses under her grisly sit-down. Crisis!

So Delphi gets a long "sleep" on the yacht and P. Burke gets it pounded through her perforated head that she's endangering Delphi. (Nurse Fleming thinks of that, thus alienating the psychomed.)

They rig a pool down there (Nurse Fleming again) and chase P. Burke back and forth. And she loves it. So naturally when they let her plug in again Delphi loves it too. Every noon beside the yacht's hydrofoils darling Delphi clips along in the blue sea they've warned her not to drink. And every night around the shoulder of the world an ill-shaped thing in a dark burrow beats its way across a sterile pool.

So presently the yacht stands up on its foils and carries Delphi to the program Mr. Cantle has waiting. It's long-range; she's scheduled for at least two decades' product life. Phase One calls for her to connect with a flock of young ultrariches who are romping loose between Brioni and Djakarta where a competitor named PEV could pick them off.

A routine luxgear op, see; no politics, no policy angles, and the main budget items are the title and the yacht, which was idle anyway. The storyline is that Delphi goes to accept some rare birds for her prince—who cares? The *point* is that the Haiti area is no longer radioactive and look!—the gods are there. And so are several new Carib West Happy Isles which can afford GTX rates, in fact two of them are GTX subsids.

But you don't want to get the idea that all these newsworthy people are wired-up robbies, for pity's sake. You don't need many if they're placed right. Delphi asks Joe about that when he comes down to Barranquilla to check her over. (P. Burke's own mouth hasn't said much for a while.)

"Are there many like me?"

"Nobody's like you, buttons. Look, are you still getting Van Allen warble?"

"I mean, like Davy. Is he a Remote?"

(Davy is the lad who is helping her collect the birds. A sincere redhead who needs a little more exposure.)

"Davy? He's one of Matt's boys, some psychojob. They haven't any channel."

"What about the real ones? Djuma van O, or Ali, or Jim Ten?"

"Djuma was born with a pile of GTX basic where her brain should be, she's nothing but a pain. Jimsy does what his astrologer tells him. Look, peanut, where do you get the idea you aren't real? You're the realest. Aren't you having joy?"

"Oh, Joe!" Flinging her little arms around him and his analyzer grids. "Oh, *me gusto mucho, muchisimo!*"

"Hey, hey." He pets her yellow head, folding the analyzer.

Three thousand miles north and five hundred feet down a forgotten hulk in a body-waldo glows.

And is she having joy. To waken out of the nightmare of being P. Burke and find herself a peri, a star-girl? On a yacht in paradise with no more to do than adorn herself and play with toys and attend revels and greet her friends—her, P. Burke, having friends!—and turn the right way for the holocams? Joy!

And it shows. One look at Delphi and the viewers know: DREAMS CAN COME TRUE.

Look at her riding pillion on Davy's sea-bike, carrying an apoplectic macaw in a silver hoop. Oh, *Morton, let's go there this winter!* Or learning the Japanese chinchona from that Kobe group, in a dress that looks like a blowtorch rising from one knee, and which should sell big in Texas. *Morton, is that real fire?* Happy, happy little girl!

And Davy. He's her pet and her baby, and she loves to help him fix his red-gold hair. (P. Burke marveling, running Delphi's fingers through the curls.) Of course Davy is one of Matt's boys—not impotent exactly, but very *very* low drive. (Nobody knows exactly what Matt does with his bitty budget, but the boys are useful and one or two have made names.) He's perfect for Delphi; in fact the psychomed lets her take him to bed, two kittens in a basket. Davy doesn't mind the fact that Delphi "sleeps" like the dead. That's when P. Burke is out of the body-waldo up at Carbondale, attending to her own depressing needs.

A funny thing about that. Most of her sleepy-time Delphi's just a gently ticking lush little vegetable waiting for P. Burke to get back on the controls. But now and again Delphi all by herself smiles a bit or stirs in her "sleep." Once she breathed a sound: "Yes."

Under Carbondale P. Burke knows nothing. She's asleep too, dreaming of Delphi, what else? But if the bushy Dr. Tesla had heard that single syllable, his bush would have turned snow white. Because Delphi is TURNED OFF.

He doesn't. Davy is too dim to notice, and Delphi's staff boss, Hopkins, wasn't monitoring.

And they've all got something else to think about now, because the cold-fire dress sells half a million copies, and not only in Texas. The GTX computers already know it. When they correlate a minor demand for macaws in Alaska the problem comes to human attention: Delphi is something special.

It's a problem, see, because Delphi is targeted on a limited consumer bracket. Now it turns out she has mass-pop potential—those macaws in

Fairbanks, man!—it's like trying to shoot mice with an ABM. A whole new ball game. Dr. Tesla and the fatherly Mr. Cantle start going around in headquarters circles and buddy-lunching together when they can get away from a seventh-level weasel boy who scares them both.

In the end it's decided to ship Delphi down to the GTX holocam enclave in Chile to try a spot on one of the mainstream shows. (Never mind why an Infanta takes up acting.) The holocam complex occupies a couple of mountains where an observatory once used the clean air. Holocam total-environment shells are very expensive and electronically superstable. Inside them actors can move freely without going off-register, and the whole scene or any selected part will show up in the viewer's home in complete three-di, so real you can look up their noses and much denser than you get from mobile rigs. You can blow a tit ten feet tall when there's no molecular skiffle around.

The enclave looks—well, take everything you know about Hollywood-Burbank and throw it away. What Delphi sees coming down is a neat giant mushroom-farm, domes of all sizes up to monsters for the big games and stuff. It's orderly. The idea that art thrives on creative flamboyance has long been torpedoed by proof that what art needs is computers. Because this showbiz has something TV and Hollywood never had—*automated inbuilt viewer feedback.* Samples, ratings, critics, polls? Forget it. With that carrier field you can get real-time response-sensor readouts from every receiver in the world, served up at your console. That started as a thingie to give the public more influence on content.

Yes.

Try it, man. You're at the console. Slice to the sex-age-educ-econ-ethno-cetera audience of your choice and start. You can't miss. Where the feedback warms up, give 'em more of that. Warm—warmer—*hot!* You've hit it—the secret itch under those hides, the dream in those hearts. You don't need to know its name. With your hand controlling all the input and your eye reading all the response, you can make them a god...and somebody'll do the same for you.

But Delphi just sees rainbows, when she gets through the degaussing ports and the field relay and takes her first look at the insides of those shells. The next thing she sees is a team of shapers and technicians descending on her, and millisecond timers everywhere. The tropical leisure is finished. She's in gigabuck mainstream now, at the funnel maw of the unceasing hose that's pumping the sight and sound and flesh and blood and sobs and laughs and dreams of *reality* into the world's happy head. Little Delphi is going plonk into a zillion homes in prime time and nothing is left to chance. Work!

And again Delphi proves apt. Of course it's really P. Burke down under Carbondale who's doing it, but who remembers that carcass? Certainly not P. Burke, she hasn't spoken through her own mouth for months. Delphi doesn't even recall dreaming of her when she wakes up.

As for the show itself, don't bother. It's gone on so long no living soul could unscramble the plotline. Delphi's trial spot has something to do with a widow and her dead husband's brother's amnesia.

The flap comes after Delphi's spots begin to flash out along the world-hose and the feedback appears. You've guessed it, of course. Sensational! As you'd say, they IDENTIFY.

The report actually says something like InskinEmp with a string of percentages, meaning that Delphi not only has it for anybody with a Y chromosome, but also for women and everything in between. It's the sweet supernatural jackpot, the million-to-one.

Remember your Harlow? A sexpot, sure. But why did bitter hausfraus in Gary and Memphis know that the vanilla-ice-cream goddess with the white hair and crazy eyebrows was *their baby girl?* And write loving letters to Jean warning her that their husbands weren't good enough for her? Why? The GTX analysts don't know either, but they know what to do with it when it happens.

(Back in his bird sanctuary the old Infante spots it without benefit of computers and gazes thoughtfully at his bride in widow's weeds. It might, he feels, be well to accelerate the completion of his studies.)

The excitement reaches down to the burrow under Carbondale where P. Burke gets two medical exams in a week and a chronically inflamed electrode is replaced. Nurse Fleming also gets an assistant who doesn't do much nursing but is very interested in access doors and identity tabs.

And in Chile, little Delphi is promoted to a new home up among the stars' residential spreads and a private jitney to carry her to work. For Hopkins there's a new computer terminal and a full-time schedule man. What is the schedule crowded with?

Things.

And here begins the trouble. You probably saw that coming too.

"What does she think she is, a goddamn *consumer rep?*" Mr. Cantle's fatherly face in Carbondale contorts.

"The girl's upset," Miss Fleming says stubbornly. "She *believes* that, what you told her about helping people and good new products."

"They are good products," Mr. Cantle snaps automatically, but his anger is under control. He hasn't got where he is by irrelevant reactions.

"She says the plastic gave her a rash and the glo-pills made her dizzy."

"Good god, she shouldn't swallow them," Dr. Tesla puts in agitatedly.

"You told her she'd use them," persists Miss Fleming.

Mr. Cantle is busy figuring how to ease this problem to the feral-faced young man. What, was it a goose that lays golden eggs?

Whatever he says to Level Seven, down in Chile the offending products vanish. And a symbol goes into Delphi's tank matrix, one that means roughly *Balance unit resistance against PR index.*

This means that Delphi's complaints will be endured as long as her Pop Response stays above a certain level. (What happens when it sinks need not concern us.) And to compensate, the price of her exposure-time rises again. She's a regular on the show now and response is still climbing.

See her under the sizzling lasers, in a holocam shell set up as a walkway accident. (The show is guesting an acupuncture school shill.)

"I don't think this new body-lift is safe," Delphi's saying. "It's made a funny blue spot on me—look, Mr. Vere."

She wiggles to show where the mini-gray pak that imparts a delicious sense of weightlessness is attached.

"So don't leave it *on*, Dee. With your meat—watch that deck-spot, it's starting to synch."

"But if I don't wear it it isn't honest. They should insulate it more or something, don't you see?"

The show's beloved old father, who is the casualty, gives a senile snigger.

"I'll tell them," Mr. Vere mutters. "Look now, as you step back bend like this so it just shows, see? And hold two beats."

Obediently Delphi turns, and through the dazzle her eyes connect with a pair of strange dark ones. She squints. A quite young man is lounging alone by the port, apparently waiting to use the chamber.

Delphi's used by now to young men looking at her with many peculiar expressions, but she isn't used to what she gets here. A jolt of something somber and knowing. Secrets.

"Eyes! Eyes, Dee!"

She moves through the routine, stealing peeks at the stranger. He stares back. He knows something.

When they let her go she comes shyly to him.

"Living wild, kitten." Cool voice, hot underneath.

"What do you mean?"

"Dumping on the product. You trying to get dead?"

"But it isn't right," she tells him. "They don't know, but I do, I've been wearing it."

His cool is jolted.

"You're out of your head."

"Oh, they'll see I'm right when they check it," she explains. "They're just so busy. When I tell them—"

He is staring down at little flower-face. His mouth opens, closes. "What are you doing in this sewer anyway? Who are you?"

Bewilderedly she says, "I'm Delphi."

"Holy Zen."

"What's wrong? Who are you, please?"

Her people are moving her out now, nodding at him.

"Sorry we ran over, Mr. Uhunh," the script girl says.

He mutters something, but it's lost as her convoy bustles her toward the flower-decked jitney.

(Hear the click of an invisible ignition-train being armed?)

"Who was he?" Delphi asks her hairman.

The hairman is bending up and down from his knees as he works.

"Paul. Isham. Three," he says and puts a comb in his mouth.

"Who's that? I can't see."

He mumbles around the comb, meaning, "Are you jiving?" Because she has to be, in the middle of the GTX enclave.

Next day there's a darkly smoldering face under a turban-towel when Delphi and the show's paraplegic go to use the carbonated pool.

She looks.

He looks.

And the next day, too.

(Hear the automatic sequencer cutting in? The system couples, the fuels begin to travel.)

Poor old Isham senior. You have to feel sorry for a man who values order:

when he begets young, genetic information is still transmitted in the old ape way. One minute it's a happy midget with a rubber duck—look around and here's this huge healthy stranger, opaquely emotional, running with god knows who. Questions are heard where there's nothing to question, and eruptions claiming to be moral outrage. When this is called to Papa's attention—it may take time, in that boardroom—Papa does what he can, but without immortality-juice the problem is worrisome.

And young Paul Isham is a bear. He's bright and articulate and tender-souled and incessantly active, and he and his friends are choking with appallment at the world their fathers made. And it hasn't taken Paul long to discover that *his* father's house has many mansions and even the GTX computers can't relate everything to everything else. He noses out a decaying project which adds up to something like, Sponsoring Marginal Creativity (the free-lance team that "discovered" Delphi was one such grantee). And from there it turns out that an agile lad named Isham can get his hands on a viable packet of GTX holocam facilities.

So here he is with his little band, way down the mushroom-farm mountain, busily spooling a show which has no relation to Delphi's. It's built on bizarre techniques and unsettling distortions pregnant with social protest. An *underground* expression to you.

All this isn't unknown to his father, of course, but so far it has done nothing more than deepen Isham senior's apprehensive frown.

Until Paul connects with Delphi.

And by the time Papa learns this, those invisible hypergolics have exploded, the energy-shells are rushing out. For Paul, you see, is the genuine article. He's serious. He dreams. He even reads—for example, *Green Mansions*—and he wept fiercely when those fiends burned Rima alive.

When he hears that some new GTX pussy is making it big, he sneers and forgets it. He's busy. He never connects the name with this little girl making her idiotic, doomed protest in the holocam chamber. This strangely simple little girl.

And she comes and looks up at him and he sees Rima, lost Rima the enchanted bird girl, and his unwired human heart goes twang.

And Rima turns out to be Delphi.

Do you need a map? The angry puzzlement. The rejection of the dissonance Rima-hustling-for-GTX-My-Father. Garbage, cannot be. The loitering around the pool to confirm the swindle...dark eyes hitting on blue wonder, jerky words exchanged in a peculiar stillness...the dreadful reorganization of the image into Rima-Delphi *in my Father's tentacles—*

You don't need a map.

Nor for Delphi either, the girl who loved her gods. She's seen their divine flesh close now, heard their unamplified voices call her name. She's played their god-games, worn their garlands. She's even become a goddess herself, though she doesn't believe it. She's not disenchanted, don't think that. She's still full of love. It's just that some crazy kind of *hope* hasn't—

Really you can skip all this, when the loving little girl on the yellow-brick road meets a Man. A real human male burning with angry compassion and grandly concerned with human justice, who reaches for her with real male arms and—boom! She loves him back with all her heart.

A happy trip, see?

Except.

Except that it's really P. Burke five thousand miles away who loves Paul. P. Burke the monster down in a dungeon smelling of electrode paste. A caricature of a woman burning, melting, obsessed with true love. Trying over twenty-double-thousand miles of hard vacuum to reach her beloved through girl-flesh numbed by an invisible film. Feeling his arms around the body he thinks is hers, fighting through shadows to give herself to him. Trying to taste and smell him through beautiful dead nostrils, to love him back with a body that goes dead in the heart of the fire.

Perhaps you get P. Burke's state of mind?

She has phases. The trying, first. And the shame. The SHAME. *I am not what thou lovest.* And the fiercer trying. And the realization that there is no, no way, none. Never. *Never...*A bit delayed, isn't it, her understanding that the bargain she made was forever? P. Burke should have noticed those stories about mortals who end up as grasshoppers.

You see the outcome—the funneling of all this agony into one dumb protoplasmic drive to fuse with Delphi. To leave, to close out the beast she is chained to. *To become Delphi.*

Of course it's impossible.

However, her torments have an effect on Paul. Delphi-as-Rima is a potent enough love object, and liberating Delphi's mind requires hours of deeply satisfying instruction in the rottenness of it all. Add in Delphi's body worshiping his flesh, burning in the fire of P. Burke's savage heart—do you wonder Paul is involved?

That's not all.

By now they're spending every spare moment together and some that aren't so spare.

"Mr. Isham, would you mind staying out of this sports sequence? The script calls for Davy here."

(Davy's still around, the exposure did him good.)

"What's the difference?" Paul yawns. "It's just an ad. I'm not blocking that thing."

Shocked silence at his two-letter word. The script girl swallows bravely.

"I'm sorry, sir, our directive is to do the *social sequence* exactly as scripted. We're having to respool the segments we did last week, Mr. Hopkins is very angry with me."

"Who the hell is Hopkins? Where is he?"

"Oh, please, Paul. *Please.*"

Paul unwraps himself, saunters back. The holocam crew nervously check their angles. The GTX boardroom has a foible about having things *pointed* at them and theirs. Cold shivers, when the image of an Isham nearly went onto the world beam beside that Dialadinner.

Worse yet, Paul has no respect for the sacred schedules which are now a full-time job for ferret boy up at headquarters. Paul keeps forgetting to bring her back on time, and poor Hopkins can't cope.

So pretty soon the boardroom data-ball has an urgent personal action-tab for Mr. Isham senior. They do it the gentle way, at first.

"I can't today, Paul."

"Why not?"

"They say I have to, it's *very* important."

He strokes the faint gold down on her narrow back. Under Carbondale, Pa., a blind mole-woman shivers.

"Important. Their importance. Making more gold. Can't you see? To them you're just a thing to get scratch with. *A huckster.* Are you going to let them screw you, Dee? Are you?"

"Oh, Paul—"

He doesn't know it, but he's seeing a weirdie; Remotes aren't hooked up to flow tears.

"Just say no, Dee. No. Integrity. You have to."

"But they say, it's my job—"

"Will you believe I can take care of you, Dee? Baby, baby, you're letting them rip us. You have to choose. Tell them, no."

"Paul... I w-will...."

And she does. Brave little Delphi (insane P. Burke). Saying, "No, please, I promised, Paul."

They try some more, still gently.

"Paul, Mr. Hopkins told me the reason they don't want us to be together so much. It's because of who you are, your father."

She thinks his father is like Mr. Cantle, maybe.

"Oh, great. Hopkins. I'll fix him. Listen, I can't think about Hopkins now. Ken came back today, he found out something."

They are lying on the high Andes meadow watching his friends dive their singing kites.

"Would you believe, on the coast the police have *electrodes in their heads?*"

She stiffens in his arms.

"Yeah, weird. I thought they only used PP on criminals and the army. Don't you see, Dee—something has to be going on. Some movement. Maybe somebody's organizing. How can we find out?" He pounds the ground behind her: "We should make *contact!* If we could only find out."

"The, the news?" she asks distractedly.

"The news." He laughs. "There's nothing in the news except what they want people to know. Half the country could burn up, and nobody would know it if they didn't want. Dee, can't you take what I'm explaining to you? They've got the whole world programmed! Total control of communication. They've got everybody's minds wired in to think what they show them and want what they give them and they give them what they're programmed to want—you can't break in or out of it, you can't get *hold* of it anywhere. I don't think they even have a plan except to keep things going round and round—and god knows what's happening to the people or the Earth or the other planets, maybe. One great big vortex of lies and garbage pouring round and round, getting bigger and bigger, and nothing can ever change. If people don't wake up soon we're through!"

He pounds her stomach softly.

"You have to break out, Dee."

"I'll try, Paul, I will—"

"You're mine. They can't have you."

And he goes to see Hopkins, who is indeed cowed.

But that night up under Carbondale the fatherly Mr. Cantle goes to see P. Burke.

P. Burke? On a cot in a utility robe like a dead camel in a tent, she cannot at first comprehend that he is telling *her* to break it off with Paul. P. Burke has never seen Paul. *Delphi* sees Paul. The fact is, P. Burke can no longer clearly recall that she exists apart from Delphi.

Mr. Cantle can scarcely believe it either, but he tries.

He points out the futility, the potential embarrassment, for Paul. That gets a dim stare from the bulk on the bed. Then he goes into her duty to GTX, her job, isn't she grateful for the opportunity, etcetera. He's very persuasive.

The cobwebby mouth of P. Burke opens and croaks.

"No."

Nothing more seems to be forthcoming.

Mr. Cantle isn't dense, he knows an immovable obstacle when he bumps one. He also knows an irresistible force: GTX. The simple solution is to lock the waldo-cabinet until Paul gets tired of waiting for Delphi to wake up. But the cost, the schedules! And there's something odd here... he eyes the corporate asset hulking on the bed and his hunch-sense prickles.

You see, Remotes don't love. They don't have real sex, the circuits designed that out from the start. So it's been assumed that it's *Paul* who is diverting himself or something with the pretty little body in Chile. P. Burke can only be doing what comes natural to any ambitious gutter-meat. It hasn't occurred to anyone that they're dealing with the real hairy thing whose shadow is blasting out of every holoshow on Earth.

Love?

Mr. Cantle frowns. The idea is grotesque. But his instinct for the fuzzy line is strong; he will recommend flexibility. And so, in Chile:

"Darling, I don't have to work tonight! And Friday too—isn't that right, Mr. Hopkins?"

"Oh, great. When does she come up for parole?"

"Mr. Isham, please be reasonable. Our schedule—surely your own production people must be needing you?"

This happens to be true. Paul goes away. Hopkins stares after him, wondering distastefully why an Isham wants to ball a waldo. How sound are those boardroom belly-fears—garble creeps, creeps in! It never occurs to Hopkins that an Isham might not know what Delphi is.

Especially with Davy crying because Paul has kicked him out of Delphi's bed.

Delphi's bed is under a real window.

"Stars," Paul says sleepily. He rolls over, pulling Delphi on top. "Are you aware that this is one of the last places on Earth where people can see the stars? Tibet, too, maybe."

"Paul..."

"Go to sleep. I want to see you sleep."

"Paul, I... I sleep so *hard*, I mean, it's a joke how hard I am to wake up. Do you mind?"

"Yes."

But finally, fearfully, she must let go. So that five thousand miles north a crazy spent creature can crawl out to gulp concentrates and fall on her cot. But not for long. It's pink dawn when Delphi's eyes open to find Paul's arms around her, his voice saying rude, tender things. He's been kept awake. The nerveless little statue that was her Delphi-body nuzzled him in the night.

Insane hope rises, is fed a couple of nights later when he tells her she called his name in her sleep.

And that day Paul's arms keep her from work and Hopkins's wails go up to headquarters where the weasel-faced lad is working his sharp tailbone off packing Delphi's program. Mr. Cantle defuses that one. But next week it happens again, to a major client. And ferret-face has connections on the technical side.

Now you can see that when you have a field of complexly heterodyned energy modulations tuned to a demand-point like Delphi, there are many problems of standwaves and lashback and skiffle of all sorts which are normally balanced out with ease by the technology of the future. By the same token they can be delicately unbalanced too, in ways that feed back into the waldo operator with striking results.

"Darling—what the hell! What's wrong? DELPHI!"

Helpless shrieks, writhings. Then the Rima-bird is lying wet and limp in his arms, her eyes enormous.

"I... I wasn't supposed to..." she gasps faintly. "They told me not to...."

"Oh, my god—*Delphi.*"

And his hard fingers are digging in her thick yellow hair. Electronically knowledgeable fingers. They freeze.

"You're a *doll!* You're one of those PP implants. They control you. I should have known. Oh, god, I should have known."

"No, Paul," she's sobbing. "No, no, no—"

"Damn them. Damn them, what they've done—you're not *you*—"

He's shaking her, crouching over her in the bed and jerking her back and forth, glaring at the pitiful beauty.

"No!" she pleads (it's not true, that dark bad dream back there). "I'm Delphi!"

"My father. Filth, pigs—damn them, damn them, damn them."

"No, no," she babbles. "They were good to me—" P. Burke underground mouthing, "They were good to me—AAH-AAAAH!"

Another agony skewers her. Up north the sharp young man wants to make sure this so-tiny interference works. Paul can scarcely hang on to her, he's crying too. "I'll kill them."

His Delphi, a wired-up slave! Spikes in her brain, electronic shackles in his bird's heart. Remember when those savages burned Rima alive?

"I'll *kill* the man that's doing this to you."

He's still saying it afterward, but she doesn't hear. She's sure he hates her now, all she wants is to die. When she finally understands that the fierceness is tenderness, she thinks it's a miracle. *He knows—and he still loves!*

How can she guess that he's got it a little bit wrong?

You can't blame Paul. Give him credit that he's even heard about pleasure-pain implants and snoops, which by their nature aren't mentioned much by those who know them most intimately. That's what he thinks is being used on Delphi, something to *control* her. And to listen—he burns at the unknown ears in their bed.

Of waldo-bodies and objects like P. Burke he has heard nothing.

So it never crosses his mind as he looks down at his violated bird, sick with fury and love, that he isn't holding *all* of her. Do you need to be told the mad resolve jelling in him now?

To free Delphi.

How? Well, he is, after all, Paul Isham III. And he even has an idea where the GTX neurolab is. In Carbondale.

But first things have to be done for Delphi, and for his own stomach. So he gives her back to Hopkins and departs in a restrained and discreet way. And the Chile staff is grateful and do not understand that his teeth don't normally show so much.

And a week passes in which Delphi is a very good, docile little ghost. They let her have the load of wildflowers Paul sends and the bland loving notes. (He's playing it coony.) And up in headquarters weasel boy feels that *his* destiny has clicked a notch onward and floats the word up that he's handy with little problems.

And no one knows what P. Burke thinks in any way whatever, except that Miss Fleming catches her flushing her food down the can and next night she faints in the pool. They haul her out and stick her with IVs. Miss Fleming frets, she's seen expressions like that before. But she wasn't around when crazies who called themselves Followers of the Fish looked through flames to life everlasting. P. Burke is seeing Heaven on the far side of death, too. Heaven is spelled P-a-u-1, but the idea's the same. *I will die and be born again in Delphi.*

Garbage, electronically speaking. No way.

Another week and Paul's madness has become a plan. (Remember, he does have friends.) He smolders, watching his love paraded by her masters. He turns out a scorching sequence for his own show. And finally, politely, he requests from Hopkins a morsel of his bird's free time, which duly arrives.

"I thought you didn't *want* me anymore," she's repeating as they wing over mountain flanks in Paul's suncar. "Now you *know*—"

"Look at me!"

His hand covers her mouth, and he's showing her a lettered card. DON'T TALK THEY CAN HEAR EVERYTHING WE SAY.

I'M TAKING YOU AWAY NOW.

She kisses his hand. He nods urgently, flipping the card.

DON'T BE AFRAID. I CAN STOP THE PAIN IF THEY TRY TO HURT YOU.

With his free hand he shakes out a silvery scrambler-mesh on a power pack. She is dumbfounded.

THIS WILL CUT THE SIGNALS AND PROTECT YOU DARLING.

She's staring at him, her head going vaguely from side to side, No.

"Yes!" He grins triumphantly. "Yes!"

For a moment she wonders. That powered mesh will cut off the field, all right. It will also cut off Delphi. But he is Paul. Paul is kissing her, she can only seek him hungrily as he sweeps the suncar through a pass.

Ahead is an old jet ramp with a shiny bullet waiting to go. (Paul also has credits and a Name.) The little GTX patrol courier is built for nothing but speed. Paul and Delphi wedge in behind the pilot's extra fuel tank, and there's no more talking when the torches start to scream.

They're screaming high over Quito before Hopkins starts to worry. He wastes another hour tracking the beeper on Paul's suncar. The suncar is sailing a pattern out to sea. By the time they're sure it's empty and Hopkins gets on the hot flue to headquarters, the fugitives are a sourceless howl above Carib West.

Up at headquarters weasel boy gets the squeal. His first impulse is to repeat his previous play, but then his brain snaps to. This one is too hot. Because, see, although in the long run they can make P. Burke do anything at all except maybe *live,* instant emergencies can be tricky. And—Paul Isham III.

"Can't you order her back?"

They're all in the GTX tower monitor station, Mr. Cantle and ferret-face and Joe and a very neat man who is Mr. Isham senior's personal eyes and ears.

"No, sir," Joe says doggedly. "We can read channels, particularly speech, but we can't interpolate organized pattern. It takes the waldo op to send one-to-one—"

"What are they saying?"

"Nothing at the moment, sir." The console jockey's eyes are closed. "I believe they are, ah, embracing."

"They're not answering," a traffic monitor says. "Still heading zero zero three zero—due north, sir."

"You're certain Kennedy is alerted not to fire on them?" the neat man asks anxiously.

"Yes, sir."

"Can't you just turn her off?" The sharp-faced lad is angry. "Pull that pig out of the controls!"

"If you cut the transmission cold you'll kill the Remote," Joe explains for the third time. "Withdrawal has to be phased right, you have to fade over to the Remote's own autonomics. Heart, breathing, cerebellum, would go blooey.

If you pull Burke out you'll probably finish her too. It's a fantastic cybersystem, you don't want to do that."

"The investment." Mr. Cantle shudders.

Weasel boy puts his hand on the console jock's shoulder, it's the contact who arranged the no-no effect for him.

"We can at least give them a warning signal, sir." He licks his lips, gives the neat man his sweet ferret smile. "We know that does no damage."

Joe frowns, Mr. Cantle sighs. The neat man is murmuring into his wrist. He looks up. "I am authorized," he says reverently, "I am authorized to, ah, direct a signal. If this is the only course. But minimal, minimal."

Sharp-face squeezes his man's shoulder.

In the silver bullet shrieking over Charleston Paul feels Delphi arch in his arms. He reaches for the mesh, hot for action. She thrashes, pushing at his hands, her eyes roll. She's afraid of that mesh despite the agony. (And she's right.) Frantically Paul fights her in the cramped space, gets it over her head. As he turns the power up she burrows free under his arm and the spasm fades.

"They're calling you again, Mr. Isham!" the pilot yells.

"Don't answer. Darling, keep this over your head damn it how can I—"

An AX90 barrels over their nose, there's a flash.

"Mr. Isham! Those are Air Force jets!"

"Forget it," Paul shouts back. "They won't fire. Darling, don't be afraid."

Another AX90 rocks them.

"Would you mind pointing your pistol at my head where they can see it, sir?" the pilot howls.

Paul does so. The AX90s take up escort formation around them. The pilot goes back to figuring how he can collect from GTX too, and after Goldsboro AB the escort peels away.

"Holding the same course." Traffic is reporting to the group around the monitor. "Apparently they've taken on enough fuel to bring them to towerport here."

"In that case it's just a question of waiting for them to dock." Mr. Cantle's fatherly manner revives a bit.

"Why can't they cut off that damn freak's life-support," the sharp young man fumes. "It's ridiculous."

"They're working on it," Cantle assures him.

What they're doing, down under Carbondale, is arguing. Miss Fleming's watchdog has summoned the bushy man to the waldo room.

"Miss Fleming, you will obey orders."

"You'll kill her if you try that, sir. I can't believe you meant it, that's why I didn't. We've already fed her enough sedative to affect heart action; if you cut any more oxygen she'll die in there."

The bushy man grimaces. "Get Dr. Quine here fast."

They wait, staring at the cabinet in which a drugged, ugly madwoman fights for consciousness, fights to hold Delphi's eyes open.

High over Richmond the silver pod starts a turn. Delphi is sagged into Paul's arm, her eyes swim up to him.

"Starting down now, baby. It'll be over soon, all you have to do is stay alive, Dee."

"...stay alive..."

The traffic monitor has caught them. "Sir! They've turned off for Carbondale—Control has contact—"

"Let's go."

But the headquarters posse is too late to intercept the courier wailing into Carbondale. And Paul's friends have come through again. The fugitives are out through the freight dock and into the neurolab admin port before the guard gets organized. At the elevator Paul's face plus his handgun get them in.

"I want Doctor—what's his name, Dee? Dee!"

"...Tesla..." She's reeling on her feet.

"Dr. Tesla. Take me down to Tesla, fast."

Intercoms are squalling around them as they whoosh down, Paul's pistol in the guard's back. When the door slides open the bushy man is there.

"I'm Tesla."

"I'm Paul Isham. *Isham.* You're going to take your flaming implants out of this girl—now. Move!"

"What?"

"You heard me. Where's your operating room? Go!"

"But—"

"Move! Do I have to burn somebody?"

Paul waves the weapon at Dr. Quine, who has just appeared.

"No, no," says Tesla hurriedly. "But I can't, you know. It's impossible, there'll be nothing left."

"You screaming well can, right now. You mess up and I'll kill you," says

Paul murderously. "Where is it, there? And wipe the feke that's on her circuits now."

He's backing them down the hall, Delphi heavy on his arm.

"Is this the place, baby? Where they did it to you?"

"Yes," she whispers, blinking at a door. "Yes..."

Because it is, see. Behind that door is the very suite where she was born.

Paul herds them through it into a gleaming hall. An inner door opens, and a nurse and a gray man rush out. And freeze.

Paul sees there's something special about that inner door. He crowds them past it and pushes it open and looks in.

Inside is a big mean-looking cabinet with its front door panels ajar.

And inside that cabinet is a poisoned carcass to whom something wonderful, unspeakable, is happening. Inside is P. Burke, the real living woman who knows that HE is there, coming closer—Paul whom she had fought to reach through forty thousand miles of ice—PAUL is here!—is yanking at the waldo doors—

The doors tear open and a monster rises up.

"Paul darling!" croaks the voice of love, and the arms of love reach for him.

And he responds.

Wouldn't you, if a gaunt she-golem flab-naked and spouting wires and blood came at you clawing with metal-studded paws—

"Get away!" He knocks wires.

It doesn't much matter which wires. P. Burke has, so to speak, her nervous system hanging out. Imagine somebody jerking a handful of your medulla—

She crashes onto the floor at his feet, flopping and roaring *PAUL-PAUL-PAUL* in rictus.

It's doubtful he recognizes his name or sees her life coming out of her eyes at him. And at the last it doesn't go to him. The eyes find Delphi, fainting by the doorway, and die.

Now of course Delphi is dead, too.

There's a total silence as Paul steps away from the thing by his foot.

"You killed her," Tesla says. "That was her."

"Your control." Paul is furious, the thought of that monster fastened into little Delphi's brain nauseates him. He sees her crumpling and holds out his arms. Not knowing she is dead.

And Delphi comes to him.

One foot before the other, not moving very well—but moving. Her darling face turns up. Paul is distracted by the terrible quiet, and when he looks down he sees only her tender little neck.

"Now you get the implants out," he warns them. Nobody moves.

"But, but she's dead," Miss Fleming whispers wildly.

Paul feels Delphi's life under his hand, they're talking about their monster. He aims his pistol at the gray man.

"You. If we aren't in your surgery when I count three, I'm burning off this man's leg."

"Mr. Isham," Tesla says desperately, "you have just killed the person who animated the body you call Delphi. Delphi herself is dead. If you release your arm you'll see what I say is true."

The tone gets through. Slowly Paul opens his arm, looks down.

"Delphi?"

She totters, sways, stays upright. Her face comes slowly up.

"Paul..." Tiny voice.

"Your crotty tricks," Paul snarls at them. "Move!"

"Look at her eyes," Dr. Quine croaks.

They look. One of Delphi's pupils fills the iris, her lips writhe weirdly.

"Shock." Paul grabs her to him. "*Fix* her!" He yells at them, aiming at Tesla.

"For god's sake...bring it in the lab." Tesla quavers.

"Good-bye-bye," says Delphi clearly. They lurch down the hall, Paul carrying her, and meet a wave of people.

Headquarters has arrived.

Joe takes one look and dives for the waldo room, running into Paul's gun.

"Oh, no, you don't."

Everybody is yelling. The little thing in his arm stirs, says plaintively, "I'm Delphi."

And all through the ensuing jabber and ranting she hangs on, keeping it up, the ghost of P. Burke or whatever whispering crazily, "Paul... Paul... Please, I'm Delphi... Paul?"

"I'm here, darling, I'm here." He's holding her in the nursing bed. Tesla talks, talks, talks unheard.

"Paul...don't sleep..." The ghost-voice whispers. Paul is in agony, he will not accept, WILL NOT believe.

Tesla runs down.

And then near midnight Delphi says roughly, "Ag-ag-ag—" and slips onto the floor, making a rough noise like a seal.

Paul screams. There's more of the *ag-ag* business and more gruesome convulsive disintegrations, until by two in the morning Delphi is nothing but a warm little bundle of vegetative functions hitched to some expensive hardware—the same that sustained her before her life began. Joe has finally persuaded Paul to let him at the waldo-cabinet. Paul stays by her long enough to see her face change in a dreadfully alien and coldly convincing way, and then he stumbles out bleakly through the group in Tesla's office.

Behind him Joe is working wet-faced, sweating to reintegrate the fantastic complex of circulation, respiration, endocrines, midbrain homeostases, the patterned flux that was a human being—it's like saving an orchestra abandoned in midair. Joe is also crying a little; he alone had truly loved P. Burke. P. Burke, now a dead pile on a table, was the greatest cybersystem he has ever known, and he never forgets her.

The end, really.

You're curious?

Sure, Delphi lives again. Next year she's back on the yacht getting sympathy for her tragic breakdown. But there's a different chick in Chile, because while Delphi's new operator is competent, you don't get two P. Burkes in a row—for which GTX is duly grateful.

The real belly-bomb of course is Paul. He was *young,* see. Fighting abstract wrong. Now life has clawed into him and he goes through gut rage and grief and grows in human wisdom and resolve. So much so that you won't be surprised, sometime later, to find him—where?

In the GTX boardroom, dummy. Using the advantage of his birth to radicalize the system. You'd call it "boring from within."

That's how he put it, and his friends couldn't agree more. It gives them a warm, confident feeling to know that Paul is up there. Sometimes one of them who's still around runs into him and gets a big hello.

And the sharp-faced lad?

Oh, he matures too. He learns fast, believe it. For instance, he's the first to learn that an obscure GTX research unit is actually getting something with their loopy temporal anomalizer project. True, he doesn't have a physics background, and he's bugged quite a few people. But he doesn't really learn about that until the day he stands where somebody points him during a test run—

—and wakes up lying on a newspaper headlined NIXON UNVEILS PHASE TWO.

Lucky he's a fast learner.

Believe it, zombie. When I say growth, I mean *growth*. Capital appreciation. You can stop sweating. There's a great future there.

TECH-ILLA SUNRISE
(.txt dot con Sangrita)

Rafael Lozano-Hemmer & Guillermo Gómez-Peña, post-Mexican double agents compiling illegal knowledge.

Guillermo Gómez-Peña is a performance artist, writer, activist, radical pedagogue, and the director of the performance troupe La Pocha Nostra. He was born in Mexico City and came to the United States in 1978. His performance work and eight books have contributed to the debates on cultural diversity, border culture, and U.S.-Mexico relations. A MacArthur Fellow and American Book Award winner, he is a regular contributor to National Public Radio. Rafael Lozano-Hemmer is a major award-winning electronic artist who develops interactive installations that are at the intersection of architecture and performance art. He has received two BAFTA British Academy Awards for Interactive Art in London, a Golden Nica at the Prix Ars Electronica in Austria, the "Artist of the Year" Rave Award in *Wired* magazine, a Rockefeller fellowship, the Trophée des Lumières in Lyon, and an International Bauhaus Award in Dessau. "Tech-Illa Sunrise," which first appeared in *Aztlán* 29, no. 1 (Spring 2004), challenges our assumptions about software, hardware, and wetware while making its point about Latino culture, the "other," and the stranglehold that some cultures seek to maintain on the promise and peril of future media.

Post-Mexican artists release recovered files of the tech-illa network. Experts believe leaked document may be false.

Dear cibernautas angloparlantes,
Ever wonder what is in the root directory of your Mexican server? Wouldn't you want to peek at the files of Chilicon Valley's most powerful sysadmin? Scary, que no? What follows is a leaked document extracted from deleted files of the tech-illa network, a rare glimpse at the webback underground's real agenda. <Warning> It is unclear at this time if this information was obtained

by hacking into the server or if it was distributed on purpose as a decoy. </Warning>. Sections in Spanglish are untranslatable. </Warning>.

I
Decompress "Mexi-cyborg" file

Nosotros, los otros...
We are all ethno-cyborgs, chiborgs, cyBorges, ciboricuas y demás. If you want to know the future of technology take a good look at us, check out Walter Mercado en Univision, a true transgenic social spammer, the mero Miami bastard son Morpheo of Captain Kirk and Liberachi.

Also, check out 60 year-old TV hostess & Venezuelan Extreme Beauty Queen Viviana de la Medianoche, with her designer body rebuilt from zero in Tijuana clandestine clinics; mil dolares, and this includes nose job, chin, inflatable chichis, removable ribs and voice change activator.

Don't forget to also research "Latino Frankenstein" sites,
Direct TV en español, and pop cultural phenomena like
el Transgenic/trans-ethnic Ricky Martin invented in Epcott,
274 year old talk show host Don Francisco;
or La criminal pop star, Gloria Trevi, who also knows the secret of
immortality...

Don't forget to carefully analyse our composite identities
We/our 207 face lifts & our 49 laser identity surgeries
We/the Mexican Orlan
We/the children of El Frankenstein de Los Mochis y La Novia de Chucky
We Los High-tecas de East LA y La Mision.com
We/our very sentimental feedback hearts
We/our rrrobotic jalapeño joystick enlargement methode
We/our identity morphing mask (we code-morphed before Transmeta's
crusoe processor and IBM's daisy project).
We/our 1960's melanina pills still sold in Cuernavaca and Acapulco for
"instant racial identity change."
Celebrity clients include Colin Powell, Michael Jackson & Salma Hayeck

We/our liposuctioned nalgas de estética infomercial bien 1970's
We/our peyote graphics engine
We/our mojado scuba technology
We/carne asada eating ebola bacteria
We/cyber-mexican flies and digital cockroaches
We/burrito powered robo-raza
We/los cyber-nacos en La Neta-scape
We R slowly corrupting your default configuration
We R alien webbacks,
and we have strapped on
our new hybrid neural implants
that enhance the adaptability
of the epistemo-loco-perceptual apparatus
to non-linear telesensory inputs.
(tongues)
You think we are getting sleepy when we are just resolving a recursive loop:
why else have fuzzy logic cochlear processors, mex-plico? We're solving
netaphysical dilemmas of sorts, tex-plico? Our bigote doubles up as an antenna
for our spread spectrum wireless LAN connection (and yes, it is I-triple-E
eight-o-two eleven and bluetooth compliant).

Question: what's the most powerful computer super-cluster?
Answer: a 512-processor machine in New Mexico called "Los Lobos". No
coincidence the cluster is programmed in "Object Oriented Chile ++" which
is radically incompatible with all your languages (you may utilize our machine
translation program Mexicorama2 to view but not edit the code).

You feel pretty hot with your overclocked gigahertz Pentium when all the
action is in our new yottaherz Sexium with speedy-g-spot inside (available
from chip maker Advanced Mexican Devices AMD).

What did you think really happens at the Mac/illa-doras?
We are reverse engineering your ass, mi nerdisteca! Porque?
You want the naked truth?

According to a spokesman from the Michoacan Institute of Technology

(MIT): "Latinos are currently interested in what (we) term 'imaginary' or 'poetical' technology. Its premise is as follows: Since most Latinos don't have access to new technologies, we imagine the access. All we have is our political imagination and our humor to interject in the conversation... It's an imaginary act of expropriation. Nuestra complejidad estético-intelectual compensa la falta de billete, mexi-comprendes?"

Have another drink compadre
Mas-turbado que nunca

II
Issue who is command <Lupita.xml>

Who do you think is your sysadmin?
It's Lupita, your service provider!

That's right, Lupita is the real motherboard, la Gran Coatlicue Digital, la Matrix Chola. Born multi-tasking and multithreading, she has protected memory and she wont grant you access privileges. Y wátchala porque se come a sus hijos! She eats her own children. She laughs at your binary code, *&%$^& when you try to digitize,*#@$!%^ scan*!~@$+(* and sample**&^^^%R# the world with a simple YES/NO, a one or a zero*^%#)(+^ black/white, in/out. Norte/Sur.

No wonder you are undergoing a crisis in representation/a crisis in masculinity/sociability/ethics. (Delete paragraph after reading it).

She has long ago dropped the binary code in favor of a recombinant self-organizing system of neural nets interconnected via EMR fields that allow for complex emergent phenomena, lighter and deeper shades of brown. El ciberespacio es café, no blanco ni negro, remember,

You try to learn Spanish w/Cybervision tapes, but it's never enough.
You try to ping her but get a 401.
You try to trace her and you get a denial of service attack.
You try to open her attachments but you get a blue screen of death
You try a portscan but you get an error type 2

You send her cookies and she hits you with the "I Love You" virus.
You send her pirated MP3s (bad Polish pop tunes) and a pair of killer porn-video glasses, and she hits you with the "I need you" virus.
You are TC (technologically correct); we are TA (technologically abusados).
We are TI: temporarily incompatible.
Empty trashcan/memoria digital/la memoria está en el dedo.
We know your sysadmin and she is mad as hell
Snooping on her registry could be your last fatal crash.

III
Decompress gastronomy file on "Tecno-canibalismo"

While your fabs produced Silicon wafers with copper deposition, we Olmechs were already going submicron with carbon-based buckminsterfullerene biocompatible processors...and eating them! Ever heard of nacho chips? Well, that happens to be the code name for our nano-EPROM-chips.

Our fat beer gut (see ../barriga.jpg) is our redundant array of lipid-soluble memory nano-chips, —digo "nano-chipos" de chipotle— that's right, tortilla co-processor wafers made in TJ/Taiwana and East Japangeles.

We eat it all, de tocho! We can assimilate "low" or "high." Nos da igual. Our diet includes everything from crappy calculators, "Target" ionizers, and wrist/phone watches (o sea, refurbished Aztechnology), to sound systems with fake fancy brands "made in Tepito" & mas y more hydraulics for our hi-preco "lowrider" carruchas. (Just check the new Made-in-Kioto "Lowrider" Mag). We specially like cables con chorizo, tamalgochis y web-os rancheros.

Why do you think the founder of Slashdot.org, the ultimate net destination for nerds, is called "CmdrTaco"? Cause that's where the action is, cross-over edible biotech computers that thrive in diverse gene-pools...

O sea, que wáchala:
Somos "techno-canibales;"
Habitamos en Chilicon Valley,
Barrio sur del DDT (Digital Divide Tardio).

See you-See me
We are heading North...
Mi querido ethernet
address 00:03:93:fb:1c:9e
Have a psycho-tropical tech-illa,
Y ponte las pilas web-on.

IV
Decompress history file on "Mexican science."

Back in the late 1930s, the theory of cybernetics was first postulated at the Instituto Nacional de Cardiología, when Mexican researcher Arturo Rosenbleuth investigated the heart's autonomy from the brain. Until then, no explanation was available as to why the heart kept beating in brain-dead "Pacheco" (mariguano) bodies. O sea, how could the corazón keep pumping without receiving instructions from the brain?

Also in Mexico City, Dr. Rosenbleuth's gringo colleague Norbert Weiner, interdisciplinary thinker extraordinaire, developed "the theory of messages and feedback" to explain self-regulation and in so doing laid the foundation for most current thought on control and communications.

Carnales, and you thought cybernetics was about hard-and soft-ware? When it was about wet-ware all along?; about corazones sangrantes, errantes, punzantes, mecánicos, hidraúlicos: about pulsating hearts que jamás siguen instrucciones de arriba; puro heart-drive ese

2 PAGES OF UNTRANSLATABLE SHAMANIC LEXICO-LOGICAL POETRY

And then Mexicans brought you color TV, thanks to Guillermo González Camarena's first patent in 1940. And followed through with the first stereo and telepresence recordings, gracias al maestro Juan Garcia Esquivel in the 50s.

Also in the 50s, Mexican wrestler hero and alternative scientist El Santo made several movies in which he clearly anticipated the Internet, lap-top computers, web cameras, see-you see-me systems and Chicano performance art.

Then in the 60's, Chicano scientists from the Michoacán Institute of Technology (MIT) working in clandestine garages throughout the US Southwest developed amazing hydraulic robotics for lowrider cars, which in retrospect make American robotics, from Moravec to SRL, frankly, frankly look naïve.

More recent accomplishments you may know about are the laboratory synthesis of pheromones (abusado con los Latin lovers) and Miguel de Icaza's Gnome project, the most admired and adopted "open source software" ever developed. However most of these breakthroughs have been ignored by the Logos Digitalis, and as of now remain unpublished by Mecánica Nacional.

TO BE CONTINUED...

V

QuetZalcua82L*1 (from "Memory bank #36582):

In 1999, Americans were arming themselves in record numbers, preparing for the Y2K blackout to be protected from looters, riots, anarchy, you know, brown people. At the same time, Subcomandante Marcos was named by Wired magazine one of the top 10 techno visionaries of our era. If you can't escape from Latinos in the privileged final frontier of cyberspace, where can you hide?

The following warning has been circulating throughout the net by cyber-terrorism watchdog groups:

"Virus Alert!! Warning!! Do not open any email sent to you if the "subject" is in any language you do not understand" Spanish, French, Spanglish, Frangle, Ingleñol...Opening these messages may corrupt your fragile sense of personal and national identity...If you have recently pointed your browser at any web site with Latino content: Zap Net, Virtual Barrio, Inter-Neta.com, Lati-Net, Salsaparagringos.net, Chihuahuas.com —a subsidiary of Taco Bell Incorporated, Ricky Martin's Menudo unplugged Page, Pocho Magazine, Pochanostra.com, or any other "Latino" web site...you may be already infected.

NSA virus researchers at the Pentagon are calling this new Silicon infection QuetZalcoat-82L or simply 'The Mexican Bug.'

The dreaded Michelangelo virus '96 and the RTM virus are harmless compared to the Mexican Bug. Like a cucaracha gang of microbites this "programa" loiters at seemingly non-threatening Latino webs: Rock en español music sites, high ethnic crafts, el Carne Asada without Meat Club, vegan burrito recipes, and sexual tourism information pages, detecting and targeting gringos with an innocent fascination for ethno-exotica.

Soon after visiting these sites you receive a 'friendly' looking e-mail, announcing a nice Mariachi Festival or advertizing a Salsa theme cruise to Baja. When you open it, a cute talking Chihuahua in a poncho and a pink sombrero appears on the screen and delivers the following message with a thick sabroso Spanish accent:

'Querido turista, curador, crítico, empresario:
There is no moral, physical or social repercussions to your actions in cyberspace. Digital technology has finally allowed us to create an inoffensive millennial mythology of the Latino, the Indigenous and the Immigrant Other. We are part of this new mythology. We are meant to cater to your most intimate fears and desires.'

*1.-Excerpt from an unsolicited e-mail by "Cyber-Vato #127" Bob Sifuentes heavily edited by the authors of this manifesto

VI.-Excerpts from the cyber-testament:

"In the beginning there was nothing,
only cyberspace,
a vast untamed, unseen cyber desert
with no water, ice, fire, or wind.
There were no animals or plants,
not even microscopic creatures.
and then we came,
El Gran Homo Digitalis.

In the absence of cardinal points,

we moved in all directions,
conquering every inch of virginal space,
naming it as we saw it,
mapping the uncharted terrain of our future.
We were young, ambitious and white,
& there was no one else around to bother us.
It was the Cambrian era of cyberspace.

Our dictum was unquestionable:
borderless "communication," that is in English,
free trade across continents & minds,
mindless interactivity,
a Theology of Interface,
unlimited belonging to a " total world,"
Our World.

Then came the Others,
brown people, tar people, e-mongrels of sorts,
speaking bizarre linguas polutas.
The cybarbarians came from the South of nothingness,
& rapidly moved North into "the zone,"
Our Zone.

In order to keep the webbacks "out,"
we constantly upgraded our systems & software
& made them increasingly expensive & complex,
but they began to pirate our programs.
We then created border fences,
intricate security codes, digital checkpoints,
but they figured all of them out.

Soon we were left with no other option
but to privatize the New World.
The "land grab era" was coming to an end
North, South, East, delete

We were then forced to utilize more severe
3765*&7563#@^+~@893201!@^@&1234
in orther to$#@$#%
& those living South of the digital divide
were#%$%$until the()65#@+8*&II..."

-Año de 2002
DT (despues de Technopalzin)
Go-Mex East Erra-fael
The year of the Stalking Fox
According to Mayan Astrology (Channel 55)

As We May Think
Vannevar Bush

Vannevar Bush (1890–1974) was a professor at the Massachusetts Institute of Technology from 1919 to just before World War II, when he took on the role of Director of the Office of Scientific Research and Development for Franklin Delano Roosevelt, which was created to coordinate research on weapons development, including oversight on the Manhattan Project and its first atomic bomb. After the war, Bush submitted to FDR his famous report, "Science, the Endless Frontier," which helped lead to the creation of the National Science Foundation. That same year, Bush was asked by the *Atlantic Monthly* to write an article on peacetime uses for military technologies developed during the war, and this famous article was the result. The article, reprinted here in its entirety, presents a number of startlingly prescient ideas, including a mechanized private file and library, called a "memex," that would store vast amounts of books, periodicals, journals, and more and make them easily retrievable.

This has not been a scientist's war; it has been a war in which all have had a part. The scientists, burying their old professional competition in the demand of a common cause, have shared greatly and learned much. It has been exhilarating to work in effective partnership. Now, for many, this appears to be approaching an end. What are the scientists to do next?

For the biologists, and particularly for the medical scientists, there can be little indecision, for their war has hardly required them to leave the old paths. Many indeed have been able to carry on their war research in their familiar peacetime laboratories. Their objectives remain much the same.

It is the physicists who have been thrown most violently off stride, who have left academic pursuits for the making of strange destructive gadgets, who have had to devise new methods for their unanticipated assignments. They have done their part on the devices that made it possible to turn back the enemy, have worked in combined effort with the physicists of our allies. They have felt within themselves the stir of achievement. They have been part of a great team. Now, as peace approaches, one asks where they will find objectives worthy of their best.

1

Of what lasting benefit has been man's use of science and of the new instruments which his research brought into existence? First, they have increased his control of his material environment. They have improved his food, his clothing, his shelter; they have increased his security and released him partly from the bondage of bare existence. They have given him increased knowledge of his own biological processes so that he has had a progressive freedom from disease and an increased span of life. They are illuminating the interactions of his physiological and psychological functions, giving the promise of an improved mental health.

Science has provided the swiftest communication between individuals; it has provided a record of ideas and has enabled man to manipulate and to make extracts from that record so that knowledge evolves and endures throughout the life of a race rather than that of an individual.

There is a growing mountain of research. But there is increased evidence that we are being bogged down today as specialization extends. The investigator is staggered by the findings and conclusions of thousands of other workers— conclusions which he cannot find time to grasp, much less to remember, as they appear. Yet specialization becomes increasingly necessary for progress, and the effort to bridge between disciplines is correspondingly superficial.

Professionally our methods of transmitting and reviewing the results of research are generations old and by now are totally inadequate for their purpose. If the aggregate time spent in writing scholarly works and in reading them could be evaluated, the ratio between these amounts of time might well be startling. Those who conscientiously attempt to keep abreast of current thought, even in restricted fields, by close and continuous reading might well shy away from an examination calculated to show how much of the previous month's efforts could be produced on call. Mendel's concept of the laws of genetics was lost to the world for a generation because his publication did not reach the few who were capable of grasping and extending it; and this sort of catastrophe is undoubtedly being repeated all about us, as truly significant attainments become lost in the mass of the inconsequential.

The difficulty seems to be, not so much that we publish unduly in view of the extent and variety of present day interests, but rather that publication has been extended far beyond our present ability to make real use of the record. The summation of human experience is being expanded at a prodigious rate, and the means we use for threading through the consequent maze to the momentarily important item is the same as was used in the days of square-rigged ships.

But there are signs of a change as new and powerful instrumentalities come into use. Photocells capable of seeing things in a physical sense, advanced photography which can record what is seen or even what is not, thermionic tubes capable of controlling potent forces under the guidance of less power than a mosquito uses to vibrate his wings, cathode ray tubes rendering visible an occurrence so brief that by comparison a microsecond is a long time, relay combinations which will carry out involved sequences of movements more reliably than any human operator and thousands of times as fast—there are plenty of mechanical aids with which to effect a transformation in scientific records.

Two centuries ago Leibnitz invented a calculating machine which embodied most of the essential features of recent keyboard devices, but it could not then come into use. The economics of the situation were against it: the labor involved in constructing it, before the days of mass production, exceeded the labor to be saved by its use, since all it could accomplish could be duplicated by sufficient use of pencil and paper. Moreover, it would have been subject to frequent breakdown, so that it could not have been depended upon; for at that time and long after, complexity and unreliability were synonymous.

Babbage, even with remarkably generous support for his time, could not produce his great arithmetical machine. His idea was sound enough, but construction and maintenance costs were then too heavy. Had a Pharaoh been given detailed and explicit designs of an automobile, and had he understood them completely, it would have taxed the resources of his kingdom to have fashioned the thousands of parts for a single car, and that car would have broken down on the first trip to Giza.

Machines with interchangeable parts can now be constructed with great economy of effort. In spite of much complexity, they perform reliably. Witness the humble typewriter, or the movie camera, or the automobile. Electrical contacts have ceased to stick when thoroughly understood. Note the automatic telephone exchange, which has hundreds of thousands of such contacts, and yet is reliable. A spider web of metal, sealed in a thin glass container, a wire heated to brilliant glow, in short, the thermionic tube of radio sets, is made by the hundred million, tossed about in packages, plugged into sockets—and it works! Its gossamer parts, the precise location and alignment involved in its construction, would have occupied a master craftsman of the guild for months; now it is built for thirty cents. The world has arrived at an age of cheap complex devices of great reliability; and something is bound to come of it.

2

A record, if it is to be useful to science, must be continuously extended, it must be stored, and above all it must be consulted. Today we make the record conventionally by writing and photography, followed by printing; but we also record on film, on wax disks, and on magnetic wires. Even if utterly new recording procedures do not appear, these present ones are certainly in the process of modification and extension.

Certainly progress in photography is not going to stop. Faster material and lenses, more automatic cameras, finer-grained sensitive compounds to allow an extension of the minicamera idea, are all imminent. Let us project this trend ahead to a logical, if not inevitable, outcome. The camera hound of the future wears on his forehead a lump a little larger than a walnut. It takes pictures 3 millimeters square, later to be projected or enlarged, which after all involves only a factor of 10 beyond present practice. The lens is of universal focus, down to any distance accommodated by the unaided eye, simply because it is of short focal length. There is a built-in photocell on the walnut such as we now have on at least one camera, which automatically adjusts exposure for a wide range of illumination. There is film in the walnut for a hundred exposures, and the spring for operating its shutter and shifting its film is wound once for all when the film clip is inserted. It produces its result in full color. It may well be stereoscopic, and record with two spaced glass eyes, for striking improvements in stereoscopic technique are just around the corner.

The cord which trips its shutter may reach down a man's sleeve within easy reach of his fingers. A quick squeeze, and the picture is taken. On a pair of ordinary glasses is a square of fine lines near the top of one lens, where it is out of the way of ordinary vision. When an object appears in that square, it is lined up for its picture. As the scientist of the future moves about the laboratory or the field, every time he looks at something worthy of the record, he trips the shutter and in it goes, without even an audible click. Is this all fantastic? The only fantastic thing about it is the idea of making as many pictures as would result from its use.

Will there be dry photography? It is already here in two forms. When Brady made his Civil War pictures, the plate had to be wet at the time of exposure. Now it has to be wet during development instead. In the future perhaps it need not be wetted at all. There have long been films impregnated with diazo dyes which form a picture without development, so that it is already there as soon as the camera has been operated. An exposure to ammonia gas destroys the unexposed dye, and the picture can then be taken out into the light and examined. The process is now slow, but someone may speed it up, and it has no grain difficulties such as now keep photographic researchers busy. Often it would be advantageous to be able to snap the camera and to look at the picture immediately.

Another process now in use is also slow, and more or less clumsy. For fifty years impregnated papers have been used which turn dark at every point where an electrical contact touches them, by reason of the chemical change thus produced in an iodine compound included in the paper. They have been used to make records, for a pointer moving across them can leave a trail behind. If the electrical potential on the pointer is varied as it moves, the line becomes light or dark in accordance with the potential.

This scheme is now used in facsimile transmission. The pointer draws a set of closely spaced lines across the paper one after another. As it moves, its potential is varied in accordance with a varying current received over wires from a distant station, where these variations are produced by a photocell which is similarly scanning a picture. At every instant the darkness of the line being drawn is made equal to the darkness of the point on the picture being observed by the photocell. Thus, when the whole picture has been covered, a replica appears at the receiving end.

A scene itself can be just as well looked over line by line by the photocell in this way as can a photograph of the scene. This whole apparatus constitutes a camera, with the added feature, which can be dispensed with if desired, of making its picture at a distance. It is slow, and the picture is poor in detail. Still, it does give another process of dry photography, in which the picture is finished as soon as it is taken.

It would be a brave man who would predict that such a process will always remain clumsy, slow, and faulty in detail. Television equipment today transmits sixteen reasonably good pictures a second, and it involves only two essential differences from the process described above. For one, the record is made by a moving beam of electrons rather than a moving pointer, for the reason that an electron beam can sweep across the picture very rapidly indeed. The other difference involves merely the use of a screen which glows momentarily when the electrons hit, rather than a chemically treated paper or film which is permanently altered. This speed is necessary in television, for motion pictures rather than stills are the object.

Use chemically treated film in place of the glowing screen, allow the apparatus to transmit one picture only rather than a succession, and a rapid camera for dry photography results. The treated film needs to be far faster in action than present examples, but it probably could be. More serious is the objection that this scheme would involve putting the film inside a vacuum chamber, for electron beams behave normally only in such a rarefied environment. This difficulty could be avoided by allowing the electron beam to play on one side of a partition, and by pressing the film against the other side, if this partition were such as to allow the electrons to go through perpendicular to its surface, and to prevent them from spreading out sideways. Such partitions, in crude form, could certainly be constructed, and they will hardly hold up the general development.

Like dry photography, microphotography still has a long way to go. The basic scheme of reducing the size of the record, and examining it by projection rather than directly, has possibilities too great to be ignored. The combination of optical projection and photographic reduction is already producing some results in microfilm for scholarly purposes, and the potentialities are highly suggestive. Today, with microfilm, reductions by a linear factor of 20 can be employed and still produce full clarity when the material is re-enlarged for examination. The limits are set by the graininess of the film, the excellence of the optical system, and the efficiency of the light sources employed. All of these are rapidly improving.

Assume a linear ratio of 100 for future use. Consider film of the same thickness as paper, although thinner film will certainly be usable. Even under these conditions there would be a total factor of 10,000 between the bulk of the ordinary record on books and its microfilm replica. The *Encyclopoedia Britannica* could be reduced to the volume of a matchbox. A library of a million volumes could be compressed into one end of a desk. If the human race has produced since the invention of movable type a total record, in the form of magazines, newspapers, books, tracts, advertising blurbs, correspondence, having a volume corresponding to a billion books, the whole affair, assembled and compressed, could be lugged off in a moving van. Mere compression, of course, is not enough; one needs not only to make and store a record but also be able to consult it, and this aspect of the matter comes later. Even the modern great library is not generally consulted; it is nibbled at by a few.

Compression is important, however, when it comes to costs. The material for the microfilm *Britannica* would cost a nickel, and it could be mailed anywhere for a cent. What would it cost to print a million copies? To print a sheet of newspaper, in a large edition, costs a small fraction of a cent. The entire material of the *Britannica* in reduced microfilm form would go on a sheet eight and one-half by eleven inches. Once it is available, with the photographic reproduction methods of the future, duplicates in large quantities could probably be turned out for a cent apiece beyond the cost of materials. The preparation of the original copy? That introduces the next aspect of the subject.

3

To make the record, we now push a pencil or tap a typewriter. Then comes the process of digestion and correction, followed by an intricate process of typesetting, printing, and distribution. To consider the first stage of the procedure, will the author of the future cease writing by hand or typewriter and talk directly to the record? He does so indirectly, by talking to a stenographer or a wax cylinder; but the elements are all present if he wishes to have his talk directly produce a typed record. All he needs to do is to take advantage of existing mechanisms and to alter his language.

At a recent World Fair a machine called a Voder was shown. A girl stroked its keys and it emitted recognizable speech. No human vocal chords entered into the procedure at any point; the keys simply combined some electrically produced vibrations and passed these on to a loud-speaker. In the Bell Laboratories there is the converse of this machine, called a Vocoder. The loudspeaker is replaced by a microphone, which picks up sound. Speak to it, and the corresponding keys move. This may be one element of the postulated system.

The other element is found in the stenotype, that somewhat disconcerting device encountered usually at public meetings. A girl strokes its keys languidly and looks about the room and sometimes at the speaker with a disquieting gaze. From it emerges a typed strip which records in a phonetically simplified language a record of what the speaker is supposed to have said. Later this strip is retyped into ordinary language, for in its nascent form it is intelligible only to the initiated. Combine these two elements, let the Vocoder run the stenotype, and the result is a machine which types when talked to.

Our present languages are not especially adapted to this sort of mechanization, it is true. It is strange that the inventors of universal languages have not seized upon the idea of producing one which better fitted the technique for transmitting and recording speech. Mechanization may yet force the issue, especially in the scientific field; whereupon scientific jargon would become still less intelligible to the layman.

One can now picture a future investigator in his laboratory. His hands are free, and he is not anchored. As he moves about and observes, he photographs and comments. Time is automatically recorded to tie the two records together. If he goes into the field, he may be connected by radio to his recorder. As he ponders over his notes in the evening, he again talks his comments into the record. His typed record, as well as his photographs, may both be in miniature, so that he projects them for examination.

Much needs to occur, however, between the collection of data and observations, the extraction of parallel material from the existing record, and the final insertion of new material into the general body of the common record. For mature thought there is no mechanical substitute. But creative thought and essentially repetitive thought are very different things. For the latter there are, and may be, powerful mechanical aids.

Adding a column of figures is a repetitive thought process, and it was long ago properly relegated to the machine. True, the machine is sometimes controlled by a keyboard, and thought of a sort enters in reading the figures and poking the corresponding keys, but even this is avoidable. Machines have been made which will read typed figures by photocells and then depress the corresponding keys; these are combinations of photocells for scanning the type, electric circuits for sorting the consequent variations, and relay circuits for interpreting the result into the action of solenoids to pull the keys down.

All this complication is needed because of the clumsy way in which we have learned to write figures. If we recorded them positionally, simply by the configuration of a set of dots on a card, the automatic reading mechanism would become comparatively simple. In fact if the dots are holes, we have the punched-card machine long ago produced by Hollorith for the purposes of the census, and now used throughout business. Some types of complex businesses could hardly operate without these machines.

Adding is only one operation. To perform arithmetical computation involves also subtraction, multiplication, and division, and in addition some method for temporary storage of results, removal from storage for further manipulation, and recording of final results by printing. Machines for these purposes are now of two types: keyboard machines for accounting and the like, manually controlled for the insertion of data, and usually automatically controlled as far as the sequence of operations is concerned; and punched-card machines in which separate operations are usually delegated to a series of machines, and the cards then transferred bodily from one to another. Both forms are very useful; but as far as complex computations are concerned, both are still in embryo.

Rapid electrical counting appeared soon after the physicists found it desirable to count cosmic rays. For their own purposes the physicists promptly constructed thermionic-tube equipment capable of counting electrical impulses at the rate of 100,000 a second. The advanced arithmetical machines of the future will be electrical in nature, and they will perform at 100 times present speeds, or more.

Moreover, they will be far more versatile than present commercial machines, so that they may readily be adapted for a wide variety of operations. They will be controlled by a control card or film, they will select their own data and manipulate it in accordance with the instructions thus inserted, they will perform complex arithmetical computations at exceedingly high speeds, and they will record results in such form as to be readily available for distribution or for later further manipulation. Such machines will have enormous appetites. One of them will take instructions and data from a whole roomful of girls armed with simple key board punches, and will deliver sheets of computed results every few minutes. There will always be plenty of things to compute in the detailed affairs of millions of people doing complicated things.

4

The repetitive processes of thought are not confined, however, to matters of arithmetic and statistics. In fact, every time one combines and records facts in accordance with established logical processes, the creative aspect of thinking is concerned only with the selection of the data and the process to be employed and the manipulation thereafter is repetitive in nature and hence a fit matter to be relegated to the machine. Not so much has been done along these lines, beyond the bounds of arithmetic, as might be done, primarily because of the economics of the situation. The needs of business and the extensive market obviously waiting assured the advent of mass-produced arithmetical machines just as soon as production methods were sufficiently advanced.

With machines for advanced analysis no such situation existed; for there was and is no extensive market; the users of advanced methods of manipulating data are a very small part of the population. There are, however, machines for solving differential equations—and functional and integral equations, for that matter. There are many special machines, such as the harmonic synthesizer which predicts the tides. There will be many more, appearing certainly first in the hands of the scientist and in small numbers.

If scientific reasoning were limited to the logical processes of arithmetic, we should not get far in our understanding of the physical world. One might as well attempt to grasp the game of poker entirely by the use of the mathematics of probability. The abacus, with its beads strung on parallel wires, led the Arabs to positional numeration and the concept of zero many centuries before the rest of the world; and it was a useful tool—so useful that it still exists.

It is a far cry from the abacus to the modern keyboard accounting machine. It will be an equal step to the arithmetical machine of the future. But even this new machine will not take the scientist where he needs to go. Relief must be secured from laborious detailed manipulation of higher mathematics as well, if the users of it are to free their brains for something more than repetitive detailed transformations in accordance with established rules. A mathematician is not a man who can readily manipulate figures; often he cannot. He is not even a man who can readily perform the transformations of equations by the use of calculus. He is primarily an individual who is skilled in the use of symbolic logic on a high plane, and especially he is a man of intuitive judgment in the choice of the manipulative processes he employs.

All else he should be able to turn over to his mechanism, just as confidently as he turns over the propelling of his car to the intricate mechanism under the hood. Only then will mathematics be practically effective in bringing the growing knowledge of atomistics to the useful solution of the advanced problems of chemistry, metallurgy, and biology. For this reason there still come more machines to handle advanced mathematics for the scientist. Some of them will be sufficiently bizarre to suit the most fastidious connoisseur of the present artifacts of civilization.

5

The scientist, however, is not the only person who manipulates data and examines the world about him by the use of logical processes, although he sometimes preserves this appearance by adopting into the fold anyone who becomes logical, much in the manner in which a British labor leader is elevated to knighthood. Whenever logical processes of thought are employed—that is, whenever thought for a time runs along an accepted groove—there is an opportunity for the machine. Formal logic used to be a keen instrument in the hands of the teacher in his trying of students' souls. It is readily possible to construct a machine which will manipulate premises in accordance with formal logic, simply by the clever use of relay circuits. Put a set of premises into such a device and turn the crank, and it will readily pass out conclusion after conclusion, all in accordance with logical law, and with no more slips than would be expected of a keyboard adding machine.

Logic can become enormously difficult, and it would undoubtedly be well to produce more assurance in its use. The machines for higher analysis have usually been equation solvers. Ideas are beginning to appear for equation transformers, which will rearrange the relationship expressed by an equation in accordance with strict and rather advanced logic. Progress is inhibited by the exceedingly crude way in which mathematicians express their relationships. They employ a symbolism which grew like Topsy and has little consistency; a strange fact in that most logical field.

A new symbolism, probably positional, must apparently precede the reduction of mathematical transformations to machine processes. Then, on beyond the strict logic of the mathematician, lies the application of logic in everyday affairs. We may some day click off arguments on a machine with the same assurance that we now enter sales on a cash register. But the machine of logic will not look like a cash register, even of the streamlined model.

So much for the manipulation of ideas and their insertion into the record. Thus far we seem to be worse off than before—for we can enormously extend the record; yet even in its present bulk we can hardly consult it. This is a much larger matter than merely the extraction of data for the purposes of scientific research; it involves the entire process by which man profits by his inheritance of acquired knowledge. The prime action of use is selection, and here we are halting indeed. There may be millions of fine thoughts, and the account of the experience on which they are based, all encased within stone walls of acceptable architectural form; but if the scholar can get at only one a week by diligent search, his syntheses are not likely to keep up with the current scene.

Selection, in this broad sense, is a stone adze in the hands of a cabinetmaker. Yet, in a narrow sense and in other areas, something has already been done mechanically on selection. The personnel officer of a factory drops a stack of a few thousand employee cards into a selecting machine, sets a code in accordance with an established convention, and produces in a short time a list of all employees who live in Trenton and know Spanish. Even such devices are much too slow when it comes, for example, to matching a set of fingerprints with one of five million on file. Selection devices of this sort will soon be speeded up from their present rate of reviewing data at a few hundred a minute. By the use of photocells and microfilm they will survey items at the rate of a thousand a second, and will print out duplicates of those selected.

This process, however, is simple selection: it proceeds by examining in turn every one of a large set of items, and by picking out those which have certain specified characteristics. There is another form of selection best illustrated by the automatic telephone exchange. You dial a number and the machine selects and connects just one of a million possible stations. It does not run over them all. It pays attention only to a class given by a first digit, then only to a subclass of this given by the second digit, and so on; and thus proceeds rapidly and almost unerringly to the selected station. It requires a few seconds to make the selection, although the process could be speeded up if increased speed were economically warranted. If necessary, it could be made extremely fast by substituting thermionic-tube switching for mechanical switching, so that the full selection could be made in one one-hundredth of a second. No one would wish to spend the money necessary to make this change in the telephone system, but the general idea is applicable elsewhere.

Take the prosaic problem of the great department store. Every time a charge sale is made, there are a number of things to be done. The inventory needs to be revised, the salesman needs to be given credit for the sale, the general accounts need an entry, and, most important, the customer needs to be charged. A central records device has been developed in which much of this work is done conveniently. The salesman places on a stand the customer's identification card, his own card, and the card taken from the article sold—all punched cards. When he pulls a lever, contacts are made through the holes, machinery at a central point makes the necessary computations and entries, and the proper receipt is printed for the salesman to pass to the customer.

But there may be ten thousand charge customers doing business with the store, and before the full operation can be completed someone has to select the right card and insert it at the central office. Now rapid selection can slide just the proper card into position in an instant or two, and return it afterward. Another difficulty occurs, however. Someone must read a total on the card, so that the machine can add its computed item to it. Conceivably the cards might be of the dry photography type I have described. Existing totals could then be read by photocell, and the new total entered by an electron beam.

The cards may be in miniature, so that they occupy little space. They must move quickly. They need not be transferred far, but merely into position so that the photocell and recorder can operate on them. Positional dots can enter the data. At the end of the month a machine can readily be made to read these and to print an ordinary bill. With tube selection, in which no mechanical parts are involved in the switches, little time need be occupied in bringing the correct card into use—a second should suffice for the entire operation. The whole record on the card may be made by magnetic dots on a steel sheet if desired, instead of dots to be observed optically, following the scheme by which Poulsen long ago put speech on a magnetic wire. This method has the advantage of simplicity and ease of erasure. By using photography, however, one can arrange to project the record in enlarged form and at a distance by using the process common in television equipment.

One can consider rapid selection of this form, and distant projection for other purposes. To be able to key one sheet of a million before an operator in a second or two, with the possibility of then adding notes thereto, is suggestive in many ways. It might even be of use in libraries, but that is another story. At any rate, there are now some interesting combinations possible. One might, for example, speak to a microphone, in the manner described in connection with the speech controlled typewriter, and thus make his selections. It would certainly beat the usual file clerk.

6

The real heart of the matter of selection, however, goes deeper than a lag in the adoption of mechanisms by libraries, or a lack of development of devices for their use. Our ineptitude in getting at the record is largely caused by the artificiality of systems of indexing. When data of any sort are placed in storage, they are filed alphabetically or numerically, and information is found (when it is) by tracing it down from subclass to subclass. It can be in only one place, unless duplicates are used; one has to have rules as to which path will locate it, and the rules are cumbersome. Having found one item, moreover, one has to emerge from the system and re-enter on a new path.

The human mind does not work that way. It operates by association. With one item in its grasp, it snaps instantly to the next that is suggested by the association of thoughts, in accordance with some intricate web of trails carried by the cells of the brain. It has other characteristics, of course; trails that are not frequently followed are prone to fade, items are not fully permanent, memory is transitory. Yet the speed of action, the intricacy of trails, the detail of mental pictures, is awe-inspiring beyond all else in nature.

Man cannot hope fully to duplicate this mental process artificially, but he certainly ought to be able to learn from it. In minor ways he may even improve, for his records have relative permanency. The first idea, however, to be drawn from the analogy concerns selection. Selection by association, rather than indexing, may yet be mechanized. One cannot hope thus to equal the speed and flexibility with which the mind follows an associative trail, but it should be possible to beat the mind decisively in regard to the permanence and clarity of the items resurrected from storage.

Consider a future device for individual use, which is a sort of mechanized private file and library. It needs a name, and, to coin one at random, "memex" will do. A memex is a device in which an individual stores all his books, records, and communications, and which is mechanized so that it may be consulted with exceeding speed and flexibility. It is an enlarged intimate supplement to his memory.

It consists of a desk, and while it can presumably be operated from a distance, it is primarily the piece of furniture at which he works. On the top are slanting translucent screens, on which material can be projected for convenient reading. There is a keyboard, and sets of buttons and levers. Otherwise it looks like an ordinary desk.

In one end is the stored material. The matter of bulk is well taken care of by improved microfilm. Only a small part of the interior of the memex is devoted to storage, the rest to mechanism. Yet if the user inserted 5000 pages of material a day it would take him hundreds of years to fill the repository, so he can be profligate and enter material freely.

Most of the memex contents are purchased on microfilm ready for insertion. Books of all sorts, pictures, current periodicals, newspapers, are thus obtained and dropped into place. Business correspondence takes the same path. And there is provision for direct entry. On the top of the memex is a transparent platen. On this are placed longhand notes, photographs, memoranda, all sorts of things. When one is in place, the depression of a lever causes it to be photographed onto the next blank space in a section of the memex film, dry photography being employed.

There is, of course, provision for consultation of the record by the usual scheme of indexing. If the user wishes to consult a certain book, he taps its code on the keyboard, and the title page of the book promptly appears before him, projected onto one of his viewing positions. Frequently-used codes are mnemonic, so that he seldom consults his code book; but when he does, a single tap of a key projects it for his use. Moreover, he has supplemental levers. On deflecting one of these levers to the right he runs through the book before him, each page in turn being projected at a speed which just allows a recognizing glance at each. If he deflects it further to the right, he steps through the book 10 pages at a time; still further at 100 pages at a time. Deflection to the left gives him the same control backwards.

A special button transfers him immediately to the first page of the index. Any given book of his library can thus be called up and consulted with far greater facility than if it were taken from a shelf. As he has several projection positions, he can leave one item in position while he calls up another. He can add marginal notes and comments, taking advantage of one possible type of dry photography, and it could even be arranged so that he can do this by a stylus scheme, such as is now employed in the telautograph seen in railroad waiting rooms, just as though he had the physical page before him.

7

All this is conventional, except for the projection forward of present-day mechanisms and gadgetry. It affords an immediate step, however, to associative indexing, the basic idea of which is a provision whereby any item may be caused at will to select immediately and automatically another. This is the essential feature of the memex. The process of tying two items together is the important thing.

When the user is building a trail, he names it, inserts the name in his code book, and taps it out on his keyboard. Before him are the two items to be joined, projected onto adjacent viewing positions. At the bottom of each there are a number of blank code spaces, and a pointer is set to indicate one of these on each item. The user taps a single key, and the items are permanently joined. In each code space appears the code word. Out of view, but also in the code space, is inserted a set of dots for photocell viewing; and on each item these dots by their positions designate the index number of the other item.

Thereafter, at any time, when one of these items is in view, the other can be instantly recalled merely by tapping a button below the corresponding code space. Moreover, when numerous items have been thus joined together to form a trail, they can be reviewed in turn, rapidly or slowly, by deflecting a lever like that used for turning the pages of a book. It is exactly as though the physical items had been gathered together from widely separated sources and bound together to form a new book. It is more than this, for any item can be joined into numerous trails.

The owner of the memex, let us say, is interested in the origin and properties of the bow and arrow. Specifically he is studying why the short Turkish bow was apparently superior to the English long bow in the skirmishes of the Crusades. He has dozens of possibly pertinent books and articles in his memex. First he runs through an encyclopedia, finds an interesting but sketchy article, leaves it projected. Next, in a history, he finds another pertinent item, and ties the two together. Thus he goes, building a trail of many items. Occasionally he inserts a comment of his own, either linking it into the main trail or joining it by a side trail to a particular item. When it becomes evident that the elastic properties of available materials had a great deal to do with the bow, he branches off on a side trail which takes him through textbooks on elasticity and tables of physical constants. He inserts a page of longhand analysis of his own. Thus he builds a trail of his interest through the maze of materials available to him.

And his trails do not fade. Several years later, his talk with a friend turns to the queer ways in which a people resist innovations, even of vital interest.

He has an example, in the fact that the outraged Europeans still failed to adopt the Turkish bow. In fact he has a trail on it. A touch brings up the code book. Tapping a few keys projects the head of the trail. A lever runs through it at will, stopping at interesting items, going off on side excursions. It is an interesting trail, pertinent to the discussion. So he sets a reproducer in action, photographs the whole trail out, and passes it to his friend for insertion in his own memex, there to be linked into the more general trail.

8

Wholly new forms of encyclopedias will appear, ready made with a mesh of associative trails running through them, ready to be dropped into the memex and there amplified. The lawyer has at his touch the associated opinions and decisions of his whole experience, and of the experience of friends and authorities. The patent attorney has on call the millions of issued patents, with familiar trails to every point of his client's interest. The physician, puzzled by a patient's reactions, strikes the trail established in studying an earlier similar case, and runs rapidly through analogous case histories, with side references to the classics for the pertinent anatomy and histology. The chemist, struggling with the synthesis of an organic compound, has all the chemical literature before him in his laboratory, with trails following the analogies of compounds, and side trails to their physical and chemical behavior.

The historian, with a vast chronological account of a people, parallels it with a skip trail which stops only on the salient items, and can follow at any time contemporary trails which lead him all over civilization at a particular epoch. There is a new profession of trail blazers, those who find delight in the task of establishing useful trails through the enormous mass of the common record. The inheritance from the master becomes not only his additions to the world's record, but for his disciples the entire scaffolding by which they were erected.

Thus science may implement the ways in which man produces, stores, and consults the record of the race. It might be striking to outline the instrumentalities of the future more spectacularly, rather than to stick closely to methods and elements now known and undergoing rapid development, as has been done here. Technical difficulties of all sorts have been ignored, certainly, but also ignored are means as yet unknown which may come any day to accelerate technical progress as violently as did the advent of the thermionic tube. In order that the picture may not be too commonplace, by reason of sticking to present-day patterns, it may be well to mention one such possibility, not to prophesy but merely to suggest, for prophecy based on extension of the known has substance, while prophecy founded on the unknown is only a doubly involved guess.

All our steps in creating or absorbing material of the record proceed through one of the senses—the tactile when we touch keys, the oral when we speak or listen, the visual when we read. Is it not possible that some day the path may be established more directly?

We know that when the eye sees, all the consequent information is transmitted to the brain by means of electrical vibrations in the channel of the optic nerve. This is an exact analogy with the electrical vibrations which occur in the cable of a television set: they convey the picture from the photocells which see it to the radio transmitter from which it is broadcast. We know further that if we can approach that cable with the proper instruments, we do not need to touch it; we can pick up those vibrations by electrical induction and thus discover and reproduce the scene which is being transmitted, just as a telephone wire may be tapped for its message.

The impulses which flow in the arm nerves of a typist convey to her fingers the translated information which reaches her eye or ear, in order that the fingers may be caused to strike the proper keys. Might not these currents be intercepted, either in the original form in which information is conveyed to the brain, or in the marvelously metamorphosed form in which they then proceed to the hand?

By bone conduction we already introduce sounds: into the nerve channels of the deaf in order that they may hear. Is it not possible that we may learn to introduce them without the present cumbersomeness of first transforming electrical vibrations to mechanical ones, which the human mechanism promptly transforms back to the electrical form? With a couple of electrodes on the skull the encephalograph now produces pen-and-ink traces which bear some relation to the electrical phenomena going on in the brain itself. True, the record is unintelligible, except as it points out certain gross misfunctioning of the cerebral mechanism; but who would now place bounds on where such a thing may lead?

In the outside world, all forms of intelligence whether of sound or sight, have been reduced to the form of varying currents in an electric circuit in order that they may be transmitted. Inside the human frame exactly the same sort of process occurs. Must we always transform to mechanical movements in order to proceed from one electrical phenomenon to another? It is a suggestive thought, but it hardly warrants prediction without losing touch with reality and immediateness.

Presumably man's spirit should be elevated if he can better review his shady past and analyze more completely and objectively his present problems. He has built a civilization so complex that he needs to mechanize his records more fully if he is to push his experiment to its logical conclusion and not merely become bogged down part way there by overtaxing his limited memory. His excursions may be more enjoyable if he can reacquire the privilege of forgetting the manifold things he does not need to have immediately at hand, with some assurance that he can find them again if they prove important.

The applications of science have built man a well-supplied house, and are teaching him to live healthily therein. They have enabled him to throw masses of people against one another with cruel weapons. They may yet allow him truly to encompass the great record and to grow in the wisdom of race experience. He may perish in conflict before he learns to wield that record for his true good. Yet, in the application of science to the needs and desires of man, it would seem to be a singularly unfortunate stage at which to terminate the process, or to lose hope as to the outcome.

Download for Free
Cory Doctorow

Cory Doctorow is a novelist, blogger, and technology activist. He is the co-editor of the popular weblog Boing Boing (www.boingboing.net), and a contributor to the *Guardian*, the *New York Times*, *Publishers Weekly*, *Wired*, and many other newspapers, magazines, and websites. He was formerly Director of European Affairs for the Electronic Frontier Foundation (www.eff.org), a nonprofit civil liberties group that defends freedom in technology law, policy, standards, and treaties. He has won the Locus and Sunburst awards and has been nominated for the Hugo, Nebula, and British Science Fiction awards. His most recent adult novel is *Makers* (Tor Books/HarperCollins UK, 2009). This essay about open access and free downloads for his novels is from his Web site and gives us a good look at his philosophy on writing, publishing, and new technologies.

There's a dangerous group of anti-copyright activists out there who pose a clear and present danger to the future of authors and publishing. They have no respect for property or laws. What's more, they're powerful and organized, and have the ears of lawmakers and the press.

I'm speaking, of course, of the legal departments at ebook publishers.

These people don't believe in copyright law. Copyright law says that when you buy a book, you own it. You can give it away, you can lend it, you can pass it on to your descendants or donate it to the local homeless shelter. Owning books has been around for longer than publishing books has. Copyright law has *always* recognized your right to own your books. When copyright laws are made—by elected officials, acting for the public good—they always safeguard this right.

But ebook publishers don't respect copyright law, and they don't believe in your right to own property. Instead, they say that when you "buy" an ebook, you're really only *licensing* that book, and that copyright law is superseded by the thousands of farcical, abusive words in the license agreement you click through on the way to sealing the deal. (Of course, the button on their website says, "Buy this book" and they talk about "ebook sales" at conferences—no one says, "License this book for your Kindle" or "Total licenses of ebooks are up from 0.00001% of all publishing to 0.0001% of all publishing, a 100-fold increase!")

I say to hell with them. You bought it, you own it. I believe in copyright law's guarantee of ownership in your books.

So you own this ebook. The license agreement (see below) is from Creative Commons and it gives you even *more* rights than you get to a regular book. Every word of it is a gift, not a confiscation. Enjoy.

What do I want from you in return? Read the book. Tell your friends. Review it on Amazon or at your local bookseller. Bring it to your book club. Assign it to your students (older students, please—that sex scene is a scorcher) (*now* I've got your attention, don't I?). As Woody Guthrie wrote:

"This song is Copyrighted in U.S., under Seal of Copyright #154085, for a period of 28 years, and anybody caught singin' it without our permission will be mighty good friends of ourn, cause we don't give a dern. Publish it. Write it. Sing it. Swing to it. Yodel it. We wrote it, that's all we wanted to do."

Oh yeah. Also: if you like it, buy it or donate a copy to a worthy, cash-strapped institution.

Why am I doing this? Because my problem isn't piracy, it's obscurity (thanks, @timoreilly for this awesome aphorism). Because free ebooks sell print books. Because I copied my ass off when I was 17 and grew up to spend practically every discretionary cent I have on books when I became an adult. Because I can't stop you from sharing it (zeroes and ones aren't ever going to get harder to copy); and because readers have shared the books they loved forever; so I might as well enlist you to the cause.

I have always dreamt of writing SF novels, since I was six years old. Now I do it. It is a goddamned dream come true, like growing up to be a cowboy or an astronaut, except that you don't get oppressed by ranchers or stuck on the launchpad in an adult diaper for 28 hours at a stretch. The idea that I'd get dyspeptic over people—*readers*—celebrating what I write is goddamned *bizarre*.

So, download this book.

Some rules of the road:

It's kind of a tradition around here that my readers convert my ebooks to their favorite formats and send them to me here, and it's one that I love! If you've converted these files to another format, send them to me and I'll host them, but before you do, make sure you read the following:

* Only one conversion per format, first come, first serve. That means that if someone's already converted the file to a Femellhebber 3000 document, that's the one you're going to find here. I just don't know enough about esoteric readers to adjudicate disputes about what the ideal format is for your favorite device.

* Make sure and include a link to the reader as well. When you send me an ebook file, make sure that you include a link to the website for the reader technology as well so that I can include it below.

* No cover art. The text of this book is freely copyable, the cover, not so much. The rights to it are controlled by my publisher, so don't include it with your file.

* No DRM. The Creative Commons license prohibits sharing the file with "DRM" (sometimes called "copy-protection") on it, and that's fine by me. Don't send me the book with DRM on it. If you're converting to a format that has a DRM option, make sure it's switched off.

Excerpt from *Makers*
Cory Doctorow

As mentioned in his full bio for "Download for Free," science fiction writer Cory Doctorow is a novelist, blogger, and technology activist. In this excerpt from Makers, *we can see Doctorow's essential optimism at work through the career of his protagonist, Suzanne Church, moving from traditional print journalism to something newer, faster, and ultimately a great deal more productive.*

That week, Suzanne tweeted constantly, filed two columns, and blogged ten or more items a day: photos, bits of discussion between Lester, Perry and Tjan, a couple videos of the Boogie Woogie Elmos doing improbable things. Turned out that there was quite a cult following for the BWE, and the news that there was a trove of some thousands of them in a Hollywood dump sent a half-dozen pilgrims winging their way across the nation to score some for the collectors' market. Perry wouldn't even take their money: "Fella," he told one persistent dealer, "I got forty *thousand* of these things. I won't miss a couple dozen. Just call it good karma."

When Tjan found out about it he pursed his lips for a moment, then said, "Let me know if someone wants to pay us money, please. I think you were right, but I'd like to have a say, all right?"

Perry looked at Suzanne, who was videoing this exchange with her keychain. Then he looked back at Tjan, "Yeah, of course. Sorry—force of habit. No harm done, though, right?"

That footage got downloaded a couple hundred times that night, but once it got slashdotted by a couple of high-profile headline aggregators, she found her server hammered with a hundred thousand requests. The Merc had the horsepower to serve them all, but you never knew: every once in a while, the web hit another tipping point and grew by an order of magnitude or so, and then all the server-provisioning—calculated to survive the old slashdottings— shredded like wet kleenex.

From: kettlewell-l@skunkworks.kodacell.com
To: schurch@sjmercury.com
Subject: Re: Embedded journalist?

This stuff is amazing. Amazing! Christ, I should put you on the payroll. Forget I wrote that. But I should. You've got a fantastic eye. I have never felt as in touch with my own business as I do at this moment. Not to mention proud! Proud—you've made me so proud of the work these guys are doing, proud to have some role in it.

Kettlebelly

She read it sitting up in her coffin, just one of several hundred emails from that day's blog-posts and column. She laughed and dropped it in her folder of correspondence to answer. It was nearly midnight, too late to get into it with Kettlewell.

Then her computer rang—the net-phone she forwarded her cellphone to when her computer was live and connected. She'd started doing that a couple years back, when soft-phones really stabilized, and her phone bills had dropped to less than twenty bucks a month, down from several hundred. It wasn't that she spent a lot of time within arm's reach of a live computer, but given that calls routed through the laptop were free, she was perfectly willing to defer her calls until she was.

"Hi Jimmy," she said—her editor, back in San Jose. 9PM Pacific time on a weeknight was still working hours for him.

"Suzanne," he said.

She waited. She'd half expected him to call with a little shower of praise, an echo of Kettlewell's note. Jimmy wasn't the most effusive editor she'd had, but it made his little moments of praise more valuable for their rarity.

"Suzanne," he said again.

"Jimmy," she said. "It's late here. What's up?"

"So, it's like this. I love your reports but it's not Silicon Valley news. It's Miami news. McClatchy handed me a thirty percent cut this morning and I'm going to the bone. I am firing a third of the newsroom today. Now, you are a stupendous writer and so I said to myself, 'I can fire her or I can bring her home and have her write about Silicon Valley again,' and I knew what the answer had to be. So I need you to come home, just wrap it up and come home."

He finished speaking and she found herself staring at her computer's screen. Her hands were gripping the laptop's edges so tightly it hurt, and the machine made a plasticky squeak as it began to bend.

"I can't do that, Jimmy. This is stuff that Silicon Valley needs to know about. This may not be what's happening *in* Silicon Valley, but it sure as shit is what's happening *to* Silicon Valley." She hated that she'd cussed—she hadn't meant to. "I know you're in a hard spot, but this is the story I need to cover right now."

"Suzanne, I'm cutting a third of the newsroom. We're going to be covering stories within driving distance of this office for the foreseeable future, and that's it. I don't disagree with a single thing you just said, but it doesn't matter: if I leave you where you are, I'll have to cut the guy who covers the school boards and the city councils. I can't do that, not if I want to remain a daily newspaper editor."

"I see," she said. "Can I think about it?"

"Think about what, Suzanne? This has not been the best day for me, I have to tell you, but I don't see what there is to think about. This newspaper no longer has correspondents who work in Miami and London and Paris and New York. As of today, that stuff comes from bloggers, or off the wire, or whatever—but not from our payroll. You work for this newspaper, so you need to come back here, because the job you're doing does not exist any longer. The job you have with us is here. You've missed the night-flight, but there's a direct flight tomorrow morning that'll have you back by lunchtime tomorrow, and we can sit down together then and talk about it, all right?"

"I think—" She felt that oh-shit-oh-shit feeling again, that needing-to-pee feeling, that tension from her toes to her nose. "Jimmy," she said. "I need a leave of absence, OK?"

"What? Suzanne, I'm sure we owe you some vacation but now isn't the time—"

"Not a vacation, Jimmy. Six months leave of absence, without pay." Her savings could cover it. She could put some banner ads on her blog. Florida was cheap. She could rent out her place in California. She was six steps into the plan and it had only taken ten seconds and she had no doubts whatsoever. She could talk to that book-agent who'd pinged her last year, see about getting an advance on a book about Kodacell.

"Are you quitting?"

"No, Jimmy—well, not unless you make me. But I need to stay here."

"The work you're doing there is fine, Suzanne, but I worked really hard to protect your job here and this isn't going to help make that happen."

"What are you saying?"

"If you want to work for the Merc, you need to fly back to San Jose, where the Merc is published. I can't make it any clearer than that."

No, he couldn't. She sympathized with him. She was really well paid by the Merc. Keeping her on would mean firing two junior writers. He'd cut her a lot of breaks along the way, too—let her feel out the Valley in her own way. It had paid off for both of them, but he'd taken the risk when a lot of people wouldn't have. She'd be a fool to walk away from all that.

She opened her mouth to tell him that she'd be on the plane in the morning, and what came out was, "Jimmy, I really appreciate all the work you've done for me, but this is the story I need to write. I'm sorry about that."

"Suzanne," he said.

"Thank you, Jimmy," she said. "I'll get back to California when I get a lull and sort out the details—my employee card and stuff."

"You know what you're doing, right?"

"Yeah," she said. "I do."

When she unscrewed her earpiece, she discovered that her neck was killing her. That made her realize that she was a forty-five-year-old woman in America without health insurance. Or regular income. She was a journalist without a journalistic organ.

She'd have to tell Kettlewell, who would no doubt offer to put her on the payroll. She couldn't do that, of course. Neutrality was hard enough to maintain, never mind being financially compromised.

She stepped out of the coffin and sniffed the salty air. Living in the coffin was expensive. She'd need to get a condo or something. A place with a kitchen where she could prep meals. She figured that Perry's building would probably have a vacancy or two.

The second business that Tjan took Perry into was even more successful than the first, and that was saying something. It only took a week for Tjan to get Perry and Lester cranking on a Kitchen Gnome design that mashed together some Homeland Security gait-recognition software with a big solid-state hard-disk and a microphone and a little camera, all packaged together in one of a couple hundred designs of a garden-gnome figurine that stood six inches tall. It could recognize every member of a household by the way they walked and play back voice-memos for each. It turned out to be a killer tool for context-sensitive reminders to kids to do the dishes, and for husbands, wives and roommates to nag each other without getting on each other's nerves. Tjan was really jazzed about it, as it tied in with some theories he had about the changing US demographic, trending towards blended households in urban centers, with three or more adults cohabiting.

"This is a rich vein," he said, rubbing his hands together. "Living communally is hard, and technology can make it easier. Roommate-ware. It's the wave of the future."

There was another Kodacell group in San Francisco, a design outfit with a bunch of stringers who could design the gnomes for them and they did great work. The gnomes were slightly lewd-looking, and they were the product of a generative algorithm that varied each one. Some of the designs that fell out of the algorithm were jaw-droppingly weird—Perry kept a three-eyed, six-armed version on his desk. They tooled up to make them by the hundred, then the thousand, then the tens of thousands. The fact that each one was different kept their margins up, but as the gnomes gained popularity their sales were steadily eroded by knockoffs, mostly from Eastern Europe.

The knockoffs weren't as cool-looking—though they were certainly weirder looking, like the offspring of a Norwegian troll and an anime robot—but they were more feature-rich. Some smart hacker in Russia was packing all kinds of functionality onto a single chip, so that their trolls cost less and did more: burglar alarms, baby-monitors, streaming Internet radio source, and low-reliability medical diagnostic that relied on quack analysis of eye pigment, tongue coating and other newage (rhymes with sewage) indicators.

Lester came back from the Dollar Store with a big bag of trolls, a dozen different models, and dumped them out on Tjan's desk, up in old foreman's offices on the catwalk above the workspaces. "Christ, would you look at these? They're selling them for less than our cost to manufacture. How do we compete with this?"

"We don't," Tjan said, and rubbed his belly. "Now we do the next thing."

"What's the next thing?" Perry said.

"Well, the first one delivered a return-on-investment at about twenty times the rate of any Kodak or Duracell business unit in the history of either company. But I'd like to shoot for thirty to forty times next, if that's all right with you. So let's go see what you've invented this week and how we can commercialize it."

Perry and Lester just looked at each other. Finally, Lester said, "Can you repeat that?"

"The typical ROI for a Kodacell unit in the old days was about four percent. If you put a hundred dollars in, you'd get a hundred and four dollars out, and it would take about a year to realize. Of course, in the old days, they wouldn't have touched a new business unless they could put a hundred million in and get a hundred and four million out. Four million bucks is four million bucks.

"But here, the company put fifty thousand into these dolls and three months later, they took seventy thousand out, after paying our salaries and bonuses. That's a forty percent ROI. Seventy thousand bucks isn't four million bucks, but forty percent is forty percent. Not to mention that our business drove similar margins in three other business units."

"I thought we'd screwed up by letting these guys eat our lunch," Lester said, indicating the dollar-store trolls.

"Nope, we got in while the margins were high, made a good return, and now we'll get out as the margins drop. That's not screwing up, that's doing the right thing. The next time around, we'll do something more capital intensive and we'll take out an even higher margin: so show me something that'll cost two hundred grand to get going and that we can pull a hundred and sixty thou's worth of profit out of for Kodacell in three months. Let's do something ambitious this time around."

Suzanne took copious notes. There'd been a couple weeks' awkwardness early on about her scribbling as they talked, or videoing with her keychain. But once she'd moved into the building with the guys, taking a condo on the next floor up, she'd become just a member of the team, albeit a member who tweeted nearly every word they uttered to a feed that was adding new subscribers by the tens of thousands.

"So, Perry, what have you got for Tjan?" she asked.

"I came up with the last one," he said, grinning—they always ended up grinning when Tjan ran down economics for them. "Let Lester take this one."

Lester looked shy—he'd never fully recovered from Suzanne turning him down, and when she was in the room, he always looked like he'd rather be somewhere else. He participated in the message boards on her blog though, the most prolific poster in a field with thousands of very prolific posters. When he posted, others listened: he was witty, charming and always right.

"Well, I've been thinking a lot about roommate-ware, 'cause I know that

Tjan's just crazy for that stuff. I've been handicapped by the fact that you guys are such excellent roomies, so I have to think back to my college days to remember what a bad roommate is like, where the friction is. Mostly, it comes down to resource contention, though: I wanna cook, but your dishes are in the sink; I wanna do laundry but your boxers are in the dryer; I wanna watch TV, but your crap is all over the living room sofa."

Living upstairs from the guys gave her fresh insight into how the Kodacell philosophy would work out. Kettlewell was really big on communal living, putting these people into each other's pockets like the old-time geek houses of pizza-eating hackers, getting that in-the-trenches camaraderie. It had taken a weekend to put the most precious stuff in her California house into storage and then turn over the keys to a realtor who'd sort out leasing it for her. The monthly check from the realtor left more than enough for her to pay the rent in Florida and then some, and once the UPS man dropped off the five boxes of personal effects she'd chosen, she was practically at home.

She sat alone over the guys' apartments in the evenings, windows open so that their muffled conversations could drift in and form the soundtrack as she wrote her columns. It made her feel curiously with, but not of, their movement—a reasonable proxy for journalistic objectivity in this age of relativism.

"Resource contention readily decomposes into a bunch of smaller problems, with distinctive solutions. Take dishes: every dishwasher should be designed with a 'clean' and a 'dirty' compartment—basically, two logical dishwashers. You take clean dishes out of the clean side, use them, and put them into the dirty side. When the dirty side is full, the clean side is empty, so you cycle the dishwasher and the clean side becomes dirty and vice-versa. I had some sketches for designs that would make this happen, but it didn't feel right: making dishwashers is too industrial for us. I either like making big chunks of art or little silver things you can carry in your pocket."

She smiled despite herself. She was drawing a half-million readers a day by doing near-to-nothing besides repeating the mind-blowing conversations around her. It had taken her a month to consider putting ads on the site—lots of feelers from blog "micro-labels" who wanted to get her under management and into their banner networks, and she broke down when one of them showed her a little spreadsheet detailing the kind of long green she could expect to bring in from a couple of little banners, with her getting the right to personally approve every advertiser in the network. The first month, she'd made more money than all but the most senior writers on the Merc. The next month, she'd outstripped her own old salary. She'd covered commercial blogs, the flamboyant attention-whores who'd bought stupid cars and ridiculous bimbos with the money, but she'd always assumed they were in a different league from a newspaper scribbler. Now she supposed all the money meant that she should make it official and phone in a resignation to Jimmy, but they'd left it pretty ambiguous as to whether she was retiring or taking a leave of absence and she was reluctant to collapse that waveform into the certainty of saying goodbye to her old life.

"So I got to thinking about snitch-tags, radio frequency ID gizmos. Remember those? When we started talking about them a decade ago, all the privacy people went crazy, totally sure that these things would be bad news. The geeks dismissed them as not understanding the technology. Supposedly, an RFID can only be read from a couple inches away—if someone wanted to find out what RFIDs you had on your person, they'd have to wand you, and you'd know about it."

"Yeah, that was bull," Perry said. "I mean, sure you can't read an RFID unless it's been excited with electromagnetic radiation, and *sure* you can't do that from a hundred yards without frying everything between you and the target. But if you had a subway turnstile with an exciter built into it, you could snipe all the tag numbers from a distant roof with a directional antenna. If those things had caught on, there'd be exciters everywhere and you'd be able to track anyone you wanted—Christ, they even put RFIDs in the hundred-dollar bill for a while! Pickpockets could have figured out whose purse was worth snatching from half a mile away!"

"All true," Lester said. "But that didn't stop these guys. There are still a couple of them around, limping along without many customers. They print the tags with inkjets, sized down to about a third the size of a grain of rice. Mostly used in supply-chain management and such. They can supply them on the cheap.

"Which brings me to my idea: Why not tag everything in a group household, and use the tags to figure out who left the dishes in the sink, who took the hammer out and didn't put it back, who put the empty milk-carton back in the fridge, and who's got the TV remote? It won't solve resource contention, but it will limit the social factors that contribute to it." He looked around at them.

"We can make it fun, you know, make cool RFID sticker designs, mod the little gnome dolls to act as terminals for getting reports."

Suzanne found herself nodding along. She could use this kind of thing, even though she lived alone, just to help her find out where she left her glasses and the TV remote.

Perry shook his head, though. "When I was a kid, I had a really bad relationship with my mom. She was really smart, but she didn't have a lot of time to reason things out with me, so often as not she'd get out of arguing with me by just changing her story. So I'd say, 'Ma, can I go to the mall this aft?' and she'd say, 'Sure, no problem.' Then when I was getting ready to leave the house, she'd ask me where I thought I was going. I'd say, 'To the mall, you said!' and she'd just deny it. Just deny it, point blank.

"I don't think she even knew she was doing it. I think when I asked her if I could go, she'd just absentmindedly say yes, but when it actually came time to go out, she'd suddenly remember all my unfinished chores, my homework, all the reasons I should stay home. I think every kid gets this from their folks, but it made me fucking crazy. So I got a mini tape recorder and I started to *tape* her when she gave me permission. I thought I'd really nail her the next time she changed her tune, play her own words back in her ear.

"So I tried it, and you know what happened? She gave me nine kinds of holy hell for wearing a wire and then she said it didn't matter what she'd said that morning, she was my mother and I had chores to do and no *how* was I going *anywhere* now that I'd started sneaking around the house with a hidden recorder. She took it away and threw it in the trash. And to top it off, she called me 'J. Edgar' for a month.

"So here's my question: How would you feel if the next time you left the dishes in the sink, I showed up with the audit trail for the dishes and waved it in your face? How would we get from that point to a happy, harmonious household? I think you've mistaken the cause for the effect. The problem with dishes in the sink isn't just that it's a pain when I want to cook a meal: it's that when you leave them in the sink, you're being inconsiderate. And the *reason* you've left them in the sink, as you've pointed out, is that putting dishes in the dishwasher is a pain in the ass: you have to bend over, you have to empty it out, and so on. If we moved the dishwasher into the kitchen cupboards and turned half of them into a dirty side and half into a clean side, then disposing of dishes would be as easy as getting them out."

Lester laughed, and so did Tjan. "Yeah, yeah—OK. Point taken. But these RFID things, they're so frigging cheap and potentially useful. I just can't believe that they've never found a single really compelling use in all this time. It just seems like an opportunity that's going to waste."

"Maybe it's a dead end. Maybe it's an ornithopter. Inventors spent hundreds of years trying to build an airplane that flew by flapping its wings, and it was all a rat-hole."

"I guess," Lester said. "But I don't like the idea."

"Like it or don't," Perry said, "doesn't affect whether it's true or not."

But Lester had a sparkle in his eye, and he disappeared into his workshop for a week, and wouldn't let them in, which was unheard of for the big, gregarious giant. He liked to drag the others in whenever he accomplished anything of note, show it off to them like a big kid.

That was Sunday. Monday, Suzanne got a call from her realtor. "Your tenants have vanished," she said.

"Vanished?" The couple who'd rented her place had been as reliable as anyone she'd ever met in the Valley. He worked at a PR agency, she worked in marketing at Google. Or maybe he worked in marketing and she was in PR at Google—whatever, they were affluent, well-spoken, and had paid the extortionate rent she'd charged without batting an eye.

"They normally paypal the rent to me on the first, but not this month. I called and left voicemail the next day, then followed up with an email. Yesterday I went by the house and it was empty. All their stuff was gone. No food in the fridge. I think they might have taken your home theater stuff, too."

"You're fucking kidding me," Suzanne said. It was 11AM in Florida and she was into her second glass of lemonade as the sun began to superheat the air. Back in California, it was 8AM. Her realtor was pulling long hours, and it wasn't her fault. "Sorry. Right. OK, what about the deposit?"

"You waived it."

She had. It hadn't seemed like a big deal at the time. The distant owner of the condo she was renting in Florida hadn't asked for one. "So I did. Now what?"

"You want to swear out a complaint against them?"

"With the police?"

"Yeah. Breach of contract. Theft, if they took the home theater. We can take them to collections, too."

Goddamned marketing people had the collective morals of a snake. All of them useless, conniving, shallow—she never should have...

"Yeah, OK. And what about the house?"

"We can find you another tenant by the end of the month, I'm sure. Maybe a little earlier. Have you thought any more about selling it?"

She hadn't, though the realtor brought it up every time they spoke. "Is now a good time?"

"Lot of new millionaires in the Valley shopping for houses, Suzanne. More than I've seen in years." She named a sum that was a third higher than the last time they'd talked it over.

"Is it peaking?"

"Who knows? It might go up, it might collapse again. But now is the best time to sell in the past ten years. You'd be smart to do it."

She took a deep breath. The Valley was dead, full of venal marketing people and buck-chasers. Here in Florida, she was on the cusp of the next thing, and it wasn't happening in the Valley: it was happening everywhere *except* the Valley, in the cheap places where innovation could happen at low rents. Leaky hot tub, incredible property taxes, and the crazy roller-coaster ride—up 20 percent this month, down 40 next. The bubble was going to burst someday and she should sell out now.

"Sell it," she said.

"You're going to be a wealthy lady," the realtor said.

"Right," Suzanne said.

"I have a buyer, Suzanne. I didn't want to pressure you. But I can sell it by Friday. Close escrow next week. Cash in hand by the fifteenth."

"Jesus," she said. "You're joking."

"No joke," the realtor said. "I've got a waiting list for houses on your block."

And so Suzanne got on an airplane that night and flew back to San Jose and took a pricey taxi back to her place. The marketdroids had left it in pretty good shape, clean and tidy, clean sheets in the linen cupboard. She made up her bed and reflected that this would be the last time she made this bed—the next time she stripped the sheets, they'd go into a long-term storage box. She'd done this before, on her way out of Detroit, packing up a life into boxes and shoving it into storage. What had Tjan said? "The self-storage industry is bigger than the recording industry, did you know that? All they do is provide a place to put stuff that we own that we can't find room for—that's superabundance."

Before bed she posted a classified on Craigslist for a couple helpers to work on boxing stuff, emailed Jimmy to see if she wanted lunch, and looked up the address for the central police station to swear out her complaint. The amp, speakers, and A/V switcher were all missing from her home theater.

She had a dozen helpers to choose from the next morning. She picked two who came with decent references, marveling that it was suddenly possible in Silicon Valley to get anyone to show up anywhere for ten bucks an hour. The police sergeant who took the complaint was sympathetic and agreed with her choice to get out of town. "I've had it with this place, too. Soon as my kids are out of highschool I'm moving back to Montana. I miss the weather."

She didn't think of the marketdroids again until the next day, when she and her helpers were boxing up the last of her things and loading them into her U-Haul. Then a BMW convertible screeched around the corner and burned rubber up to her door.

The woman marketdroid was driving, looking crazy and disheveled, eyes red-rimmed, one heel broken off of her shoes.

"What the FUCK is your problem, lady?" she said, as she leapt out of her car and stalked toward Suzanne.

Instinctively, Suzanne shrank back and dropped the box of books she was holding. It spilled out over her lawn.

"Fiona?" she said. "What's happened?"

"I was *arrested.* They came to my workplace and led me out in handcuffs. I had to make *bail.*"

Suzanne's stomach shrank to a little pebble, impossibly heavy. "What was I supposed to do? You two took off with my home theater!"

"What home theater? Everything was right where you left it when I went. I haven't lived here in *weeks.* Tom left me last month and I moved out."

"You moved out?"

"Yeah, bitch, I *moved out.* Tom was your tenant, not me. If he ripped something off, that's between you and him."

"Look, Fiona, wait, hold up a second. I tried to call you, I sent you email. No one was paying the rent, no one told me that you'd moved out, and no one answered when I tried to find out what had happened."

"That sounds like an *explanation,*" she said, hissing. "I'm waiting for a fucking *apology.* They took me to *prison.*"

Suzanne knew that the local lockup was a long way from prison. "I apologize," she said. "Can I get you a cup of coffee? Would you like to use the shower or anything?"

The woman glared at her a moment longer, then slowly folded in on herself, collapsing, coughing and sobbing on the lawn.

Suzanne stood with her arms at her sides for a moment. Her Craigslist helpers had gone home, so she was all alone, and this woman, whom she'd met only once before, in passing, was clearly having some real problems. Not the kind of thing she dealt with a lot—her life didn't include much person-to-person hand-holding.

But what can you do? She knelt beside Fiona in the grass and took her hand. "Let's get you inside, OK?"

At first it was as though she hadn't heard, but slowly she straightened up and let Suzanne lead her into the house. She was twenty-two, twenty-three, young enough to be Suzanne's daughter if Suzanne had gone in for that sort of thing. Suzanne helped her to the sofa and sat her down amid the boxes still waiting to go into the U-Haul. The kitchen was packed up, but she had a couple bottles of Diet Coke in the cooler and she handed one to the girl.

"I'm really sorry, Fiona. Why didn't you answer my calls or email?"

She looked at Suzanne, her eyes lost in streaks of mascara. "I don't know. I didn't want to talk about it. He lost his job last month and kind of went crazy, told me he didn't want the responsibility anymore. What responsibility? But he told me to go, told me it would be best for both of us if we were apart. I thought it was another girl, but I don't know. Maybe it was just craziness. Everyone I know out here is crazy. They all work a hundred hours a week, they get fired or quit their jobs every five months. Everything is so expensive. My rent is three-quarters of my salary."

"It's really hard," Suzanne said, thinking of the easy, lazy days in Florida, the hackers' idyll that Perry and Lester enjoyed in their workshops.

"Tom was on antidepressants, but he didn't like taking them. When he was on them, he was pretty good, but when he went off, he turned into...I don't know. He'd cry a lot, and shout. It wasn't a good relationship, but we moved out here from Oregon together, and I'd known him all my life. He was a little moody before, but not like he was here."

"When did you speak to him last?" Suzanne had found a couple of blister-packs of anti-depressants in the medicine chest. She hoped that wasn't Tom's only supply.

"We haven't spoken since I moved out."

An hour later, the mystery was solved. The police went to Tom's workplace and discovered that he'd been fired the week before. They tried the GPS in his car and it finked him out as being in a ghost mall's parking lot near his old office. He was dead behind the wheel, a gun in his hand, shot through the heart.

Suzanne took the call and though she tried to keep her end of the conversation quiet and neutral, Fiona—still on the sofa, drinking the warm, flat Coke—knew. She let out a moan like a dog that's been kicked, and then a scream. For Suzanne, it was all unreal, senseless. The cops told her that her home theater components were found in the trunk of the car. No note.

"God, oh God, Jesus, you selfish shit fucking bastard," Fiona sobbed. Awkwardly, Suzanne sat down beside her and took her into a one-armed hug. Her helpers were meeting her at the self-storage the next day to help her unload the U-Haul.

"Do you have someone who can stay with you tonight?" Suzanne asked, praying the answer was yes. She had a house to move out of. Christ, she felt so cold-blooded, but she was on a goddamned schedule.

"Yes, I guess." Fiona scrubbed at her eyes with her fists. "Sure."

Suzanne sighed. The lie was plain. "Who?"

Fiona stood up and smoothed out her skirt. "I'm sorry," she said, and started for the door.

Groaning inwardly, Suzanne blocked her. "You'll stay on the sofa," she said. "You're not driving in this state. I'll order in pizza. Pepperoni mushroom OK?"

Looking defeated, Fiona turned on her heel and went back to the sofa.

Over pizza, Suzanne pulled a few details out of her. Tom had fallen into a funk when the layoffs had started in his office—they were endemic across the Valley, another bust was upon them. His behavior had grown worse and worse, and she'd finally left, or been thrown out, it wasn't clear. She was on thin ice at Google, and they were laying people off too, and she was convinced that being led out in handcuffs would be the straw that broke the camel's back.

"I should move back to Oregon," she said, dropping her slice back on the box-top.

Suzanne had heard a lot of people talk about giving up on the Valley since she'd moved there. It was a common thing, being beaten down by life in the Bay

394 | FUTURE MEDIA

Area. You were supposed to insert a pep talk here, something about hanging in, about the opportunities here.

"Yes," she said, "that's a good idea. You're young, and there's a life for you there. You can start something up, or go to work for someone else's startup." It felt weird coming out of her mouth, like a betrayal of the Valley, of some tribal loyalty to this tech-Mecca. But after all, wasn't she selling up and moving east?

"There's nothing in Oregon," Fiona said, snuffling.

"There's something everywhere. Let me tell you about some friends of mine in Florida," and she told her, and as she told her, she told herself. Hearing it spoken aloud, even after having written about it and written about it, and been there and DONE it, it was different. She came to understand how fucking *cool* it all was, this new, entrepreneurial, inventive, amazing thing she was engaged in. She'd loved the contrast of nimble software companies when compared with gigantic, brutal auto companies, but what her boys were doing, it made the software companies look like lumbering lummoxes, crashing around with their fifty employees and their big purpose-built offices.

Fiona was disbelieving, then interested, then excited. "They just make this stuff, do it, then make something else?"

"Exactly—no permanence except for the team, and they support each other, live and work together. You'd think that because they live and work together that they don't have any balance, but it's the opposite: they book off work at four or sometimes earlier, go to movies, go out and have fun, read books, play catch. It's amazing. I'm never coming back here."

And she never would.

She told her editor about this. She told her friends who came to a send-off party at a bar she used to go to when she went into the office a lot. She told her cab driver who picked her up to take her to the airport and she told the bemused engineer who sat next to her all the way back to Miami. She had the presence of mind not to tell the couple who bought her house for a sum of money that seemed to have at least one extra zero at the end—maybe two.

And so when she got back to Miami, she hardly noticed the incredible obesity of the man who took the money for the gas in her leased car—now that she was here for the long haul she'd have to look into getting Lester to help her buy a used Smart-car from a junker lot—and the tin roofs of the shantytowns she passed looked tropical and quaint. The smell of swamp and salt, the pea-soup humidity, the bass thunder of the boom-cars in the traffic around her—it was like some kind of sweet homecoming for her.

Tjan was in the condo when she got home and he spotted her from the balcony, where he'd been sunning himself, and helped her bring up her suitcases of things she couldn't bear to put in storage.

"Come down to our place for a cup of coffee once you're settled in," he said, leaving her. She sluiced off the airplane grease that had filled her pores on the long flight from San Jose to Miami, and changed into a cheap sun-dress and a pair of flip-flops that she'd bought at the Thunderbird Flea Market, and headed down to their place.

Tjan opened the door with a flourish and she stepped in and stopped short. When she'd left, the place had been a reflection of their jumbled lives: gizmos, dishes, parts, tools and clothes strewn everywhere in a kind of joyful, eye-watering hyper-mess, like an enormous kitchen junk-drawer.

Now the place was *spotless*—and what's more, it was *minimalist*. The floor was not only clean, it was visible. Lining the walls were translucent white plastic tubs stacked to the ceiling.

"You like it?"

"It's amazing," she said. "Like Ikea meets *Barbarella*. What happened here?"

Tjan did a little two-step. "It was Lester's idea. Have a look in the boxes."

She pulled a couple of the tubs out. They were jam-packed with books, tools, cruft and crud—all the crap that had previously cluttered the shelves and the floor and the sofa and the coffee table.

"Watch this," he said. He unvelcroed a wireless keyboard from the side of the TV and began to type: T-H-E C-O... The field autocompleted itself: THE COUNT OF MONTE CRISTO, and brought up a picture of a beaten-up paperback along with links to web-stores, reviews, and the full text. Tjan gestured with his chin and she saw that the front of one of the tubs was pulsing with a soft blue glow. Tjan went and pulled open the tub and fished for a second before producing the book.

"Try it," he said, handing her the keyboard. She began to type experimentally: U-N and up came UNDERWEAR (14). "No way," she said.

"Way," Tjan said, and hit return, bringing up a thumbnail gallery of fourteen pairs of underwear. He tabbed over each, picked out a pair of Simpsons boxers, and hit return. A different tub started glowing.

396 | FUTURE MEDIA

"Lester finally found a socially beneficial use for RFIDs. We're going to get rich!"

"I don't think I understand," she said.

"Come on," he said. "Let's get to the junkyard. Lester explains this really well."

He did, too, losing all of the shyness she remembered, his eyes glowing, his sausage-thick fingers dancing.

"Have you ever alphabetized your hard drive? I mean, have you ever spent any time concerning yourself with where on your hard drive your files are stored, which sectors contain which files? Computers abstract away the tedious, physical properties of files and leave us with handles that we use to persistently refer to them, regardless of which part of the hard drive currently holds those particular bits. So I thought, with RFIDs, you could do this with the real world, just tag everything and have your furniture keep track of where it is.

"One of the big barriers to roommate harmony is the correct disposition of stuff. When you leave your book on the sofa, I have to move it before I can sit down and watch TV. Then you come after me and ask me where I put your book. Then we have a fight. There's stuff that you don't know where it goes, and stuff that you don't know where it's been put, and stuff that has nowhere to put it. But with tags and a smart chest of drawers, you can just put your stuff wherever there's room and ask the physical space to keep track of what's where from moment to moment.

"There's still the problem of getting everything tagged and described, but that's a service business opportunity, and where you've got other shared identifiers like ISBNs you could use a cameraphone to snap the barcodes and look them up against public databases. The whole thing could be coordinated around 'spring cleaning' events where you go through your stuff and photograph it, tag it, describe it—good for your insurance and for forensics if you get robbed, too."

He stopped and beamed, folding his fingers over his belly. "So, that's it, basically."

Perry slapped him on the shoulder and Tjan drummed his forefingers like a heavy-metal drummer on the side of the workbench they were gathered around.

They were all waiting for her. "Well, it's very cool," she said, at last. "But, the whole white-plastic-tub thing. It makes your apartment look like an Ikea showroom. Kind of inhumanly minimalist. We're Americans, we like celebrating our stuff."

"Well, OK, fair enough," Lester said, nodding. "You don't have to put everything away, of course. And you can still have all the decor you want. This is about clutter control."

"Exactly," Perry said. "Come check out Lester's lab."

"OK, this is pretty perfect," Suzanne said. The clutter was gone, disappeared into the white tubs that were stacked high on every shelf, leaving the work-surfaces clear. But Lester's works-in-progress, his keepsakes, his sculptures and triptychs were still out, looking like venerated museum pieces in the stark tidiness that prevailed otherwise.

Tjan took her through the spreadsheets. "There are ten teams that do closet-organizing in the network, and a bunch of shippers, packers, movers, and storage experts. A few furniture companies. We adopted the interface from some free software inventory-management apps that were built for illiterate service employees. Lots of big pictures and autocompletion. And we've bought a hundred RFID printers from a company that was so grateful for a new customer that they're shipping us 150 of them, so we can print these things at about a million per hour. The plan is to start our sales through the consultants at the same time as we start showing at trade-shows for furniture companies. We've already got a huge order from a couple of local old-folks' homes."

They walked to the IHOP to have a celebratory lunch. Being back in Florida felt just right to her. Francis, the leader of the paramilitary wing of the AARP, threw them a salute and blew her a kiss, and even Lester's nursing junkie friend seemed to be in a good mood.

When they were done, they brought take-out bags for the junkie and Francis in the shantytown.

"I want to make some technology for those guys," Perry said as they sat in front of Francis's RV drinking cowboy coffee cooked over a banked wood-stove off to one side. "Roommate-ware for homeless people."

Francis uncrossed his bony ankles and scratched at his mosquito bites. "A lot of people think that we don't buy stuff, but it's not true," he said. "I shop hard for bargains, but there's lots of stuff I spend more on because of my lifestyle than I would if I had a real house and steady electricity. When I had a chest-freezer, I could bulk buy ground round for about a tenth of what I pay now when I go to the grocery store and get enough for one night's dinner. The alternative is using propane to keep the fridge going overnight, and that's not cheap, either. So I'm a kind of premium customer. Back at Boeing, we loved the people who made small orders, because we could charge them such a premium for custom work, while the big airlines wanted stuff done so cheap that half the time we lost money on the deal."

Perry nodded. "There you have it—roommate-ware for homeless people, a great and untapped market."

Suzanne cocked her head and looked at him. "You're sounding awfully commerce-oriented for a pure and unsullied engineer, you know?"

He ducked his head and grinned and looked about twelve years old. "It's infectious. Those little kitchen gnomes, we sold nearly a half-million of those things, not to mention all the spin-offs. That's a half-million *lives*—a half-million *households*—that we changed just by thinking up something cool and making it real. These RFID things of Lester's—we'll sign a couple million customers with those. People will change everything about how they live from moment to moment because of something Lester thought up in my junkyard over there."

"Well, there's thirty million of us living in what the social workers call 'marginal housing,'" Francis said, grinning wryly. He had a funny smile that Suzanne had found adorable until he explained that he had an untreated dental abscess that he couldn't afford to get fixed. "So that's a lot of difference you could make."

"Yeah," Perry said. "Yeah, it sure is."

That night, she found herself still blogging and answering emails—they always piled up when she travelled and took a couple of late nights to clear out—after 9PM, sitting alone in a pool of light in the back corner of Lester's workshop that she had staked out as her office. She yawned and stretched and listened to her old back crackle. She hated feeling old, and late nights made her feel old—feel every extra ounce of fat on her tummy, feel the lines bracketing her mouth and the little bag of skin under her chin.

She stood up and pulled on a light jacket and began to switch off lights and get ready to head home. As she poked her head in Tjan's office, she saw that she wasn't the only one working late.

"Hey, you," she said. "Isn't it time you got going?"

He jumped like he'd been stuck with a pin and gave a little yelp. "Sorry," he said, "didn't hear you."

He had a cardboard box on his desk and had been filling it with his personal effects—little one-off inventions the guys had made for him, personal fetishes and tchotchkes, a framed picture of his kids.

"What's up?"

He sighed and cracked his knuckles. "Might as well tell you now as tomorrow morning. I'm resigning."

She felt a flash of anger and then forced it down and forcibly replaced it with professional distance and curiosity. Mentally she licked her pencil-tip and flipped to a blank page in her reporter's notebook.

"Oh yes?"

"I've had another offer, in Westchester County. Westinghouse has spun out its own version of Kodacell and they're looking for a new vice-president to run the division. That's me."

"Good job," she said. "Congratulations, Mr. Vice-President."

He shook his head. "I emailed Kettlewell half an hour ago. I'm leaving in the morning. I'm going to say goodbye to the guys over breakfast."

"Not much notice," she said.

"Nope," he said, a note of anger creeping into his voice. "My contract lets Kodacell fire me on one day's notice, so I insisted on the right to quit on the same terms. Maybe Kettlewell will get his lawyers to write better boilerplate from here on in."

When she had an angry interview, she habitually changed the subject to something sensitive: angry people often say more than they intend to. She did it instinctively, not really meaning to psy-ops Tjan, whom she thought of as a friend, but not letting that get in the way of the story. "Westinghouse is doing what, exactly?"

"It'll be as big as Kodacell's operation in a year," he said. "George Westinghouse personally funded Tesla's research, you know. The company understands funding individual entrepreneurs. I'm going to be training the talent scouts and mentoring the financial people, then turning them loose to sign up entrepreneurs for the Westinghouse network. There's a competitive market for garage inventors now." He laughed. "Go ahead and print that," he said. "Blog it tonight. There's competition now. We're giving two points more equity and charging half a point less on equity than the Kodacell network."

"That's amazing, Tjan. I hope you'll keep in touch with me—I'd love to follow your story."

"Count on it," he said. He laughed. "I'm getting a week off every eight weeks to scout Russia. They've got an incredible culture of entrepreneurship."

"Plus you'll get to see your kids," Suzanne said. "That's really good."

"Plus, I'll get to see my kids," he admitted.

"How much money is Westinghouse putting into the project?" she asked, replacing her notional notebook with a real one, pulled from her purse.

"I don't have numbers, but they've shut down the whole appliances division to clear the budget for it." She nodded—she'd seen news of the layoffs on the wires. Mass demonstrations, people out of work after twenty years' service. "So it's a big budget."

"They must have been impressed with the quarterlies from Kodacell."

Tjan folded down the flaps on his box and drummed his fingers on it, squinting at her. "You're joking, right?"

"What do you mean?"

"Suzanne, they were impressed by *you*. Everyone knows that quarterly numbers are easy to cook—anything less than two annual reports is as likely to be enronning as real fortune-making. But *your* dispatches from here—they're what sold them. It's what's convincing *everyone*. Kettlewell said that three-quarters of his new recruits come on board after reading your descriptions of this place. That's how *I* ended up here."

She shook her head. "That's very flattering, Tjan, but—"

He waved her off and then, surprisingly, came around the desk and hugged her. "But nothing, Suzanne. Kettlewell, Lester, Perry—they're all basically big kids. Full of enthusiasm and invention, but they've got the emotional maturity and sense of scale of hyperactive five-year-olds. You and me, we're grownups. People take us seriously. It's easy to get a kid excited, but when a grownup chimes in you know there's some there there."

Suzanne recovered herself after a second and put away her notepad. "I'm just the person who writes it all down. You people are making it happen."

"In ten years' time, they'll remember you and not us," Tjan said. "You should get Kettlewell to put you on the payroll."

Kettlewell himself turned up the next day. Suzanne had developed an intuitive sense of the flighttimes from the west coast and so for a second she couldn't figure out how he could possibly be standing there—nothing in the sky could get him from San Jose to Miami for a 7AM arrival.

"Private jet," he said, and had the grace to look slightly embarrassed. "Kodak had eight of them and Duracell had five. We've been trying to sell them all off but no one wants a used jet these days, not even Saudi princes or Columbian drug-lords."

"So, basically, it was going to waste."

He smiled and looked eighteen—she really did feel like the only grownup sometimes—and said, "Zackly—it's practically environmental. Where's Tjan?"

"Downstairs saying goodbye to the guys, I think."

"OK," he said. "Are you coming?"

She grabbed her notebook and a pen and beat him out the door of her rented condo.

"What's this all about," Tjan said, looking wary. The guys were hang-dog and curious looking, slightly in awe of Kettlewell, who did little to put them at their ease—he was staring intensely at Tjan.

"Exit interview," he said. "Company policy."

Tjan rolled his eyes. "Come on," he said. "I've got a flight to catch in an hour."

"I could give you a lift," Kettlewell said.

"You want to do the exit interview between here and the airport?"

"I could give you a lift to JFK. I've got the jet warmed up and waiting."

Sometimes, Suzanne managed to forget that Kodacell was a multi-billion-dollar operation and that Kettlewell was at its helm, but other times the point was very clear.

"Come on," he said, "we'll make a day of it. We can stop on the way and pick up some barbecue to eat on the plane. I'll even let you keep your seat in the reclining position during take-off and landing. Hell, you can turn your cell-phone on—just don't tell the Transport Security Administration!"

Tjan looked cornered, then resigned. "Sounds good to me," he said, and Kettlewell shouldered one of the two huge duffel-bags that were sitting by the door.

"Hi, Kettlewell," Perry said.

Kettlewell set down the duffel. "Sorry, sorry. Lester, Perry, it's really good to see you. I'll bring Suzanne back tonight and we'll all go out for dinner, OK?"

Suzanne blinked. "I'm coming along?"

"I sure hope so," Kettlewell said.

Perry and Lester accompanied them down in the elevator.

"Private jet, huh?" Perry said. "Never been in one of those."

Kettlewell told them about his adventures trying to sell off Kodacell's private air force.

"Send one of them our way, then," Lester said.

"Do you fly?" Kettlewell said.

"No," Perry said. "Lester wants to take it apart. Right, Les?"

Lester nodded. "Lots of cool junk in a private jet."

"These things are worth millions, guys," Kettlewell said.

"No, someone *paid* millions for them," Perry said. "They're *worth* whatever you can sell them for."

Kettlewell laughed. "You've had an influence around here, Tjan," he said. Tjan managed a small, tight smile.

Kettlewell had a driver waiting outside the building who loaded the duffels into the spacious trunk of a spotless dark town-car whose doors chunked shut with an expensive sound.

"I want you to know that I'm really not angry at all, OK?" Kettlewell said.

Tjan nodded. He had the look of a man who was steeling himself for a turn in an interrogation chamber. He'd barely said a word since Kettlewell arrived. For his part, Kettlewell appeared oblivious to all of this, though Suzanne was pretty sure that he understood exactly how uncomfortable this was making Tjan.

"The thing is, six months ago, nearly everyone was convinced that I was a fucking moron, that I was about to piss away ten billion dollars of other people's money on a stupid doomed idea. Now they're copying me and poaching my best people. So this is good news for me, though I'm going to have to find a new business manager for those two before they get picked up for turning planes into component pieces."

Suzanne's PDA vibrated whenever the number of online news stories mentioning her or Kodacell or Kettlewell increased or decreased sharply. She used to try to read everything, but it was impossible to keep up—now all she wanted was to keep track of whether the interestingness-index was on the uptick or downtick.

It had started to buzz that morning and the pitch had increased steadily until it was actually uncomfortable in her pocket. Irritated, she yanked it out and was about to switch it off when the lead article caught her eye.

KODACELL LOSES TJAN TO WESTINGHOUSE

The by-line was Freddy. Feeling like a character in a horror movie who can't resist the compulsion to look under the bed, Suzanne thumbed the PDA's wheel and brought up the whole article.

> Kodacell business-manager Tjan Lee Tang, whose adventures we've followed through Suzanne Church's gushing, besotted blog posts

She looked away and reflexively reached toward the delete button. The innuendo that she was romantically involved with one or more of the guys had circulated on her blog's message boards and around the diggdots ever since she'd started writing about them. No woman could possibly be writing about this stuff because it was important—she had to be "with the band," a groupie or a whore.

Combine that with Rat-Toothed Freddy's sneering tone and she was instantly sent into heart-thundering rage. She deleted the post and looked out the window. Her pager buzzed some more and she looked down. The same article, being picked up on blogs, on some of the bigger diggdots, and an AP wire.

She forced herself to re-open it.

> has been hired to head up a new business unit on behalf of the multinational giant Westinghouse. The appointment stands as more proof of Church's power to cloud men's minds with pretty empty words about the half-baked dot-com schemes that have oozed out of Silicon Valley and into every empty and dead American suburb.

It was hypnotic, like staring into the eyes of a serpent. Her pulse actually thudded in her ears for a second before she took a few deep breaths and calmed down enough to finish the article, which was just more of the same: nasty personal attacks, sniping, and innuendo. Freddy even managed to imply that she was screwing all of them—and Kettlewell besides.

Kettlewell leaned over her shoulder and read.

"You should send him an email," he said. "That's disgusting. That's not reportage."

"Never get into a pissing match with a skunk," she said. "What Freddy wants is for me to send him mail that he can publish along with more snarky commentary. When the guy you're arguing with controls the venue you're arguing in, you can't possibly win."

"So blog him," Kettlewell said. "Correct the record."

"The record is correct," she said. "It's never been incorrect. I've written an exhaustive record that is there for everyone to see. If people believe this, no amount of correction will help."

Kettlewell made a face like a little boy who'd been told he couldn't have a toy. "That guy is poison," he said. "Those quote marks around blog."

"Let him add his quote marks," she said. "My daily readership is higher than the Merc's paid circulation this week." It was true. After a short uphill climb from her new URL, she'd accumulated enough readers that the advertising revenue dwarfed her old salary at the Merc, an astonishing happenstance that nevertheless kept her bank account full. She clicked a little. "Besides, look at this, there are three dozen links pointing at this story so far and all of them are critical of him. We don't need to stick up for ourselves—the world will."

Saying it calmed her and now they were at the airport. They cruised into a private gate, away from the militarized gulag that fronted Miami International. A courteous security guard waved them through and the driver confidently piloted the car up to a wheeled jetway beside a cute, stubby little toy jet. On the side, in cursive script, was the plane's name: Suzanne.

She looked accusatorially at Kettlewell.

"It was called that when I bought the company," he said, expressionless but somehow mirthful behind his curved surfer shades. "But I kept it because I liked the private joke."

"Just no one tell Freddy that you've got an airplane with my name on it or we'll never hear the fucking end of it."

She covered her mouth, regretting her language, and Kettlewell laughed, and so did Tjan, and somehow the ice was broken between them.

"No *way* flying this thing is cost-effective," Tjan said. "Your CFO should be kicking your ass."

"It's a little indulgence," Kettlewell said, bounding up the steps and shaking hands with a small, neat woman pilot, an African-American with corn-rows peeking out under her smart peaked cap. "Once you've flown in your own bird, you never go back."

"This is a *monstrosity*," Tjan said as he boarded. "What this thing eats up in hangar fees alone would be enough to bankroll three or four teams." He settled into an oversized Barcalounger of a seat and accepted a glass of orange juice that the pilot poured for him. "Thank you, and no offense."

"None taken," she said. "I agree one hundred percent."

"See," Tjan said.

Suzanne took her own seat and her own glass and buckled in and watched the two of them, warming up for the main event, realizing that she'd been brought along as a kind of opening act.

"They paying you more?"

"Yup," Tjan said. "All on the back-end. Half a point on every dollar brought in by a team I coach or whose members I mentor."

Kettlewell whistled. "That's a big share," he said.

"If I can make my numbers, I'll take home a million this year."

"You'll make those numbers. Good negotiations. Why didn't you ask us for the same deal?"

"Would you have given it to me?"

"You're a star," Kettlewell said, nodding at Suzanne, whose invisibility to the conversation popped like a bubble. "Thanks to her."

"Thanks, Suzanne," Tjan said.

Suzanne blushed. "Come on, guys."

Tjan shook his head. "She doesn't really understand. It's actually kind of charming."

"We might have matched the offer."

"You guys are first to market. You've got a lot of procedures in place. I wanted to reinvent some wheels."

"We're too *conservative* for you?"

Tjan grinned wickedly. "Oh yes," he said. "I'm going to do business in *Russia*."

Kettlewell grunted, and pounded his orange juice. Around them, the jet's windows flashed white as they broke through the clouds and the ten-thousand-foot bell sounded.

"How the hell are you going to make anything that doesn't collapse under its own weight in Russia?"

"The corruption's a problem, sure," Tjan said. "But it's offset by the entrepreneurship. Some of those cats make the Chinese look lazy and unimaginative. It's a shame that so much of their efforts have been centered on graft, but there's no reason they couldn't be focused on making an honest ruble."

They fell into a discussion of the minutiae of Perry and Lester's businesses, franker than any business discussion she'd ever heard. Tjan talked about the places where they'd screwed up, and places where they'd scored big, and about all the plans he'd made for Westinghouse, the connections he had in Russia. He even talked about his kids and his ex in St. Petersburg, and Kettlewell admitted that he'd known about them already.

For Kettlewell's part, he opened the proverbial kimono wide, telling Tjan about conflicts within the board of directors, poisonous holdovers from the pre-Kodacell days who sabotaged the company from within with petty bureaucracy, even the problems he was having with his family over the long hours they were working. He opened the minibar and cracked a bottle of champagne to toast Tjan's new job, and they mixed it with more orange juice, and then there were bagels and schmear, fresh fruit, power bars, and canned Starbucks coffees with deadly amounts of sugar and caffeine.

When Kettlewell disappeared into the tiny—but marble-appointed—bathroom, Suzanne found herself sitting alone with Tjan, almost knee to knee, lightheaded from lack of sleep and champagne and altitude.

"Some trip," she said.

"You're the best," he said, wobbling a little. "You know that? Just the best. The stuff you write about these guys, it makes me want to stand up and salute. You make us all seem so fucking *glorious*. We're going to end up taking over the world because you inspire us so. Maybe I shouldn't tell you this, because you're not very self-conscious about it right now, but Suzanne, you won't believe it because you're so goddamned modest, too. It's what makes your writing so right, so believable—"

Kettlewell stepped out of the bathroom. "Touching down soon," he said, and patted them each on the shoulder as he took his seat. "So that's about it, then," he said, and leaned back and closed his eyes. Suzanne was accustomed to thinking of him as twenty-something, the boyish age of the magazine cover portraits from the start of his career. Now, eyes closed on his private jet, harsh upper atmosphere sun painting his face, his crow's-feet and the deep vertical brackets around his mouth revealed him for someone pushing a youthful forty, kept young by exercise and fun and the animation of his ideas.

"Guess so," Tjan said, slumping. "This has been one of the memorable experiences of my life, Kettlewell, Suzanne. Not entirely pleasant, but pleasant on the whole. A magical time in the clouds."

"Once you've flown private, you'll never go back to coach," Kettlewell said, smiling, eyes still closed. "You still think my CFO should spank me for not selling this thing?"

"No," Tjan said. "In ten years, if we do our jobs, there won't be five companies on earth that can afford this kind of thing—it'll be like building a cathedral after the Protestant Reformation. While we have the chance, we should keep these things in the sky. But you should give one to Lester and Perry to take apart."

"I was planning to," Kettlewell said. "Thanks."

Suzanne and Kettlewell got off the plane and Tjan didn't look back when they'd landed at JFK. "Should we go into town and get some bialy to bring back to Miami?" Kettlewell said, squinting at the bright day on the tarmac.

"Bring deli to Miami?"

"Right, right," he said. "Forget I asked. Besides, we'd have to charter a chopper to get into Manhattan and back without dying in traffic."

Something about the light through the open hatch or the sound or the smell—something indefinably New York—made her yearn for Miami. The great cities of commerce like New York and San Francisco seemed too real for her, while the suburbs of Florida were a kind of endless summer camp, a dreamtime where anything was possible.

"Let's go," she said. The champagne buzz had crashed and she had a touch of headache. "I'm bushed."

"Me too," Kettlewell said. "I left San Jose last night to get into Miami before Tjan left. Not much sleep. Gonna put my seat back and catch some winks, if that's OK?"

"Good plan," Suzanne said.

Embarrassingly, when were fully reclined, their seats nearly touched, forming something like a double bed. Suzanne lay awake in the hum of the jets for a while, conscious of the breathing human beside her, the first man she'd done anything like share a bed with in at least a year. The last thing she remembered was the ten-thousand-foot bell going off and then she slipped away into sleep.

The Future of the World Wide Web
Timothy Berners-Lee

A graduate of Oxford University, Tim Berners-Lee invented the World Wide Web, an Internet-based hypermedia initiative for global information sharing, while at CERN, the European Particle Physics Laboratory, in 1989. He wrote the first Web client and server in 1990. His specifications of URIs, HTTP, and HTML were refined as Web technology spread. He is the 3Com Founders Professor of Engineering in the School of Engineering, with a joint appointment in the Department of Electrical Engineering and Computer Science at the Laboratory for Computer Science and Artificial Intelligence (CSAIL) at the Massachusetts Institute of Technology (MIT), where he also heads the Decentralized Information Group (DIG). He is also a Professor in the Electronics and Computer Science Department at the University of Southampton, UK. He is the Director of the World Wide Web Consortium (W3C), a Web standards organization founded in 1994 that develops interoperable technologies (specifications, guidelines, software, and tools) to lead the Web to its full potential. He is a founding Director of the Web Science Trust (WST), launched in 2009 to promote research and education in Web Science, the multidisciplinary study of humanity connected by technology.

"The Future of the Web," reprinted here in its entirety, is an address to the U.S. House of Representatives Committee on Energy and Commerce Subcommittee on Telecommunications and the Internet that Berners-Lee gave in March 2007. In this address, Berners-Lee predicts that the future of the Web will include more and better data integration along with ever greater accessibility through a variety of devices and that Web applications will become ever more ubiquitous, able to be found in home and office walls, automobile dashboards, and even refrigerator doors. Just a few years have passed since this address to the House Committee was made, and you will not be surprised to look around and see that Berners-Lee has been spot on in terms of his predicted trends.

Testimony of Sir Timothy Berners-Lee
CSAIL Decentralized Information Group
Massachusetts Institute of Technology

Before the
United States House of Representatives

Committee on Energy and Commerce
Subcommittee on Telecommunications and the Internet
Hearing on the "Digital Future of the United States:
Part I—The Future of the World Wide Web"

This document on the Web: [http://dig.csail.mit.edu/2007/03/01-ushouse-future-of-the-web]

Chairman Markey, Ranking Member Upton, and Members of the Committee. It is my honor to appear before you today to discuss the future of the World Wide Web. I would like to offer some of my experience of having designed the original foundations of the Web, what I've learned from watching it grow, and some of the exciting and challenging developments I see in the future of the Web. Though I was privileged to lead the effort that gave rise to the Web in the mid-1990s, it has long passed the point of being something designed by a single person or even a single organization. It has become a public resource upon which many individuals, communities, companies and governments depend. And, from its beginning, it is a medium that has been created and sustained by the cooperative efforts of people all over the world.

To introduce myself, I should mention that I studied Physics at Oxford, but on graduating discovered the new world of microprocessors and joined the electronics and computer science industry for several years. In 1980, I worked on a contract at CERN, the European Particle Physics Laboratory, and wrote for my own benefit a simple program for tracking the various parts of the project using linked note cards. In 1984 I returned to CERN for ten years, during which time I found the need for a universal information system, and developed the World Wide Web as a side project in 1990. In 1994, the need for coordination of the Web became paramount, and I left to come to MIT, which became the first of now three international host institutes for the World Wide Consortium (W3C). I have directed W3C since that time. I hold the 3Com Founders chair at MIT where I pursue research on advanced Web technologies with the MIT Decentralized Information Group. The testimony I offer here today is purely my own opinion and does not necessarily reflect the views of the World Wide Web Consortium or any of its Members.

The special care we extend to the World Wide Web comes from a long tradition that democracies have of protecting their vital communications channels. We nurture and protect our information networks because they stand at the core of our economies, our democracies, and our cultural and personal lives. Of course, the imperative to assure the free flow of information has only grown given the global nature of the Internet and Web. As a Federal judge said in defense of freedom of expression on the Internet:

> The Internet is a far more speech-enhancing medium than print, the village green, or the mails.... The Internet may fairly be regarded as a never-ending worldwide conversation. [1]

Therefore it is incumbent on all of us to understand what our role is in fostering continued growth, innovation, and vitality of the World Wide Web. I am gratified that the United States and many other democracies around the world have taken up this challenge. My hope today is to help you to explore the role this committee and this Congress has in building upon the great advances that are in store for the Web.

I. Foundations of the World Wide Web

The success of the World Wide Web, itself built on the open Internet, has depended on three critical factors: 1) unlimited links from any part of the Web to any other; 2) open technical standards as the basis for continued growth of innovation applications; and 3) separation of network layers, enabling independent innovation for network transport, routing and information applications. Today these characteristics of the Web are easily overlooked as obvious, self-maintaining, or just unimportant. All who use the Web to publish or access information take it for granted that any Web page on the planet will be accessible to anyone who has an Internet connection, regardless of whether it is over a dialup modem or a high speed multi-megabit per second digital access line. The last decade has seen so many new ecommerce startups, some of which have formed the foundations of the new economy, that we now expect that the next blockbuster Web site or the new homepage for your kid's local soccer team will just appear on the Web without any difficulty.

Today I will speak primarily about the World Wide Web. I hesitate to point out that the Web is just one of the many applications that run on top of the Internet. As with other Internet applications such as email, instant messaging, and voice over IP, the Web would have been impossible to create without the Internet itself operating as an open platform. [2]

A. Universal linking: Anyone can connect to anyone, any page can link to any page

How did the Web grow from nothing to the scale it is at today? From a technical perspective, the Web is a large collection of Web pages (written in the standard HTML format), linked to other pages (with the linked documents named using the URI standard), and accessed over the Internet (using the HTTP network protocol). In simple terms, the Web has grown because it's easy to write a Web page and easy to link to other pages. The story of the growth of the World Wide Web can be measured by the number of Web pages that are published and the number of links between pages. Starting with one page and one site just about 15 years ago, there are now over 100,000,000 Web sites [3] with an estimated over 8 billion publicly accessible pages as of 2005. What makes it easy to create links from one page to another is that there is no limit to the number of pages or number of links possible on the Web. Adding a Web page requires no coordination with any central authority, and has an extremely low, often zero, additional cost. What's more, the protocol that allows us to follow these links (HTTP) is a non-discriminatory protocol. It allows us to follow any link at all, regardless of content or ownership. So, because it's so easy to write a Web page, link to another page, and follow these links around, people have done a lot of this. Adding a page provides content, but adding a link provides the organization, structure and endorsement to information on the Web which turn the content as a whole into something of great value.

A current example of the low barriers to reading, writing and linking on the Web is the world of blogs. Blogs hardly existed five years ago, but have become an enormously popular means of expression for everything from politics to local news, to art and science. The low barriers to publishing pages and abundance of linking ability have come together, most recently with blogs, to create an open platform for expression and exchange of all kinds. [4] The promise of being able to reach anyone over a communications system that will carry virtually anything (any type of information) is somewhat like other infrastructures we depend upon: the mail system, the road system, and the telephone system. It stands in contrast to more closed systems such as the broadcast or cable television networks. Those closed systems perform valuable functions as well, but their impact in society is different and less pervasive.

The universality and flexibility of the Web's linking architecture has a unique capacity to break down boundaries of distance, language, and domains of knowledge. These traditional barriers fall away because the cost and complexity of a link is unaffected by most boundaries that divide other media. It's as easy to link from information about commercial law in the United States to commercial law in China, as it is to make the same link from Massachusetts' Commercial Code to that of Michigan. These links work even though they have to traverse boundaries of distance, network operators, computer operating systems, and a host of other technical details that previously served to divide information. The Web's ability to allow people to forge links is why we refer to it as an abstract information space, rather than simply a network. Other open systems such as the mails, the roads or the telephones come to perform a function in society that transcends their simple technical characteristics. In these systems, phone calls from the wireline networks travel seamlessly to wireless providers. Mails from one country traverse borders with minimal friction, and the cars we buy work on any roads we can find. Open infrastructures become general purpose infrastructure on top of which large scale social systems are built. The Web takes this openness one step further and enables a continually evolving set of new services that combine information at a global scale previously not possible. This universality has been the key enabler of innovation on the Web and will continue to be so in the future.

B. Open Foundation for Information-driven Innovation

The Web has not only been a venue for the free exchange of ideas, but also it has been a platform for the creation of a wide and unanticipated variety of new services. Commercial applications including eBay, Google, Yahoo, and Amazon.com are but a few examples of the extraordinary innovation that is possible because of the open, standards-based, royalty-free technology that makes up the Web. Whether developing an auction site, a search engine, or a new way of selling consumer goods, e-commerce entrepreneurs have been able develop new services with confidence that they will be available for use by anyone with an Internet connection and a Web browser, regardless of operating system, computer hardware, or the ISP chosen by that user. [5] Innovation in the non-commercial and government domains has been equally robust. Early Web sites such as Thomas have led the way in efforts to make the legislative process more open and transparent, and non-commercial sites such as the Wikipedia have pioneered new collaborate styles of information sharing. The flexibility and openness inherent in Web standards also make this medium a powerful foundation on which to build services and applications that are truly accessible for people with disabilities, as well as people who need to transform content for purposes other than that for which it was originally intended.

The lesson from the proliferation of new applications and services on top of the Web infrastructure is that innovation will happen provided it has a platform of open technical standards, a flexible, scalable architecture, and access to these standards on royalty-free ($0 fee patent licenses) terms. At the World Wide Web Consortium, we will only standardize technology if it can be implemented on a royalty-free basis. So, all who contribute to the development of technical standards at the W3C are required to agree to provide royalty-free licenses to any patents they may hold if those patents would block compliance with the standard. [6] Consider as a comparison the very successful Apple iTunes+iPod music distribution environment. This integration of hardware, software, Web service shows an intriguing mix of proprietary technology and open standards. The iTunes environment consists of two parts: sales of music and videos, and distribution of podcasts. The sale of music is managed by a proprietary platform run by Apple with the aim of preventing copyright infringement. However, because Apple uses closed, non-standard technology for its copy protection (known as Digital Rights Management), the growth is seen as limited. In fact, Apple CEO Steve Jobs recently wrote that the market for online music sales is being limited by the lack of open access to DRM technology. [7] By contrast, the podcast component of iTunes is growing quite dramatically, providing a means for many small and large audio and video distributors to share or sell their wares on the Web. Unlike the music and video sales, podcasts are based on open standards, assuring that it's easy to create, edit and distribute the podcast content.

C. Separation of Layers

When, seventeen years ago, I designed the Web, I did not have to ask anyone's permission. The Web, as a new application, rolled out over the existing Internet without any changes to the Internet itself. This is the genius of the design of the Internet, for which I take no credit. Applying the age old wisdom of design with interchangeable parts and separation of concerns, each component of the Internet and the applications that run on top of it are able to develop and improve independently. This separation of layers allows simultaneous but autonomous innovation to occur at many levels all at once. One team of engineers can concentrate on developing the best possible wireless data service, while another can learn how to squeeze more and more bits through fiber optic cable. At the same time, application developers such as myself can develop new protocols and services such as voice over IP, instant messaging, and peer-to-peer networks. Because of the open nature of the Internet's design, all of these continue to work well together even as each one is improving itself.

II. Looking forward

Having described how the Web got to where it is, let us shift to the question of where it might go from here. I hope that I've already persuaded you that the evolution of the Web is not in the hands of any one person, me or anyone else. But I'd like to highlight three areas in which I expect exciting developments in the near future. First, the Web will get better and better at helping us to manage, integrate, and analyze data. Today, the Web is quite effective at helping us to publish and discover documents, but the individual information elements within those documents (whether it be the date of any event, the price of an item on a catalog page, or a mathematical formula) cannot be handled directly as data. Today you can see the data with your browser, but can't get other computer programs to manipulate or analyze it without going through a lot of manual effort yourself. As this problem is solved, we can expect that Web as a whole to look more like a large database or spreadsheet, rather than just a set of linked documents. Second, the Web will be accessible from a growing diversity of networks (wireless, wireline, satellite, etc.) and will be available on an ever increasing number of different types of devices. Finally, in a related trend, Web applications will become a more and more ubiquitous throughout our human environment, with walls, automobile dashboards, refrigerator doors all serving as displays giving us a window onto the Web.

A. Data Integration

Digital information about nearly every aspect of our lives is being created at an astonishing rate. Locked within all of this data is the key to knowledge about how to cure diseases, create business value, and govern our world more effectively. The good news is that a number of technical innovations (RDF which is to data what HTML is to documents, and the Web Ontology Language [OWL] which allows us to express how data sources connect together) along with more openness in information sharing practices are moving the World Wide Web toward what we call the Semantic Web. Progress toward better data integration will happen through use of the key piece of technology that made the World Wide Web so successful: the link. The power of the Web today, including the ability to find the pages we're looking for, derives from the fact that documents are put on the Web in standard form, and then linked together. The Semantic Web will enable better data integration by allowing everyone who puts individual items of data on the Web to link them with other pieces of data using standard formats.

To appreciate the need for better data integration, compare the enormous volume of experimental data produced in commercial and academic drug discovery laboratories around the world, as against the stagnant pace of drug discovery. While market and regulatory factors play a role here, life science researchers are coming to the conclusion that in many cases no single lab, no single library, no single genomic data repository contains the information necessary to discover new drugs. Rather, the information necessary to understand the complex interactions between diseases, biological processes in the human body, and the vast array of chemical agents is spread out across the world in a myriad of databases, spreadsheets, and documents.

Scientists are not the only ones who need better data integration. Consider the investment and finance sector, a marketplace in which profit is generated, in large part, from having the right information, at the right time, and reaching correct conclusions based on analysis and insight drawn from that information. Successful investment strategies are based on finding patterns and trends in an increasingly diverse set of information sources (news, market data, historical trends, commodity prices, etc.). Leading edge financial information providers are now developing services that allow users to easily integrate the data they have, about their own portfolios or internal market models, with the information delivered by the information service. The unique value creation is in the integration services, not in the raw data itself or even in the software tools, most of which will be built on open source components.

New data integration capabilities, when directed at personal information, pose substantial privacy challenges which are hardly addressed by today's privacy laws. The technology of today's Web already helps reveal far more about individuals, their behavior, their reading interest, political views, personal associations, group affiliations, and even health and financial status. In some cases, this personal information is revealed by clever integration of individual pieces of data on the Web that provide clues to otherwise unavailable information. In other cases, people actually reveal a lot about themselves, but with the intent that it only used in certain contexts by certain people. These shifts in the way we relate to personal information require serious consideration in many aspects of our social and legal lives. While we are only just beginning to see these shifts, now is the time to examine a range of legal and technical options that will preserve our fundamental privacy values for the future without unduly stifling beneficial new information processing and sharing capabilities. Our research group at MIT is investigating new technologies to make the most of the Semantic Web, as well as both technical and public policy models that will help bring increased transparency and accountability to the World Wide Web and other large scale information systems. [8] Our belief is that in order to protect privacy and other public policy values, we need to research and develop new technical mechanisms that provide great transparency into the ways in which information in the system is used, and provide accountability for those uses with respect to whatever are the prevailing rules.

B. Network Diversity and Device Independence

The Web has always been accessible from a variety of devices over a variety of networks. From early on, one could browse the Web from a Macintosh, a Windows PC or a Linux-based computer. However, for a long time the dominant mode of using the Web was from some desktop or laptop computer with a reasonably large display. Increasingly, people will use non-PC devices that have either much smaller or much larger displays, and will reach the Internet through a growing diversity of networks. At one end of this spectrum, the devices will seem more like cell phones. At the other end, they will seem more like large screen TVs. There are, of course, technical challenges associated with squeezing a Web page designed for a 17 inch screen into the two to four inch display available on a mobile phone or PDA. Some of these will be solved through common standards and some through innovative new interface techniques. All of this means more convenience for users and more opportunity for new Web services that are tailored to people who are somewhere other than their desks.

Growth in access networks and Web-enabled applications presents a number of important opportunities. For example, more robust, redundant network services together with innovative uses of community-based social networks on the Web are coming to play an increasing role in areas such as emergency planning and notification. [9] Reports about ad hoc communication networks supporting disaster relief efforts are just one illustration of the benefit of the openness, flexibility and accessibility of the Internet and Web. This one area is a microcosm of many of the issues that we are discussing today, because in order to work well it requires seamless integration of diverse types of data; repurposing that data instantly into valid formats for a myriad of different Web devices; and including appropriate captions, descriptions, and other necessary accessibility information. I would encourage all Web sites designers to ensure that their material conforms not only to W3C standards, but also to guidelines for accessibility for people with disabilities, and for mobile access.

C. Ubiquitous Web Applications

In the future, the Web will seem like it's everywhere, not just on our desktop or mobile device. As LCD technology becomes cheaper, walls of rooms, and even walls of buildings, will become display surfaces for information from the Web. Much of the information that we receive today through a specialized application such as a database or a spreadsheet will come directly from the Web. Pervasive and ubiquitous web applications hold much opportunity for innovation and social enrichment. They also pose significant public policy challenges. Nearly all of the information displayed is speech but is being done in public, possibly in a manner accessible to children. Some of this information is bound to be personal, raising privacy questions. Finally, inasmuch as this new ubiquitous face of the Web is public, it will shape the nature of the public spaces we work, shop, do politics, and socialize in.

D. The Web is Not Complete

Progress in the evolution of the Web to date has been quite gratifying to me. But the Web is by no means finished.

The Web, and everything which happens on it, rest on two things: technological protocols, and social conventions. The technological protocols, like HTTP and HTML, determine how computers interact. Social conventions, such as the incentive to make links to valuable resources, or the rules of engagement in a social networking Web site, are about how people like to, and are allowed to, interact.

As the Web passes through its first decade of widespread use, we still know surprisingly little about these complex technical and social mechanisms. We have only scratched the surface of what could be realized with deeper scientific investigation into its design, operation and impact on society. Robust technical design, innovative business decisions, and sound public policy judgment all require that we are aware of the complex interactions between technology and society. We call this awareness Web Science: the science and engineering of this massive system for the common good. [10] In order to galvanize Web Science research and education efforts, MIT and the University of Southampton in the United Kingdom have created the Web Science Research Initiative. In concert with an international Scientific Advisory Council of distinguished computer scientists, social scientists, and legal scholars, WSRI will help create an intellectual foundation, educational atmosphere, and resource base to allow researchers to take the Web seriously as an object of scientific enquiry and engineering innovation.

III. Conclusion

So how do we plan for a better future, better for society?

We ensure that that both technological protocols and social conventions respect basic values. That Web remains a universal platform: independent of any specific hardware device, software platform, language, culture, or disability. That the Web does not become controlled by a single company—or a single country.

By adherence to these principles we can ensure that Web technology, like the Internet, continues to serve as a foundation for bigger things to come. It is my hope, Chairman Markey, members of the committee, that an understanding of the nature of the Web will guide you in your future work, and that the public at large can count on you to hold these values to the best of your ability. I am grateful for the opportunity to appear before you and am ready to help your efforts in future.

Notes

[1] American Civil Liberties Union v. Reno, 929 F. Supp. 824, 844 (E.D. Pa. 1996) (Dalzell, J.)

[2] Kapor, M. and Weitzner, D. "Social and Industrial Policy for Public Networks: Visions for the Future." Harasim and Walls, eds. Global Networks: Computers and International Communication. Oxford University Press. Oxford. (1994)

[3] Netcraft February 2007 Web Server Survey. http://news.netcraft.com/archives/web_server_survey.html

[4] Weinberger, D. Small Pieces Loosely Joined: A Unified Theory of the Web. Perseus Books. (2002)

[5] Note that due to failure by some browser vendors to comply fully with standards, Web site developers sometimes have to go to extra trouble to make it so that their sites actually work properly on all browsers.

[6] Overview and Summary of the W3C Patent Policy, http://www.w3.org/2004/02/05-patentsummary.html. W3C Patent Policy. D. Weitzner, Standards, Patents and the Dynamics of Innovation on the World Wide Web. http://www.w3.org/2004/10/patents-standards-innovation.html

[7] Jobs wrote on the Apple Web site: "Imagine a world where every online store sells DRM-free music encoded in open licensable formats. In such a world, any player can play music purchased from any store, and any store can sell music which is playable on all players. This is clearly the best alternative for consumers, and Apple would embrace it in a heartbeat. If the big four music companies would license Apple their music without the requirement that it be protected with a DRM, we would switch to selling only DRM-free music on our iTunes store. Every iPod ever made will play this DRM-free music," Steve Jobs, Thoughts on Music (February 6, 2007), http://www.apple.com/hotnews/thoughtsonmusic/

[8] Weitzner, Abelson, Berners-Lee, Hanson, Hendler, Kagal, McGuinness, Sussman, Waterman, Transparent Accountable Data Mining: New Strategies for Privacy Protection; MIT CSAIL Technical Report MIT-CSAIL-TR-2006-007 (27 January 2006).

[9] B. Shneiderman, and J. Preece, PUBLIC HEALTH: 911.gov, Science 315 (5814), 944 (16 February 2007)

[10] "Creating a Science of the Web" Tim Berners-Lee, Wendy Hall, James Hendler, Nigel Shadbolt, Daniel J. Weitzner. Science 313, 11 August 2006. And see the Web Science Research Initiative, http://www.webscience.org/

Excerpt from *Understanding Media*
Automation: Learning a Living
Marshall McLuhan

Marshall McLuhan (1911–1980) was the first media scholar to achieve mainstream recognition for his work. His *Understanding Media: The Extensions of Man* (McGraw-Hill, 1964), was a global bestseller and introduced the idea that "the medium is the message" to millions. In this final chapter of that book, McLuhan predicts the instantaneous retrieval of information as well as a global network that operates much as the human central nervous system does, receiving messages and sending them continuously and so operating as a single, unified system. He adds that "men are suddenly nomadic gatherers of knowledge, nomadic as never before," and anyone who has spent a few hours in an evening surfing the Internet for one particular bit of knowledge and wound up discovering dozens more can appreciate what McLuhan sees coming when he talks about "self-employment and artistic autonomy," near the end of this chapter.

A newspaper headline recently read, "Little Red Schoolhouse Dies When Good Road Built." One-room schools, with all subjects being taught to all the same time, simply dissolve when better transportation permits specialized spaces and specialized teaching. At the extreme of speeded up movement, however, specialism of space and subject disappears once more. With automation, it is not only jobs that appear, and complex roles that reappear. Centuries of specialist stress in pedagogy and in the arrangement of data now end with the instantaneous retrieval of information made possible by electricity. Automation is information and it not only ends jobs in the world of work, it ends subjects in the world of learning. It does not end the world of learning. The future of work consists of earning a living in the automation age. This is a familiar pattern in electric technology in general. It ends the old dichotomies between culture and technology, between art and commerce, and between work and leisure. Whereas in the mechanical age of fragmentation leisure had been the absence of work, or mere idleness, the reverse is true in the electric age. As the age of information demands the simultaneous use of all our faculties, we discover that we are most at leisure when we are most intensely involved, very much as with the artists in all ages.

In terms of the industrial age, it can be pointed out that the difference between the previous mechanical age and the new electric age appears in the different kinds of inventories. Since electricity, inventories are made up not so much of goods in storage as of materials in continuous process of transformation at spatially removed sites. For electricity not only gives primacy to process, whether in making or in learning, but it makes independent the source of energy from the location of the process. In entertainment media, we speak of this fact as "mass media" because the source of the program and the process of experiencing it are independent in space, yet simultaneous in time. In industry this basic fact causes the scientific revolution that is called "automation" or "cybernation."

In education the conventional division of the curriculum into subjects is already as outdated as the medieval trivium and quadrivium after the Renaissance. Any subject taken in depth at once relates to other subjects. Arithmetic in grade three or nine, when taught in terms of number theory, symbolic logic, and cultural history, ceases to be mere practice in problems. Continued in their present patterns of fragmented unrelation, our school curricula will insure a citizenry unable to understand the cybernated world in which they live.

Most scientists are quite aware that since we have acquired some knowledge of electricity it is not possible to speak of atoms as pieces of matter. Again, as more is known about electrical "discharges" and energy, there is less and less tendency to speak of electricity as a thing that "flows" like water through a wire, or is "contained" in a battery. Rather, the tendency is to speak of electricity as painters speak of space; namely, that it is a variable condition that involves the special positions of two or more bodies. There is no longer any tendency to speak of electricity as "contained" in anything. Painters have long known that objects are not contained in space, but that they generate their own spaces. It was the dawning awareness of this in the mathematical world a century ago that enabled Lewis Carroll, the Oxford mathematician, to contrive *Alice in Wonderland*, in which times and spaces are neither uniform nor continuous, as they had seemed to be since the arrival of Renaissance perspective. As for the speed of light, that is merely the speed of total causality.

It is a principal aspect of the electric age that it establishes a global network that has much of the character of our central nervous system. Our central nervous system is not merely an electric network, but it constitutes a single unified field of experience. As biologists point out, the brain is the interacting place where all kinds of impressions and experiences can be exchanged and translated, enabling us to *react to the world as a whole*. Naturally, when electric technology comes into play, the utmost variety and extent of operations in industry and society quickly assume a unified posture. Yet this organic unity of interprocess that electromagnetism inspires in the most diverse and specialized areas and organs of action is quite the opposite of organization in a mechanized society. Mechanization of any process is achieved by fragmentation, beginning with the mechanization of writing by movable types, which has been called the "mono-fracture of manufacture."

The electric telegraph, when crossed with typography, created the strange new form of the modern newspaper. Any page of the telegraph press is a surrealistic mosaic of bits of "human interest" in vivid interaction. Such was the art form of Chaplin and the early silent movies. Here, too, an extreme speed-up of mechanization, an assembly line of still shots on celluloid, led to a strange reversal. The movie mechanism, aided by the electric light, created the illusion of organic form and movement as much as a fixed position had created the illusion of perspective on a flat surface five hundred years before.

The same thing happens less superficially when the electric principle crosses the mechanical lines of industrial organization. Automation retains only as much of the mechanical character as the motorcar kept of the forms of the horse and the carriage. Yet people discuss automation as if we had not passed the oat barrier, and as if the horse-vote at the next poll would sweep away the automation regime.

Automation is not an extension of the mechanical principles of fragmentation and separation of operations. It is rather the invasion of the mechanical world by the instantaneous character of electricity. That is why those involved in automation insist that it is a way of thinking, as much as it is a way of doing. Instant synchronization of numerous operations has ended the old mechanical pattern of setting up operations in lineal sequence. The assembly line has gone the way of the stag line. Nor is it just the lineal and sequential aspect of mechanical analysis that has been erased by the electric speed-up and exact synchronizing of information that is automation.

Automation or cybernation deals with all the units and components of the industrial and marketing process exactly as radio or TV combine the individuals in the audience into new interprocess. The new kind of interrelation in both industry and entertainment is the result of the electric instant speed. Our new electric technology now extends the instant processing of knowledge by interrelation that has long occurred within our central nervous system. It is that same speed that constitutes "organic unity" and ends the mechanical age that had gone into high gear with Gutenberg. Automation brings in real "mass production," not in terms of size, but of an instant inclusive embrace. Such is also the character of "mass media." They are an indication, not of the size of their audiences, but of the fact that everybody becomes involved in them at the same time. Thus commodity industries under automation share the same structural character of the entertainment industries in the degree that both approximate the condition of instant information. Automation affects not just production, but every phase of consumption and marketing; for the consumer becomes producer in the automation circuit, quite as much as the reader of the mosaic telegraph press makes his own news, or just is his own news.

But there is a component in the automation story that is as basic as tactility to the TV image. It is the fact that, in any automatic machine, or galaxy of machines and functions, the generation and transmission of power is quite separate from the work operation that uses the power. The same is true in all servo-mechanist structures that involve feedback. The source of energy is separate from the process of translation of information, or the applying of knowledge. This is obvious in the telegraph, where the energy and channel are quite independent of whether the written code is French or German. The same separation of power and process obtains in automated industry, or in "cybernation." The electric energy can be applied indifferently and quickly to many kinds of tasks.

Such was never the case in the mechanical systems. The power and the work done were always in direct relation, whether it was hand and hammer, water and wheel, horse and cart, or steam and piston. Electricity brought a strange elasticity in this matter, much as light itself illuminates a total field and does not dictate what shall be done. The same light can make possible a multiplicity of tasks, just as with electric power. Light is a nonspecialist kind of energy or power that is identical with information and knowledge. Such is also the relation of electricity to automation, since both energy and information can be applied in a great variety of ways. Grasp of this fact is indispensable to the understanding of the electronic age, and of automation in particular. Energy and production now tend to fuse with information and learning. Marketing and consumption tend to become one with learning, enlightenment, and the intake of information. This is all part of the electric implosion that now follows or succeeds the centuries of explosion and increasing specialism. The electronic age is literally one of illumination. Just as light is at once energy and information, so electric automation unites production, consumption, and learning in an inextricable process. For this reason, teachers are already the largest employee group in the U.S. economy, and may well become the only group.

The very same process of automation that causes a withdrawal of the present work force from industry causes learning itself to become the principal kind of production and consumption. Hence the folly of alarm about unemployment. Paid learning is already becoming both the dominant employment and the source of new wealth in our society. This is the new *role* for men in society, whereas the older mechanistic idea of "jobs," or fragmented tasks and specialist slots for "workers," becomes meaningless under automation.

It has often been said by engineers that, as information levels rise, almost any sort of material can be adapted to any sort of use. This principle is the key to the understanding of electric automation, in the case of electricity, as energy for production becomes independent of the work operation, there is not only the speed that makes for total and organic interplay, but there is, also, the fact that electricity is sheer information that, in actual practice, illuminates all it touches. Any process that approaches instant interrelation of a total field tends to raise itself to the level of conscious awareness, so that computers seem to "think." In fact, they are highly specialized at present, and quite lacking in the full process of interrelation that makes for consciousness. Obviously, they can be made to simulate the process of consciousness, just as our electric global networks now begin to simulate the condition of our central nervous system. But a conscious computer would still be one that was an extension of our consciousness, as a telescope is an extension of our eyes, or as a ventriloquist's dummy is an extension of the ventriloquist.

Automation certainly assumes the servomechanism and the computer. That is to say, it assumes electricity as store and expediter of information. These traits of store, or "memory," and accelerator are the basic features of any medium of communication whatever. In the case of electricity, it is not corporeal substance that is stored or moved, but perception and information. As for technological acceleration, it now approaches the speed of light. All nonelectric media had merely hastened things a bit. The wheel, the road, the ship, the airplane, and even the space rocket are utterly lacking in the character of instant movement. Is it strange, then, that electricity should confer on all previous human organization a completely new character? The very toil of man now becomes a kind of enlightenment. As unfallen Adam in the Garden of Eden was appointed the task of the contemplation and naming of creatures, so with automation. We have now only to name and program a process or a product in order for it to be accomplished. Is it not rather like the case of Al Capp's Schmoos? One had only to look at a Schmoo and think longingly of pork chops or caviar, and the Schmoo ecstatically transformed itself into the object of desire. Automation brings us into the world of the Schmoo. The custom-built supplants the mass-produced.

Let us, as the Chinese say, move our chairs closer to the fire and see what we are saying. The electric changes associated with automation have nothing to do with ideologies or social programs. If they had, they could be delayed or controlled. Instead, the technological extension of our central nervous system that we can call the electric media began more than a century ago, subliminally. Subliminal have been the effects. Subliminal they remain. At no period in human culture have men understood the psychic mechanisms involved in invention and technology. Today it is the instant speed of electric information that, for the first time, permits easy recognition of the patterns and the formal contours of change and development. The entire world, past and present, now reveals itself to us like a growing plant in an enormously accelerated movie. Electric speed is synonymous with light and with the understanding of causes. So, with the use of electricity in previously mechanized situations, men easily discover causal connections and patterns that were quite unobservable at the slower rates of mechanical change. If we play backward the long development of literacy and printing and their effects on social experience and organization, we can easily see how these forms brought about that high degree of social uniformity and homogeneity of society that is indispensable for mechanical industry. Play them backward, and we get just that shock of unfamiliarity in the familiar that is necessary for the understanding of the life of forms. Electricity compels us to play our mechanical development backward, for it reverses much of that development. Mechanization depends on the breaking up of processes into homogenized but unrelated bits. Electricity unifies these fragments once more because its speed of operation requires a high degree of interdependence among all phases of any operation. It is this electric speed-up and interdependence that has ended the assembly line in industry.

This same need for organic interrelation, brought in by the electric speed of synchronization, now requires us to perform, industry-by-industry, and country-by-country, exactly the same organic interrelating that was first effected in the individual automated unit. Electric speed requires organic structuring of the global economy quite as much as early mechanization by print and by road led to the acceptance of national unity. Let us not forget that nationalism was a mighty invention and revolution that, in the Renaissance, wiped out many of the local regions and loyalties. It was a revolution achieved almost entirely by the speed-up of information by means of uniform movable types. Nationalism cut across most of the traditional power and cultural groupings that had slowly grown up in various regions. Multi-nationalism had long deprived Europe of its economic unity. The Common Market came to it only with the Second War. War is accelerated social change, as an explosion is an accelerated chemical reaction and movement of matter. With electric speeds governing industry and social life, explosion in the sense of crash development becomes normal. On the other hand, the old-fashioned kind of "war" becomes as impracticable as playing hopscotch with bulldozers. Organic interdependence means that disruption of any part of the organism can prove fatal to the whole. Every industry has had to "rethink through" (the awkwardness of this phrase betrays the painfulness of the process), function by function, its place in the economy. But automation forces not only industry and town planners, but government and even education, to come into some relation to social facts.

The various military branches have had to come into line with automation very quickly. The unwieldy mechanical forms of military organization have gone. Small teams of experts have replaced the citizen armies of yesterday even faster than they have taken over the reorganization of industry. Uniformly trained and homogenized citizenry, so long in preparation and so necessary to a mechanized society, is becoming quite a burden and problem to an automated society, for automation and electricity require depth approaches in all fields and at all times. Hence the sudden rejection of standardized goods and scenery and living and education in America since the Second War. It is a switch imposed by electric technology in general, and by the TV image in particular.

Automation was first felt and seen on a large scale in the chemical industries of gas, coal, oil, and metallic ores. The large changes in these operations made possible by electric energy have now, by means of the computer, begun to invade every kind of white-collar and management area. Many people, in consequence, have begun to look on the whole of society as a single unified machine for creating wealth. Such has been the normal outlook of the stockbroker, manipulating shares and information with the cooperation of the electric media of press, radio, telephone, and teletype. But the peculiar and abstract manipulation of information as a means of creating wealth is no longer a monopoly of the stockbroker. It is now shared by every engineer and by the entire communications industries. With electricity as energizer and synchronizer, all aspects of production, consumption, and organization become incidental to communications. The very idea of communication as interplay is inherent in the electrical, which combines both energy and information in its intensive manifold.

Anybody who begins to examine the pattern of automation finds that perfecting the individual machine by making it automatic involves "feedback." That means introducing an information loop or circuit, where before there had been merely a one-way flow or mechanical sequence. Feedback is the end of the lineality that came into the Western world with the alphabet and the continuous forms of Euclidean space. Feedback or dialogue between the mechanism and its environment brings a further weaving of individual machines into a galaxy of such machines throughout the entire plant. There follows a still further weaving of individual plants and factories into the entire industrial matrix of materials and services of a culture. Naturally, this last stage encounters the entire world of policy, since to deal with the whole industrial complex as an organic system affects employment, security, education, and polities, demanding full understanding in advance of coming structural change. There is no room for witless assumptions and subliminal factors in such electrical and instant organizations.

As artists began a century ago to construct their works backward, *starting with the effect,* so now with industry and planning. In general, electric speed-up requires complete knowledge of ultimate effects. Mechanical speed-ups, however radical in their reshaping of personal and social life, still were allowed to happen sequentially. Men could, for the most part, get through a normal life span on the basis of a single set of skills. That is not at all the case with electric speed-up. The acquiring of new basic knowledge and skill by senior executives in middle age is one of the most common needs and harrowing facts of electric technology. The senior executives, or "big wheels," as they are archaically and ironically designated, are among the hardest pressed and most persistently harassed groups in human history. Electricity has not only demanded ever deeper knowledge and faster interplay, but has made the harmonizing of production schedules as rigorous as that demanded of the members of a large symphony orchestra. And the satisfactions are just as few for the big executives as for the symphonists, since a player in a big orchestra can hear nothing of the music that reaches the audience. He gets only noise.

The result of electric speed-up in industry at large is the creation of intense sensitivity to the interrelation and interprocess of the whole, so as to call for ever-new types of organization and talent. Viewed from the old perspectives of the machine age, this electric network of plants and processes seems brittle and tight. In fact, it is not mechanical, and it does begin to develop the sensitivity and pliability of the human organism. But it also demands the same varied nutriment and nursing as the animal organism.

With the instant and complex interprocesses of the organic form, automated industry also acquires the power of adaptability to multiple uses. A machine set up for the automatic production of electric bulbs represents a combination of processes that were previously managed by several machines. With a single attendant, it can run as continuously as a tree in its intake and output.

But, unlike the tree, it has a built-in system of jigs and fixtures that can be shifted to cause the machine to turn out a whole range of products from radio tubes and glass tumblers to Christmas-tree ornaments. Although an automated plant is almost like a tree in respect to the continuous intake and output, it is a tree that can change from oak to maple to walnut as required. It is part of the automation or electric logic that specialism is no longer limited to just one specialty. The automatic machine may work in a specialist way, but it is not limited to one line. As with our hands and fingers that are capable of many tasks, the automatic unit incorporates a power of adaptation that was quite lacking in the pre-electric and mechanical stage of technology. As *anything* becomes more complex, it becomes less specialized. Man is more complex and less specialized than a dinosaur. The older mechanical operations were designed to be more efficient as they became larger and more specialized. The electric and automated unit, however, is quite otherwise. A new automatic machine for making automobile tailpipes is about the size of two or three office desks. The computer control panel is the size of a lectern. It has in it no dies, no fixtures, no settings of any kind, but rather certain general-purpose things like grippers, benders, and advancers. On this machine, starting with lengths of ordinary pipe, it is possible to make eighty different kinds of tailpipe in succession, as rapidly, as easily, and as cheaply as it is to make eighty of the same kind. And the characteristic of electric automation is all in this direction of return to the general-purpose handicraft flexibility that our own hands possess. The programming can now include endless changes of program. It is the electric feedback, or dialogue pattern, of the automatic and computer-programmed "machine" that marks it off from the older mechanical principle of one-way movement.

This computer offers a model that has the characteristics shared by all automation. From the point of intake of materials the output of the finished product, the operations tend to be independently, as well as interdependently, automatic. The synchronized concert of operations is under the control of gauges and instruments that can be varied from the control-panel boards that are themselves electronic. The material of intake is relatively uniform in shape, size, and chemical properties, as likewise the material of the output. But the processing under these conditions permits use of the highest level of capacity for any needed period. It is, as compared with the older machines, the difference between an oboe in an orchestra and the same tone on an electronic music instrument. With the electronic music instrument, any tone can be made available in any intensity and for any length of time. Note that the older symphony orchestra was, by comparison, a machine of separate instruments *that gave the effect of organic unity.* With the electronic instrument, one *starts* with organic unity as an immediate fact of perfect synchronization. This makes the attempt to create the effect of organic unity quite pointless. Electronic music must seek other goals.

Such is also the harsh logic of industrial automation. All that we had previously achieved mechanically by great exertion and coordination can now be done electrically without effort. Hence the specter of joblessness and propertylessness in the electric age. Wealth and work become information factors, and totally new structures are needed to run a business or relate it to social needs and markets. With the electric technology, the new kinds of instant interdependence and interprocess that take over production also enter the market and social organizations. For this reason, markets and education designed to cope with the products of servile toil and mechanical production are no longer adequate. Our education has long ago acquired the fragmentary and piece-meal character of mechanism. It is now under increasing pressure to acquire the depth and interrelation that are indispensable in the all-at-once world of electric organization. Paradoxically, automation makes liberal education mandatory.

The electric age of servomechanisms suddenly releases men from the mechanical and specialist servitude of the preceding machine age. As the machine and the motorcar released the horse and projected it onto the plane of entertainment, so does automation with men. We are suddenly threatened with a liberation that taxes our inner resources of self-employment and imaginative participation in society. This would seem to be a fate that calls men to the role of artist in society. It has the effect of making most people realize how much they had come to depend on the fragmentalized and repetitive routines of the mechanical era. Thousands of years ago man, the nomadic food-gatherer, had taken up positional, or relatively sedentary, tasks. He began to specialize. The development of writing and printing were major stages of that process. They were supremely specialist in separating the roles of knowledge from the roles of action, even though at times it could appear that "the pen is mightier than the sword." But with electricity and automation, the technology of fragmented processes suddenly fused with the human dialogue and the need for over-all consideration of human unity. Men are suddenly nomadic gatherers of knowledge, nomadic as never before, informed as never before, free from fragmentary specialism as never before—but also involved in the total social process as never before; since with electricity we extend our central nervous system globally, instantly interrelating every human experience. Long accustomed to such a state in stock-market news or front-page sensations, we can grasp the meaning of this new dimension more readily when it is pointed out that it is possible to "fly" unbuilt airplanes on computers. The specifications of a plane can be programmed and the plane tested under a variety of extreme conditions before it has left the drafting board. So with new products and new organizations of many kinds. We can now by computer deal with complex social needs with the same architectural certainty that we previously attempted in private housing. Industry as a whole has become the unit of reckoning, and so with society, politics, and education as wholes.

Electric means of storing and moving information with speed and precision make the largest units quite as manageable as small ones. Thus the automation of a plant or of an entire industry offers a small model of the changes that must occur in society from the same electric technology. Total interdependence is the starting fact. Nevertheless, the range of choice in design, stress, and goal within that total field of electromagnetic interprocess is very much greater than it ever could have been under mechanization.

Since electric energy is independent of the place or kind of work-operation, it creates patterns of decentralism and diversity in the work to be done. This is a logic that appears plainly enough in the difference between firelight and electric light, for example. Persons grouped around a fire or candle for warmth or light are less able to pursue independent thoughts, or even tasks, than people supplied with electric light. In the same way, the social and educational patterns latent in automation are those of self-employment and artistic autonomy. Panic about automation as a threat of uniformity on a world scale is the projection into the future of mechanical standardization and specialism, which are now past.